Map represents county boundaries that were drawn in 1974.

SCOTLAND

NORTHERN
IRELAND

ENGLAND

IRELAND

Birton
(James Fraser)

Flaxborough
(Colin Watson)

Comerbourne,
Comerford,
Midshire
(Ellis
Peters)

Norchester,
Northshire
(Alan Hunter)

Melford,
Melfordshire
(John Bingham)

WALES

Alderley,
Westshire
(James Anderson)

Berebury,
Calleshire
(Catherine Aird)

Wellbridge,
Southshire
(Michael Allen)

Markhampton,
Didford Magna,
Yewbury,
Markshire
(Cyril Hare)

Kingsmarkham,
Sussex
(Ruth Rendell)

Long Dream
(Michael Innes)

Fortrow
(Peter Alding)

A READER'S GUIDE TO

THE
CLASSIC
BRITISH
MYSTERY

A READER'S GUIDE TO
THE CLASSIC BRITISH MYSTERY

SUSAN OLEKSIW

G.K. Hall & Co.
Boston

For Michael

Library of Congress Cataloging in Publication Data

Oleksiw, Susan
   A reader's guide to the classic British mystery/Susan Oleksiw.
     p. cm.
   ISBN 0-8161-8787-8
   1. Detective and mystery stories, English—Stories, plots, etc.
2. Detective and mystery stories, English—Bibliography.
3. Bibliography—Best books—Detective and mystery stories.
4. English fiction—20th century—Stories, plots, etc. 5. English
fiction—20th century—Bibliography. 6. Bibliography—Best books
—English fiction.   I. Title.
PR888.D4O4   1988
823'.0872'09—dc19   88-1735

This publication is printed on permanent/durable acid-free paper
MANUFACTURED IN THE UNITED STATES OF AMERICA

Contents

Preface

Several years ago I began keeping notes and lists of the various mysteries my husband and I had read and of those we wanted to locate. I was not the only one doing this, and I soon found myself sharing my lists with other readers I met in mystery bookstores. This book is the result.

I have gathered here the works of authors who write what has come to be called the classic British mystery, be it a novel of detection, police procedure, romance, or suspense. I originally intended to include only the novel of detection but was reminded as I selected titles that the vast majority of writers known for their stories of detection rarely change the tone dramatically when they adopt the form of another type, such as the police procedural. Further, lovers of the mystery novel often prefer to read all the works of one congenial author before moving on to another. The authors covered here, therefore, belong to that school of writing which has become known as a standard in genre writing.

There are 121 authors, listed alphabetically. Under each author, I have listed all titles published up to 1985. If the list of an author's mystery novels to this date is incomplete, the author's name is marked with an asterisk. The bibliography is limited to novels and novellas, excluding short stories, plays, and science fiction (the only borderline cases are the Petros novels by James Anderson). Under each author, titles are listed chronologically by series character. This means that under the listing for Agatha Christie, for example, Hercule Poirot's books are listed first, since he was the first series character introduced by Christie; these are followed by those with Ariadne Oliver, then by Tommy and Tuppence, Colonel Race, Superintendent Battle, and, finally, Miss Jane Marple. At the end of these

I have listed the novels without a series character, again, in the order of the time of the story. The reason for choosing this manner of organization will be obvious to readers who have tried to follow the biography of their favorite characters.

In arranging the titles chronologically I have relied on the internal evidence of the novels. Some authors give precise dates for the action of the story; others write of a world without time; and still others change the age of the characters as well as history to suit the story. I have arranged these as best I can, and I hope readers who have a better idea will let me know. The order of the novels in the list of annotations is followed in the sections on period, location, setting, miscellaneous information, and classics of the genre.

I have read all the novels listed here except those marked with an asterisk. The purpose of the annotations is to give the reader the flavor of the story without giving away the ending or passing judgment on the story. For the most part the novels are all available through public libraries, though many of them are out of print. With one exception (Fergus Hume's The Mystery of a Hansom Cab), all the titles were first published after 1900.

Working on this book brought me many new friends, fellow lovers of the mystery novel. Martha Hamilton and Donald York of the Cambridge Public Library located several titles for me, suggested authors to include here, and loaned me books from their own collections. Susan Innocenti of the Beverly Public Library also loaned me books and suggested authors to include. I have enjoyed their books and adopted most of their suggestions. Dorothy Keller of the Interlibrary Loan Department of the Boston Public Library has tracked down books from Maine to California, leaving me amazed at the network among libraries stretching across the country.

A good friend as well as a fine librarian, Susan Senecal Turner first helped me find several hard-to-locate titles. My editor, Borgna Brunner, has been patient and attentive throughout. At the outset, Ara Salibian asked perceptive questions that guided me in developing the book, and Cecile Watters provided thoughtful and gentle copyediting.

Most important through all of this has been Suzanne Nichelson of the Interlibrary Loan Department of the Beverly Public Library. Suzanne cheerfully searched for, found, and borrowed mysteries for me month after month. Her response to research questions related to the British mystery novel was equally pleasant and thorough. To her in particular and to all those who helped me complete this book, I am most grateful.

I began writing this book with my husband, Michael, in mind, who still thinks that there is no more pleasant way to spend one's leisure than in reading mysteries. May he find here enough books for many years to come.

1

Creators and Characters

Herbert Adams
Catherine Aird
Peter Alding
Michael Allen
Margery Allingham
Delano Ames

James Anderson

J.R.L. Anderson

Jeffrey Ashford
Marian Babson
H.C. Bailey

Brian Ball
Robert Barnard
Francis Beeding

Josephine Bell

Jimmie Haswell
Inspector C.D. Sloan
Inspector Robert Fusil
Superintendent Ben Spence
Albert Campion
Jane and Dagobert Brown
Corporal Juan Llorca
Inspector Wilkins
Mikael Petros
Colonel Peter Blair
Inspector Piet Deventer
Inspector Don Kerry
Douglas Perkins
Reggie Fortune
Joshua Clunk

Superintendent Perry Trethowan
Thomas Preston
Colonel Alistair Granby
Inspector Wilkins
Ronald Briercliffe
Inspector George Martin
Dr. David Wintringham
Superintendent Steven Mitchell
Claud Warrington-Reeve
Dr. Henry Frost
Miss Amy Tupper

1

E.C. Bentley	Philip Trent
Anthony Berkeley	Roger Sheringham
	Ambrose Chitterwick
John Bingham	Kenneth Ducane (Vandoren)
	Superintendent John Brock
Gavin Black	Paul Harris
Lionel Black	Emma Greaves
	Kate Theobald
	Superintendent Francis Foy
Nicholas Blake	Nigel Strangeways
John and Emery Bonett	Professor Mandrake
	Inspector Salvador Borges
Christianna Brand	Inspector Cockrill
	Superintendent Charlesworth
Simon Brett	Charles Paris
Leo Bruce	Sergeant William Beef
	Carolus Deene
W. J. Burley	Dr. Henry Pym
	Superintendent Charles Wycliffe
Henry Calvin	John Carlyle and Dai Owen
Edward Candy	Inspector Burnivel
Youngman Carter	Albert Campion
Sarah Caudwell	Professor Hilary Tamar
G.K. Chesterton	
Agatha Christie	Hercule Poirot
	Ariadne Oliver
	Tommy and Tuppence Beresford
	Colonel Race
	Superintendent Battle
	Miss Jane Marple
Douglas Clark	Superintendent George Masters
V.C. Clinton-Baddeley	Dr. R.V. Davie
Edmund Crispin	Gervase Fen
Freeman Wills Crofts	Inspector Joseph French
Gordon Daviot	Inspector Alan Grant
Detection Club	
D.M. Devine	
Dominic Devine	
Colin Dexter	Inspector Morse
Peter Dickinson	Superintendent James Pibble
Eilís Dillon	Professor Daly
	Inspector Mike Kenny

Margaret Erskine	Inspector Septimus Finch
J. Jefferson Farjeon	
E.X. Ferrars	Toby Dyke
	Superintendent Ditteridge
	Virginia Freer
	Professor Andrew Basnett
A. Fielding	Inspector Pointer
Nigel FitzGerald	Superintendent Duffy
	Alan Russell
J.S. Fletcher	Ronald Camberwell
Dick Francis	Sid Halley
Antonia Fraser	Jemima Shore
James Fraser	Inspector Bill Aveyard
R. Austin Freeman	Dr. John Thorndyke
Jonathan Gash	Lovejoy
Michael Gilbert	Inspector Hazlerigg
	Sergeant Patrick Petrella
Kenneth Giles	Inspector Harry James
Martha Grimes	Superintendent Richard Jury
Cyril Hare	Inspector Mallett
	Francis Pettigrew
S.T. Haymon	Inspector Benjamin Jurnet
Georgette Heyer	Superintendent Hannasyde
	Inspector Hemingway
Reginald Hill	Superintendent Andrew Dalziel
	Inspector Peter Pascoe
James Hilton. See Glen Trevor.	
John Buxton Hilton	Inspector Thomas Brunt
	Superintendent Simon Kenworthy
Kenneth Hopkins	Gerald Lee
	Dr. William Blow and
	Prof. Gideon Manciple
S.B. Hough	Inspector John Brentford
P.M. Hubbard	
Fergus Hume	
Alan Hunter	Superintendent George Gently
Francis Iles	
Michael Innes	Sir John Appleby
	Inspector Thomas Cadover
	Charles Honeybath
P.D. James	Superintendent Adam Dalgliesh
	Cordelia Gray

J.G. Jeffreys. See Jeremy Sturrock.
Roderic Jeffries   Inspector Enrique Alvarez
Romilly and Katherine John
H.R.F. Keating   Inspector Ganesh Ghote
                                Mrs. Craggs
C.H.B. Kitchin   Malcolm Warren
Ronald A. Knox   Miles Bredon
Elizabeth Lemarchand   Superintendent Tom Pollard
E.C.R. Lorac   Superintendent Macdonald
Peter Lovesey   Sergeant Cribb
Philip MacDonald   Colonel Anthony Gethryn
                                Superintendent Arnold Pike
Jessica Mann   Professor Thea Crawford
                                Tamara Hoyland
Ngaio Marsh   Superintendent Roderick Alleyn
J.C. Masterman   Ernst Brendel
Anthony Matthews. See Lionel Black.
A. A. Milne
Gladys Mitchell   Dame Beatrice Adela
                                Lestrange Bradley
Gwen Moffat   Miss Melinda Pink
Anne Morice   Tessa Crichton
Patricia Moyes   Superintendent Henry Tibbett and
                                Emily Tibbett
Simon Nash   Adam Ludlow and
                                Inspector Montero
Anthony Oliver   Lizzie Thomas and John Webber
Emma Page   Inspector Kelsey
Frank Parrish   Dan Mallett
John Penn   Superintendent George Thorne
Anne Perry   Inspector Thomas Pitt and
                                Charlotte E. Pitt
Ellis Peters   Brother Cadfael
                                Superintendent George Felse and
                                Bunty and Dominic Felse
Stella Phillips   Inspector Matthew Furnival
Martin Porlock
Sheila Radley   Inspector Douglas Quantrill
Ruth Rendell   Inspector Reginald Wexford
John Rhode   Dr. Lancelot Priestley
Jonathan Ross   Superintendent George Rogers
Patrick Ruell

Dorothy L. Sayers	Lord Peter Wimsey
John Sherwood	Celia Grant
Dorothy Simpson	Inspector Luke Thanet
Jeremy Sturrock	Jeremy Sturrock
Julian Symons	Inspector Bland
	Inspector Crambo
Josephine Tey	Inspector Alan Grant
Leslie Thomas	
June Thomson	Inspector Finch/Rudd
Leonard Tourney	Matthew Stock
Glen Trevor	
Michael Underwood	Superintendent Simon Manton
	Martin Ainsworth
	Rosa Epton
	Sergeant Nick Attwell
Roy Vickers	Inspector Kyle
Henry Wade	Inspector John Poole
	Major Faide
	Inspector Henry Lott
	Constable John Bragg
Colin Watson	Inspector Walter Purbright
Patricia Wentworth	Maud Silver
R. J. White	Inspector David Brock
David Williams	Mark Treasure
Colin Wilson	
Sara Woods	Antony Maitland
Margaret Yorke	Dr. Patrick Grant

2

Novels of Detection, Mystery, and Suspense

Herbert Adams*

The Crooked Lip
London: Methuen, 1926.
Philadelphia: Lippincott, 1926.

Jimmie Haswell

A businessman is taking his grown daughter on her first trip through Britain, traveling by train. Before they arrive at their destination, the father is murdered, leaving his daughter, who was raised in France, alone in a strange country.

The Golden Ape
London: Methuen, 1930.
Philadelphia: Lippincott, 1930.

Jimmie Haswell

Donald Wade has trouble opening the door to his flat, but he perseveres, enters, and confronts a young woman, who appears to have ransacked the place. Looking around him, he determines that the flat is not his and the woman not a typical burglar. By the time he figures out who she is, the owner of the flat is dead and the police want to question Donald.

The Woman in Black
London: Methuen, 1933.
Philadelphia: Lippincott, 1932.

Jimmie Haswell

From a poor background in Manchester, Beresford Wilson has worked his way up to become a successful London journalist. Then, accused of murdering his wife, from whom he has lived apart, he is tried and acquitted. On the night of his release from prison, he is shot.

Catherine Aird

The Religious Body
London: Macdonald, 1966.
New York: Doubleday, 1966.

Inspector C.D. Sloan

No one expects to find murder in a convent in the twentieth century, but that is exactly what Sloan is called in to investigate when a nun is found dead. The police must not only find a murderer but also do so with the help of a group of women sometimes reluctant, sometimes wary, and sometimes hostile to participating in a police investigation.

Henrietta Who?
London: Macdonald, 1968.
New York: Doubleday, 1968.

Inspector C.D. Sloan

A hit-and-run car accident leaves Sloan with the expected problem of identifying the driver of the car and the unexpected complication of identifying the victim, who was until her death a reserved widow uneventfully raising her daughter in the quiet village of Larking.

The Complete Steel
London: Macdonald, 1969.

The Stately Home Murder
New York: Doubleday, 1970.

Inspector C.D. Sloan

A sunny Sunday afternoon is the perfect time to explore the long-secret treasures of the stately home Ornum House, but one enterprising day-tripper discovers a secret that was not meant for public view--a corpse. Sloan journeys into the world of the contemporary aristocracy and its still-considerable network of supporters.

A Late Phoenix
London: Collins, 1970.
New York: Doubleday, 1971.

Inspector C.D. Sloan

Excavation of a Saxon site and surrounding area bombed in World War II before rebuilding of the area can be undertaken leads to the discovery of two bodies, but neither can be tied to the history of the site.

His Burial Too
London: Collins, 1973.
New York: Doubleday, 1973.

Inspector C.D. Sloan

A member of a prestigious research and development firm is found dead in a Saxon church tower, which had been effectively sealed. The solution to this variation on the locked-room mystery is both intelligent and clever.

Slight Mourning
London: Collins, 1975.
New York: Doubleday, 1976.

Inspector C.D. Sloan

The quiet village of Constance Parva changes slowly if at all. But late one night, the owner of the manor dies suddenly in a car accident, and that is the first in a series of shocks the village residents must absorb.

Parting Breath
London: Collins, 1977.
New York: Doubleday, 1978.

Inspector C. D. Sloan

An academic setting is certain to include extremes in character and conduct, and the University of Calleshire is no exception. The trouble begins with a student sit-in and moves on to murder and more.

Some Die Eloquent
London: Collins, 1979.
New York: Doubleday, 1980.

Inspector C.D. Sloan

A chemistry teacher at a girls' school plans to retire soon, but instead she dies of causes related to diabetes. This would seem to be a sad end to a quiet but contented life, until the police learn that she had a quarter of a million pounds in her bank account.

Passing Strange
London: Collins, 1980.
New York: Doubleday, 1981.

Inspector C.D. Sloan

Every year the Almstone Horticultural Society holds its show at the Priory estate, a tradition that everyone hopes will continue after the estate changes hands in the near future. This year, however, there are signs of deeper problems, including murder.

Last Respects
London: Collins, 1982.
New York: Doubleday, 1982.

Inspector C.D. Sloan

The coastal town of Edsway, long neglected and declining, begins to show signs of rejuvenation, and residents now have greater ambitions for the future. The only sour note is the discovery of the body of a well-dressed man out at sea.

Harm's Way
London: Collins, 1984.
New York: Doubleday, 1984.

Inspector C.D. Sloan

Two members of the Berebury Country Footpaths Society set out to inspect the paths chosen for the society's next walk and find a piece of a human body. The problem then is to find the rest of the body, which must be on one of the nearby farms.

A Most Contagious Game
London: Macdonald, 1967.
New York: Doubleday, 1967.

Thomas Harding has retired to the country to recover from a heart attack, but is beginning to wonder if he'll die of boredom instead. Deciding to mod ernize his home, he pokes around and uncovers a priest's hole and a skeleton. Intrigued, Harding sets out to solve a two-hundred-year-old murder.

Peter Alding*

The C. I. D. Room
London: Long, 1967.

All Leads Negative
New York: Harper, 1967.

Inspector Robert Fusil

A carefully packed and guarded shipment of gold charms is not as safe as was thought: one of the boxes is missing when the shipment is unloaded. Assigned to investigate the case, particularly the loading of the consignment, is a young detective constable with women and adventure on his mind as much as his job.

Murder among Thieves
London: Long, 1969.
New York: McCall, 1970.

Inspector Robert Fusil

Five professional criminals plan and execute successfully a dangerous armored car robbery, relying on both careful planning and violence to protect them. Not long afterward, the bodies of the members of the gang begin to appear unexpectedly, one by one.

Guilt without Proof
London: Long, 1970.
New York: McCall, 1971.

Inspector Robert Fusil

Three men hijack a lorry carrying whiskey, and the police at first cynically expect it to disappear into London. Instead, the search for the lorry and its load leads the police to Fortrow liquor stores and suppliers, revealing a well-planned if illegal venture.

Despite the Evidence
London: Long, 1971.
New York: Saturday Review Press, 1972.

Inspector Robert Fusil

The police are frustrated by a rash of petty thefts in a factory, and Constable Kerr has his own problems. He stops to help a man in a car accident and is knocked out. When he recovers in the hospital, he is told that the man in the accident is perfectly all right and that he, Kerr, was knocked out by a falling branch. Kerr knows this is nonsense, but has trouble getting anyone to believe him.

Field of Fire
London: Long, 1973.

Inspector Robert Fusil

Fortrow hasn't had a state visit in several years, and now there will be two visits within nine days. The visitors are an officer of the Czech Communist party and the president of an African nation, and a London gang plans to assassinate one of the men. The other crimes and accidents in the area get pushed aside for these visits, except for one: a man drives into the river and drowns, with two of the car windows open on a cold evening.

Six Days to Death
London: Long, 1975.

Inspector Robert Fusil

Police Constable Brady is quiet, stolid, and hard working. When he unexpectedly becomes a hero by interrupting a bank robbery, his life changes. He receives an award and his neighbors treat him with new respect. Then, several months later, a criminal sends him a threatening letter, giving him only six days to live.

Murder Is Suspected
London: Long, 1977.
New York: Walker, 1977.

Inspector Robert Fusil

A hit-and-run accident usually leads the police down a dead-end road, but this time the trail leads back to the police. Inspector Fusil must deal with codes of honor and dishonor in trying to solve a number of crimes that become more and more tightly intertwined.

Ransom Town
London: Long, 1979.
New York: Walker, 1979.

Inspector Robert Fusil

A bungled bank robbery, a ransom demand, and a suicide appear at first to have nothing in common, but the relentless digging of Fusil and his men slowly uncovers some slim but strong connections. The emphasis is less on the story of the suspects than on the persistence of Fusil.

A Man Condemned
London: Hale, 1981.
New York: Walker, 1981.

Inspector Robert Fusil

Inspector Fusil has his usual complex of disparate crimes to solve. He has been assigned the task of protecting a rich Iranian who is not well liked in Britain; a gang steals £125,000 in an armed robbery; and a constable is found dead in a car accident, apparently drunk at the wheel.

Betrayal by Death
London: Hale, 1982.
New York: Walker, 1982.

Inspector Robert Fusil

Nine young boys have disappeared over the past few weeks, but the police have no clues. In addition, the police are swamped with other problems: burglaries, bank robberies, car thefts, among other crimes. Fusil finally recognizes a number of coincidences and then relentlessly pursues the child killer.

Michael Allen

Spence in Petal Park
London: Constable, 1977.

Spence and the Holiday Murders
New York: Walker, 1978.

Superintendent Ben Spence

Rich and handsome Roger Parnell is not disturbed that friends and acquaintances sometimes dislike him. After he is found dead, the police accept a certain amount of jealousy in his relationships with others. But a little digging uncovers another side of his character, making jealousy only a veneer of a deeper hatred and fear.

Spence at the Blue Bazaar
London: Constable, 1979.
New York: Walker, 1979.

Superintendent Ben Spence

A beautiful woman returns to her village home as a stripper. Unrecognized by the people of her childhood, she remembers them and their secrets. Soon she discovers another: the identity of the person who viciously murdered two villagers many years ago.

Spence at Marlby Manor
New York: Walker, 1982.

Superintendent Ben Spence

A series of accidents besets Lady Dinnister and finally culminates in the death of a member of her household. Allen gives the reader the full cast of characters and suspects of the stately home, from the titled widow and her family to the surly gardener.

Margery Allingham

The Crime at Black Dudley
London: Jarrolds, 1929.

The Black Dudley Murder
New York: Doubleday, 1930.

Albert Campion

A quiet country weekend goes awry. The main ingredients include an old family ritual, sinister businessmen, and naive but well-meaning guests.

Mystery Mile
London: Heinemann, 1930.
Rev. ed. Harmondsworth, Engl.: Penguin, 1968.
New York: Doubleday, 1930.

Albert Campion

Judge Lobbett has escaped four attempts on his life in the United States and has decided he might be safer in England. He escapes another attempt before his son and daughter manage to hide him away in a manor house in a village, where he can indulge his love of history and folklore.

Death of a Ghost
London: Heinemann, 1934.
New York: Doubleday, 1934.

Albert Campion

In 1930 members of the art world gather at the annual exhibition of a dead painter's work, keeping alive his memory as well as their own grudges. The rivalries of the guests and participants finally become too intense to conceal behind social niceties, and one of the guests is murdered--only a few feet from Albert Campion.

Police at the Funeral
London: Heinemann, 1931.
New York: Doubleday, 1932.

Albert Campion

An old widow of a Cambridge professor maintains her home and way of life according to the standards of the 1870s, which is considered a barely tolerable hardship by her now elderly children living with her. The secrets and arguments of the isolated family lead first to a disappearance and then to a murder.

Flowers for the Judge
London: Heinemann, 1936.
New York: Doubleday, 1936.

Legacy in Blood
New York: Mercury, 1949.

Albert Campion

In 1911 Tom Barnabas, partner in the Barnabas and Company publishing house, disappeared on his way to work. In 1931 Paul R. Brande, a director of the firm and a cousin of Tom Barnabas, has also disappeared, but only for a few days. He is soon found--dead.

Look to the Lady
London: Jarrolds, 1931.

The Gyrth Chalice Mystery
New York: Doubleday, 1931.

Albert Campion

A chalice dating from before the Conquest has been guarded religiously by the Gyrth family since that date, but its fate now rests partly in the hands of a tramp and partly in the hands of Albert Campion. A unique treasure, the chalice is now the object of an intense search by a secret group of millionaire art collectors hoping to acquire it.

Sweet Danger
London: Heinemann, 1933.

Kingdom of Death
New York: Doubleday, 1933.

The Fear Sign
New York: Mcfadden, 1961.

Albert Campion

A massive earthquake in Europe has the unexpected result of giving a tiny kingdom about six hundred yards of coastline, and the kingdom belongs to a near-extinct line among the British aristocracy. Unfortunately, no one seems to have documents to prove it, so Campion and his friends, at the request of the government, are sent in search of them and encounter others doing the same.

The Case of the Late Pig
London: Hodder, 1937.

In: **Mr. Campion: Criminologist**
New York: Doubleday, 1936.

Albert Campion

In January 1936, Campion attends the funeral of an old classmate, who had once taken a knife to Campion and bullied just about everyone he met. Not many people are going to miss Pig Peters, and so Campion dismisses him from his mind--until June. Then he sees Pig Peters again, dead for not more than twelve hours this time.

Dancers in Mourning
London: Heinemann, 1937.
New York: Doubleday, 1937.

Who Killed Chloe?
New York: Avon, 1943.

Albert Campion

A series of practical jokes begins to unnerve the lead actor in a successful play. When he moves to his country estate with friends for the weekend in order to relax, the jokes continue. Asked to find the joker, Campion becomes personally involved.

The Fashion in Shrouds
London: Heinemann, 1938.
Rev. ed. London: Heinemann, 1965.
New York: Doubleday, 1938.

Albert Campion

Georgia Wells is a successful actress but very unlucky in her personal life. Divorced once, she then became engaged but her fiancé suddenly disappeared. More than two years later his body is found. Then her current husband dies. Campion needs to solve this mystery quickly because Georgia's eye has turned to another adoring man.

Traitor's Purse
London: Heinemann, 1941.
New York: Doubleday, 1941.

The Sabotage Murder Mystery
New York: Avon, 1942.

Albert Campion

Campion is accused of assaulting a policeman, but he has lost his memory. The only thing he can remember is that the number 15 is of vital importance. He must struggle to recover his memory in time to defeat a sinister enemy.

Coroner's Pidgin
London: Heinemann, 1945.

Pearls before Swine
New York: Doubleday, 1945.

Albert Campion

Home from his war service, Campion is anxious to get to the country for a holiday when he discovers Lugg, his manservant, and an elderly woman depositing a corpse in his bed. Soon half the neighborhood seems to be engaged in the problem of disposing of the body, and it is some time before they are willing to tell the whole story to the police. Even then, certain details are changed in the telling.

More Work for the Undertaker
London: Heinemann, 1949.
Rev. ed. London: Heinemann, 1968.
New York: Doubleday, 1949.

Albert Campion

Professor Palinode, the essayist, and his wife, the poet, may be remembered long after their deaths, but their aging children are reduced to living as boarders in what was once their family home. In a neighborhood ruined by a quick decline, Campion searches for a poisoner and the writer of poison-pen letters.

The Tiger in the Smoke
London: Chatto, 1952.
New York: Doubleday, 1952.

Albert Campion

Widowed at the age of twenty, Meg Elginbrodde is preparing to marry again, five years later, when she first receives in the mail a photograph of her late husband on a street in contemporary London. Convinced that he is alive, she can think of no reason for him to stay away from her.

The Beckoning Lady
London: Chatto, 1955.

The Estate of the Beckoning Lady
New York: Doubleday, 1955.

Albert Campion

Friends and relatives gather in the summer countryside, walking the lanes, lazing in the meadows, and completely blind to the corpse lying only a few feet away. After several days the body is finally noticed. The search for the murderer only partly disrupts the various house parties being held in the area.

Hide My Eyes
London: Chatto, 1958.

Tether's End
New York: Doubleday, 1958.

Ten Were Missing
New York: Dell, 1959.

Albert Campion

Unresolved and unconnected events of the past come to the fore as a young country girl seeks a long-lost aunt and the police seek an answer to several long-forgotten crimes. Campion understandably remains skeptical as he helps police track down the most tenuous of clues.

The China Governess
London: Chatto, 1962.
New York: Doubleday, 1962.

Albert Campion

In one of the worst sections of London, the government has managed to restore and build anew part of the neighborhood destroyed in the war. Now the area is plagued by senseless and cruel vandalism that seems directed at driving out the new residents. The ties to the old neighborhood wind through the years and over miles to reach beyond contemporary London.

The Mind Readers
London: Chatto, 1965.
New York: Morrow, 1965.

Albert Campion

A syndicate of businessmen has joined with the navy to investigate a new form of communication. Their secrecy, however, distresses the wives of the scientists and poses problems of its own.

Cargo of Eagles
London: Chatto, 1968.
New York: Morrow, 1968.

Albert Campion

The village of Saltey in Essex first became known as a place of ill omen in the Middle Ages, and later became known for its receptivity to smugglers and others escaping from London. The villagers seem content with any reputation that keeps away outsiders, and it is therefore little wonder that a doctor who has inherited a house in Saltey receives poison-pen letters and an escaped convict decides to head for the village.

The White Cottage Mystery
London: Jarrolds, 1928.
Rev. ed. London: Chatto, 1975.

The owner of a manor house is murdered in a nearby cottage at dusk, with members of the household in various parts of the cottage and a policeman on the road outside. The trail of the murderer leads to Europe and back to the village.

Black Plumes
London: Heinemann, 1940.
New York: Doubleday, 1940.

The family owners of the Ivory Art Gallery are slowly being demoralized by recurrent acts of vandalism against valuable works of art. To make matters worse, the head of the gallery is in China, and the business is being run by an assortment of relatives and staff members. Then the acting head is murdered and a member of the staff disappears.

Take Two at Bedtime (2 novellas)
Kingswood, Engl: World's Work, 1950.

Deadly Duo
New York: Doubleday, 1949.

Wanted: Someone Innocent. Gillian Brayton faced a bleak life as a milliner's
assistant until she attends a school reunion and is swept up by Rita Raven,
an old friend Gillian barely remembers. Rita insists that meeting her again
is a great joy and promptly offers her a job as secretary (for which Gillian
is not qualified). It takes only a few minutes after her arrival at Rita's
plush home for Gillian to realize that something is terribly wrong: the servants despise Rita and her husband is nowhere to be seen.

Last Act. Mathilde Zoffany may no longer be on the stage but she still
performs a role and commands the attention of her audience. Devoted to a
grandson and adopted granddaughter, she gives love and attention in her
style. Suspicious of a second grandson, however, she calls the police for
protection, convinced he means to have his inheritance soon under French
law, regardless of her wishes.

No Love Lost (2 novellas)
Kingswoods, Engl.: World's Work, 1954.
New York: Doubleday, 1954.

The Patient at Peacocks Hall. Dr. Ann Fowler has made a life for herself
in a small country practice, forgetting the man who jilted her for a movie
actress, or so she thinks. The past begins to return in a series of coincidences until she is face to face with the actress and then with her old lover.

Safer than Love. Elizabeth Lane is preparing to face the dismal state of her
marriage when her old boyfriend, Andy, arrives in town to stand in for the
vacationing doctor. Between Andy's final declaration of love and the townspeople's insatiable desire to know why she married Victor Lane, Elizabeth
begins to see that her marriage must fail, though she entered it precisely
because she thought it would be safe.

Delano Ames*

She Shall Have Murder
London: Hodder, 1948.
New York: Rinehart, 1949.

Jane and Dagobert Brown

An elderly and slightly paranoid client of a staid law firm is found murdered in her sleep. Despite carefully questioning and searching, Dagobert Brown keeps returning to the members of the law firm as suspects, all of whom knew the client through her regular chatty visits.

Murder Begins at Home
London: Hodder, 1949.
New York: Rinehart, 1950.

Jane and Dagobert Brown

On their way to Detroit, Jane and Dagobert Brown arrive in Palo Alto, New Mexico, where now lives the almost mythical Miranda Ross, Dagobert's "war experience." Now married and living on a ranch with various relatives, Miranda is cool to Dagobert's telephone call, but invites the Browns for the weekend. Miranda is talked about with awe by everyone as the woman too good to be true, but the Browns never see her. On the morning after they arrive, Miranda is dead.

Corpse Diplomatique
London: Hodder, 1950.
New York: Rinehart, 1951.

Jane and Dagobert Brown

Still seeking meaningful work in life and hoping to persuade his wife to write a novel, Dagobert takes Jane to Nice so that he can study Provençal. The accidental death of a long-time resident of the Browns' pension gives Dagobert an additional interest in the French coast.

Death of a Fellow Traveller
London: Hodder, 1950.
New York: Rinehart, 1950.

Nobody Wore Black
New York: Dell, 1951.

Jane and Dagobert Brown

Bored with his surroundings, where he watches his neighbors and their regular visitors including a man with a limp and two Great Danes, and hoping to inspire Jane to write another novel, Dagobert takes his wife to a tiny village in Cornwall, where they are nearly knocked down by two Great Danes. Then the dogs' owner dies, and Dagobert is off looking for the murderer. He is especially hoping for spies.

The Body on Page One
London: Hodder, 1951.
New York: Rinehart, 1951.

Jane and Dagobert Brown

Jane has always wanted to open one of her books with a body on page one, but she does not like the sight of a corpse. Indeed, so distracted is she by a neighbor's temporary corpse that she fails to notice that someone has been searching the Browns' apartment. When there is finally a body, a real one, the murder victim is not the person expected (or hoped for), and the shock drives out all other concerns, including the love letters being sent to Dagobert.

Murder, Maestro, Please
London: Hodder, 1952.
New York: Rinehart, 1952.

Jane and Dagobert Brown

Vacationing in the Pyrenees, the Browns join a group of British and American tourists gathering for a music festival. Overshadowing the music is the murder of a British tourist. To solve this crime, Dagobert must cope with spies, missing bicycles, a child prodigy, and a harpsichordist temporarily coming out of retirement, so to speak.

No Mourning for the Matador
London: Hodder, 1953.
New York: Washburn, 1953.

Jane and Dagobert Brown

Denis St. John has won the admiration of many in Spain, which is hard for an English bullfighter, but at least one person is glad to see him killed by a bull in the ring. His performance was visibly below standard, mystifying his friends and fans. Then Dagobert discovers by chance later that night one reason for St. John's sloppy and deadly performance.

Crime, Gentlemen, Please
London: Hodder, 1954.

Coffin for Christopher
New York: Washburn, 1954.

Jane and Dagobert Brown

A charming scoundrel periodically returns home to his wife and child. On his last return, he runs through his wife's money and is later found dead from an overdose of sleeping pills. The consensus among those who knew him is that his suicide was the only decent thing he ever did. Then the Browns find a letter sent to the dead man from France at an obscure London address, received only two hours before his death.

Landscape with Corpse
London: Hodder, 1955.
New York: Washburn, 1955.

Jane and Dagobert Brown

When Norman Bloomfield discovered the village of Paraiso de Mar and its local saint, Santa Serafina, he found a mission in life. He glorified the saint and introduced modern plumbing. His death during a festival for the saint, therefore, seemed fitting, or a judgment, depending on the point of view.

Crime Out of Mind
London: Hodder, 1956.
New York: Washburn, 1956.

Jane and Dagobert Brown

A beautiful young woman falls off a verandah to her death and her uncle identifies her body, advising the police that he is in fact her husband, not her uncle. The Baron von Jenbach is not the only one acting strangely: a laconic American tourist seems about to bolt from every conversation, a Hungarian pretends to be British, and a British singer is, like most other women who come to the hotel, thrown into a tizzy by the baron.

She Wouldn't Say Who
London: Hodder, 1957.
New York: Washburn, 1958.

Jane and Dagobert Brown

Dagobert decides that Jane really wants to be a suburban housewife, so he promptly gets a job and settles Jane into a home, made available when the husband-owner ran off with a secretary. In a few months, Jane and Dagobert's life shows striking parallels with the life of the previous residents of The Nid: Jane learns that Dagobert is involved with another woman, an actress, as well as an entire theater group.

Lucky Jane
London: Hodder, 1959.

For Old Crime's Sake
Philadelphia: Lippincott, 1959.

Jane and Dagobert Brown

Dagobert begins a new career by entering as many contests as possible. In Jane's name he wins a trip to the Mediterranean island of Tabarca. Jane is one of seven lucky winners, but by the time the winners reach France, there are only six. Then they notice that their bus is being followed by a man on a motor scooter.

The Man in the Tricorn Hat
London: Methuen, 1960.
Chicago: Regnery, 1966.

Corporal Juan Llorca

The sleepy coastal village of Madrigal is discovered by American and European tourists, who bring with them their own brand of trouble. An artist who settles there for the light and scenery becomes involved with other tourists, and all of them seem to be hiding the real reason for their interest in Madrigal.

The Man with Three Jaguars
London: Methuen, 1961.
Chicago: Regnery, 1967.

Sergeant Juan Llorca

In a booming tourist town on the Mediterranean coast, the rich foreigners are forgiven much, but not everything. Late one night a Britisher is killed by a hit-and-run driver, and the police know only that the car appears to have been a Jaguar. Unfortunately, one of the British residents owns three.

The Man with Three Chins
London: Methuen, 1965.
Chicago: Regnery, 1968.

Sergeant Juan Llorca

Sent to the small town of Benijacar to help with the annual festival, Sergeant Llorca meets a servant girl waiting for her lover late at night on a private estate. Then he is hit on the head and barely escapes a pack of guard dogs. In the morning he returns to the estate to report as much as he can tactfully to the owner and finds, instead, a corpse.

No Traveller Returns
London: Nicholson, 1934.

After receiving a disturbing telegram, Bob Hazard returns to Jamaica after twelve years. On the ship to the island, a drunk approaches Hazard and insists on talking to him before two passengers take the drunk away. Later the drunken Joseph Meyers falls overboard and Hazard's room is ransacked. The only item missing is a manuscript on voodoo.

James Anderson

The Affair of the Blood-stained Egg Cosy
London: Constable, 1975.
New York: McKay, 1977.

Inspector Wilkins

The earl and countess of Burford are host to several guests who are strangers to each other and in different walks of life. Nevertheless, the earl assumes he can entertain his personal guests while the diplomats present conduct their business discreetly. He is very wrong.

The Affair of the Mutilated Mink Coat
New York: Avon, 1982.

Inspector Wilkins

Lord and Lady Burford have a policy on house parties (keep them small) to avoid disasters (like the last big party), but they are once again facing a group of disparate guests: a film idol and producer want to look over the house for a movie location; a cousin and her husband have arrived from Australia; and the countess's daughter has invited two beaus in order to choose the one she will marry. The Burfords cannot keep the different groups apart.

Assassin
London: Constable, 1969.
New York: Simon, 1971.

Mikael Josef Petros

Mikael Petros has been condemned to death for murder, but only days before he is to die he is offered the opportunity to live--if he agrees to assassinate the president of a neighboring country to which Petros's country is closely linked. Petros agrees, and to ensure his compliance, his rescuers give him an injection that will prove fatal if he does not get the antidote by a certain date. Petros has twelve weeks in which to carry out the assassination.

The Abolition of Death
London: Constable, 1974.
New York: Walker, 1975.

Mikael Joseph Petros

Petros has served a prison sentence for assassinating the president of a European nation, but he now knows that he will never be free of the sentence of hatred people feel for him. He is again offered the opportunity to redeem himself, by carrying out a secret mission for the government. A scientist in another country has learned how to stop the aging process and is about to hand over this knowledge to a dictator.

The Alpha List
London: Constable, 1972.
New York: Walker, 1973.

The police discover a new twist to the crime of blackmail: someone is threatening innocent people with disclosing information that could harm another innocent person. The victim is asked to pay, not in money, but in information damaging to a more important victim. The blackmailer is leaving a trail of small lives shattered for enormous greed.

Appearance of Evil
London: Constable, 1977.

Matt Greenwood has gracelessly accepted his lot as a librarian in a small college library in New Mexico when he sees the announcement of the candidacy of Victor Feverstone for the governorship of a western state. Matt is stunned; he remembers an incident that took place twenty years ago and convinced him that Feverstone was a communist agent. When Matt next discovers that there may be only two people left alive who know Victor's secret, he travels to England to prevent the murder he is certain Victor has planned.

Angel of Death*
London: Constable, 1978.

Assault and Matrimony
London: Muller, 1980.
New York: Doubleday, 1981.

After twenty-four years of marriage, Sylvia has decided to murder her husband. This by itself might be shocking enough, but the day before, Edgar decided to murder Sylvia. The crisis of more than twenty years finally looms when Sylvia and Edgar learn they are going to have new neighbors, people decidedly out of step with their image of the neighborhood. Edgar wants to move out and Sylvia wants to buy the house next door.

Auriol*
London: Muller, 1982.

J.R.L. Anderson

Death on the Rocks
London: Gollancz, 1973.
New York: Stein, 1975.

Major Peter James Blair

Sailing for home, Blair notices a figure lying on the rocks. Coming closer, he realizes she must be dead and goes for help. Two days after the inquest, his cottage is burgled, and after another two days, he receives a bomb in the mail. Someone is very upset over the suicide of a secretary in an advertising agency.

Death in the Thames
London: Gollancz, 1974.
New York: Stein, 1975.

Major Peter James Blair

George Judd has spent years fishing a particular spot on the Thames, so people on shore expect to see his punt, but not empty and in the middle of the river. After a week police finally find his body--upstream. But he did not die of drowning and his fishing rod is still missing. Even worse, there is little in the area, except for a tiny village and a stately home housing an industrial think-tank, to catch anyone's interest.

Death in the North Sea
London: Gollancz, 1975.
New York: Stein, 1976.

Colonel Peter James Blair

A Dutch freighter stops to rescue a man adrift in a dinghy, but the first two rescuers are killed by a bomb attached to the body in the boat. As the police try to make sense of this, others begin to wonder about the danger to the rest of the North Sea ships and to the oil rigs not far away.

Death in the Desert
London: Gollancz, 1976.
New York: Stein, 1977.

Colonel Peter James Blair

A college student takes a summer job in a small African nation and narrowly escapes death. After that his life is never the same, though his later brushes with death are less dramatic. Colonel Blair must sort through student pranks to find the thread leading back to Africa.

Death in the City
London: Gollancz, 1977.
New York: Scribner, 1982.

Colonel Peter James Blair

The body of a middle-aged man is found buried in the mud of the Thames, his pockets weighted down with unspent bullets. The police soon learn that the ammunition is Belgian and was never supplied to the British army. Anderson's tale moves on to international shipping, political ambition, and the rewards of sailing.

Death in the Caribbean
London: Gollancz, 1977.
New York: Stein, 1977.

Colonel Peter James Blair

In answer to a request for help, Blair travels to the island of Nueva to assist in the sale of small British arms to the government. While he is dining with one of the island's main figures, an earthquake strikes the area, wiping out buildings and crops. But the Caribs in the hills insist there was no earthquake: something is happening in the caves near a large estate.

Death in the Greenhouse
London: Gollancz, 1978.
New York: Scribner, 1983.

Colonel Peter James Blair

A former member of the colonial service is found murdered in his greenhouse. Known as a quiet man with no enemies, he had spent his retirement growing exotic African plants, and some of these seem to be the only property missing at his death. Colonel Blair must travel to Africa for a solution.

Death in a High Latitude
London: Gollancz, 1981.
New York: Scribner, 1984.

Colonel Peter James Blair

The Cambridge Museum of Cartography is home to a large collection of special materials, including a seventeenth-century map called Baffin's Map. Of little contemporary use, Baffin's Map is suddenly the center of attention: the keeper who last worked with it dies suddenly, the map disappears, and the executive of a large oil company is kidnapped and offered in exchange for the original map.

A Sprig of Sea Lavender
London: Gollancz, 1978.
New York: St. Martin, 1979.

Inspector Piet Deventer

A young woman carrying only an artist's portfolio boards a train at Mark's Tey and arrives in London dead. When the police search for clues to her death, they find only the paintings, one of which may be a hitherto unknown Constable, and a sprig of sea lavender. Inspector Deventer uses this little information to uncover a darker side of the art world.

Festival
London: Gollancz, 1979.
New York: St. Martin, 1979.

Chief Constable Piet Deventer

Deventer's resources as a man and as a police officer are stretched almost to the limits when his nine-month-old daughter is kidnapped. At the same time the police must deal with a rock music festival and its attendant petty crime. In this instance, however, the web of crime grows, drawing in larger numbers of people and even some important public figures.

Reckoning in Ice
London: Gollancz, 1971.

Richard Garston, an accountant, is wondering why he was called in to review procedures at International Metals when the chairman, a venerable and brilliant scientist, invites him to Scotland. There Garston hears that the chairman's recent secret work has been discovered. This unsettling discovery and reports in the financial newspapers have led the chairman to conclude that someone is planning to steal his work and reap huge profits. Garston agrees to help, and ultimately sails across the North Atlantic in a twenty-five-foot boat to confront a group of investors in Greenland.

The Nine-spoked Wheel
London: Gollancz, 1975.

A student archaeologist is crushed underneath one of the Great Stones at Avebury, which appears to have fallen over during excavation. Although this is both tragic and a Newtonian challenge, the head of the dig, Dr. Arbolent, is much more concerned with his investigations and finds. Indeed, he insists he is on the verge of proving that the Etruscans came from Britain.

Redundancy Pay
London: Gollancz, 1976.

Death in the Channel
New York: Stein, 1976.

David Grendon, a successful accountant, suddenly finds himself unemployed. Disillusioned by the money chase, he turns to an honest life of hard work, and returns to a Devon fishing village. But the police are looking for an unidentified stranger in the same area, one who stole a sixteenth-century chalice from a village church, and David is, frankly, suspicious.

Jeffrey Ashford

Investigations Are Proceeding
London: Long, 1961.

The D.I.
New York: Harper, 1962.

Inspector Don Kerry

The divisional police are shocked when a mild police constable, known for his easygoing manner and love of his job, is arrested for a brutal crime. He is quickly convicted, and the police shift their attention to a missing person, suicide, and murder. But the case of Constable Oldfield does not end: the police watch Mrs. Oldfield's life fall apart and begin to doubt her husband's guilt.

Enquiries Are Continuing
London: Long, 1964.

The Superintendent's Room
New York: Harper, 1965.

Inspector Don Kerry

A new superintendent throws the police off their stride, complicating their investigations into two crimes committed against children. A few slip-ups by others working with the police lead to clearly drawn lines, and police work begins to suffer. And then the police are suspected of clear violations of the law in an arson case and its investigation.

Counsel for the Defence
London: Long, 1960.
New York: Harper, 1960.

A daring bank robbery stumps the police at first, but careful police work eventually pays off. Then the police discover they have a more dangerous opponent in the criminals' barrister.

The Burden of Proof
London: Long, 1962.
New York: Harper, 1962.

Roger Ventnor surprised his friends by giving up his hedonistic life after the death of his father and settling down to farm the family estate. When a former girlfriend is found dead and pregnant in an empty house on the estate, Roger does not seem an unlikely suspect.

Will Anyone Who Saw the Accident ...
London: Long, 1963.
New York: Harper, 1963.

Hit and Run
London: Arrow, 1966.

A young man named Steve leaves a party at which he has had far too much
to drink and after his girlfriend has gone off with another man. Later in an
accident a man is killed, but Steve cannot remember if he had an accident,
though he knows he had trouble driving home.

The Hands of Innocence
London: Long, 1965.
New York: Walker, 1966.

Convicted and sentenced to prison for the murder of two young girls, George
Krammer escapes from prison with the intent of proving himself cured of the
sick passions that drove him to his crimes. After kidnapping a young girl,
he takes her to the isolated home of a widow and there struggles to prove
himself cured.

Consider the Evidence
London: Long, 1966.
New York: Walker, 1966.

The police manage to connect the known criminal Haggard with a particularly
violent crime, but Haggard is determined to be acquitted. He is, but at a
cost that sends a policeman to prison and forces another to prove him innocent of any illegal conduct.

Forget What You Saw
London: Long, 1967.
New York: Walker, 1967.

Harry Brissom sees only success stretching out in front of him--a good future
as a barrister and marriage to a woman who will advance his career, though
his mother-in-law is a formidable and selfish woman. Then Harry witnesses
an accident in which a woman is killed. For the driver this is bad enough,

but for his associates this could be a disaster--Simon, the driver, knows how to short-circuit bank alarms and his associates need him for their next job. They cannot afford to let Harry put Simon in prison, and so they begin to apply pressure, first to Harry, then to his friends and family.

Prisoner at the Bar
London: Long, 1969.
New York: Walker, 1969.

Robert Bladen, a barrister, believes in doing his duty as a citizen, even when it might be uncomfortable for him. Therefore, when a man is killed in a lover's lane on a night when Bladen was there with a married woman, he so informs the police. The police, however, find his behavior curious.

To Protect the Guilty
London: Long, 1970.
New York: Walker, 1970.

After serving two years for vehicular homicide, Jim Parker faces a bleak future, but he is determined that he and his wife will succeed, even if their new farm is suffering from years of neglect. Jim's determination is doubted, however, when he calls the police to report a stolen lorry hidden in an unused barn on his property.

Bent Copper
London: Long, 1971.
New York: Walker, 1971.

Inspector Parker wants to win promotion, but to do so he needs to have a better record in his home district, an area that seems to have been singled out for a crime spree by a number of criminals. On top of this, he doesn't seem to know how to handle some of his men, particularly a young, idealistic one.

A Man Will Be Kidnapped Tomorrow
London: Long, 1972.
New York: Walker, 1972.

Four students at Ruffbridge University convince themselves that the police fabricated evidence against their fellow students. The four decide to take drastic action to release the confined students. They kidnap an ordinary citizen and hold her for ransom--the other students. But despite their careful planning, things go wrong almost from the beginning.

The Double Run
London: Long, 1973.
New York: Walker, 1973.

When Hilary Ryan loses his job with an auto company, he assumes he will get back at his former employers and quickly get another job. But he can't do either, and he soon faces a challenge he is not prepared for: what is he willing to do to make enough money to survive?

The Colour of Violence
London: Long, 1974.
New York: Walker, 1974.

A series of chance events brings two sets of people to the same apartment on a Saturday evening. After his wife leaves him, writer George Armitage moves into the city and deepens his new friendships. After careful planning, Weir and his cronies are ready for a burglary that is a crook's dream.

Three Layers of Guilt
London: Long, 1975.
New York: Walker, 1976.

Thirty years after he saved another man's life, Harry Miles asks the man, now a millionaire, for help in finding a job. He soon joins an estate in which no one trusts another, and the other workers resent the obvious improvements Miles makes. Certainly, no one seems pleased to learn that Miles once risked his life for another.

Slow Down the World
London: Long, 1976.
New York: Walker, 1976.

The career that race-car driver Jim Brice has built for himself is shattered by an accident during a race. When Brice tries to rebuild his life, he is first drawn to the world of crime and then shocked by what he has become part of.

Hostage to Death
London: Long, 1977.
New York: Walker, 1977.

Five bank robbers are trapped in a bank, with twenty-two hostages and thousands of pounds inside and dozens of police outside. When the robbers finally release the hostages and surrender, thousands of pounds are gone and one robber is missing.

The Anger of Fear
London: Long, 1978.
New York: Walker, 1979.

Police Constable Athana is an eager young detective who gets the chance to prove himself when a security plan goes awry and he uncovers questionable behavior by some of his colleagues. Ashford focuses on the intricacies of a force in which the members run the full range in character.

A Recipe for Murder
London: Long, 1980.
New York: Walker, 1980.

A rich woman bored with her novelist husband and a self-made man bored with his rich wife try to escape their unhappy marriages together, but only get in deeper in another, fatal deception.

The Loss of the Culion
London: Collins, 1981.
New York: Walker, 1981.

Bill Stevens seems to be the only man with a conscience on board the Culion, but when the ship sinks in the Indian Ocean, he is reported lost, after panicking and endangering the rest of the crew. After his unexpected return to England, Stevens sets out to regain his reputation and uncover the reason for the sinking of the Culion.

Guilt with Honour
London: Collins, 1982.
New York: Walker, 1982.

At a bird hunt, royalty and aristocracy spread out across the fields, moving slowly. As they stalk their prey, a middle-aged man is stalking the hunters. When he shoots, the prince is pushed out of the way and the man flees. But one of the guests, a race-car driver, insists that the attacker was not shooting at the prince, and no one believes him.

A Sense of Loyalty
London: Collins, 1983.
New York: Walker, 1984.

Industrial espionage is not a crime in England, which leaves HI Motors with only one recourse: hire a private agent to identify the employee who is giving the competition information that could ruin HI Motors. As the agent moves closer to his quarry, loyalty to the company conflicts with loyalty to other values.

Presumption of Guilt
London: Collins, 1984.
New York: Walker, 1985.

Angus Sterne agrees to drive a car from Spain to England and to carry papers for it that will enable him to avoid customs duties. All goes well until he arrives at the rendezvous in England. No one claims the car and Angus, therefore, has to keep it until someone does.

An Ideal Crime
London: Collins, 1985.
New York: Walker, 1986.

Jim Thorpe is willing to forgo much in order to finish his law degree, studying during the day and working as a security guard at night for Fifield
Vaults. When his employer's daughter invites him for dinner, he is glad of
the break. But that is also the night when burglars break into Fifield, plun-
der the vaults, and kill the guard on duty. When the police decide it was
an inside job, Jim is the obvious suspect.

Marian Babson

Cover-up Story*
London: Collins, 1971.

Douglas Perkins

Murder on Show
London: Collins, 1972.

Douglas Perkins

Douglas Perkins enters the strange world of cat lovers when he becomes the
public relations officer for an exhibition entitled Cats through the Ages. He
wends his way through temperamental owners, opportunistic sponsors, bemused
felines, and two large tigers. As the distinction between master and pet
blurs, Douglas's job gets trickier, and on the morning of the opening he
finds that a security guard has been knocked out and a gold statue of Dick
Whittington's cat stolen.

Pretty Lady
London: Collins, 1973.

Denny is a happy young man, with good friends and a family. Then he meets
Merelda, an aging actress married to a rich industrialist. Merelda has finally

acknowledged her resentment of her husband and begun to plan a murder to free herself. A chance meeting with Denny is the final step in her plan.

Unfair Exchange
London: Collins, 1974.
New York: Walker, 1986.

Zita Falbridge is preparing for her husband's absence for three weeks on a business trip when his ex-wife, the beautiful and irresponsible Caroline, maneuvers her into taking her daughter, Fanny, from a still-earlier marriage. Zita quickly learns, as David warned she would, that Fanny is a difficult child. In addition, Zita must worry about the man watching the house. Then Fanny runs away. Caroline declares the child kidnapped, is suspiciously unworried, and drags Zita off to rescue the child.

The Stalking Lamb*
London: Collins, 1974.

Murder Sails at Midnight
London: Collins, 1975.

Mrs. Abercrombie, still in her wheelchair but slowly recovering, is helped by a nurse, who is now a rich woman in her own right. Susan Emery, who limps, has only a few days left before she inherits a large estate, and Gloria Pontini has earned her own money and success. One of these women is Mr. Butler's quarry, scheduled to die while their cruise ship crosses the Atlantic.

There Must Be Some Mistake*
London: Collins, 1975.

Untimely Guest
London: Collins, 1976.

Ten years ago Dee Dee eloped with her sister's fiancé. The girl's father chased the pair, and his sudden death afterward was attributed to the shock of his daughter's behavior. Bridget, the jilted sister, entered a convent, and Dee Dee ultimately left her husband, Terence, who went on living with his in-laws. Now Bridie has left the convent, and Dee Dee has a new fiancé.

Murder, Murder, Little Star
London: Collins, 1977.
New York: Walker, 1980.

Mrs. Frances Armitage, a widow with two grown children, lands a job as a chaperone to a child movie star. Her illusions about a glamorous job in the movie industry are dispelled by the bratty child's behavior, but after an attempt on the child's life, Frances begins to think she is the only friend the child has.

The Lord Mayor of Death
London: Collins, 1977.
New York: Walker, 1979.

The annual Lord Mayor's Show is a spectacular parade drawing thousands of London children. But behind the carnival atmosphere, a mother searches wildly for her missing daughter and the police search methodically for a man with a grudge and a bomb.

Tightrope for Three
London: Collins, 1978.

The fog creeping over Dartmoor cuts off several people from the rest of the world: a businessman having a liaison with his secretary awaits a helicopter to take him back to London for an important business coup; his wife in a cottage nearby is worried about her daughter's appendicitis; and a vicious killer who has just escaped from prison is counting himself lucky for stumbling on them all.

So Soon Done For
London: Collins, 1979.

The residents of the exclusive neighborhood of Crozier Crescent wake up one morning to find the home of a neighbor occupied by squatters--a hippie earth mother and her three children. The police point out that only the owners, who are away, can evict the family. Then two men join the group. The neighbors try to mobilize against the family, but instead the squatters create unsuspected tensions among the residents, eliciting uneasy tolerance from some and malevolence from others.

The Twelve Deaths of Christmas
London: Collins, 1979.
New York: Walker, 1980.

A random killer terrorizes London in the days before Christmas, leaving no clues and suggesting no motive. After each crime, the murderer returns to a cozy home in a West End lodging house, safe once again from the world outside.

Queue Here for Murder
London: Collins, 1980.

Line Up for Murder
New York: Walker, 1981.

Lining up in advance for the annual department store sale is an honored tradition that occasionally attracts dishonorable characters. This tale gives the reader a sidewalk view of the changing face of London.

Dangerous to Know
London: Collins, 1980.
New York: Walker, 1981.

The London Record has all the problems of a big-city newspaper: declining circulation, rising costs, and angry readers. Two reporters have been killed, apparently in the line of duty, and the editors are now wondering what stories are so dangerous to their reporters: business investigations, the psychic in high society, the guests at the fat farm, or the game of musical beds being played among the newspaper staff.

Bejewelled Death
London: Collins, 1981.
New York: Walker, 1982.

Carrying museum jewels to London in a hatbox seems a good idea until the young curator counts three other identical hatboxes among her fellow travelers. When she arrives at her London hotel, she has the wrong hatbox and the jewels are gone. She enlists the aid of three of her traveling companions to track down the jewels.

Death Warmed Up
London: Collins, 1982.
New York: Walker, 1982.

After struggling to build her catering service, Jean Ainley finds more to
worry about than financial solvency. Her clients begin to act as though an
invitation to lunch were an opportunity to murder. Between suspicious diners
and a wayward staff, Ainley sorts out murders and menus.

Death beside the Sea
London: Collins, 1982.
New York: Walker, 1983.

The August Bank Holiday is anything but a holiday for club owners and residents in the coastal resorts. Like many others, Trudi Kane, bar pianist,
must worry about aggressive patrons, late hours, and the occasional marauding
motorcycle gang. In addition, she has a starer in her audience and a malicious child resident in her theatrical digs. And someone among them all
may be the murderer of a young woman.

A Fool for Murder
London: Collins, 1983.
New York: Walker, 1984.

Pressed by his family to face up to his age and make provisions for his relatives and children, Wilmer Creighleigh plans to meet with his solicitor on
his return from a lecture tour in America. But his ultimate solution to family
problems is totally unexpected and seems destined to lead to murder.

The Cruise of a Deathtime
London: Collins, 1983.
New York: Walker, 1984.

The Empress Josephine gets off to a poor start on its cruise across the
Atlantic Ocean to Africa when one of the crew misses the ship's departure.
This is followed by the discovery of two dead passengers, and after that
captain and crew wonder if anyone will survive the trip.

A Trail of Ashes
London: Collins, 1984.
New York: Walker, 1985.

A young widow with two children decides to spend the summer in New England with her sister in order to recover from her husband's death. Instead of idyllic rural life, however, she settles into a town under a strain. Her sister, overwrought, is clearly worried about her husband, who looks seriously ill from overworking.

Death Swap
London: Collins, 1984.
New York: Walker, 1985.

Arnold Harper is persuaded to take his family to England for three months, swapping his house in New Hampshire (see above title) for a home outside London. He looks forward to long days doing research in London's famed libraries while his wife and children enjoy English life. Unfortunately, problems with his new neighbors and a series of accidents make his wife wonder if he'll live through the summer.

Death in Fashion
London: Collins, 1985.
New York: Walker, 1986.

In the frenetic and competitive world of high fashion Decemo Designers suffers its share of mishaps as the staff and models prepare for their major show. A funeral wreath arrives instead of the ordered flowers; the studio's most important dress is ruined in an accident; and two buyers have a violent quarrel during the show. Then the accidents become personal, and it is soon evident that lives are in danger.

H.C. Bailey*

Shadow on the Wall
London: Gollancz, 1934.
New York: Doubleday, 1934.

Reggie Fortune

London society has a number of deaths that are unsettling but can't be
proved to be murder. First, Mrs. Poynta shoots herself, then her husband
crashes his military aircraft, and then a Mr. Luttrell is killed in a fall from
a window the morning after a charity ball. Lady Rosnay, fortunately, is
only slightly injured when she is knocked down at the ball, which is held in
her home, but her tiara is apparently stolen though she doesn't mention it.

The Great Game
London: Gollancz, 1939.
New York: Doubleday, 1939.

Reggie Fortune

The quiet of a June evening is broken by the sound of the Mary bell ringing
twice. Since there is no church service scheduled and since the Mary bell is
rung to announce the parson's death, those who hear the bell run to the
church, where they find the parson running for help for a woman lying on
the church floor. The only person who doesn't hear the bell and come running is the one person who said she was just there.

The Bishop's Crime
London: Gollancz, 1940.
New York: Doubleday, 1941.

Reggie Fortune

Bishop Rankin, young and humanitarian, clashes with the other members of
Badon Cathedral soon after his arrival there when he suggests selling some
of the library books to fund his good works. On top of this his two young
children have their own ideas about a proper childhood, and the police trace
the corpse of a criminal to the cathedral.

Mr. Fortune Finds a Pig
London: Gollancz, 1943.
New York: Doubleday, 1943.

Reggie Fortune

The medical authorities are beginning to worry in a remote village in Wales after fifteen evacuated children come down with a strange fever. The local doctors diagnose it as typhus and blame the woman in charge of the children. But Reggie Fortune wonders: he has never seen a case of typhus in Britain, the children were inspected two weeks earlier by the public health nurse, and there are no pigs in the area.

Clunk's Claimant
London: Gollancz, 1937.

The Twittering Bird Mystery
New York: Doubleday, 1937.

Joshua Clunk

The Lade family nurtured their large housing estate until the last generation, when William Lade turned over the management to his real estate agent, Mr. Platt. Since then, the property has gone steadily downhill under the selfish eye of the agent. After twenty years there are certainly many who hate him: the tenants, the people in his office, and perhaps the owners of the estate, for they must have had some reason to leave everything so entirely in Platt's hands, and he is not a man to inspire affection.

The Veron Mystery
London: Gollancz, 1939.

Mr. Clunk's Text
New York: Doubleday, 1939.

Joshua Clunk

Joseph Axton made money the wrong way, by buying and selling farmland.
He then built a mansion and retired to enjoy his wealth, but village society
wants nothing to do with him. When he is critically injured in a fall from
his horse, his housekeeper insists that the vultures are moving in to steal his
estate while he is too weak to resist. Unexpectedly he dies, and so does his
housekeeper.

The Little Captain
London: Gollancz, 1941.

Orphan Ann
New York: Doubleday, 1941.

Joshua Clunk

Sister Martha surrounds her home for orphan girls with privacy and discre-
tion, or perhaps secrecy and suspicion. A chance inquiry by a patron of
the home and the death of a nightclub dancer lead Joshua Clunk to investigate the home, to find out exactly what is happening to orphan girls of good
background.

Dead Man's Shoes
London: Gollancz, 1942.

Nobody's Vineyard
New York: Doubleday, 1942.

Joshua Clunk

The coastal village of Calbay has little to recommend it, though some of
the less scrupulous find it convenient for them. When an orphan who works
for a pub owner is found dead in the ocean, the assumption by the local
reporter and townspeople is that his death must somehow be connected with
his surly employer, Mr. Bryony, who insists he is being maligned.

Slippery Ann
London: Gollancz, 1944.

The Queen of Spades
New York: Doubleday, 1944.

Joshua Clunk

The quiet town of Sturton Bay is beset with incidents that appear to be
harmless but leave the police worried. Miss Parker, secretary to the manager
of the docks, falls into a quarry; a new resident, last seen hanging around
a hotel, disappears; and two youngsters find a dead body in a cave. Those
involved in the incidents as witnesses or friends are nervous and reticent, but
the police cannot break down their stories.

The Wrong Man
London: Macdonald, 1946.
New York: Doubleday, 1945.

Joshua Clunk

Anxious to thank the wife of the soldier who saved his life, the American
Colonel Baker travels to a small village in England to meet Mrs. Thirl. She
is surprisingly young and disturbingly misinformed about her husband's current

state. At the inn where he is staying, Colonel Baker meets a British major also said to be a friend of Bill Thirl. But to the colonel's eye, this major and Thirl are unlikely to have been friends.

Brian Ball*

Death of a Low-Handicap Man
London: Barker, 1974.
New York: Walker, 1978.

The pleasant Sunday golf games at Wolvers are interrupted when one of the players is suddenly murdered. Police Constable Root, an avid golfer, is immediately confronted with the task of finding the murderer--amid a course full of friends and acquaintances.

Montenegrin Gold
London: Barker, 1974.
New York: Walker, 1978.

Within a few days, Charles Copley loses his job and then his father. As he sinks into alcohol and self-pity at the turn his life has taken, he gets tangled in a web of hatred and intrigue reaching back thirty years to a war that never ended, though soldiers like his father quietly retired from an active role.

Robert Barnard

Sheer Torture
London: Collins, 1981.

Death by Sheer Torture
New York: Scribner, 1982.

Inspector Perry Trethowan

At his father's death, Detective Inspector Trethowan returns home, but not to mourn. One of his slightly crazy relatives has murdered his equally crazy father by a method designed to ensure the family's notoriety for at least one more generation.

Death and the Princess
London: Collins, 1982.
New York: Scribner, 1982.

Superintendent Perry Trethowan

The young Princess Helena has led the circumscribed life of a dutiful if distant member of the royal family, and though somewhat silly, she is certainly harmless. Yet Scotland Yard has been tipped that she could be in danger, and the deaths of two men closely associated with her seemed to confirm the tips.

The Missing Brontë
London: Collins, 1983.

The Case of the Missing Brontë
New York: Scribner, 1983.

Superintendent Perry Trethowan

When a retired schoolteacher discovers what might be a missing Brontë manuscript, she modestly attempts to identify it with the help of experts. Unfortunately, others are less patient and less scrupulous in determining the future of the manuscript, and soon Trethowan is following a trail of burglary, assault, and worse.

A Little Local Murder
London: Collins, 1976.
New York: Scribner, 1983.

The casual interest of a radio producer in recording a visit to the village of Twytching injects new life into the boring routine of the villagers. But for some the competition to be included in the radio program becomes too intense, leading to murder and an entirely new image for the pastoral town.

Death of an Old Goat
London: Collins, 1977.
New York: Walker, 1977.

Professor Belville-Smith is unhappily traveling around Australia, giving his lectures on Jane Austen to university groups as little interested in him as he is in them. But in Drummondale, all that changes.

Death on the High C's
London: Collins, 1977.
New York: Walker, 1978.

The members of the Northern Opera Company have learned to tolerate each other, but when a new singer of exceptional ability joins the company, the jealousies grow. The mounting tension propels the singers to a great performance, and one of them to murder.

Blood Brotherhood
London: Collins, 1977.
New York: Walker, 1978.

A small group of church men and women gather at an Anglican community for a symposium on the role of the church in the modern world, but they bring too much of the world with them. One of the brothers is murdered and the local police seem inept and clumsy.

Unruly Son
London: Collins, 1978.

Death of a Mystery Writer
New York: Scribner, 1979.

To please his daughter, Sir Oliver Fairleigh-Stubbs, a successful mystery writer, agrees to be pleasant to one and all during his birthday party. But his new demeanor comes too late to assuage at least one of the many friends and relatives he has offended over the years. Unraveling the murder means unraveling the web of hostility that ensnares the family.

Posthumous Papers
London: Collins, 1979.

Death of a Literary Widow
New York: Scribner, 1980.

Walter Machin has been dead for some time, his books forgotten, but his memory kept alive by a widow and an ex-wife, who share a house. Now the literary world has rediscovered Machin's work, and each former wife thinks she has the right to benefit exclusively.

Death in a Cold Climate
London: Collins, 1980.
New York: Scribner, 1981.

A young foreigner in the Norwegian town of Tromsø walks off to keep an appointment and never returns; his body is found months later. The only information the police have is that the dead man spoke briefly with a number of students in a café in the hours before he disappeared.

Mother's Boys
London: Collins, 1981.

Death of a Perfect Mother
New York: Scribner, 1981.

For twenty years, Lillian Hodsden lived her life exactly as she pleased, un-
aware that others merely tolerated her callous behavior. No one is surprised
when she is murdered, and the more the police probe, the more suspects
they find, and the murkier the murder becomes.

Little Victims
London: Collins, 1983.

School for Murder
New York: Scribner, 1984.

Burleigh School, a mediocre private school for boys, has attracted over the
years an eccentric and second-rate group of teachers and students. A streak
of malice runs through several of the boys, and no one is personally unhappy
or terribly shocked at the murder of one in particular.

Corpse in a Gilded Cage
London: Collins, 1984.
New York: Scribner, 1984.

Perce and Elsie Spender, a quiet working-class couple from Clapham, inherit
a title and an estate. After trying out the life of an earl and countess for
a few weeks, they decide to go back to the life they have always known.
But their children do not so readily agree, and soon a murder prevents anyone from going anywhere.

Out of the Blackout
London: Collins, 1985.
New York: Scribner, 1985.

Evacuated to the countryside in 1941, young Simon is glad to forget London
and its dangers, but as he grows up he begins to wonder why no one ever

claimed him and why he knew, as a five-year-old, to conceal his name. Over more than twenty years, Simon slowly learns about his past and the death that sent him to freedom.

Disposal of the Living
London: Collins, 1985.

Fête Fatale
New York: Scribner, 1985.

The women of Hexton-on-Weir take their responsibility for the life of the village seriously. Thus, when the new vicar turns out to be high church and celibate, the women decide to take action, and the annual village fête ends with a murder.

Francis Beeding*

The Seven Sleepers
London: Hutchinson, 1925.
Boston: Little, Brown, 1925.

Thomas Preston

Thomas Preston is a salesman for the family hardware business and traveling in Europe when his trunk is mistakenly sent to Geneva. Since the woman he loves is there, he takes this as an omen and sets off. During his first night he is mistaken for someone else and handed a secret document. The next day he is invited to a rendezvous. Curious, Preston decides to follow the trail meant for another. After all, he has already identified three of the seven names on the document.

The Hidden Kingdom
London: Hodder, 1927.
Boston: Little, Brown, 1927.

Thomas Preston

While on a sales trip to Spain, Preston encounters the followers of the arch-villain Professor Kreutzemark and is trapped into figuring out the professor's latest scheme. All that is known is that the professor is staying in Barcelona with a man who raises bulls for the bullfights and that he is interested in a medieval manuscript.

The Six Proud Walkers
London: Hodder, 1928.
Boston: Little, Brown, 1928.

Colonel Alistair Granby

During a walk along the Appian Way, a young British tourist is accosted by a madman, witnesses a murder, steals a horse for his escape, is kidnapped and then drugged, and escapes again by jumping off a roof. So begins an adventure for young Mr. Carroll, who is more concerned with mustering the courage to propose marriage to the woman he loves.

Pretty Sinister
London: Hodder, 1929.
Boston: Little, Brown, 1929.

Colonel Alistair Granby

Colonel Granby, trying to unravel a cryptic message on a cigarette pack, and a young friend from the Foreign Office looking for a lost love team up inadvertently to dodge foreign agents, from Geneva to London and northward.

The Five Flamboys
London: Hodder, 1929.
Boston: Little, Brown, 1929.

Colonel Alistair Granby

When a moneylender is killed on the Isle of Wight, the Foreign Office steps in to cover up his death, for Angus McGuffie, born Shadrach Lowenstein, was in the process of sending vital information to the government. Now Colonel Granby must get the information himself, and he chooses a startling route, traveling to Geneva to find the identity of the five flamboys, the only source of fear ever acknowledged by McGuffie.

The League of Discontent
London: Hodder, 1930.
Boston: Little, Brown, 1930.

Colonel Alistair Granby

A French miller who once worked for the British government as an agent comes out of retirement to sell information to his old employers, but he dies before Granby can reach him. Raising suspicions about his death is the presence nearby of an Italian assassin released from prison during a general amnesty and a financier convicted in England of fraud.

The Four Amourers
London: Hodder, 1930.
Boston: Little, Brown, 1930.

Colonel Alistair Granby

Traveling through Spain, Colonel Granby and his friend John Baxter see a man barely escape death. Rescuing him, they listen to a tale of blackmail and fear. Then he dies, Granby disposes of the body, and the two men move on. In Madrid a few days later, Baxter realizes that their disposal of the body did not go unnoticed and his role unappreciated.

The Nine Waxed Faces
London: Hodder, 1936.
New York: Harper, 1936.

Colonel Alistair Granby

Bob Hardcastle is sent to Europe to investigate an agent in Italy who insists
he has important information for the British. Hardcastle arranges to meet
the agent-artist in Innsbruck, but the agent has trouble crossing the border.
By the time Hardcastle, with the help of a secret Austrian organization,
reaches Bertholdi, he is mad, raving nonsensically.

The Ten Holy Horrors
London: Hodder, 1939.
New York: Harper, 1939.

Colonel Alistair Granby

In the darkening days of 1938, an afternoon tea party for the constituents
of a Conservative MP on the terrace of the House of Commons is the unlikely
setting for a meeting of warring factions of Ukrainians. This is the beginning of a hunt by Colonel Granby for an infamous Nazi agent.

The Twelve Disguises
London: Hodder, 1942.
New York: Harper, 1942.

Colonel Alistair Granby

General Creighton may be difficult to work with and ungracious when he is
right, which he always is, but no one wants to go through the war without
him. When he insists on being smuggled into France, the top officials must
agree. When he disappears in France without a trace, the officials know they
must find him.

Death Walks in Eastrepps
London: Hodder, 1931.
New York: Mystery League, 1931.

Inspector Wilkins

The quiet coastal village of Eastrepps is the unexpected site of a senseless murder--and then another. Fearing a homicidal maniac is on the loose, the local police and Scotland Yard pursue every possible lead, ferreting out the sometimes well-known secrets of the villagers, high and low, but there is still no murderer.

Murder Intended
London: Hodder, 1932.
Boston: Little, Brown, 1932.

Inspector Wilkins

With a perverse sense of humor, a man leaves his parsimonious wife a small fortune, on the understanding that all of her heirs attend a dinner party annually. When the old woman cannot attend one year, the guests begin to lightly discuss murder, including the old woman's. Soon after, the dinner guests begin to die off, one by one.

The Three Fishers
London: Hodder, 1931.
Boston: Little, Brown, 1931.

Ronald Briercliffe

Cashiered from his regiment for drinking, Roland Briercliffe is given the opportunity to redeem himself by joining the intelligence branch. His assignment is to watch over Francis Wyndham, a former British agent who discovered after the war that crime was more lucrative than government work.

No Fury
London: Hodder, 1937.

Murdered: One by One
New York: Harper, 1937.

Inspector George Martin

Valerie Beauchamp is a successful romantic novelist who turns a cold and mean face to everyone except Arthur Scott-Digby, for Valerie has fallen madly in love with a man she knows only through his letters. She arranges to meet him, but he does not appear. Then she learns the truth about her Arthur and about her friends, the members of the local literary society who look down on her and her writing.

The Little White Hag
London: Hutchinson, 1926.
Boston: Little, Brown, 1926.

Robert Quexter, a quiet American with an overseas bank, lets a fellow American share his hotel room during a stopover in Dijon. Though the man behaves oddly, Quexter is thinking more of the various meetings he will attend at the League of Nations in Geneva. Indeed, he is especially interested in the meetings on drug trafficking, but these are nothing compared to the tangle of criminal activity he falls into because of his chance meeting in Dijon.

The House of Dr. Edwardes
London: Hodder, 1927.
Boston: Little, Brown, 1928.

Spellbound
Cleveland: World, 1945.

Beeding uses the many myths and superstitions associated with an asylum for the mentally ill to create a world as illusory as it is mysterious. A medieval castle in an isolated valley in France is the home of a renowned doctor specializing in the treatment of the mentally ill. Constance Sedgwick arrives to take up her first post only to learn that the famous doctor is gone and a new one has taken his place.

The Emerald Clasp
London: Hodder, 1933.
Boston: Little, Brown, 1933.

After fifteen years of caring for her invalid mother, Rosamund Shipley inherits a large estate and income, and goes off to see something of the world
before she is too old. Traveling with an old friend in France, she is flattered by the attentions of Marian's gentleman friend. Marian is thereby
driven to suicide, and Rosamund falls in love with and marries Guy. The
sadness of Marian's death is compounded a few months later when Rosamund
is informed that Marian had left her her pearl necklace but had had to pawn
the pearls in the last year of her life.

The Big Fish
London: Hodder, 1938.

Heads off at Midnight
New York: Harper, 1938.

A young student's reverie is broken by screams in the middle of the night.
He rushes out to find a dead body in the garden of the home of his uncle,
the Peruvian minister. When he returns a few moments later, the corpse is
still there but its head is gone. The Peruvian minister must draw on the
wisdom of his scholarly friends to make sense of this crime.

Josephine Bell*

Fall over Cliff
London: Longmans, 1938.
New York: Macmillan, 1956.

Dr. David Wintringham

Mrs. Medlicott is dying, and her relatives are waiting to inherit her fortune.
Years earlier she brought together her surviving relatives, told them how
much they would get, and hoped they would visit her if they wished. Then
they started dying off, one by one, from a swimming accident, a traffic accident, and diabetes, and then, just when the old woman is only hours away

from death herself, from a fall over a cliff. And the last one is obviously not an accident.

Death at Half-Term
London: Longmans, 1939.

Curtain Call for a Corpse
New York: Macmillan, 1965.

Dr. David Wintringham

Danbury School customarily presents a play for the parents of students at the end of term in the summer, but this year the school has had to hire a theater troupe. Now, in addition to the usual chaos of a parents' weekend, the headmaster must deal with thievery and murder among the actors.

Death at the Medical Board
London: Longmans, 1944.
New York: Ballantine, 1964.

Dr. David Wintringham

Ursula Frinton is determined to be accepted by the medical board for war work, and her family is just as determined to prevent her from qualifying. Armed with a letter from a heart specialist, Ursula passes her medical exam and challenges the letters sent by local doctors on her poor health. But someone's determination is stronger still, for Ursula dies suddenly at the medical board.

Death in Clairvoyance
London: Longmans, 1949.

Dr. David Wintringham

Mrs. Odette Hamilton has come to Summerton for a rest after an eight-month ordeal. She and her friend attend a costume ball for the tourists, during which she has a vision of a man in a clown suit being killed by another man in a clown suit. When she warns her friend, they look through the crowd and find five guests with clown suits. Nevertheless, they cannot alter fate: a man dies just as Odette predicted.

The Summer School Mystery
London: Methuen, 1950.

Dr. David Wintringham

Students from the prestigious music schools of London gather at Falconbury for a summer session. They get off to a slow start when some of the students are late to arrive. Indeed, Belinda Power sent her instruments well ahead of her and her fiancé has already arrived. During the first practice, however, the man who is taking Belinda's place in the orchestra finds that she has in fact arrived--dead.

Bones in the Barrow
London: Methuen, 1953.
New York: Macmillan, 1955.

Dr. David Wintringham

On a fog-bound train, a young clerk sees for an instant a woman in a slum apartment struck and killed. He tells the police, but nothing happens. Then a builder and his apprentice find human bones on a roof. The police look again and this time focus on a lodger who rented a room in the area where the clerk saw the murder. The lodger is a street hawker of cat's meat with his own refrigerator.

The China Roundabout
London: Hodder, 1956.

Murder on the Merry-Go-Round
New York: Ballantine, 1965.

Dr. David Wintringham

Mrs. Forrestal had not seen her brother for some time when he died, but she recognized everything in the flat in his house, which he had turned into a boardinghouse. Only one thing is missing: a china merry-go-round that had delighted them both as children. Trying to find this antique toy disturbs the tenants and anyone else who knew about it. But Mrs. Forrestal wants to find it anyway.

The Seeing Eye
London: Hodder, 1958.

Dr. David Wintringham and Superintendent Steven Mitchell

A noted art critic is found dead after an exhibit at the Westminster Art Gallery. The police first suspect a known burglar, but as they investigate they discover that the late Oswald Burke was in some way related or connected to several of the more noticeable guests at the exhibit. Indispensable in their search for answers is a sketch pad and drawings by Tom Drummond, an art student who sketched the other guests during the exhibit.

The Port of London Murders
London: Longmans, 1938.
New York: Macmillan, 1958.

Inspector Steven Mitchell

The dying neighborhoods near the wharves along the Thames harbor those struggling to make a living from the river beside those who have made this their last stop in a long and expensive fall from affluence. The sudden death of one of their number leads Scotland Yard on a dangerous path among those who live and work on the river.

Easy Prey
London: Hodder, 1959.
New York: Macmillan, 1959.

Superintendent Steven Mitchell and Claud Warrington-Reeve

Reg and Mavis Holmes are congratulating themselves on their luck in finding a roomer who also enjoys sitting with their baby. Then one evening they come home to a house filled with gas. Miss Trubb is taken to a hospital in time, and Reg and Mavis learn that she was once convicted of murdering a child. Somehow, reason Reg and Mavis, this doesn't seem possible.

A Well-known Face
London: Hodder, 1960.
New York: Washburn, 1960.

Superintendent Steven Mitchell and Claud Warrington-Reeve

Dr. Andrew Fuller is struck off the medical register when he is convicted of unprofessional conduct with a patient and he moves to South America. On the morning his wife seeks a lawyer to represent her in her divorce proceedings, her gardener finds the doctor dead in the dining room.

A Flat Tyre in Fulham
London: Hodder, 1963.

Fiasco in Fulham
New York: Macmillan, 1963.

Room for a Body
New York: Ballantine, 1964.

Superintendent Steven Mitchell and Claud Warrington-Reeve

When a car thief abandons a stolen car to be used in a robbery, he leaves behind one complication that eventually leads police to several crimes: a flat tire.

The Upfold Witch
London: Hodder, 1964.
New York: Macmillan, 1964.

Dr. Henry Frost

Dr. and Mrs. Frost choose Upfold village as their retirement home, and on the surface it seems to be the quintessential English village. They soon learn that this village conceals a secret that touches everyone, a secret that few want to talk about openly.

Death on the Reserve
London: Hodder, 1966.
New York: Macmillan, 1966.

Dr. Henry Frost

Fauldmere Nature Reserve is an ideal spot for birdwatchers and hikers,
though it is isolated and grim. The warden watches over every square foot,
but when two young people fail to return from the reserve, no one knows
anything about them or their hike.

Wolf! Wolf!
London: Hodder, 1979.
New York: Walker, 1980.

Miss Amy Tupper

Strolling up and down a hospital corridor, Amy Tupper sees a well-known
murderer getting into the elevator. Next day, the corpse of a nurse is found
in an empty cupboard. While Tupper pursues her criminal, the police suspect
a Pakistani pharmacist.

A Question of Inheritance
London: Hodder, 1980.
New York: Walker, 1981.

Miss Amy Tupper

Florence Bennet foolishly agreed to marry an older man to provide him with
a son, but the marriage is cold. On the only night she is alone with her
baby son without servants or husband at home, the baby dies a crib death.
Terrified and miserable, Florence flees, managing to get to Naples undetected.

To Let: Furnished
London: Methuen, 1952.

Stranger on a Cliff
New York: Ace, 1964.

With her children in school and her husband in the United States, Rosamund Townsend decides to rent a house in the country and chooses a beautiful manor house in Dorset. She takes to the villagers, and they to her, telling her bit by bit the history of the house and its owners. And suddenly, Rosamund realizes that she is not a stranger here--her past is tied to the manor house and its old family.

Fires at Fairlawn
London: Methuen, 1954.

Margaret and Tom Seeley move happily into an old mansion with plans to renovate and subdivide the old house into three homes. Their plans proceed on schedule, but all who come to the house refer darkly to the last owner's death. Curious, Margaret discreetly asks questions only to learn that someone else is interested in the old house and has succeeded in breaking in.

Death in Retirement
London: Methuèn, 1956.
New York: Macmillan, 1956.

Gillian Clayton is very grateful to her aunt, Dr. Clayton, for giving her a home after the death of her parents, but now she is ready to move on and marry Max. Dr. Clayton resists. When Max finds a couple to live with Dr. Clayton, she becomes less predictable. Gillian attributes this to the consequences of forty years as a missionary in India and advancing old age, but she is still worried.

Double Doom
London: Hodder, 1957.
New York: Macmillan, 1958.

The morning newspapers carry the obituaries of middle-aged twins, but only one is dead and the other is in the hospital. Anxious to spare his patient, Dr. Goddard orders that the surviving twin not be allowed to see any papers.

Someone disregards the doctor's orders, however, and the second twin dies of a heart attack, apparently from seeing his own obituary.

The House above the River
London: Hodder, 1959.

Waiting for the fog to lift so they can continue their sailing trip along the French coast, Giles Armitage and his friends meet a British couple staying in a chateau nearby. To Giles's shock, Mrs. Davenport turns out to be the woman who jilted him eight years ago. Now Miriam desperately claims that she is afraid for her life, that her husband is trying to kill her. Miriam's dramatic cries for help remind Giles of her earlier selfishness and her lies.

New People at the Hollies
London: Hodder, 1961.
New York: Macmillan, 1961.

A rambling Victorian house is turned into a home for the elderly, and at first only two boys, living next door, notice that something unusual is going on. The nurses are entirely proper to doctors and patients, but have another side in private. Then one of the residents dies, apparently of natural causes, with blood on her hand and on her nightgown but with no signs of injury. Mr. Coltman, one of the elderly residents, undertakes an investigation, though he is dismissed as senile.

Adventure with Crime
London: Hodder, 1962.

Frances Aldridge decides a short trip in the United States should help her finally get over the death of her husband, so she sets out to discover America. And she does. Her hotel room is broken into, fellow travelers delight and confuse her, passing acquaintances act in a downright suspicious manner, and she is smitten by a charming young man.

The Hunter and the Trapped
London: Hodder, 1963.

Simon Fawcett attracts his students to the point of blind loyalty, but he remains aloof from them. When Penelope Dane falls in love with him, he turns her away with a declaration of his love for a married woman. But what he feels for Mrs. Allingham is not love, and the shallowness and cruelty of his character lead to blackmail and murder.

No Escape
London: Hodder, 1965.
New York: Macmillan, 1966.

A young doctor pulls an apparent suicide from the Thames, but she does not behave like a suicide. Clearly she is afraid, and he arranges for her to go to his hospital for treatment. Dr. Long is not the only person concerned with the young woman: in addition to the press, there is a man who claims to be a friend of her employer and who takes a special interest in one of the nurses attending the woman.

The Catalyst
London: Hodder, 1966.
New York: Macmillan, 1967.

Hugh Wilmot is taking his wife and sister-in-law to Greece, a country he has long wanted to visit. Once there, however, the Greek sun dispels the shadows in their lives, letting them see how little they like each other.

Death of a Con Man
London: Hodder, 1968.
Philadelphia: Lippincott, 1968.

An accident between a car and a chartered coach leaves only one person seriously injured. He is rushed to the hospital and given a transfusion, but his condition still deteriorates. It is immediately evident that he has been given the wrong blood type, although it is the type noted in his diary.

The Wilberforce Legacy
London: Hodder, 1969.
New York: Walker, 1969.

Colonel Wilberforce is living out his last years in a declining Caribbean hotel when he receives word of the visit of two distant relatives. After their arrival one man is dead and another has disappeared. Untangling the murder means digging into the past and into other crimes best forgotten.

The Fennister Affair
London: Hodder, 1969.
New York: Stein, 1978.

The night before Sally Combes joins a cruise ship in Bermuda a woman disappears, and her distraught husband leaves the ship. Though the passengers are reluctant to talk about the woman's death, for obvious reasons, Sally feels, the ship's officers are even more unforthcoming when Sally presents them with a suicide note she found in her cabin. It was signed by the missing woman.

A Hole in the Ground
London: Hodder, 1971.
New York: Ace, 1973.

Dr. Martin Filton returns to a Cornish village where he vacationed twenty years earlier. An incident that he had passed off comes back to him when he takes a path by an old tin mine and sees again a face he saw twenty years ago. During that first visit he had helped a young woman who had been out shooting rabbits. Now he is helping another young woman who is investigating a mine vent. But the face is the same.

A Hydra with Six Heads
London: Hodder, 1970.
New York: Stein, 1977.

Dr. Roy Cartwright is substituting for another doctor in London for a month before taking up a post in Hampshire. The time passes peacefully enough until an unattractive woman patient accuses him of attacking her. Roy is about to complain loudly when his receptionist whispers that the same woman made the same charge against another doctor in the group.

Death of a Poison-Tongue
London: Hodder, 1972.
New York: Stein, 1977.

Althea Swinford is looking forward to studying at Polford University. On the train ride to the school, she meets an older woman who adroitly gleans information from her, tries to drug her with candy, and speaks Turkish. Althea learns from this woman and the vicar that the village is being torn apart by vicious rumors that have no basis in fact but still hurt. The poison-tongued villager is slowly becoming known, Althea's fellow passengers insist.

A Pigeon among the Cats
London: Hodder, 1974.
New York: Stein, 1977.

Retired schoolmistress Rose Lawler settles down for a bus tour of Italy, ready to relax and take what comes. What comes is Gwen Chilton, a self-centered young woman who has left her husband and expects everyone to sympathize with her. What also comes is Owen Strong, a middle-aged wanderer who knows Italy well and pops up every now and then. Rose is not drawn to either one, but cannot always get away from them.

Victim
London: Hodder, 1975.
New York: Walker, 1976.

Mrs. Mellanby has sensibly decided that her large Edwardian home is too much for her at her age and she is ready to sell. Not only will this mean moving to a smaller house, but it will also mean a tidy profit. Unfortunately, Mrs. Mellanby forgot to reckon with the opposition of the Residents' Protection Society or with the virulence of their objections.

The Trouble in Hunter Ward
London: Hodder, 1976.
New York: Walker, 1977.

St. Edmund's Hospital is preparing for a strike when the staff will have to do without telephone, elevators, clean linen, and the regular food service. These problems pale beside the arrival of Miss Enid Hallet, a former nurse who has lost many positions because of her malicious and uncontrollable tongue.

Such a Nice Client
London: Hodder, 1977.

Stroke of Death
New York: Walker, 1977.

Lucy Summers is a physiotherapist who undertakes a new case with the enthusiasm of the newly trained, but when she first meets Mr. Lawrence she is shocked. He is obviously hungry, but his daughter-in-law insists that the old man refuses food. Is he senile or being starved to death?

A Swan-Song Betrayed
London: Hodder, 1978.

Treachery in Type
New York: Walker, 1980.

After thirty years of silence, the elderly Mrs. Grosshouse is ready to write another novel, to the dismay of her friends. Not everyone is skeptical, however, and before the old woman can finish the book to her satisfaction, the novel is published by another and wins praise from the critics.

The Innocent
London: Hodder, 1983.

A Deadly Place to Stay
New York: Walker, 1983.

A teenaged girl runs away from home and arrives in London with almost no money and no skill in city living. Needing a place to stay, she accepts the invitation of a stranger to stay with the Holy Group. She does not know that others have accepted such an offer and have never left.

E.C. Bentley

Trent's Last Case
London: Nelson, 1913.
Rev. ed. New York: Knopf, 1929.

The Woman in Black
New York: Century, 1913.

Philip Trent

The sudden death of Sigsbee Manderson sends shock waves through the world financial community, and a newspaper editor sets painter-detective Philip Trent on the long quest for the murderer. Clues and characters abound in Bentley's classic novel of the "infallible sleuth."

Trent's Own Case
London: Constable, 1936.
New York: Knopf, 1936.

Philip Trent

When James Randolph, a financier and philanthropist, is found shot to death, the police have many suspects--including Philip Trent. While Trent investigates the murder, the police investigate him and one of his closest friends. Written with H. Warner Allen.

Elephant's Work
London: Hodder, 1950.
New York: Knopf, 1950.

The Chill
New York: Dell, 1953.

A railway accident leaves Mr. Severn with amnesia and the passport of a master criminal. Plucked from the wreckage by two men he does not recognize, Severn is charmed by his fugitive friends and aids them in their crimes--until he finally remembers who he is.

Anthony Berkeley*

The Poisoned Chocolates Case
London: Collins, 1929.
New York: Doubleday, 1929.

Roger Sheringham and Ambrose Chitterwick

In this gentle satire of mystery novels and detectives, the members of the newly founded Crimes Circle are invited to solve a particularly baffling murder. During their meetings over the next several evenings, each member offers a solution. The problem is this: A man receives a box of chocolates as a sample from the maker. Disliking candy, he gives the box to an acquaintance, who gives the box to his wife, who is thus poisoned to death.

Panic Party
London: Hodder, 1934.

Mr. Pidgeon's Island
New York: Doubleday, 1934.

Roger Sheringham

When Guy Pidgeon, an Oxford don, inherits a fortune, he gives free rein to his imagination and eccentricities. He buys a yacht and invites an odd assortment of friends and strangers, idle aristocrats and second-rate novelists, to sail with him to a desert island. He then strands his guests on the island, finally telling them that one among them is a murderer. In truth, he and a friend created this jaunt to see how these people would behave under severe stress.

The Piccadilly Murder
London: Collins, 1929.
New York: Doubleday, 1930.

Ambrose Chitterwick

Rarely do the police have an eyewitness to a genteel murder by poison, but
that seems to be what Mr. Chitterwick is. Thrilled by his new importance,
he studies the methods of the police in putting together their case and becomes increasingly uncomfortable with their choice of a suspect. Finally,
his self-assurance is shaken by a wholly unexpected figure.

Trial and Error
London: Hodder, 1937.
New York: Doubleday, 1937.

Ambrose Chitterwick

Faced with only a year to live, Lawrence Todhunter decides to do the world
some good in his last few months. He settles on murder, the elimination of
a person sufficiently wicked to merit such a death. He carefully chooses his
victim and plans his crime--but murder is harder than he expected.

John Bingham

The Double Agent
London: Gollancz, 1966.
New York: Dutton, 1967.

Kenneth Ducane (Vandoren)

In the past men faced the hardship of personal loss by going on safari; today
they join the secret service. These are the cynical words of Ducane to his
newest recruit, Reginald Sugden. But for Sugden, the death of the woman
he loved is only part of the reason he is willing to turn his sales trips to the
USSR into a spy mission. The Russians take the bait and blackmail him into

spying for them while the British watch. And so, step by step, Sugden slips
into a no man's land of violence, suspicion, and betrayal.

Vulture in the Sun
London: Gollancz, 1971.

Kenneth Ducane (Vandoren)

When Tom Carter is sent to Cyprus to fill in for Frank Baker so the agent
can have a rest, he knows that the job will go badly. And it does. Frank
is killed by a bomb after promising to let Tom have important information,
leaving Tom to make what he can of Baker's lover, Hellena, owners of the
hotel where Tom is staying, and agents for the various Turkish, Greek, and
Cypriot factions.

God's Defector
London: Macmillan, 1976.

Ministry of Death
New York: Walker, 1977.

Kenneth Ducane (Vandoren)

Father Lawrence Brown is highly regarded by his parishioners until he leaves
the church to marry one of them. Only then does he realize the danger he
represents to certain members of his parish, men who can no longer count
on the sanctity of the confessional to protect them.

Brock and the Defector
London: Gollancz, 1982.
New York: Doubleday, 1982.

Superintendent John Brock and Kenneth Ducane (Vandoren)

Alice Robins thinks life is going well for her and her lover, Alexis Schorin,
a Soviet agent who has agreed to serve as a double agent. Then Schorin is

recalled to Moscow and instead chooses to defect. Fleeing to the country-side, the two lovers are pursued by Soviets and someone they don't expect.

Brock
London: Gollancz, 1981.

Superintendent John Brock

Brock returns to his hometown of Melford, expecting tranquillity and uncom-plicated people after London and Belfast. Instead, he arrives when the town is teetering on the brink of a crime wave: a third rape, an upstanding citizen blackmailed for his peculiar tastes, and two residents planning two separate murders.

My Name Is Michael Sibley
London: Gollancz, 1952.
New York: Dodd, Mead, 1952.

Michael Sibley, narrator of this tale of a murder investigation, is a newspaper reporter who finds himself the chief suspect in a murder case. Rattled, he begins to conceal minor details of his recent life, all the while wondering who has in fact murdered the man he knew since school and despised secretly for years. The longer the investigation goes on, however, the guiltier Sibley looks to the police.

Five Roundabouts to Heaven
London: Gollancz, 1953.

The Tender Poisoner
New York: Dodd, Mead, 1953.

In the halcyon days of the 1930s, a group of British and northern European students became close friends while studying French at a summer school. Over the next several years the ties they created grew stronger and the need of some to break them stronger still. One murder is planned, accidental death missed, and another murder completed.

The Third Skin
London: Gollancz, 1954.
New York: Dodd, Mead, 1954.

Murder Is a Witch
New York: Dell, 1957.

Les Marshall is a minor clerk in a newspaper office. To impress his girl-friend, he asks for and gets a raise, which he doesn't deserve. Growing greedier, he helps a friend in a burglary. So begins the nightmare that peels away the protective layers of conceit and arrogance, leaving him as vulnerable as a child.

The Paton Street Case
London: Gollancz, 1955.

Inspector Morgan's Dilemma
New York: Dodd, Mead, 1956.

When a furniture shop owned by a Jewish refugee couple is destroyed by arson, a corpse is found in the apartment above. The man had died, however, from a blow to the head before the fire. Inspector Morgan is reluctant to pursue the Steiners, owners of the building, but the path of his investigation keeps returning to them.

Marion
London: Gollancz, 1958.

Murder off the Road
New York: Dodd, Mead, 1957.

David Shepton is called to investigate a murder in a building he left only moments before, after consoling a woman who lost her fiancé. Neither incident seems out of the ordinary, but each seems incomplete in its bald facts.

Murder Plan Six
London: Gollancz, 1958.
New York: Dodd, Mead, 1959.

Victor Hartmann, a publisher, receives a series of tapes in the mail from an author called Michael Barlow, who explains in detail that his identity is false and he intends to commit a murder. Barlow will not identify the victim or himself, but the story will serve for his next book.

Night's Black Agent
London: Gollancz, 1961.
New York: Dodd, Mead, 1961.

Mr. Green is a hateful man, for he takes it upon himself to ruin other people who refuse to be blackmailed. He is also clever, for he attacks his victim through someone the victim cares for, thus separating himself from the immediate crime. After watching him destroy three families, a relative of one decides to track down the anonymous Green and exact his own revenge.

A Case of Libel
London: Gollancz, 1963.

The Sunday News is struggling with rising costs and declining circulation. In addition, the owner, a playboy, cares little for the newspaper and hires an editor to either save the paper or shut it down. The other members of the staff know what this can mean. There is no crime, but there is a puzzle to solve.

A Fragment of Fear
London: Gollancz, 1965.
New York: Dutton, 1966.

Mrs. Lucy Dawson is one of many elderly English ladies who visit Italy every year, and when she is found dead, the hotel owner is understandably reluctant to talk about her violent death. But that does not explain the same reluctance among her fellow guests at the Bower Hotel in England, where she lived for the rest of the year. James Compton, a writer, thought her death might make an interesting story, but he had not thought there would be anything in her life or death that people would want to hide.

I Love, I Kill
London: Gollancz, 1968.

Good Old Charlie
New York: Simon, 1968.

In Durrington, Charles Maither had watched the woman he loved marry an actor he despised. So to Durrington and provincial theater he returned, to exact an unusual revenge. He will make Paul King, a second-rate actor, into a success and then be there when King abandons his provincial wife for a more suitable companion for a star.

The Marriage Bureau Murders
London: Macmillan, 1977.

Ineffectual and unattractive, Sidney Shaw is overjoyed one day when his wife leaves him, perhaps unnerved by the occasional flash of malice in his eyes. Then he quits his job and sets up the Sure Friendship Bureau, looking forward to helping men and women find happiness. There are a few exceptions, however, and those he keeps in a special file. Those are the hunted and Sidney's Hound, the one who carries out the kill for the hunter.

Deadly Picnic
London: Macmillan, 1980.

A close friendship between two police officers and their wives begins to unravel at a picnic in the country, foreshadowing the early retirement of one and a career disappointment for the other. More pressing is the news that a criminal they sent to prison is out and has been seen in the neighborhood of the policeman he once threatened with revenge.

Gavin Black

Suddenly at Singapore ... *
London: Collins, 1961.

Paul Harris

Dead Man Calling
London: Collins, 1962.
New York: Harper, 1962.

Paul Harris

Paul Harris is anxious to win a license to manufacture diesel engines and follows the agent arranging the sale to his hotel room. Harris arrives just as Mikos is stabbed to death in the next room. When he later informs Mikos's secretary, she flees and he follows her, to the intense curiosity of Japanese travelers. A young student attaches himself to Harris and thereafter reappears at regular intervals.

A Dragon for Christmas
London: Collins, 1963.
New York: Harper, 1963.

Paul Harris

Harris enters China to sell a small motor to the Chinese, but even before he disembarks he is warned by another visiting businessman that his life is in danger. He later meets a Scotsman who defected to the Chinese ten years earlier and now wants to leave; he also meets a childhood friend who wants to stay. And all of them know that the welcome extended to the businessmen is a thin and fragile veneer.

The Eyes around Me
London: Collins, 1964.
New York: Harper, 1964.

Paul Harris

The world of the rich in Hong Kong attracts many but satisfies few. Ella Bain has more money than she knows what to do with, two failed marriages, and a love for whiskey. She is also known for a generous if sometimes vulgar heart, which makes her murder all the more surprising to her friends and her only surviving relative.

You Want to Die, Johnny?
London: Collins, 1966.
New York: Harper, 1966.

Paul Harris

The daughter of the British resident of the tiny nation of Bintan has so offended public opinion in the United States that she is forcibly brought home by her father. On the final leg of their journey to Bintan, their small plane is shot at during landing, which seems to be an indictment of the girl's behavior with an American rock star.

A Wind of Death
London: Collins, 1967.
New York: Harper, 1967.

Paul Harris

Paul Harris's willingness to help an American agent by collecting information for him backfires when he fails to bring back the expected information. Instead Harris discovers that one of his men has been doing business with North Vietnam (selling guns) and the American military think Harris is in on it.

The Cold Jungle
London: Collins, 1969.
New York: Harper, 1969.

Paul Harris

Paul Harris is ready to order four new ships for his business, and shipyard owners are going to extravagant lengths to win the contract. The competition turns nasty after Paul commits himself to a Scottish shipyard owned by an old friend. Soon his friend is dead in a car accident, and companies are pushing hard for his signature, all except his friend's company.

A Time for Pirates
London: Collins, 1971.
New York: Harper, 1971.

Paul Harris

Tensions between Chinese and Malays are growing, with rioters armed and well coordinated for their "spontaneous" demonstrations. A chance encounter with the wife of a visiting European leaves Paul fearing even worse developments. A Chinese firm, not known for its evenhandedness, has found oil and has no intention of sharing it or the profits with the Malaysian government.

The Bitter Tea
London: Collins, 1973.
New York: Harper, 1972.

Paul Harris

Concerned about the decline of his shipyard in Scotland and his business in Asia, Harris decides to take a few days to think outside Kuala Lumpur. He arrives at his favorite spot to find it transformed by a new gambling casino and just in time to witness an attack on a visiting dignitary from China.

The Golden Cockatrice
London: Collins, 1974.
New York: Harper, 1975.

Paul Harris

Someone is trying to drive Paul Harris out of business by undercutting his prices on large loads carried in Indonesian waters. Suspicious that the new company is a front for a Hong Kong marine tycoon, Harris hires a lawyer of dubious reputation to ferret out information. (Copyright note: the British and U.S. versions of the book differ substantially.)

A Big Wind for Summer
London: Collins, 1975.
New York: Harper, 1976.

Gale Force
London: Fontana, 1978.

Paul Harris

A letter from an old woman who once knew his parents in Malaysia draws Harris to Scotland. Claiming that she has an original Renoir, the woman insists that only Harris can sell it for her. This seems unlikely until Harris takes stock of the other island residents he has met.

A Moon for Killers*
London: Collins, 1976.

Killer Moon
London: Fontana, 1977.

Paul Harris

Night Run from Java*
London: Collins, 1979.

Paul Harris

The Fatal Shadow*
London: Collins, 1983.

Lionel Black

Chance to Die*
London: Cassell, 1965.

Emma Greaves

The Bait
London: Cassell, 1966.

Emma Greaves

A number of prostitutes are murdered in London, but one of the bodies is that of a government agent and the murder only an imitation of the prostitute killings. The government decides to play along with the pretense, hoping to draw out the murderer of the agent if not of the prostitutes.

Two Ladies in Verona*
London: Cassell, 1967.

The Lady Is a Spy
New York: Paperback Library, 1969.

Emma Greaves

Swinging Murder
London: Cassell, 1969.
New York: Walker, 1969.

Kate Theobald

The eleventh earl of Wilmington, who wants to share his good fortune by inheritance, hosts a big party for everyone he knows (as well as some strangers). The festivities are hardly dampened by the discovery in the garden of the body of one of the earl's lawyers. Naturally, the earl becomes the prime suspect when he cavalierly admits to paying the lawyer £1,000 not to produce a document proving the existence of another heir to the estate. (First U. S. edition published under the name Anthony Matthews.)

Death Has Green Fingers
London: Collins, 1971.
New York: Walker, 1971.

Kate Theobald

On a weekend in the country, Kate and Henry Theobald are introduced to the complexities of rose growing and hybridization. They are impressed with the keen competition among rose growers and even wonder if it can lead to murder. (First U.S. edition published under the name Anthony Matthews.)

Death by Hoax
London: Collins, 1974.
New York: Avon, 1978.

Kate Theobald

During the summer doldrums, Kate Theobald is sent to investigate a series of hoaxes in a seaside community. Not expecting to find more than a tale of shattered nerves and flaring tempers, Kate is well ahead of the police when the joker pulls off a murder.

A Healthy Way to Die
London: Collins, 1976.
New York: Avon, 1979.

Kate Theobald

Kate is assigned what she expects to be the pleasant task of spending a week at an exclusive health farm, where she meets a tycoon, a pop singer, an American columnist, and assorted rich matrons. All is lovely until the dieting begins to take its toll, prompting Kate to imagine tension between the owners, furtive glances and worse among others. It is not her imagination when she finds a young tycoon hanging in his bedroom.

The Penny Murders
London: Collins, 1979.
New York: Avon, 1980.

Kate Theobald

Two successful businessmen have long engaged in a personal rivalry in the arena of numismatics, but their personal gratification turns sour when one is murdered and certain coins in his collection disappear.

The Eve of the Wedding
London: Collins, 1980.
New York: Avon, 1981.

Kate Theobald

A party for a bride and groom brings together a large crowd of relatives and friends, including Henry and Kate Theobald. As the evening wears on, quaint wedding customs turn sour; the bride runs off in tears; and someone finds a corpse in the library.

Breakaway
London: Collins, 1970.

Flood
New York: Stein, 1971.

Inspector Francis Foy

A bank robbery in London and the threat of a massive flood in the Fens in Norfolk bring together two disparate groups: the criminals attempting to flee the country after the robbery and the farm families struggling to save their homes and land.

Ransom for a Nude
London: Collins, 1972.
New York: Stein, 1972.

Superintendent Francis Foy

Sir David Bullen opened his home to transients and the needy after the war and has been trying to keep the free home going ever since. When an art dealer finds an unknown Velasquez in Sir David's attic, Sir David is ecstatic with plans for expansion to be paid for by the sale of the painting. Other people, however, have other ideas. One plans to hold the painting for ransom, and another manages to pull off a highly intelligent theft.

The Life and Death of Peter Wade
London: Collins, 1973.
New York: Stein, 1974

Superintendent Francis Foy

Peter Wade was a womanizer and wildly successful second-rate actor, who fell
to his death from his balcony during a party. When writer Johnny Trott is
offered the job of writing the actor's biography, he at first assumes that the
publisher wants a pornographic account and turns down the job. Reassured
that the publisher wants a straight book, Johnny begins work, and what he
finds out about Wade is far worse than the pornographic tales of his life.

A Provincial Crime*
London: Cassell, 1960.

Outbreak
London: Cassell, 1968.
New York: Stein, 1968.

A businessman arrives in London from South America, with a cold. When he
finally seeks medical help, the doctors diagnose smallpox. Moving quickly to
avert an epidemic, the medical officers trace the man's contacts, but instead
of business meetings, the man has been visiting nightclubs and gambling clubs.
When the officers go to his apartment, they find a terrified woman and a
briefcase full of money.

Arafat Is Next!
London: Collins, 1975.
New York: Stein, 1975.

When Anthony Dunton is killed by a terrorist's bomb meant for another, his
brothers decide to seek revenge against the man they hold ultimately responsible: Yasir Arafat.

The Foursome
London: Collins, 1978.

George Chapman has a successful business and a beautiful home, but his wife, Ella, is cold and George, therefore, regularly seeks other women. When he meets Gladys Kemp, she is too wonderful to let go, so he brings her home. George, Ella, and Gladys set up housekeeping together, with George insisting this will work, Gladys willing to get along, and Ella determined to drive Gladys out of her home. Then the threesome becomes a foursome.

Nicholas Blake

A Question of Proof
London: Collins, 1935.
New York: Harper, 1935.

Nigel Strangeways

During Sports Day at a boys' prep school one of the students is murdered, his body left to be found later. When the police arrive, they begin a full-scale investigation, much to the delight of the boys and the consternation and fear of the schoolmasters, who wonder what else the police will bring to light.

Thou Shell of Death
London: Collins, 1936.

Shell of Death
New York: Harper, 1936.

Nigel Strangeways

A legendary airman, Fergus O'Brien, has retired to the countryside, in part to work on a new design and in part to withdraw from an adoring public. Just before Christmas he receives three letters threatening his murder on Boxing Day. To keep an eye on his enemies, O'Brien invites all those with a reason to hate him to his home for Christmas.

There's Trouble Brewing
London: Collins, 1937.
New York: Harper, 1937.

Nigel Strangeways

Eustace Bunnett is a domineering, vindictive man, so when his dog is found in one of the coppers in his brewery, the people who know Bunnett consider it a humane release for the poor animal. But Bunnett wants the culprit caught. Before an investigation can get under way, there is another body in the copper.

The Beast Must Die
London: Collins, 1938.
New York: Harper, 1938.

Nigel Strangeways

Long recognized as one of Blake's best, this is the classic tale of revenge. A writer suspends his grief for his dead son by plotting the murder of the man who killed him, recording in a journal his efforts to identify, locate, and murder the guilty man.

The Smiler with the Knife
London: Collins, 1939.
New York: Harper, 1939.

Nigel Strangeways

The quiet Devonshire countryside conceals the usual ghosts and rural sins, but in one village the gentry and others with money and background have another secret: an underground political movement that means secret leaders and arms shipments, and a reliable labor force.

Malice in Wonderland
London: Collins, 1940.

The Summer Camp Mystery
New York: Harper, 1940.

Malice with Murder
New York: Pyramid, 1964.

Nigel Strangeways

The planned weeks of delight and relaxation at the Wonderland Holiday Club go awry for dozens of guests when they become the victim of a practical joker who announces himself as the Mad Hatter. Three people are held under water while swimming, sports equipment is ruined, and the guests get edgy. Then the newspapers get hold of the story.

The Case of the Abominable Snowman
London: Collins, 1941.

The Corpse in the Snowman
New York: Harper, 1941.

Nigel Strangeways

An idle parlor game of calling up the ghost of a seventeenth-century bishop who died in Easterham Manor produces a surprising effect: the family cat goes wild. The experience unsettles the family and guests, adding to the already palpable tension in the house.

Minute for Murder
London: Collins, 1947.
New York: Harper, 1948.

Nigel Strangeways

In the zany Ministry of Morale, an odd collection of writers and editors boosts the morale of war-weary Britons. Indeed, there is little real dissension until a former member of the ministry returns from his glorious exploits in Germany and his former lover is not glad of his return.

Head of a Traveler
London: Collins, 1949.
New York: Harper, 1949.

Nigel Strangeways

A headless corpse is found in the Thames River not far from the home of a famous poet. Robert Seaton lives in a charming house on the river with his family in what would seem to be an idyllic life. He rents a cottage to a painter and his daughter, who barely conceals her problems, and his wife, Janet Seaton, employs a dwarf of limited capacities as a household servant.

The Dreadful Hollow
London: Collins, 1953.
New York: Harper, 1953.

Nigel Strangeways

Sir Archibald Blick is worried about the village of Prior's Umborne, an odd concern for a financial force in London. The villagers are the object of a poison-pen campaign, some letters so painful and terrifying as to drive the recipient to commit suicide. For Sir Archibald, this is bad for business, particularly for the factory he is backing in a town nearby.

The Whisper in the Gloom
London: Collins, 1954.
New York: Harper, 1954.

Catch and Kill
New York: Bestseller, 1955.

Nigel Strangeways

Desperate to pass on a new discovery, a police informant gives a slip of
paper to a child in a park just before he dies. And so Bert Hale and his
gang of friends are plunged into a world of crime and violence, succeeding
where the police have failed and threatening to expose a criminal gang.
The police are close behind the boys, however, trying to catch up with them
before the criminals lose patience and turn on the children.

End of Chapter
London: Collins, 1957.
New York: Harper, 1957.

Nigel Strangeways

General Thoresby has written an autobiography that goes beyond safe limits
in its comments about other military figures and only under duress is he
persuaded to remove the offending passages. But the passages show up in
page proofs sent from the printer and must be again taken out. Then after
thousands of copies have been distributed, the publishers learn that the
passages are still in the text. Someone is out to ruin the staid publishing
house of Wenham and Geraldine.

The Widow's Cruise
London: Collins, 1959.
New York: Harper, 1959.

Nigel Strangeways

A cruise around the Greek islands brings together tourists old and young,
serious and frivolous, of many nationalities. Beneath the veneer of the holi-

day spirit lie the resentments of those who have met before and the pain of one who cannot forget the past.

The Worm of Death
London: Collins, 1961.
New York: Harper, 1961.

Nigel Strangeways

Dr. Piers Loudron, a patriarch and doctor now facing his last years, disappears. His body is found in the Thames, and the likely suspects in his murder are his four grown children, all of whom seem to have harbored enough anger and frustration to account for their father's death.

The Sad Variety
London: Collins, 1964.
New York: Harper, 1964.

Nigel Strangeways

A snowstorm holds several guests at a country estate, but not before the daughter of one of the guests, a famous scientist, is kidnapped. Efforts to find her are hampered by the needs of other guests to keep their own affairs secret.

The Morning after Death
London: Collins, 1966.
New York: Harper, 1966.

Nigel Strangeways

Josiah Ahlberg, a professor in the Classics Department at Cabot University in Boston is little interested in the opinion of his half brothers, who also teach at the university, and the opinion of others in his field. His disdain for others is legendary, but his murder takes everyone by surprise. The obvious suspect is one of his brothers, or perhaps a student he accused of plagiarism, or possibly the student's sister.

The Private Wound
London: Collins, 1968.
New York: Harper, 1968.

In 1939, a young British novelist settles in an Irish village to work on his
latest book. Although the outsider is accepted by some, he is threatened and
warned to leave by others. Soon embroiled in a love affair, he is the first
to be suspected when his lover is found murdered.

A Tangled Web
London: Collins, 1956.
New York: Harper, 1956.

Death and Daisy Bland
New York: Dell, 1960.

A charming young man of good family runs away with a working girl. Deeply
in love, she does not ask where his money comes from, and, equally in love,
he does not want to tell her. Their carefree life of occasional riches comes
to an unexpected end when a policeman is shot during a burglary attempt.

A Penknife in My Heart
London: Collins, 1958.
New York: Harper, 1958.

Stuart Hammer overhears Ned Stowe talking in a pub and recognizes a trapped man. Ned is trapped in a dead marriage, and Stuart is trapped by his
uncle. For Stuart, Ned is an opportunity, and Stuart thus proposes to the
unhappy man that they help each other out of their predicaments.

The Deadly Joker
London: Collins, 1963.

John and Jenny Waterson move to a quiet village in Dorset, expecting solitude
and time for Jenny to recover from her breakdown; instead they step into a
world subtly dominated by a practical joker who leaves ill will and distrust
behind him. The first jokes seem innocuous; the poison-pen letters that come
next are meant to hurt.

John and Emery Bonett

Dead Lion
London: Joseph, 1949.
New York: Doubleday, 1949.

Professor Mandrake

The death of a successful literary critic and radio personality at first is accepted as an accident, but his nephew thinks that more than one person might have wanted to murder the critic. Moreover, the more the nephew learns, the more he thinks his uncle's murder might have been justified.

A Banner for Pegasus
London: Joseph, 1951.

Not in the Script
New York: Doubleday, 1951.

Professor Mandrake

A film cast and crew in a small English village alternately amuse and annoy the residents, who in turn confuse and stymie the film people. Despite their differences, both sides are happy with the progress of the movie--until one of the main figures turns up dead.

No Grave for a Lady
London: Joseph, 1960.
New York: Doubleday, 1959.

Professor Mandrake

Lotte Liselotte still has the charm and some of the beauty of her earlier days when she enchanted audiences and fascinated Hitler. But she reserves her charm for a select few, and after only a few days at a resort some of the guests despise her and others have been swept away by her. And only Lotte considers it a game.

Better Dead
London: Joseph, 1964.

Better Off Dead
New York: Doubleday, 1964.

Inspector Salvador Borges

Rocadamor is home to a number of European expatriates who have learned to
live in a foreign country with fellow exiles. The only discordant note comes
from Ferdy, a Britisher who runs a popular bar and makes a point of learning
all he can about his fellow expatriates.

The Private Face of Murder
London: Joseph, 1966.
New York: Doubleday, 1966.

Inspector Salvador Borges

The fishing village of Calatrava is home to a British colony from the film and
theater world. Some of the British find it hard to adjust to the languid life
of a Spanish resort. The boredom of a young former actress and the ambitions of a washed-up actor lead to blackmail and then murder.

This Side Murder?
London: Joseph, 1967.

Murder on the Costa Brava
New York: Walker, 1968.

Inspector Salvador Borges

A thoroughly despicable journalist is sent to a resort hotel in Spain to dig
up stories for his newspaper. He is quick to alienate every one he meets,
including members of the hotel staff. It is little wonder that he is soon
murdered.

The Sound of Murder
London: Harrap, 1970.
New York: Walker, 1971

Inspector Salvador Borges

Halberd Corsair became a millionaire by shrewd and hard-nosed business prac-
tices. The truth of this suddenly becomes apparent one Friday as he ends
his week by planning to bankrupt one enterprise, shut down another, fire a
few employees, and deny a loan to a relative. One of the intended victims
murders Corsair during the weekend.

No Time to Kill
London: Harrap, 1972.
New York: Walker, 1972.

Inspector Salvador Borges

The Cala Felix, a hotel with bungalows, is a small community of British tourists and part-time residents. Their isolation does not protect them from surprise guests: an up-and-coming writer runs into a successful writer only
recently thought to be dead. And the isolation sometimes costs residents
their lives: a couple who have just made their wills drown in a boating
accident nearby.

Perish the Thought*
London: Hale, 1984.

Inspector Salvador Borges

Christianna Brand*

Heads You Lose
London: Lane, 1941.
New York: Dodd, Mead, 1942.

Inspector Cockrill

Someone in the village of Pigeonsford has a deep and abiding hatred for
women, though they be blameless. First a kitchen maid is murdered, then a
middle-aged spinster--two women who couldn't be more unlike each other.

Green for Danger
London: Lane, 1945.
New York: Dodd, Mead, 1944.

Inspector Cockrill

In an English hospital during World War II, the army brings together a group
of doctors, nurses, and other staff who view the war as a catalyst in their
lives. One among them is also carrying on a private war and is led to mur-
der--in full view of doctors and nurses during an operation.

Suddenly at His Residence
London: Bodley, 1947.

The Crooked Wreath
New York: Dodd, Mead, 1946.

Inspector Cockrill

Sir Richard March has outlived three sons and one wife, but he is happy with
his second wife (his former mistress) and his several grandchildren. Of a
very different generation from his younger relatives, Sir Richard often disap-
proves of their behavior and threatens to change his will, most often during
his annual memorial ritual to his late wife. This year, however, he sounds
serious.

Death of Jezebel
London: Bodley, 1948.
New York: Dodd, Mead, 1948.

Inspector Cockrill and Inspector Charlesworth

A young man from Malaya kills himself in London during the war after he finds out that his girlfriend has been unfaithful. His friends remember how he died, and when they get together after seven years, one of them decides that this is the time for revenge.

London Particular
London: Joseph, 1952.

Fog of Doubt
New York: Scribner, 1953.

Inspector Cockrill and Inspector Charlesworth

The murder of a foreign visitor in a doctor's home could have been committed by any member of the household, including the slightly mad grandmother. Brand called this her favorite novel.

Tour de Force
London: Joseph, 1955.
New York: Scribner, 1955.

Inspector Cockrill

A guided tour to Italy brings together the usual assortment of British tourists, who stumble through hotels and cathedrals, complaining happily about the food and the heat. The mood changes, however, with the murder of one of their own.

Death in High Heels
London: Lane, 1941.
New York: Scribner, 1954.

Inspector Charlesworth

A ladies' dress shop isn't an orderly, placid place at the best of times, and on this particular morning two of the salesgirls are using oxalic acid to clean a hat, unsuccessfully, and wondering who will be sent to oversee the new branch in Deauville. Most in the store are hoping Miss Gregory will be chosen, thus eliminating one thorn in their sides and leading to the promotion of Miss Doon. Sad to say, Miss Doon dies first.

The Rose in Darkness
London: Joseph, 1979.

Superintendent Charlesworth

Sari Morne's trip to a suburban cinema to see the one and only movie of her film career turns into a nightmare when she thinks she is being followed. Stopped by a fallen tree, the former actress sees another car and driver on the other side of the tree. They swap cars and Sari arrives home safe but scared. In the morning, her friends doubt her story, so she shows one of them the car and finds a corpse in the back seat.

Cat and Mouse
London: Joseph, 1950.
New York: Knopf, 1950.

Inspector Chucky

Miss Friendly-wise, also known as Tinka Jones, sob sister for Girls Together magazine, is drawn to her native Wales for a holiday after answering a number of letters from an avid if shy and lonely reader in a remote area around Swansea. On impulse, Tinka visits her correspondent, arriving at an isolated mountain home. But the owner, Mr. Carlyon, though he is just as the shy Amista described him, insists he has no wife and that he lives alone with his two servants.

The Honey Harlot*
London: Allen, 1978.

Simon Brett

Cast, in Order of Disappearance
London: Gollancz, 1975.
New York: Scribner, 1975.

Charles Paris

When Sally Nash goes on trial for prostitution among theater people, one of London's biggest theater tycoons quietly disappears after breaking off his relationship with his girlfriend. His girlfriend, however, points out the illogic of this and frantically tries to find him.

So Much Blood
London: Gollancz, 1976.
New York: Scribner, 1977.

Charles Paris

Paris will never be a star, but he manages to win a chance to do a one-man show on Thomas Hood in Edinburgh. There he is drawn to a group of drama students, one of whose number recently died in a manner that piques Paris's curiosity.

Star Trap
London: Gollancz, 1977.
New York: Scribner, 1977.

Charles Paris

The backers of the musical comedy She Stoops to Conquer get nervous when there are two accidents to the cast in the first weeks of rehearsal. The backers wonder if someone is trying to sabotage their production and put them out of business.

An Amateur Corpse
London: Gollancz, 1978.
New York: Scribner, 1978.

Charles Paris

Charles has agreed to critique the performance of an amateur dramatic society, one of whose members is the young (second) wife of an advertising client of Charles. To his distress, Charles thinks the actors are provincial amateurs and that his client-friend is having marital problems. When his friend is arrested for his wife's murder, Charles, feeling guilty for not standing by him, decides to do what he can to help.

A Comedian Dies
London: Gollancz, 1979.
New York: Scribner, 1979.

Charles Paris

Bill Peaky is moving up the ladder of success quickly until he is electrocuted at the beginning of his act in a seaside resort. The audience is stunned at the tragedy, and Charles is disappointed when the death is declared an accident.

The Dead Side of the Mike
London: Gollancz, 1980.
New York: Scribner, 1980.

Charles Paris

The BBC attracts an odd assortment of personalities, which is part of what makes it an interesting place to work. Charles is even agreeable to joining a committee on features until a young studio manager dies. Somehow, Charles just doesn't think it's suicide.

Situation Tragedy
London: Gollancz, 1981.
New York: Scribner, 1981.

Charles Paris

Competition in a television series is always intense, but someone in the new comedy "The Strutters" seems bent on eliminating its members one by one. First, the acid-tongued production assistant dies from a fall, then the director dies in a car accident, and then an author dies.

Murder Unprompted
London: Gollancz, 1982.
New York: Scribner, 1982.

Charles Paris

Charles lands a small but respectable part in a new play being produced in Taunton. When a London producer agrees to bring the play to London if he can choose the cast, the normal tensions of a dramatic cast explode with rivalry, revenge, and ambition.

Murder in the Title
London: Gollancz, 1983.
New York: Scribner, 1983.

Charles Paris

In a provincial theater production, Charles has the innocuous role of the murder victim after he has been killed. All he has to do is fall down dead, but even this seems to be too much for Charles until he realizes that some-one in the cast or crew wants his performance to be totally realistic.

Not Dead, Only Resting
London: Gollancz, 1984.
New York: Scribner, 1984.

Charles Paris

When Paris is out of work for several weeks, a fellow actor offers him a job redecorating the flat of an owner of a restaurant patronized by theater and television people. Charles accepts, and on his first day, he and his friend find the mutilated body of someone they know.

Dead Giveaway
London: Gollancz, 1985.
New York: Scribner, 1986.

Charles Paris

Paris gets a job on a television game show, as a man with a profession that must be identified by famous celebrities. Bemoaning his failure to rank among the celebrities, he accepts the job, counting on free drinks and a paycheck.

A Shock to the System
London: Macmillan, 1984.
New York: Scribner, 1985.

Graham Marshall was pushed and groomed for success and enjoyed each step in his rise in station. From his birth to lower-middle-class parents to assistant personnel head of an international oil company, Graham had expected all that came to him, until the day that the next reward was inexplicably denied him. On that day Graham committed a murder and, to his surprise, got away with it. This opened up new vistas for him and another path to success.

Dead Romantic
London: Macmillan, 1985.
New York: Scribner, 1986.

Young Paul Grigson falls in love with his private tutor, Madeleine Severn,
who has fallen in love with Bernard Hopkins, another teacher at the private
language school. One of them must, and does, die, murdered in a secluded
cottage.

Leo Bruce*

Case for Three Detectives
London: Bles, 1936.
New York: Stokes, 1937.

Sergeant William Beef

Dr. Thurston and his wife are having a small house party when a woman's
scream shatters the night. The guests rush to Mrs. Thurston's room, break
down the door, and find her dead. Dr. Thurston brings in three detectives
to solve the crime: Lord Simon Plimsoll, M. Amer Picon, and Monsignor Smith.
Meanwhile, Sergeant Beef, the village constable, struggles stolidly with the
crime.

Case without a Corpse
London: Bles, 1937.
New York: Stokes, 1937.

Sergeant William Beef

Beef's evening dart game is interrupted by a young man who rushes in and
confesses to murder. Before Beef can take the matter in hand, the stranger
commits suicide, leaving Beef with a case without a corpse. In the end, Beef
is so pleased with his success in this case that he decides to go into business
as a detective if he is not promoted to Scotland Yard.

Case with No Solution
London: Bles, 1939.

Case with No Conclusion
Chicago: Academy, 1984.

Sergeant William Beef

Sergeant Beef begins his career as a private detective in London when he is asked by a young man to save his brother from a charge of murder. The morning after a dinner party for family and friends, one of the guests reappears in the library--dead.

Case with Four Clowns
London: Davies, 1939.
New York: Stokes, 1939.

Sergeant William Beef

Beef's nephew, Albert Stiles, reports in a letter to his uncle that the fortuneteller of a circus where he works has predicted a murder. Beef gladly journeys to Yorkshire to look things over, enters a circus seething with anger, and settles down to await murder among bareback riders, trapeze artists, and lion tamers.

Case with Ropes and Rings
London: Nicholson, 1940.
Chicago: Academy, 1980.

Sergeant William Beef

The tragic death by hanging of the son of the marquess of Edenbridge seems to Sergeant Beef to be the perfect case for him, especially since he doesn't believe it was suicide. Reluctantly, Lionel Townsend, Beef's chronicler, introduces him to a teacher at Penshurst, the boy's school, and Beef joins the staff of the exclusive public school to look for a murderer.

Case for Sergeant Beef
London: Nicholson, 1947.
Chicago: Academy, 1980.

Sergeant William Beef

A retired watchmaker decides to leave his mark on the world by executing the perfect murder, so he plans carefully and keeps copious notes. He succeeds, as far as the police are concerned, but his sister calls in Sergeant Beef.

Neck and Neck
London: Gollancz, 1951.
Chicago: Academy, 1980.

Sergeant William Beef

The tables are turned on Lionel Townsend, Beef's chronicler, when he is called home and told that his aunt has been murdered. As the heirs to the large estate, Lionel and his brother, along with their cousins, are the obvious suspects.

Cold Blood
London: Gollancz, 1952.
Chicago: Academy, 1980.

Sergeant William Beef

Sergeant Beef gets an opportunity to raise the level of his clientele when he is called in to investigate the murder of the rich and elderly Cosmo Ducrow. In an isolated country estate, Ducrow is found dead in the morning outside the house, his head knocked in by a croquet mallet.

Our Jubilee Is Death
London: Davies, 1959.
Chicago: Academy, 1986.

Carolus Deene

Few people are a better candidate for murder than the popular novelist Lil-lianne Bomberger, whose streak of malice torments her nieces and nephew, her secretary, and her servants. When she is found buried on the beach with only her head showing, no one mourns her loss, except perhaps one of her publishers.

Furious Old Women
London: Davies, 1960.
Chicago: Academy, 1983.

Carolus Deene

An elderly woman active in the affairs of the village church is beaten to death in the churchyard. Apparently a senseless crime of violence and rob-bery, the crime incenses the victim's sister, who insists it is a parish matter and the perpetrator should hang for it.

Jack on the Gallows Tree
London: Davies, 1960.
Chicago: Academy, 1983.

Carolus Deene

The placid life of Buddington-on-the-Hill, an inland health resort popular with the elderly well-to-do, is jolted by the discovery of the murder of an elderly woman. Immediately afterward, the body of another woman is found. Stran-gled within a few hours of each other, the women had no known connection between them.

Die All, Die Merrily
London: Davies, 1961.
New York: British Book Centre, 1961.

Carolus Deene

Lady Drumbone has spent several years in Parliament embarrassing the government and is now in a peck of trouble. Her nephew has committed suicide, after tape-recording a confession of murder committed only a few hours before. His aunt has not handed this over to the police, and at least one part of the recording calls for closer attention.

A Bone and a Hank of Hair
London: Davies, 1961.
New York: British Book Centre, 1961.

Carolus Deene

When Mrs. Chalk arrives to visit her cousin, the woman's husband tells her that his wife has left him. Mrs. Chalk is certain something more serious has happened but leaves quietly. While waiting for a train to take her home, she questions a villager about her cousin and the cousin's husband, and receives in turn a description of Mrs. Rathbone not at all like her cousin, making Mrs. Chalk wonder how many Mrs. Rathbones there are.

Nothing Like Blood
London: Davies, 1962.
Chicago: Academy, 1985.

Carolus Deene

The well-to-do residents of a guest house on the coast are naturally unsettled over two deaths among their number. The first to die was an old woman given little time to live by her doctor; the second was a younger woman who, according to eyewitnesses, dived from her balcony to the rocks below. The guests talk about the deaths as though both might have been murder.

Crack of Doom
London: Davies, 1963.

Such Is Death
New York: London House, 1963.

Carolus Deene

A murderer plans the perfect crime, one that is untraceable but offers complete intellectual satisfaction. The victim will be chosen at random and all other details of the crime will lead nowhere. The person chosen as victim, however, turns out to be a perfect choice for some.

Death in Albert Park
London: Allen, 1964.
New York: Scribner, 1979.

Carolus Deene

In a quiet suburb of London, three women, apparently chosen at random, are murdered within weeks of each other in Albert Park. The quiet streets of this gray Victorian neighborhood lose their aura of safety as the police attempt to identify the most elusive of murderers--the random, serial murderer.

Death at Hallows End
London: Allen, 1965.
New York: British Book Centre, 1966.

Carolus Deene

Old Grossiter realizes one day that his vast wealth will go to his next of kin, two nephews barely known to him, unless he directs otherwise. He investigates his nephews and concludes that he had better leave everything to charity. He so instructs his solicitor, demanding that the man bring him the will at once. Duncan Humby dutifully sets off the next day and disappears less than a mile from the nephews' farm, where Grossiter is staying. That night Grossiter dies.

Death at St. Asprey's School
London: Allen, 1967.
Chicago: Academy, 1984.

Carolus Deene

A series of bizarre incidents upsets an English preparatory school for boys. Small pets are found dead and an instructor is injured. The headmaster gives in to growing fear and calls in Carolus Deene.

Death with Blue Ribbon
London: Allen, 1969.
New York: British Book Centre, 1970.

Carolus Deene

Yves Rolland has crawled his way to the top of the restaurant business, where one morning he meets two men not unlike himself. Threatened with ruin unless he pays them, Rolland throws the men out and refuses to be intimidated, but to no avail. A guest becomes sick with food poisoning; a famous gourmand makes her annual visit, and she is also poisoned. Then she dies, and Rolland wishes he had paid the protection money in the first place.

Death in the Middle Watch
London: Allen, 1974.

Carolus Deene

Mr. Porteus is worried about his cruise business, and for good reason. Last year on the <u>Summer Queen</u> a man died and was buried at sea. The doctor, though seasick, issued a certificate. Now Mr. Porteus is receiving threatening letters about the next cruise of the same ship. He is right to worry, for on the first night out a crew member thinks he hears a man going overboard.

W. J. Burley

A Taste of Power
London: Gollancz, 1966.

Dr. Henry Pym

The Huntley-May grammar school has undergone the usual change in teachers of late, and one among the staff has taken the trouble to learn a great deal about the teachers and students. Poison-pen letters arrive with disturbing regularity and with enough distorted truth to command attention. Though no violence is threatened, the teachers suspect danger. Their suspicions are confirmed by an unusual warning of what might happen.

Death in Willow Pattern
London: Gollancz, 1969.
New York: Walker, 1970.

Dr. Henry Pym

Sir Francis Leigh and two other members of his family are receiving poison-pen letters accusing Sir Francis of the abduction and murder of two local girls who have disappeared. This seems silly though malicious, but the letter writer goes on to point out that one of Sir Francis's ancestors was guilty of precisely the same crime. Indeed, there are remarkable parallels between the alleged crimes.

Three-Toed Pussy
London: Gollancz, 1968.

Superintendent Charles Wycliffe

In a village that one resident calls a refuge for intelligent cowards, a young woman is murdered, her body left in a manner to emphasize her physical deformity--one foot is missing two toes. Everyone connected with the dead woman--and she had many men friends--seems to be well above ordinary violence, prone to the literary life even in a remote Cornish village.

To Kill a Cat
London: Gollancz, 1970.
New York: Walker, 1970.

Superintendent Charles Wycliffe

During a holiday on the coast, Wycliffe helps the local police investigate the death of a young woman. The more Wycliffe learns, the more contradictory becomes the picture of the murder and the character of the victim.

Guilt Edged
London: Gollancz, 1971.
New York: Walker, 1972.

Superintendent Charles Wycliffe

The wife of a prominent businessman is found in the river, but none of her relatives is visibly upset. The only concern is shown by her brother, an MP who wants the matter handled quickly, quietly, and efficiently.

Death in a Salubrious Place
London: Gollancz, 1973.
New York: Walker, 1973.

Superintendent Charles Wycliffe

A young island woman is murdered and her body left in a quarry. To the fishermen and tradespeople, the year-round residents of the island, the murderer can be only the rock singer who has recently settled in their midst with his entourage.

Death in Stanley Street
London: Gollancz, 1974.
New York: Walker, 1974.

Superintendent Charles Wycliffe

The murder of a prostitute is clearly not an ordinary crime: great care has been taken to arrange the scene of the crime and the woman was known to be intelligent, educated, and expensive. Tracing her identity is embarrassing for people in her past as well as in the present.

Wycliffe and the Pea-Green Boat
London: Gollancz, 1975.
New York: Walker, 1975.

Superintendent Charles Wycliffe

The members of the Tremain family have never gotten along well with each other or outsiders. In the 1950s two cousins were drawn to the same woman, and one was convicted of murdering her out of jealousy. Twenty years later the other cousin is charged with murdering his father out of greed. Certainly the Tremains exhibit the consequences of harboring the baser passions for many years.

Wycliffe and the Schoolgirls
London: Gollancz, 1976.
New York: Walker, 1976.

Superintendent Charles Wycliffe

A nightclub singer is murdered and a week later a nurse is attacked on her way to work. The police can find no connection between the women, except that they had met as schoolgirls years ago.

Wycliffe and the Scapegoat
London: Gollancz, 1978.
New York: Doubleday, 1979.

Superintendent Charles Wycliffe

Jonathan Riddle lives estranged from his family and his community. When he disappears on a Friday evening in October, the townspeople are happy to speculate on his whereabouts. They are especially fond of the idea of his taking the place of the life-sized figure called the Scapegoat, which is attached to a wheel that is sent burning into the ocean on All-Hallows Eve.

Wycliffe in Paul's Court
London: Gollancz, 1980.
New York: Doubleday, 1980.

Superintendent Charles Wycliffe

The charm of the neighborhood of Paul's Court conceals many of the usual tensions among neighbors, but no one expects discord to go so far as the murder of one of their own. A youngster is found murdered, and another neighbor is found dead; the police suspect the deaths are linked.

Wycliffe's Wild Goose Chase
London: Gollancz, 1982.
New York: Doubleday, 1982.

Superintendent Charles Wycliffe

Wycliffe finds a gun on a beach and traces it to its original owner. The gun had been stolen two years earlier, and its recovery suggests that other stolen property may now be located. Seeking the dealer who appraised the gun for the owner, Wycliffe finds him in his office--dead from a gunshot.

Wycliffe and the Beales
London: Gollancz, 1983.
New York: Doubleday, 1984.

Superintendent Charles Wycliffe

Bunny Newcombe is the village odd-job man, accepted but generally invisible to the other residents. After his mother dies, however, he changes, becoming in outer appearance a tramp. Then he is murdered, and no one can imagine why anyone would kill a harmless man like Bunny.

Wycliffe and the Four Jacks
London: Gollancz, 1985.
New York: Doubleday, 1986.

Superintendent Charles Wycliffe

In a resort village, tourists and residents follow their separate paths, and the death of a bar girl hardly relates to anyone beyond her own circle, or so people think. There is one in the village who is uncomfortable with the time of her death: it is too close to reminders of certain dates he has been receiving in the mail, four Jacks, each marked with a date.

The Schoolmaster
London: Gollancz, 1977.
New York: Walker, 1977.

When the wife of a schoolteacher leaves him for another man, the teacher's orderly life unravels. Then the woman's lover is murdered, and the teacher drifts into the past and an earlier death.

Charles and Elizabeth
London: Gollancz, 1979.
New York: Walker, 1981.

Wandering through the Cornish countryside, Brian Kenyon, a teacher, explores an old mansion. He thinks he sees a young woman in Victorian dress and a garden of an earlier day. Researching the family, he learns that the people and voices must date from over a hundred years ago. Brian is not disturbed by this, but his employers insist on psychiatric treatment.

The House of Care
London: Gollancz, 1981.
New York: Walker, 1982.

Laura Care is a student of the occult, which she expects to use to prove the identity of her mother's murderer. According to the police, however, Deborah Care fell from a tower sixteen years ago. Laura, who grew up with a stepmother and assorted relatives, disagrees strongly with the police and is determined to unveil every secret and exact every penalty from her relatives.

Henry Calvin*

The Chosen Instrument
London: Hutchinson, 1969.

Boka Lives
New York: Harper, 1969.

John Carlyle and Dai Owen

John Carlyle and Dai Owen agree to build a road on the island nation of Tatra, having been assured that it is a quiet and orderly country. But in their first few days, they are almost crushed by a rock slide, witness a riot, and face questions from every guard they meet.

The Poison Chasers
London: Hutchinson, 1971.

John Carlyle and Dai Owen

A remote corner of Scotland has been chosen for the site of an antipollution research station, and the few inhabitants of the area are pleased at the prospect of industry coming into the area. Nevertheless, things do not go well.

Three construction workers are killed; then a fence is put up and guard dogs make the rounds with the security guards. This seems far too much security for a construction job in a remote village of two hundred people and no crime.

It's Different Abroad
London: Hutchinson, 1963.
New York: Harper, 1963.

A schoolteacher on her first trip outside Scotland, Helen McLeish arrives in France hoping for some of the fun she has missed in life. Instead of fun, she stumbles from one misadventure to another, dodging petty criminals and bickering relatives who secretly consider her a mildly hysterical spinster.

Edward Candy*

Which Doctor?
London: Gollancz, 1953.
New York: Rinehart, 1954.

Inspector Burnivel

Dr. Martin Sandeman may be a good physician, but his manner and character alienate the people who must work with him. When he is found dead on the morning of a major medical conference, no one is distressed. More distressing is the disappearance of an orphan from one of the wards.

Bones of Contention
London: Gollancz, 1954.
New York: Doubleday, 1983.

Inspector Burnivel

The routine of a small medical museum is interrupted when a skeleton arrives from an anonymous donor. The curator of the collection dies while trying to identify the donor, and the delicate balance between personal feelings and professional attitudes is hopelessly upset.

Words for Murder Perhaps
London: Gollancz, 1971.
New York: Doubleday, 1984.

Superintendent Burnivel

Stifled in his professional and personal life, Mr. Roberts decides to offer a course on crime fiction, and soon real life is imitating a crime novel. A beautiful young widow joins his class, his ex-wife's husband disappears, and a visiting professor is murdered.

Scene Changing
London: Gollancz, 1977.

Jeff Renshaw, university teacher, has written a modest novel about an old man and a girl along the lines of Lolita, and Patrick Marchant, successful stage adapter, wants to dramatize it. Marchant's sister and colleagues are opposed to the idea, and even Jeff Renshaw doesn't take the offer seriously at first.

Youngman Carter

Mr. Campion's ... Farthing
London: Heinemann, 1969.
New York: Morrow, 1969.

Albert Campion

Miss Charlotte Cambric offers weekend visits to international guests at her Victorian mansion, built by a famous eccentric uncle. But business is erratic, and a rich competitor wants to buy her out. Then a Russian scientist disappears from Miss Cambric's estate.

Mr. Campion's Falcon
London: Heinemann, 1970.

Mr. Campion's Quarry
New York: Morrow, 1971.

Albert Campion

A quiet middle-aged man dies of natural causes in a resort hotel, and soon afterward the hotel manager is found dead. There seems to be no connection between the two men, but their deaths send ripples into the world of oil and government and even archaeology.

Sarah Caudwell

Thus Was Adonis Murdered
London: Collins, 1981.
New York: Scribner, 1981.

Professor Hilary Tamar

To strengthen her spirit before she gives an account of herself to the Inland Revenue, Julia Larwood, barrister, takes a ten-day trip to Venice. To pass the time, she looks among her fellow passengers for a suitable diversion and alights upon a gorgeous young man.

The Shortest Way to Hades
London: Century, 1984.
New York: Scribner, 1985.

Professor Hilary Tamar

Five young barristers need all their tact and skill to bring about an agreement among the several heirs of a large estate. As soon as the lawyers seem to have settled everything, however, one of the heirs dies in an accident after writing to one of the barristers.

G.K. Chesterton*

The Man Who Was Thursday
London: Simpkin, 1908.
New York: Dodd, Mead, 1908.

In this tale, subtitled <u>A Nightmare</u>, scholars have traced Chesterton's personal emotional history as well as a theologian's dialogue with the Bible. The Central Anarchist Council has seven members, each named after a day of the week; their leader is Sunday. As the story begins, members of the London branch meet to elect a successor to their representative to the council, who has just died. Their representative has been named Thursday.

Four Faultless Felons (4 novellas)
London: Cassell, 1930.
New York: Dodd, Mead, 1930.

<u>The Moderate Murderer</u>. In the colonial district of Polybia, near Egypt, the Viscount Tallboys arrives to take over the governorship. He brings with him his niece and nephew, and his nephew's tutor. He also brings a compromise from the British government that is certain to upset the natives of Polybia.

<u>The Honest Quack.</u> The poet-painter Walter Windrush builds his life around an unusual tree, praising its uniqueness to anyone and everyone. He eventually buys the land, builds a house, and constructs a wall around the tree. After that he won't let anyone in to see it. A doctor-friend finally decides he must see this tree.

<u>The Ecstatic Thief</u>. Lord Normandale is bemoaning the fate (his own) of a rich, self-made businessman who is cursed with three ungrateful sons; this is the first his secretary has ever heard of a third son. She soon has an opportunity to meet him.

<u>The Loyal Traitor</u>. The royal house and government of Pavonia, an enlightened European state, is threatened by an underground movement called the Brotherhood of the Word. No one knows quite what this is, except that it seems to portend revolution and to attract some reputable citizens.

Agatha Christie

The Mysterious Affair at Styles
London: Lane, 1920.
New York: Dodd, Mead, 1920.

Hercule Poirot

For many years after her husband's death, Mrs. Cavendish has lived contentedly at Styles Court with her two stepsons and a companion. After she marries her companion's distant relative, Alfred Inglethorp, life begins to change. Everyone seems to want her money or to suspect others of wanting it. Little wonder that she is found to be dying of poison in her locked bedroom.

The Murder on the Links
London: Lane, 1923.
New York: Dodd, Mead, 1923.

Hercule Poirot

Poirot receives an urgent letter calling him to France, but when he arrives the man who sent for him is dead. The body was found in a shallow grave, wearing only a long raincoat over underclothing. His wife is found bound and gagged in the house, knowing only that her husband was kidnapped late at night.

The Murder of Roger Ackroyd
London: Collins, 1926.
New York: Dodd, Mead, 1926.

Hercule Poirot

Roger Ackroyd has waited a year for Mrs. Ferrars to mourn her husband and accept a marriage proposal. When she finally tells him why she cannot marry him, he is shocked. When she is later found dead, he decides he must confide in someone.

The Big Four
London: Collins, 1927.
New York: Dodd, Mead, 1927.

Hercule Poirot

A begrimed and delirious man stumbles into Poirot's apartment, reciting the detective's address before passing out. When he recovers, he narrates a tale of the Big Four, four archcriminals who intend to destroy the order of the world.

The Mystery of the Blue Train
London: Collins, 1928.
New York: Dodd, Mead, 1928.

Hercule Poirot

The Blue Train from London to the Riviera is carrying Katherine Grey on her first journey in her new life as a rich woman rather than a companion to rich women. The train also carries Ruth Kettering, a rich woman who has just left her titled but irresponsible husband, and a woman who longs to be rich like the others. Before the train arrives, one woman is dead and a priceless jewel is missing.

Peril at End House
London: Collins, 1932.
New York: Dodd, Mead, 1932.

Hercule Poirot

Nick Buckley, named after her grandfather, has inherited End House and little else, but she seems happy with her lot, so much so that she carelessly ignores several near-fatal accidents. After a fourth near miss, she is persuaded to take precautions.

Lord Edgware Dies
London: Collins, 1933.

Thirteen at Dinner
New York: Dodd, Mead, 1933.

Hercule Poirot

Jane Wilkinson is a successful actress who has no trouble attracting admirers. Unfortunately, she married one of them and now wants a divorce. After first refusing, Lord Edgware agrees to a divorce and tells Jane's emissary so. Later that evening, however, while his wife is attending a dinner party, Lord Edgware is murdered, and the butler insists Jane did it.

Murder on the Orient Express
London: Collins, 1934.

Murder in the Calais Coach
New York: Dodd, Mead, 1934.

Hercule Poirot

As the Orient Express winds its way through a snowy Yugoslavia the passengers in the Istanbul-Calais coach settle in for a long journey. Before the first night is out, one of them will be dead, and there will be too many clues and too many suspects for the murder.

Three Act Tragedy
London: Collins, 1935.

Murder in Three Acts
New York: Dodd, Mead, 1934.

Hercule Poirot

Sir Charles Cartwright, a retired actor, is entertaining houseguests before dinner when the vicar, a likable fellow, drops dead with his cocktail in his hand. Everyone is astonished, but the death is declared natural. Some weeks later, a psychiatrist who was at the same party dies in Yorkshire in the same manner: he drops dead while holding his drink.

Death in the Clouds
London: Collins, 1935.

Death in the Air
New York: Dodd, Mead, 1935.

Hercule Poirot

A short flight from Paris to Croydon ends in tragedy when one of the passengers is murdered just before landing. Beside the body is what appears to be a poisoned African dart. In a crowded compartment with only eighteen seats, it hardly seems possible that the passenger could have been killed with the dart.

The ABC Murders
London: Collins, 1936.
New York: Dodd, Mead, 1936.

The Alphabet Murders
New York: Pocket Books, 1966.

Hercule Poirot

Poirot receives a letter warning him of an impending crime and challenging him to catch the criminal. The note, giving the place and date of the crime, is only the first for the murderer, who signs himself A.B.C., a reference to the standard railway guide.

Murder in Mesopotamia
London: Collins, 1936.
New York: Dodd, Mead, 1936.

Hercule Poirot

A nurse on a temporary assignment in Iraq is asked to take the case of the wife of an archaeologist conducting a dig in the area. Told that the patient has "fancies," the nurse expects alcohol or drugs. After she meets Mrs. Leidner, the nurse is convinced that her patient is afraid.

Cards on the Table
London: Collins, 1936.
New York: Dodd, Mead, 1937.

Hercule Poirot

A rich collector, Mr. Shaitana prefers a unique collection: people who commit murder. He invites four master sleuths (H. Poirot, A. Oliver, Supt. Battle, and Col. Race) to dinner to meet four members of his collection. Before the evening is out, Mr. Shaitana has been murdered by one of his respectable dinner guests.

Dumb Witness
London: Collins, 1937.

Poirot Loses a Client
New York: Dodd, Mead, 1937.

Hercule Poirot

Emily Arundell knows that her young relatives visit her only to ensure their place in her will, and she accepts this and their right to a share of the family money after her death--until one night during their visit she trips over her dog's ball and falls down the stairs. Scared yet pensive, she writes Poirot and her solicitor, changing her will. The letter to Poirot doesn't reach him until two months after her death and after her estate has passed to a surprise heir.

Death on the Nile
London: Collins, 1937.
New York: Dodd, Mead, 1938.

Hercule Poirot

Linnet Ridgeway seems to have everything: beauty, brains, and money. But her friend Jacquelin has something Linnet doesn't have: a man she loves passionately. Linnet steals her friend's fiancé and they journey to Egypt for their honeymoon, which is punctuated by unpleasant encounters with Jackie. Nevertheless, Linnet and her husband embark on a cruise up the Nile, sharing their holiday with several who are intensely jealous of Linnet and others who hate or fear her.

Appointment with Death
London: Collins, 1938.
New York: Dodd, Mead, 1938.

Hercule Poirot

Tourists in the Middle East can't help noticing Mrs. Boynton and her family. The old woman, rich and ugly, takes a perverse pleasure in controlling her family and thwarting their plans, leaving all but her daughter-in-law thoroughly cowed. Even outsiders drawn to the family by pity, curiosity, or affection are not safe from the old woman's malice.

Hercule Poirot's Christmas
London: Collins, 1938.

Murder for Christmas
New York: Dodd, Mead, 1939.

A Holiday for Murder
New York: Avon, 1947.

Hercule Poirot

Old Mr. Simeon Lee is looking forward to having all his children and their families around him at Christmas, including the son who ran off years ago and the son who became a painter. But it only sounds heartwarming. Greedy, cruel, and manipulative, Mr. Lee is looking forward to watching the sparks fly among his sons and their families.

Sad Cypress
London: Collins, 1940.
New York: Dodd, Mead, 1940.

Hercule Poirot

Mrs. Welman dies as expected, but without leaving a will, so her entire estate passes to her niece, Elinor. Elinor sets out to do the right thing by those close to Mrs. Welman, even for Mary Gerrard, the lodgekeeper's daughter. Then Mary dies, and Elinor's feelings for Mary make her the obvious suspect.

One, Two, Buckle My Shoe
London: Collins, 1940.

The Patriotic Murders
New York: Dodd, Mead, 1941.

An Overdose of Death
New York: Dell, 1953.

Hercule Poirot

An ordinary morning at the dentist's office turns out to be less than normal
when the dentist is found dead. Since his patients included an important
financier, Chief Inspector Japp is assigned to the case. The police suspect
murder until one of the patients dies later in the day. Then they suspect
that the dentist committed suicide after accidentally mistreating a patient.
This theory isn't very satisfactory either.

Evil under the Sun
London: Collins, 1941.
New York: Dodd, Mead, 1941.

Hercule Poirot

The holiday atmosphere of the Jolly Roger Hotel grows tense with the arrival
of Arlena Marshall and her husband and stepdaughter. To several of the men,
she is simply a beautiful woman to look at; to one man, she is the awaited
lover; and to others, both men and women, she is evil, the kind of person
who enjoys disrupting other people's lives.

Five Little Pigs
London: Collins, 1943.

Murder in Retrospect
New York: Dodd, Mead, 1942.

Hercule Poirot

Sixteen years ago Caroline Crale was convicted of murdering her husband, Amyas Crale, a famous painter. Now their daughter wants to know who was really guilty. Sixteen years ago Amyas had been painting a rich young heiress, one of many women he had brief affairs with, and entertaining other guests--his younger sister, a friend, and the friend's brother, who lived nearby.

The Hollow
London: Collins, 1946.
New York: Dodd, Mead, 1946.

Murder after Hours
New York: Dell, 1954.

Hercule Poirot

Dr. John Christow and his wife, Gerda, are expecting only a quiet weekend in the country with Lady Angketell. John, of course, is hoping for time to be with Henrietta, his lover. After dinner on his first evening, he unexpectedly runs into Veronica Cray, an actress he loved almost seventeen years ago. The complaints he has had about his life finally come to a head, and he must face the three women who have been important in his life.

Taken at the Flood
London: Collins, 1948.

There Is a Tide...
New York: Dodd, Mead, 1948.

Hercule Poirot

Gordon Cloade was very good to his close relatives and their families, taking care of their bills and supporting them in their less-lucrative ventures. Then Gordon remarries a young widow and dies in an air raid. Unfortunately, Gordon forgot to make a new will, so his new wife gets everything just when his relatives need money more than ever. Then Mrs. Cloade decides to live with her tightfisted brother.

Mrs. McGinty's Dead
London: Collins, 1952.
New York: Dodd, Mead, 1952.

Blood Will Tell
New York: Detective Book Club, 1952.

Hercule Poirot and Ariadne Oliver

Mrs. McGinty is a widow and a village charwoman, reliable, pleasant, and not well-off. Her murder is a surprise to everyone, and a jury convicts her paying guest, a diffident young man, of murder and robbery. Not everyone is satisfied, however, so Poirot moves into a chaotic guest house, studying the life of a charwoman and searching for a murderer.

After the Funeral
London: Collins, 1953.

Funerals Are Fatal
New York: Dodd, Mead, 1953.

Murder at the Gallop
London: Fontana, 1963.

Hercule Poirot

What is left of the large Abernethie family gathers at the death of the oldest
son, Richard, who died suddenly after mourning the death of his son.
Richard had been generous in his will, and everyone seems satisfied except
his sister, Cora. Unchanged after twenty years, Cora disingenuously asks,
"It was murder, wasn't it?"

Hickory Dickory Dock
London: Collins, 1955.

Hickory Dickory Death
New York: Dodd, Mead, 1955.

Hercule Poirot

At a student hostel catering to foreign students in a wide range of scholarly
subjects, there is a growing unease over a series of petty thefts. Students
lose cheap jewelry, slacks, even a cookbook. When one of the residents
finally confesses, the confession covers only some of the stolen items.

Dead Man's Folly
London: Collins, 1956.
New York: Dodd, Mead, 1956.

Hercule Poirot and Ariadne Oliver

The new owners of Nosse Hall have agreed to host a fête and a murder hunt as part of it, to be staged by the detective writer Mrs. Ariadne Oliver. After a number of people have suggested changes, however, Mrs. Oliver begins to wonder if someone is planning a real murder.

Cat among the Pigeons
London: Collins, 1959.
New York: Dodd, Mead, 1960.

Hercule Poirot

The headmistress of Meadowbank, a school for girls, is used to coping with crises, but not murder. When one of the instructors is killed, the girls are delighted at the prospect of a murder investigation, and the teachers are wary. Some are worried about the princess from a Near Eastern country, and others are worried about the niece of a pilot who died in a revolution in the princess's country.

The Clocks
London: Collins, 1963.
New York: Dodd, Mead, 1964.

Hercule Poirot and Ariadne Oliver

Sheila Webb's quiet life as a secretary-typist is jolted when she arrives at a client's home and discovers a body in the sitting room. Just as she is about to scream, the owner of the house arrives, a blind woman who later insists she did not call for a secretary. In addition to the corpse, someone has added several clocks to Miss Pebmarsh's sitting room, none set for the correct time.

Third Girl
London: Collins, 1966.
New York: Dodd, Mead, 1967.

Hercule Poirot and Ariadne Oliver

A young girl announces to Poirot that she may have committed a murder, but
decides not to ask for his help. Poirot tracks her down and learns that there
are two possible murders to consider. In addition, the girl has disappeared,
friends and relatives are reticent, and there is a suicide in the girl's apartment building.

Hallowe'en Party
London: Collins, 1969.
New York: Dodd, Mead, 1969.

Hercule Poirot and Ariadne Oliver

Mothers and children have gathered to decorate for a Hallowe'en party.
During the afternoon, one of the kids insists she once saw a murder, even
though no one will believe her tale. After the party is over that evening,
the child is found dead.

Elephants Can Remember
London: Collins, 1972.
New York: Dodd, Mead, 1972.

Hercule Poirot and Ariadne Oliver

Mrs. Oliver is used to inane questions and fulsome praise from some of the
people she meets, but she is thrown off her stride by Mrs. Burton-Cox, whose
son is engaged to marry Mrs. Oliver's goddaughter. Mrs. Burton-Cox wants
to know the truth about her prospective daughter-in-law's background: Did
the father shoot the mother, or did the mother shoot the father? Mrs.
Oliver is at first shocked and then curious.

Curtain
London: Collins, 1975.
New York: Dodd, Mead, 1975.

Hercule Poirot

Poirot has returned to Styles Court, which is now a guest house. After looking over his fellow guests, he learns that one has been involved with or somehow related to five murders. From this Poirot concludes that there will be murder again at Styles Court.

The Pale Horse
London: Collins, 1961.
New York: Dodd, Mead, 1962.

Ariadne Oliver

A priest in a poor neighborhood is called to the side of a dying woman, who urges him to bring an evil to an end. The priest agrees, the woman dies, and the priest leaves for home. He is murdered in an alley, and the police find in his shoe a list of names that have no apparent relation to each other.

The Secret Adversary
London: Lane, 1922.
New York: Dodd, Mead, 1922.

Tommy and Tuppence Beresford

Although World War I is over, a young woman who escaped death on the Lusitania with important documents is still being sought, and the number of people searching for her seems to increase with each year. The disturbing question is why she doesn't simply turn the documents over to the government.

N or M?
London: Collins, 1941.
New York: Dodd, Mead, 1941.

Tommy and Tuppence Beresford

An agent is killed just as he is about to discover the identity of one of Hitler's most important agents. Tommy Beresford takes the agent's place and is soon living with the most unlikely group of suspects.

By the Pricking of My Thumbs
London: Collins, 1968.
New York: Dodd, Mead, 1968.

Tommy and Tuppence Beresford

Aunt Ada is old but feisty right until the end, as Tommy and Tuppence learn on their last visit to her in a nursing home. When they return to clear up her room, they are sad to note the loss of another guest in the nursing home, Mrs. Lancaster, who had told Tuppence a strange tale of a child hidden behind a fireplace. Mrs. Lancaster had given Aunt Ada a painting of the house with the child, and Tuppence muses over it until she realizes that she recognizes the house. She decides to track down the house.

Postern of Fate
London: Collins, 1973.
New York: Dodd, Mead, 1973.

Tommy and Tuppence Beresford

In their new home, Tuppence discovers a message in a children's book left behind by the previous owners: "Mary Jane did not die naturally. It was one of us. I think I know which one." Tuppence decides to trace the child and the murder.

The Man in the Brown Suit
London: Lane, 1924.
New York: Dodd, Mead, 1924.

Colonel Race

Anne Beddingfield, cast out into the world, sets out to meet adventure.
Instead, she sees an accident in a tube station: a man falls onto the rails and
dies, pronounced dead by a man claiming to be a doctor. Anne finds a scrap
of paper belonging to the dead man, and this and something about the way
the doctor examined the body stick in her mind.

Sparkling Cyanide
London: Collins, 1945.

Remembered Death
New York: Dodd, Mead, 1945

Colonel Race

Rosemary Barton dies a horrible death from cyanide poisoning at her own
birthday party; it is accepted as suicide. Several months later, her husband,
George, receives an anonymous letter claiming that Rosemary's death wasn't
a suicide. George looks again at the guest list for the party and decides to
gather the guests together again.

The Secret of Chimneys
London: Lane, 1925.
New York: Dodd, Mead, 1925.

Superintendent Battle

The ninth marquis of Caterham has inherited not only the stately home of
Chimneys but also the custom of holding important diplomatic meetings there.
Resigned, Lord Caterham watches as his home is invaded by Foreign Office
personnel and diplomats from Herzoslovakia to arrange the restoration of the
Herzoslovakian monarchy for the benefit of the British economy. The only
danger to their plan is a South African adventurer, who has the memoirs of
a dead Herzoslovakian statesman and is turning them over to a publisher.

The Seven Dials Mystery
London: Collins, 1929.
New York: Dodd, Mead, 1929.

Superintendent Battle

Chimneys is once again full of houseguests, many from the Foreign Office. But this is a younger group, brought together at first by the tenants. The guests decide to play a practical joke on one of their number with eight alarm clocks set for 6:30 a.m. In the morning, instead of seeing Gerry rousted out of bed by the clocks, however, his friends wait in vain for any reaction. Gerry was murdered in the night and is only the first of the houseguests to die.

Murder Is Easy
London: Collins, 1939.

Easy to Kill
New York: Dodd, Mead, 1939.

Superintendent Battle

A retired police officer from Asia returns home to England and encounters crime on his first day. On the train to London an old woman tells him she is going to Scotland Yard to report a series of murders in her village and to predict that the next victim will be Dr. Humbley. Mr. Fitzwilliam dismisses his traveling companion's story until he later learns that she was killed by a hit-and-run driver and that Dr. Humbley died just as she said he would.

Towards Zero
London: Collins, 1944.
New York: Dodd, Mead, 1944.

Superintendent Battle

The month of September draws an assorted group to Lady Tressilian's home in Saltcreek: her late husband's ward and his new wife, Kay; the ward's ex-wife, Audrey; and their friends. Among these and the other guests, one has a carefully worked-out plan for murder.

The Murder at the Vicarage
London: Collins, 1930.
New York: Dodd, Mead, 1930.

Miss Jane Marple

The vicarage of St. Mary Mead fairly percolates with gossip and speculation on the unseemly behavior of the village residents, much to the discomfort of the vicar. Least liked in the neighborhood is Colonel Protheroe, who argues with other church officers, insists on going over the church books with the vicar, harasses a visiting archaeologist, nearly comes to blows with a painter, and finally ends up dead in the vicar's study.

The Body in the Library
London: Collins, 1942.
New York: Dodd, Mead, 1942.

Miss Jane Marple

Colonel and Mrs. Bantry are awakened one morning with the news that there is a body in the library--the body of a blond, flamboyantly dressed young woman, not at all a good match for the library of Gossington Hall. The trail leads to a resort hotel, where the woman worked as a dancer and had become friends of one of the guests, a rich old man with not long to live.

The Moving Finger
London: Collins, 1943.
New York: Dodd, Mead, 1942.

The Case of the Moving Finger
New York: Avon, 1948.

Miss Jane Marple

Several people in Lymstock have received poison-pen letters. Some think the letters silly, some are shocked, and still others are worried about the person behind them. Most people take them in stride until the solicitor's wife is found dead after receiving a letter about her second son.

A Murder Is Announced
London: Collins, 1950.
New York: Dodd, Mead, 1950.

Miss Jane Marple

The residents of Chipping Cleghorn open their Friday morning papers to read "A Murder Is Announced," giving a place and the date as that evening. Accepting the notice as an invitation, various villagers arrive at Little Paddocks, the address given in the paper. Promptly at 6:30 p.m. the lights go out and a shot is fired. When the lights go on again, there is a murder victim on the floor.

They Do It with Mirrors
London: Collins, 1952.

Murder with Mirrors
New York: Dodd, Mead, 1952.

Miss Jane Marple

Carrie Louise and her sister, Ruth, have grown wealthy through their marriages, and Ruth is now worried about Carrie and her band of miscellaneous relatives. Now married to a man committed to saving young delinquents, Carrie lives with patients and staff, grown stepchildren and spouses, and her own children. And some of them definitely don't like her.

A Pocket Full of Rye
London: Collins, 1953.
New York: Dodd, Mead, 1954.

Miss Jane Marple

Rex Fortescue sips his morning tea in the office and instantly goes into convulsions. When the newspapers report his death and that he had rye in his pocket, only Miss Marple perceives the significance of the grain. Still there are two other murders before the rhyme and reason are clear and the murderer confronted.

4:50 from Paddington
London: Collins, 1957.

What Mrs. McGillicuddy Saw!
New York: Dodd, Mead, 1957.

Murder, She Said
New York: Pocket Books, 1961.

Miss Jane Marple

Mrs. McGillicuddy looks out the window of her first-class carriage into the window of another train moving alongside and is met with the sight of a man strangling a young woman. The trains part, the conductor doubts her story, and Mrs. McGillicuddy travels on, reporting her story to her friend Miss Marple. The newspapers carry no report of a corpse on a train or in the vicinity of the strangling, so Miss Marple sets out to find both body and murderer.

The Mirror Crack'd from Side to Side
London: Collins, 1962.

The Mirror Crack'd
New York: Dodd, Mead, 1963.

Miss Jane Marple

The village of St. Mary Mead is all agog over the arrival of a famous actress and her husband, who have taken over Gossington Hall. During a fête, some of the local residents are invited to meet the famous actress, but the party ends abruptly when one of the guests dies, apparently after an unexpected attack.

A Caribbean Mystery
London: Collins, 1964.
New York: Dodd, Mead, 1965.

Miss Jane Marple

Major Palgrave has a host of stories for his listeners, ranging from adventure tales set in the African jungle to medical stories about a murderer. He even has a photograph of a suspected murderer, but he is interrupted before he can show it to Miss Marple. Sad to say, he dies not long afterward, in his sleep.

At Bertram's Hotel
London: Collins, 1965.
New York: Dodd, Mead, 1966.

Miss Jane Marple

Bertram's Hotel clings to the Edwardian way of life, still serving afternoon tea to dowagers of the aristocracy and various religions. And all because it is good for business, providing foreign tourists with a real remnant of old England. Nevertheless, the quaint English guests can sometimes pose a problem, particularly when they are not what they seem. A canon gets lost, a guardian loses his young charge, and the police are worried about a series of robberies.

Nemesis
London: Collins, 1971.
New York: Dodd, Mead, 1971.

Miss Jane Marple

An ally from an earlier case in the West Indies, Mr. Rafiel, leaves Jane a charge to investigate a crime. He does not give her any details of the crime, but trusts her intuition and judgment. Miss Marple agrees to be guided from beyond the grave by letters left with a solicitor, to be posted to her according to a schedule set up by Mr. Rafiel before he died.

Sleeping Murder
London: Collins, 1976.
New York: Dodd, Mead, 1976.

Miss Jane Marple

In Jane Marple's last case, she advises a young couple to forgo their curiosity and let sleeping murders lie. A young woman only recently married rents a house on the coast and then discovers that she knows things about it that no one has mentioned to her. She discovers that she once lived in the house briefly, and her dreams and fears tell her she witnessed a murder there. But the police have no record of a suspicious death at the house.

Death Comes as the End
London: Collins, 1945.
New York: Dodd, Mead, 1944.

This is a tale of jealousy and greed in Egypt in 2000 B.C. Imhotep arrives home at his extensive estates with a beautiful concubine, Nofret, naively hoping the stormy reaction among his sons and their families will be short-lived. It is not. Nofret grows more arrogant as time passes, and eventually Imhotep turns on his eldest son and his wife, denouncing them and warning the rest of the family not to harm Nofret. Soon afterward, Nofret is murdered.

The Sittaford Mystery
London: Collins, 1931.

Murder at Hazelmoor
New York: Dodd, Mead, 1931.

A widow and her daughter have rented Sittaford House, on the edge of Dartmoor, causing the few people in the area to wonder why. This topic is quickly replaced by another one. During a seance at Sittaford House, a spirit reports the murder of the owner of the house, who has moved into a nearby town. An impending snowstorm makes it impossible for the neighbors to verify this news from beyond.

Why Didn't They Ask Evans?
London: Collins, 1934.

The Boomerang Clue
New York: Dodd, Mead, 1935.

Bobby Jones and Dr. Thomas are playing golf when they look over a cliff and see a man who must have just fallen. The doctor goes for help and Bobby stays with the dying man, whose last words are "Why didn't they ask Evans?"

Ten Little Niggers
London: Collins, 1939.

And Then There Were None
New York: Dodd, Mead, 1940.

Ten Little Indians
New York: Pocket Books, 1965.

Ten people unknown to each other are brought to Indian Island, off the coast of Devon, under different pretexts. On their first evening, a voice accuses each one of a specific murder. One by one the guests die until there is no one left: ten murders without a murderer.

Crooked House
London: Collins, 1949.
New York: Dodd, Mead, 1949.

Young Charlie Hayward finds his engagement put on hold when his fiancée's grandfather dies of poison. He was obviously murdered and the favorite suspect is his second wife, a woman fifty years his junior who is in love with the children's tutor. Both family and some police hope she is the murderer, since finding guilt in any other member of the family would be awkward and embarrassing.

They Came to Baghdad
London: Collins, 1951.
New York: Dodd, Mead, 1951.

In 1950 they are coming to Baghdad for many different reasons: political
leaders for a conference, agents for what they can learn and do, young men
who need work, and Victoria Jones, who has both imagination and common
sense, the second to get her out of the jams the first quality gets her into.
Victoria travels to Baghdad after she is smitten with a young man in London.
She is soon almost broke and harboring a criminal in her bedroom.

Destination Unknown
London: Collins, 1954.

So Many Steps to Death
New York: Dodd, Mead, 1955.

Her only child dead and her marriage over, Hilary Craven flies to Morocco
to escape. Preparing to commit suicide, she is invited by a stranger to try
a more imaginative path to death--impersonating a woman who has apparently
defected to an Iron Curtain country. Hilary agrees.

Ordeal by Innocence
London: Collins, 1958.
New York: Dodd, Mead, 1959.

A series of small accidents prevents Arthur Calgary from learning of his
encounter with a man later charged with murder. When Calgary finally learns
that he was the young man's alibi, the man has already died in prison.
Calgary therefore takes his news to the family of the dead man, unprepared
for their ambivalence. For if Jack did not kill his mother, as Arthur can
prove, then who in the household did?

Endless Night
London: Collins, 1967.
New York: Dodd, Mead, 1968.

Young Michael Rogers stops drifting aimlessly through life on the day he
sees Gipsy's Acre, an old house thought to be cursed. There he also meets

a woman named Ellie and confides in her his fantasies. But Ellie is rich, rich enough to make his fantasies come true, and so begins their life together in defiance of family, friends, and Gypsy warnings.

Passenger to Frankfurt
London: Collins, 1970.
New York: Dodd, Mead, 1970.

Regardless of the consequences for his diplomatic career, Sir Stafford Nye has enjoyed cultivating the unpredictable in his life. So when a young woman proposes in the Frankfurt airport that he give her his cape and passport, he decides to oblige. When he finally makes it back to England, he finds that his engagement with the unknown woman is not over--indeed, he is in this deeper than in his own work.

Douglas Clark

Nobody's Perfect
London: Cassell, 1969.
New York: Stein, 1969.

Inspector George Masters

The well-liked president of a pharmaceutical company is found dead from a drug overdose. Although the man was evidently murdered, Masters and his colleagues cannot find anyone among the eight hundred employees who might have reason to kill the president.

Death after Evensong
London: Cassell, 1969.
New York: Stein, 1970.

Inspector George Masters

The vicar is often the heart and soul of the village but not in Rooksby. Vicar Parseloe is intensely disliked by many, even considered a menace to the community. It is almost a relief when he is found dead, apparently shot to death in a schoolroom.

Sweet Poison
London: Cassell, 1970.

Inspector George Masters

Mrs. Fay Partridge is a rich young widow determined to enjoy herself, so when she suddenly dies of toxic necrosis of the liver, all are surprised but few mourn. Even more surprising is the death of her two poodles on the same day, from the same cause.

Deadly Pattern
London: Cassell, 1970.
New York: Stein, 1970.

Inspector George Masters

The coastal resort of Finstoft is the unexpected site for a series of murders of respectable, middle-aged women. The insularity that had for long protected the townspeople from the outside world now seems to be shielding the murderer, and the police must trace the changes in the village over the last forty years before they can understand the motive for the murders.

Sick to Death
London: Cassell, 1971.
New York: Stein, 1971.

Inspector George Masters

Sally Bowker is a beautiful and happy young woman, liked by all and successful in her business with two friends. Sadly, she dies in a diabetic coma. Her doctor refuses to accept this as inevitable and begins to investigate, finding that the last insulin she took was useless. There is no sign of tampering with the bottle containing the insulin and no discernible motive for murder among those who knew her.

Premedicated Murder
London: Gollancz, 1975.
New York: Scribner, 1976.

Superintendent George Masters

Roger Harte never let his crippling war injuries hold him back and he easily won the admiration of his community. His nearest neighbor, however, was Milton Rencory, a self-made man no one liked even though Harte v·ged people to be considerate of him. When Harte is found dead in Rencory's home from an obscure poison, the conclusion seems obvious to the local police and Harte's friends.

Dread and Water
London: Gollancz, 1976.
New York: Harper, 1984.

Superintendent George Masters

Three scientists from a research center die in separate mountaineering accidents, and the police are called in to discover if there is any connection between their deaths. In addition to murder, the Scotland Yard team finds a community rife with ambition and rivalry.

The Gimmel Flask
London: Gollancz, 1977.
New York: Dell, 1982.

Superintendent George Masters

The senior partner in the largest firm of auctioneers and estate agents in East Anglia is murdered, and there is no evidence of how it was done. A man of regular habits, the senior partner held to his strict schedule right up to the day he died.

Table D'Hote
London: Gollancz, 1977.
New York: Harper, 1984.

Superintendent George Masters

Wanda Mace invites her lover and his wife to her home for an extended visit, but during a dinner party the husband is called away and his wife feels too sick to stay up. The next morning Wanda discovers her houseguest dead, and two doctors can find no reason for her sudden death.

The Libertines
London: Gollancz, 1978.

Superintendent George Masters

Right after World War II a group of men formed the Libertines, a cricket club, and kept up their annual meetings at the farm of one of the members. At first, only one member was a misfit, and the others learned to put up with him. Now, several of the members are feeling uncomfortable at the meetings, and the game is losing its appeal.

Heberden's Seat
London: Gollancz, 1979.
New York: Harper, 1984.

Superintendent George Masters

On their way back to London, Masters and Green stop in a deserted church-yard to enjoy the solitude while they wait for a repair truck--until they find a body in a well. When they report their finding to the local police, they are told that two other men are missing and the area is plagued by an arsonist.

Golden Rain
London: Gollancz, 1980.
New York: Dell, 1982.

Superintendent George Masters

The young headmistress of a private girls' boarding school is poisoned. At first the police suspect an accident or suicide, but the more they investigate, the more convinced they are that the woman was murdered.

Poacher's Bag
London: Gollancz, 1980.
New York: Harper, 1983

Superintendent George Masters

Masters and Green investigate the death of an inventor who was the unlikely victim of a poacher's rifle. Even though the poacher admits firing the fatal shot, Masters's mother-in-law, who was engaged to the victim, insists that her fiancé was murdered by someone else.

The Longest Pleasure
London: Gollancz, 1981.
New York: Morrow, 1981.

Superintendant George Masters

A series of outbreaks of botulism in widely separate parts of Great Britain poses a threat to people's health and the national economy. With nothing to pursue but scientific evidence, Masters and Green set out to identify and stop a random but scientific murderer.

Roast Eggs
London: Gollancz, 1981.
New York: Dodd, Mead, 1981.

Superintendant George Masters

A successful businessman is charged with murdering his wife though the police have little evidence. When the trial seems to be going in his favor, the police call in Masters and Green, who are given only a court transcript to work with and only a weekend in which to ensure the man's conviction for murder.

Shelf Life
London: Gollancz, 1982.
New York: Harper, 1983.

Superintendent George Masters

The village of Colesworth is having its usual share of troubles--vagrancy, vandalism, and petty theft. Things get out of hand when a youngster is arrested for drunkenness and dies while in police custody. Masters and Green unravel a carefully planned murder and trace it to a most unlikely murderer.

The Monday Theory
London: Gollancz, 1983.
New York: Harper, 1985.

Superintendent George Masters

An acid-tongued newspaper columnist and her lover are found dead in a lonely cottage, apparently poisoned. Even though the police can rule out accident and suicide, they can't find a motive for murder.

Vicious Circle
London: Gollancz, 1983.
New York: Harper, 1985.

Superintendent George Masters

When an autocratic matriarch dies from an overdose of medication, the obvious conclusion is that death must have been accidental. But there are two problems with this: her doctor took elaborate precautions to prevent an overdose, and the dead woman was related to every local official who might be involved in investigating her death.

Dead Letter
London: Gollancz, 1984.
New York: Harper, 1985.

Superintendent George Masters

An old army buddy writes to Inspector Green, describing a murder he witnessed and asking for help. The writer does not sign his name, however,
because a high-level policeman is involved in the murder. With only the
letter to go on, Masters and Green must identify the writer, the location of
the murder, the victim, and the implicated policeman.

Bouquet Garni
London: Gollancz, 1984.

Superintendent George Masters

The employees of the Garden of Eden nursery come to work one morning to
find that part of the nursery has been vandalized, ruining thousands of
dollars worth of seeds. The next day the residents of Beverton learn that
three women have died of three different poisons. Two of the women worked
at the nursery, but no one can tell how the three were poisoned.

Jewelled Eye
London: Gollancz, 1985.

Superintendent George Masters

Rutland Laboratories, a pharmaceutical company, is on the verge of perfecting
a cure for cancer when one of its top scientists disappears during a walking
tour in Somerset. The police begin a low-key investigation, drawing on the
assistance of an ex-convict and uncovering a plot by Libyans to gain control
of the scientific breakthrough.

Performance
London: Gollancz, 1985.
New York: Harper, 1986.

Superintendent George Masters

Eleven women have been murdered in the last eleven months in the Northern
Counties. No matter how carefully the Scotland Yard team reexamines the
evidence, the men can find only two factors linking the eleven deaths: each
victim had recently achieved a personal triumph, and each had been murdered
within three days after the full moon.

V.C. Clinton-Baddeley

Death's Bright Dart
London: Gollancz, 1967.
New York: Morrow, 1970.

Dr. R.V. Davie

A Cambridge college sponsors a small conference, but several of the participants seem to have something other than scholarship on their minds. During
a day of lectures, a scientist drops dead during his lecture, not long after
telling Dr. Davie, a professor and detective novel buff, that he feared for
his life.

My Foe Outstretch'd beneath the Tree
London: Gollancz, 1968.
New York: Morrow, 1968.

Dr. R.V. Davie

During a brief trip to London, Dr. Davie looks forward to a quiet stay at
his London club and the pleasures of being with like-minded men: occasional
solitude, engaging conversation, and camaraderie. What Davie finds, however,
is quite different: eavesdropping, clandestine affairs, and murder.

Only a Matter of Time
London: Gollancz, 1969.
New York: Morrow, 1970.

Dr. R.V. Davie

King's Lacy is gaining a reputation for its annual music festival, and this and china figurines are the chief pleasures for Robert Coppleston, who lives with his mother and expects no social life of his own. His failure to appear for an evening festival performance, therefore, is very strange. Even stranger was his phone call earlier in the day to an officer in the electronics firm where he works, insisting that he had to see the officer at once.

No Case for the Police
London: Gollancz, 1970.
New York: Morrow, 1970.

Dr. R.V. Davie

Dr. Davie returns to his childhood home to serve as literary executor for an old friend. When he goes through his late friend's papers, he finds a notebook with an unsettling story in it. Though at first inclined to put aside the notebook, he becomes curious about it when he realizes that others in the village are prodding him to take certain actions.

To Study a Long Silence
London: Gollancz, 1972.
New York: Harper, 1984.

Dr. R.V. Davie

Dr. Davie attends a drama school production of a commedia dell'arte play, and rates it fairly high. He is very surprised when he is called by the police to make a statement about his evening. According to the police, near the end of the performance one of the actors was killed and the murder may have been committed in full view of the audience.

Edmund Crispin

The Moving Toyshop
London: Gollancz, 1946.
Philadelphia: Lippincott, 1946.

Gervase Fen

Late one evening in 1938, Richard Cadogan, poet and gun-fancier, travels to Oxford for a holiday, stumbling across a toyshop whose proprietor has left the door unlocked. Looking in to make sure all is well, the poet discovers the body of an elderly woman, gets hit on the head, and awakes in a closet. He escapes and eventually returns with the police, only to find a grocery store where the toyshop had been only hours before.

The Case of the Gilded Fly
London: Gollancz, 1944.

Obsequies at Oxford
Philadelphia: Lippincott, 1945.

Gervase Fen

Circumstances bring a group of professional actors and actresses to an Oxford theater, where the conflicts of London finally come to a head. At the center of the turmoil is Yseut Haskell, a young actress of mediocre talent and great wealth, who considers legitimate any effort to improve her position in the theater.

Holy Disorders
London: Gollancz, 1945.
Philadelphia: Lippincott, 1946.

Gervase Fen

Geoffrey Vintner, famous composer and organist, insists on living a quiet
life and concentrating on his music. He is glad to be invited to take over
the services at Tolnbridge Cathedral, but disturbed that his predecessor seems
to have been maliciously removed. When he receives a letter warning him
to stay away from Tolnbridge, he begins to wish he had never accepted the
offer.

Swan Song
London: Gollancz, 1977.
New York: Walker, 1980.

Dead and Dumb
Philadelphia: Lippincott, 1947.

Gervase Fen

Producing an opera is not an easy task, and the presence of Edwin
Shorthouse in the company can push even the most hardened trouper to the
brink of despair. When Shorthouse is found dead, the consensus is that he
was a fully deserving victim, and the murderer made a good choice.

Love Lies Bleeding
London: Gollancz, 1948.
Philadelphia: Lippincott, 1948.

Gervase Fen

The usual complement of eccentric teachers and high-spirited boys seems to
have gotten out of hand at Castrevenford School when a girl from a neighboring school disappears and someone breaks into the chemistry department.
Invited to deliver a speech to the students, Gervase Fen arrives in time to
observe some of the strange goings-on, but not soon enough to prevent
murder.

Buried for Pleasure
London: Gollancz, 1948.
Philadelphia: Lippincott, 1949.

Gervase Fen

Fen has just completed a definitive edition of Langland and, to preserve his sanity, has decided he needs a change of interest. He is therefore standing for Parliament in a rural district where the inhabitants may be even less sane than he is. To keep his mind off the vulgar techniques of electioneering, Fen assists in the investigation of a woman who was murdered through the mail and casts a paternal eye over several young and unhappy local residents.

Frequent Hearses
London: Gollancz, 1950.

Sudden Vengeance
New York: Dodd, Mead, 1950.

Gervase Fen

Fen agrees to consult on a movie about Alexander Pope, but even before filming begins there are serious problems among cast and crew. An actress signed to a small part commits suicide, but few care. Then a cameraman drops dead in a script conference.

The Long Divorce
London: Gollancz, 1951.
New York: Dodd, Mead, 1951.

A Noose for Her
New York: Mercury, 1952.

Gervase Fen

The picturesque village of Cotten Abbas is in the grip of an anonymous letter writer. Someone is sending two kinds of letters: one obscene, the other revealing embarrassing secrets. Few are surprised that the secrets are known, for this is after all a village, but most are wondering about the purpose of the letters. Then one of the recipients commits suicide and a foreign schoolteacher is murdered.

The Glimpses of the Moon
London: Gollancz, 1977.
New York: Walker, 1978.

Gervase Fen

Fen becomes involved in a murder that has already been satisfactorily settled by the police. Nevertheless, with a journalist and retired major, Fen moves from witness to witness, interrupting obscure plans for revenge and becoming an accessory after the fact of murder.

Freeman Wills Crofts

Inspector French's Greatest Case
London: Collins, 1925.
New York: Seltzer, 1925.

Inspector Joseph French

A young man finds the chief clerk of a diamond business dead and the safe empty, diamonds and cash gone. There is no sign of violence or force and few signs of anything else that might help the police. This is the first of French's cases solved by meticulous and methodical investigation.

Inspector French and the Cheyne Mystery
London: Collins, 1926.

The Cheyne Mystery
New York: Boni, 1926.

Inspector Joseph French

Maxwell Cheyne lives the quiet life of a country gentleman and writer. He is flattered when a man seeks him out in a hotel restaurant to compliment him on his war service and his writing. Unfortunately, the man drugs him during lunch. When Cheyne wakes up, he finds nothing missing from his wallet. When he arrives home, he finds his home apparently has been burglarized, but nothing has been taken.

Inspector French and the Starvel Tragedy
London: Collins, 1927.

The Starvel Hollow Tragedy
New York: Harper, 1927.

Inspector Joseph French

On one of her rare trips away from her uncle's house, Ruth Averill is called home, only to learn that her uncle's home burned to the ground, killing him and two servants. Then the police learn that the old man kept most of his money in cash in the house.

The Sea Mystery
London: Collins, 1928.
New York: Harper, 1928.

Inspector Joseph French

A father and son fishing in Burry Inlet find a crate with a corpse in it. Step by step, Inspector French traces the crate through its trip to the inlet, from a bridge, delivered there by a truck, and so on, until he identifies the sender, the corpse, and the murderer.

The Box Office Murders
London: Collins, 1929.

The Purple Sickle Murders
New York: Harper, 1929.

Inspector Joseph French

A young woman is found drowned in a quarry south of London and her friend
is later found drowned at sea. These deaths are only two in a series of
deaths of young women who work in box offices for movie theaters and other
places of amusement.

Sir John Magill's Last Journey
London: Collins, 1930.
New York: Harper, 1930.

Inspector Joseph French

When Sir John Magill retired from his linen-manufacturing business, he handed it all over to his son, moved to London, and stayed there. One day he
announces that he is going to Northern Ireland to try out his new invention,
and that is the last his family ever hears of him. He never arrives at his
hotel or his son's home, though he can be traced up to a half-hour before
he was supposed to meet his son.

Mystery in the Channel
London: Collins, 1931.

Mystery in the English Channel
New York: Harper, 1931.

Inspector Joseph French

A steamer passes a yacht drifting in the Channel with only two people on
board, both men dressed in business suits and both shot to death. Inspector
French traces the men to the financial world of London, but the trail returns
repeatedly to the sea.

Death on the Way
London: Collins, 1932.

Double Death
New York: Harper, 1932.

Inspector Joseph French

The young engineers and their assistants on a railroad job are careful about checking their work. One evening two men spot a body on the tracks but cannot stop an approaching train in time. After careful investigation, the authorities conclude that no one can be blamed for the accident. Then a coastal guard comes to the police with an unsettling story.

Sudden Death*
London: Collins, 1932.
New York: Harper, 1932.

Inspector Joseph French

The Hog's Back Mystery
London: Hodder, 1933.

The Strange Case of Dr. Earle
New York: Dodd, Mead, 1933.

Inspector Joseph French

Dr. Earle regularly enjoys his newspaper after dinner while his wife does the dishes. One evening when they have houseguests, Dr. Earle settles into his chair to read, but is gone ten minutes later, apparently still wearing his slippers. A rapid search of the neighborhood fails to locate him.

The 12:30 from Croydon*
London: Hodder, 1934.

Willful and Premeditated
New York: Dodd, Mead, 1934.

Inspector Joseph French

Mystery on Southampton Water
London: Hodder, 1934.

Crime on the Solent
New York: Dodd, Mead, 1934.

Inspector Joseph French

The depression has taken its highest toll and businesses are recovering. In the cement-manufacturing business, however, the recovery of the Joymount Company is threatened by a competing company, Chayle, on the Isle of Wight. Chayle has a new product that is taking over the market, and when the Joymount chemist cannot figure out the formula, he decides to burgle the offices of the competing company.

Crime at Guildford
London: Collins, 1935.

The Crime at Nornes
New York: Dodd, Mead, 1935.

Inspector Joseph French

Worried about the effects of the depression on their firm, directors and officers of a London jeweler gather at a country estate to plan the future of the firm. Before they can begin their work, however, one man is killed. The next day the firm's gems are gone.

Man Overboard
London: Collins, 1936.
New York: Dodd, Mead, 1936.

Cold-blooded Murder
New York: Avon, 1947.

Inspector Joseph French

Pamela Grey and Jack Penrose are waiting until they have enough money before they marry. Then two assistants in a chemical company approach them with a proposition to promote and sell a new formula that will revolutionize the petrol industry. Convinced of the legitimacy of the formula, Pamela and Jack agree to use their connections with well-to-do relatives to find a backer.

The Loss of the Jane Vosper
London: Collins, 1936.
New York: Dodd, Mead, 1936.

Inspector Joseph French

The Jane Vosper goes down in heavy seas after a series of unexplained explosions, taking with her more than her cargo. For one of the main insurance companies, the insurance payment could alter the future of the company. For the officers of the ship, the loss of the Vosper could be the end of their careers and perhaps worse. Every party in the inquiry is justifiably worried.

Found Floating
London: Hodder, 1937.
New York: Dodd, Mead, 1937.

Inspector Joseph French

William Carrington is prepared to finally hand over the reins of the family business to his nephew from Australia, a stranger to England and the family. But no one takes to the newcomer, and he doesn't seem to care for his new relatives. When food poisoning strikes the entire family, a doctor advises them to take a sea voyage in order to recover fully.

The End of Andrew Harrison
London: Hodder, 1938.

Future Alibi
New York: Dodd, Mead, 1938.

Inspector Joseph French

It is said that Andrew Harrison will do anything to make money, but he certainly won't do much to get along with his family. His wife and children are close to despising him, as do his business associates. When he disappears, his family is suspicious and the stock market shaken. When he reappears, the market soars and suspicion spreads.

Antidote to Venom
London: Hodder, 1938.
New York: Dodd, Mead, 1939.

Inspector Joseph French

George Surridge would probably be a completely happy man if his wife, Clarissa, were less greedy and more charitable. As it is, she has him, the director of a large zoo, living up to if not beyond his means. His one outlet, gambling, has its own drawbacks. All at once, it seems, he begins to hope his rich aunt will die, he meets a young widow, and a retired professor is injured while working with one of the poisonous snakes in the zoo.

Fatal Venture
London: Hodder, 1939.

Tragedy in the Hollow
New York: Dodd, Mead, 1939.

Inspector Joseph French

A lawyer and a travel agent set up a cruise business, finding both ship and backers. Together they thwart competitors trying to cash in on their idea: a floating gambling casino touring the British Isles.

Golden Ashes
London: Hodder, 1940.
New York: Dodd, Mead, 1940.

Inspector Joseph French

When a distant cousin from America inherits a family estate with its many valuable collections, he looks forward to an active social life. When the local society ignores him, he becomes morose and moves to Europe. Soon after, his ancestral home is burned to the ground.

Fear Comes to Chalfont
London: Hodder, 1942.
New York: Dodd, Mead, 1942.

Inspector Joseph French

Richard and Julia Elton married for convenience: he to improve his social position, she to escape sudden poverty. The marriage soon turns sour, and Julia falls in love with another man. Then Richard is murdered.

The Affair at Little Wokeham
London: Hodder, 1943.

Double Tragedy
New York: Dodd, Mead, 1943.

Inspector Joseph French

Bernard and Christina Winnington are finding their agreement to live with
their rich uncle in exchange for a legacy a hard bargain. Their sister,
Bellissa, is finding her new husband, Guy Plant, also difficult to live with,
for different reasons. Guy has speculated and lost on the stock exchange,
and needs money badly. He is desperate--until he discovers a petty theft
in his office.

James Tarrant, Adventurer*
London: Hodder, 1941.

Circumstantial Evidence
New York: Dodd, Mead, 1941.

Inspector Joseph French

The Losing Game
London: Hodder, 1941.

A Losing Game
New York: Dodd, Mead, 1941.

Inspector Joseph French

Albert Reeve has a modest business as a moneylender and a more lucrative
sideline as a blackmailer. He notices one day that after almost ten successful
years in the business, he is blackmailing people who happen to live close to
him. Two in particular have no money of their own.

Death of a Train
London: Hodder, 1946.
New York: Dodd, Mead, 1947.

Inspector Joseph French

Britain has a limited supply of radio valves and other war supplies and
must therefore move them safely to where they are needed most. The highest
levels of government develop a plan for a special train in extreme secrecy,
but the train is derailed in transit, leaving the government facing the possibility of a high-level spy.

Enemy Unseen
London: Hodder, 1945.
New York: Dodd, Mead, 1945.

Inspector Joseph French

The residents of St. Pols, a Cornish village on the coast, are proud of their
role in the Home Guard. The local commanding officer, however, is worried
about two thefts of wire and hand grenades from the supply shed. The thefts
are investigated and forgotten until an elderly man is killed on the beach
by an explosion.

Silence for the Murderer
London: Hodder, 1949.
New York: Dodd, Mead, 1948.

Superintendent Joseph French

Dulcie Heath has waited six years for Frank Roscoe to return and begin a
new life with her. When he finally arrives, he looks beaten and afraid.
The two begin a new life, but it is quite different from what Dulcie had in
mind.

French Strikes Oil
London: Hodder, 1952.

Dark Journey
New York: Dodd, Mead, 1951.

Superintendent Joseph French

A man discovers evidence of oil on his father's estate and tries to persuade his father and siblings to cash in on this find. Before he can convince anyone, however, the brother who wants to preserve the ancestral land from oil rigs is killed in a train accident.

Anything to Declare*
London: Hodder, 1957.

Superintendent Joseph French

The Cask
London: Collins, 1920.
New York: Seltzer, 1924.

In 1912 a large cask arrives at a London port, but before it can be unloaded, several gold sovereigns fall out of it. Inside are more sovereigns and a human hand. When the police arrive to investigate, the cask is gone. This book established Crofts's style and ushered in the Golden Age of the detective story.

The Ponson Case
London: Collins, 1921.
New York: Boni, 1927.

Sir William Ponson, a self-made man, is also amiable and forgiving. He has retired with his wife, his childhood sweetheart, to a country manor and made peace with his scholarly son. He is also fond of his indolent and irresponsible nephew. Nevertheless, late one night he drowns in a nearby river, after apparently setting out to visit a doctor-friend on the other shore.

The Pit-Prop Syndicate
London: Collins, 1922.
New York: Seltzer, 1925.

While traveling in the Rhone Valley in France, Seymour Merriman runs low
on gas and follows a lorry in order to get assistance. When he finally catches up with the lorry, he sees that it is disguised. Curious, Merriman and a
friend begin to investigate the lorry, its driver, and his associates.

The Groote Park Murder
London: Collins, 1923.
New York: Seltzer, 1925.

A man is found dead on the railroad tracks, the obvious victim of a moving
train. Identified as Albert Smith, an employee of a local store, the man
had no close friends and no admirers. But he did have unsuspected wealth.
He also seems to have had a number of witnesses to his activities in the
last night of his life, and these come forward tardily but inevitably.

Gordon Daviot

The Man in the Queue
London: Methuen, 1929.
New York: Dutton, 1929.

Inspector Alan Grant

Hundreds of Londoners are willing to stand in line for the chance to see
the last performance of a popular play, but when the doors open and the
line moves forward, one man slumps to his knees and falls over. For him
the line had another purpose. The police have on their hands the body of
a prosperous young man with no identification who was killed in front of
dozens of witnesses--none of whom saw a thing. (See Josephine Tey for two
other editions of this book.)

Detection Club*

"The Scoop" and "Behind the Screen"
London: Gollancz, 1983.
New York: Harper, 1983.

Behind the Screen. Paul Dudden insinuates himself into the Ellis household
as a paying guest and then begins a campaign to dominate the family. His
efforts do not go unnoticed, and he is finally found stabbed to death on
the living room floor. (First serialized in the Listener in 1930.)

The Scoop. In newspaper competition, the scoop is everything, and the Morning Star has a big one when a reporter discovers the weapon used in the
murder of a woman in a lonely cottage. He also recollects having seen it
recently in a shop. He hurriedly writes his story on the ride back to his
office, but he never arrives. He is found stabbed to death in the train station, the murder weapon gone. (First serialized in the Listener in 1931.)

The Floating Admiral
London: Hodder, 1931.
New York: Doubleday, 1932.

Admiral Penistone spent his career sailing in Asia, finally retiring to a home
on the gentle River Whyn. Unfortunately, his retirement does not last long,
for his body is found in the vicar's rowboat floating along the river. Dressed
in evening clothes, the admiral lies on the vicar's hat; he has been stabbed.

Ask a Policeman
London: Macmillan, 1933.
New York: Morrow, 1933.

The self-made millionaire-journalist Lord Comstock, loved by none and feared
by many, is found dead in his library after a morning of several unexpected
visitors, including an angry archbishop, an assistant commissioner of police,
and the chief government whip.

Double Death*
London: Gollancz, 1939.

D.M. Devine

My Brother's Killer
London: Collins, 1961.
New York: Dodd, Mead, 1962.

Late one foggy night, Oliver Barnett calls his brother at home, asking him
to come back to the office. When Simon arrives, he finds Oliver dead. So
begins Simon's determination to find out why his brother was killed and to
defend him in the face of the many smaller unpleasant revelations that ensue
from his death.

Doctors Also Die
London: Collins, 1962.
New York: Dodd, Mead, 1963.

After the death of his partner, Dr. Turner settles again into the familiar
routine of a successful practice. But others in the town are not willing to
let the late Dr. Henderson rest. For Provost Hackett this is an opportunity
to extend his personal power over another doctor; for others it is an opportunity to escape what had seemed like a never-ending misery.

The Royston Affair
London: Collins, 1964.
New York: Dodd, Mead, 1965.

After several years of hostile silence, attorney Mark Lovell receives a letter
from his father asking him to come home. On the night of his arrival, everyone he meets is uncomfortable at the sight of him, recalling his departure
over the Royston case and the charge of perjury he made against his half
brother. Surprised that his father is not at home to greet him, Mark visits
his old haunts but by the time he finally meets his father, the old man is
dead.

His Own Appointed Day
London: Collins, 1965.
New York: Walker, 1966.

A bright student in the local high school suddenly turns into a delinquent
and then disappears. Convinced he is better off elsewhere, his sister only
reluctantly tells the police of his disappearance. Then the stories about
him grow, and she decides to find out if they are true and what really happened to him.

Devil at Your Elbow
London: Collins, 1966.
New York: Walker, 1967.

Universities are notorious for harboring controversies with a life of their
own, and Hardgate University is no exception. The ambitions of certain
professors and administrators to remove Professor Haxton are fed by an anonymous tip that he mishandled university funds. A bitter, reclusive man,
Haxton makes a poor showing at his defense. When he is later found dead,
the general assumption is that he committed suicide, but this seems oddly
out of character for Haxton.

The Fifth Cord
London: Collins, 1967.
New York: Walker, 1967.

A schoolteacher is attacked late one evening, but her assailant is driven
off. The police find the business card of a local funeral director with the
number 1 written on it and assume it fell from the murderer's pocket. Then
another woman is murdered, a business card is found pinned to her night-
dress, and the card has the number 2 written on it.

Death Is My Bridegroom
London: Collins, 1969.
New York: Walker, 1969.

Branchfield University authorities have a lot on their minds: protesting students, dissenting professors, and unhappy benefactors. The last is of particular concern because the daughter of the university's largest benefactor

is barely managing to stay in school. Then she disappears, and events take on a purpose unexpected by the academics.

Dominic Devine

This Is Your Death
London: Collins, 1982.
New York: St. Martin, 1982.

Geoffrey Wallis is a successful novelist who has patiently manipulated and controlled everyone in his life. Then in 1962 his brother comes to visit. The brother seems to have a hold over him, and some are certain that Geoffrey will murder Lionel. There is indeed murder, but Lionel is not the victim.

The Sleeping Tiger
London: Collins, 1968.
New York: Walker, 1968.

John Prescott accepts the world as it comes. When his friend Peter is found dead, he accepts the verdict of suicide and the reasons given. When he later marries Peter's fiancée, he accepts her promises of fidelity. Not until he is charged with two murders does he begin to search for a murderer and for answers to questions he never asked before.

Illegal Tender
London: Collins, 1970.
New York: Walker, 1970.

No one has ever given much credit to Ruth Elder, certainly not her parents or friends. Yet she is important enough to murder after carelessly bragging that she "found" an odd piece of paper in one of the offices.

Dead Trouble
London: Collins, 1971.
New York: Doubleday, 1971.

Alma Vallance goes to Paris after she is jilted by her fiancé and there falls
in love with a Briton, who openly confesses to being something of a rogue.
When he visits her in England and continues to pursue her, her family is
suspicious of him but unable to deter Alma's interest in the man.

Three Green Bottles
London: Collins, 1972.
New York: Doubleday, 1972.

A teenaged girl is strangled on the golf course, and the police have no clues
to her murderer. Then a doctor with a history of mental illness is found
dead at the base of a cliff near the murder scene. The police think this is
the end of the case of the teenaged girl.

Sunk without Trace
London: Collins, 1978.
New York: St. Martin, 1979.

On her mother's death, a young woman learns that she is illegitimate and
sets out to find her father. Returning to the town of her birth, she gets a
job in city hall, and soon learns enough to unsettle smug civil servants and
crusty politicians.

Colin Dexter

Last Bus to Woodstock
London: Macmillan, 1975.
New York: St. Martin, 1975.

Inspector Morse

Two young women are hitchhiking early in the evening; a few hours later one is found dead in the courtyard of a pub. What the police first learn about her is of little help: she is one of many young secretaries employed in the area, living a modest and sometimes carefree life with her peers.

Last Seen Wearing
London: Macmillan, 1976.
New York: St. Martin, 1976.

Inspector Morse

Two years after an attractive schoolgirl disappears, she sends a letter to her parents. The police again set out to find her, but the investigating officer is killed. The police investigation leads to the girl's respectable school and to another death.

The Silent World of Nicholas Quinn
London: Macmillan, 1977.
New York: St. Martin, 1977.

Inspector Morse

Members of the Foreign Examinations Syndicate must have impeccable credentials, both personal and professional, in order to maintain their reputation with academic institutions. When one of the members is murdered, therefore, it seems improbable at first that his death can have anything to do with the syndicate.

Service of All the Dead
London: Macmillan, 1979.
New York: St. Martin, 1980.

Inspector Morse

The parish of St. Frideswide's seems overburdened with sin in this tale of a churchwarden who pilfers, a vicar who behaves suspiciously with youngsters, and a church organist who is involved with a married woman. The sins quickly escalate to blackmail and murder.

The Dead of Jericho
London: Macmillan, 1981.
New York: St. Martin, 1981.

Inspector Morse

A successful teacher and businesswoman is found hanged after the police receive an anonymous call. The evidence points to suicide, but there is soon another death in the same neighborhood and this one is definitely not suicide.

The Riddle of the Third Mile
London: Macmillan, 1983.
New York: St. Martin, 1983.

Inspector Morse

The predictable life of Dr. Browne-Smith comes to an unpredicted end, and no one cares that his end was sudden, unexpected, and violent.
Browne-Smith's nearly forty years in academe supply numerous prospective murderers, but the motive goes back even further than that.

Peter Dickinson

Skin Deep
London: Hodder, 1968.

The Glass-sided Ants' Nest
New York: Harper, 1968.

Superintendent James Pibble

After World War II only a few members of the Ku tribe survive, and a Briton decides to move them all back to London. The daughter of a missionary joins the tribe, now living in a London house. She is accepted into the tribe as a man, becomes an anthropologist, and lives quietly among her new community. For almost twenty years all goes well, until the chief of the tribe is murdered according to the rituals of the Ku.

A Pride of Heroes
London: Hodder, 1969.

The Old English Peep Show
New York: Harper, 1969.

Superintendent James Pibble

The suicide of a servant for an eccentric aristocratic family hardly seems to warrant a superintendent from Scotland Yard, but that is what the family asks for and gets. Unfortunately for the family, it isn't long before Superintendent Pibble is seeing through one deception after another, behind the larger charade of a stately home open to tourists.

The Seals
London: Hodder, 1970.

The Sinful Stones
New York: Harper, 1970.

Superintendent James Pibble

Sir Francis has won two Nobel Prizes and lived into his nineties. Now living in a religious community on an island, he is convinced someone is trying to steal his autobiography. Furthermore, he insists that only Pibble can help him, even though Sir Francis seems to have tried hard not to find Pibble.

Sleep and His Brother
London: Hodder, 1971.
New York: Harper, 1971.

James Pibble

Most charitable institutions have a difficult time raising funds for their day-to-day existence, but the McNair Foundation has had a windfall. In fact, the foundation for sick children has more money than it can spend, and some members of the foundation are uncomfortable about this.

The Lizard in the Cup
London: Hodder, 1972.
New York: Harper, 1972.

James Pibble

T. Thanatos, a Greek millionaire, wins the concession to develop the tourist trade on an island in the West Indies, beating out other interests that include the Mafia. Now there is talk that these interests intend to take their revenge, and Mr. Thanatos poses the problem to his houseguests, leaving them to devise a plan for his safety.

One Foot in the Grave
London: Hodder, 1979.
New York: Pantheon, 1979.

James Pibble

Consigned to a slow decline in a nursing home, Pibble decides to commit suicide and thereby reclaim his dignity. But before he can carry out the last step in his plan, he discovers a body, dead, where he had hoped to die. As his favorite nurse frequently notes, Pibble is still very much the detective.

A Summer in the Twenties
London: Hodder, 1981.
New York: Pantheon, 1981.

In 1926 people are expecting a general strike in response to a coal mine owner's lockout of the miners. Tom Hankey, a student at Oxford, is drawn into the preparations for the strike by his father's desire to keep his part of the train system going, by the ambitions of a university friend to build a national network to fight the strike threat, and by two young women who are on opposite sides of the strike.

The Poison Oracle
London: Hodder, 1974.
New York: Pantheon, 1974.

In a still-medieval Arab kingdom, a modern sultan supports the psycholinguistic investigations of a British researcher, maintains a zoo, and welcomes into his palace a beautiful hijacker of a Japanese airliner. When the clash of old and new finally leads to murder, the only witness is a chimpanzee trained by the psycholinguist.

The Lively Dead
London: Hodder, 1975.
New York: Pantheon, 1975.

Committed to confronting oppression in the state and dry rot in the timbers, young Lydia Timms is trying to restore her boardinghouse and care for her husband and child when her mildly odd tenants become odder and even ominous. The nice old lady who recently died of a fall, for example, had a secret life that her daughter in prison knew nothing about.

King and Joker
London: Hodder, 1976.
New York: Pantheon, 1976.

With a slight recasting of history, the author presents us with an entirely different royal family. In the transparent yet secretive world of the contemporary royal, an unknown person is playing practical jokes on the royal family and its staff. At first the jokes seem harmless though unpleasant, but they soon turn nasty and reveal an insider's knowledge of the royal household.

Walking Dead
London: Hodder, 1977.
New York: Pantheon, 1978.

David Foxe works for a private research lab and is used to secrecy in his work, so he is not especially surprised at some of the behavior he encounters in his new posting in the Caribbean. He is intrigued, however, by the efforts of some of the natives to rig the test results of some of the rats he is training and testing.

The Seventh Raven
London: Gollancz, 1981.
New York: Dutton, 1981.

In one London neighborhood, the highlight of the year is a children's opera performed in the church, with a cast of 100 youngsters. This year the cast is 101 after the wife of the ambassador from a small third world country persuades the producers of the opera to add her son to the cast. When an attempt to kidnap the boy goes wrong, the women running the rehearsal and the children find themselves confronting a band of terrorists, who decide to hold everyone in the church hostage.

The Last Houseparty
London: Bodley, 1982.
New York: Pantheon, 1982.

The stately home of the Snailwoods is now overrun by day-trippers, but memories of its period of glory live on. The restoration of a magnificent clock on the estate helps the last member of the family to finally unravel a double crime from the family's last, great days in the 1930s.

Hindsight
London: Bodley, 1983.
New York: Pantheon, 1983.

A novelist decides to use his own childhood as background for a mystery novel, but as he works on his story and discusses it with another writer, he peels away layers of time and naïveté that had long concealed a real murder and a real murderer.

Death of a Unicorn
London: Bodley, 1984.
New York: Pantheon, 1984.

In 1952 a young woman is offered a job as a society writer by a man she meets at a party, and through this chance opportunity she finds a life for herself. The man becomes her lover and is later killed. She puts the past behind her and becomes a successful writer, until thirty years later a phone call from an old colleague brings back questions she had forgotten about and left unanswered.

Eilís Dillon

Death at Crane's Court
London: Faber, 1953.
New York: Walker, 1963.

Professor Daly and Inspector Mike Kenny

Crane's Court is both a tourist hotel and a charming retirement home, serving both short-term guests and long-term residents. Into this placid environment a new owner brings a distaste for his guests, an ineptness for the business, and a malicious pleasure in manipulating the staff.

Death in the Quadrangle
London: Faber, 1956.
New York: British Book Centre, 1962.

Professor Daly and Inspector Mike Kenny

The retired Professor Daly is delighted to be invited to deliver a series of lectures on the novel at King's University, but he is chagrined to learn soon after his arrival that he was invited for nonscholarly reasons. The president of the university has been receiving threatening letters and admits that he has so antagonized the faculty members that any one of them could be the culprit.

Sent to His Account
London: Faber, 1954.
New York: British Book Centre, 1961.

The quiet and austere life of a Dublin accountant is turned upside down when he inherits the country estate and baronetcy of a distant cousin. When he tours the property for the first time, he finds that he may also have inherited a role in a feud between the villagers and a Dublin businessman.

Margaret Erskine

And Being Dead
London: Bles, 1938.

The Limping Man
New York: Doubleday, 1939.

The Painted Mask
New York: Ace, 1972.

Inspector Septimus Finch

No one is unhappy about the death of Kenneth Dean, a portrait painter whose
body is washed up on the coast with fresh water in the lungs. Yet no one
seems relieved at his death. A lawyer thinks Dean may have been murdered
by mistake, and that he, the lawyer, was the intended victim. Others are
more concerned about the limping man who is heard at night going through
the village but is never seen.

The Whispering House
London: Hammond, 1947.

The Voice of the House
New York: Doubleday, 1947.

Inspector Septimus Finch

A rainstorm strands Finch on the moors near an old mansion, where he seeks
refuge. Invited in, he is announced as though expected. This interlude in
his holiday brings him two murders and a strange, old family whose members
are evidently waiting for something evil to happen.

I Knew MacBean
London: Hammond, 1948.
New York: Doubleday, 1948.

Caravan of Night
New York: Ace, 1972.

Inspector Septimus Finch

Inspector Finch overhears what seems to be a casual remark by the driver
of a hearse to a woman standing on the sidewalk nearby. Startled by the
implications of the remark, he eventually traces the hearse to an empty store,
locates the coffin, and finds it empty with air holes in the cover. The police
trace the coffin to a squatter in the home of a once well-to-do family, whose
owner now serves the community by taking in the down-and-out, criminal or
otherwise.

Give up the Ghost
London: Hammond, 1949.
New York: Doubleday, 1949.

Inspector Septimus Finch

The police in Camborough receive a drawing of a dead man on a cross, a
dead woman on the ground, and an old woman sitting on a bag of money.
A note asks why only the young should die. Then three old women are killed, a copy of the drawing pinned to the clothes of each victim. The police
are stymied. Members of the Pleyden family, which owns the factory and
much else in the area, decide to help the police by organizing a vigilante
group.

The Disappearing Bridegroom
London: Hammond, 1950.

The Silver Ladies
New York: Doubleday, 1951.

Inspector Septimus Finch

On the night of Helen Simpson's coming-of-age party, her chaperone, who seemed to come with the mansion purchased by Helen's father, passes the time by telling the girl's fortune, and before another day is gone, her more uncomfortable predictions seem to be coming true. A retired burglar comes to the house and soon dies, Helen disappears, and the hangers-on face a new future.

Death of Our Dear One
London: Hammond, 1952.

Look behind You Lady
New York: Doubleday, 1952.

Don't Look behind You
New York: Ace, 1972.

Inspector Septimus Finch

Freddie Dawes, a young policeman, inherits his uncle's mansion, which has been turned into a residential club. He also inherits a substantial sum of money on one condition, which the family solicitor alone knows and can judge. Freddie therefore determines to be a responsible, prudent heir until his friend, Septimus Finch, points out that the uncle also left Freddie a collection of people to be sorted out, the remaining residents of Fletton House, one of whom must have a secret.

Dead by Now
London: Hammond, 1953.
New York: Doubleday, 1954.

Inspector Septimus Finch

The long-neglected Luxuria Theatre in Grovely Wood is considered the perfect
site for family housing until a letter to the local paper points out that the
theater has a ghost, that of its owner, who committed suicide on the night
his actress-wife died in the theater. Her children and grandchildren still
own the theater, though it has been closed since her death. When a policeman sees the ghost, it is definitely time to investigate.

Fatal Relations
London: Hammond, 1955.

Old Mrs. Ommanney Is Dead
New York: Doubleday, 1955.

The Dead Don't Speak
New York: Detective Book Club, 1955.

Inspector Septimus Finch

Hammerford is a picturesque village to the average tourist, but it takes on
a disturbing quality to those who look closely--emptiness. Villagers have
closed their windows, bolted their doors, and avoided their gardens, all because a practical joker has played a number of pranks that seem harmless
but are not funny.

The Voice of Murder
London: Hodder, 1956.
New York: Doubleday, 1956.

Inspector Septimus Finch

Alice Glen-Carr retained her mental acuity right up until the night she died,
completely unexpectedly. Now her relatives converge on her home; they are

as educated and as sophisticated as Alice's money could make them, but they cannot explain the mystery of her death.

Sleep No More
London: Hodder, 1958.
New York: Ace, 1969.

Inspector Septimus Finch

Just about everyone has reason to celebrate Loretta Stourbridge's decision to remarry. Her late husband's various relations will then receive their legacies, now that the estate is no longer tied to his widow. But someone seems to have forgotten this on the night of the house party for relatives to meet Loretta's fiancé; the party ends in murder.

The House of the Enchantress
London: Hodder, 1959.

A Graveyard Plot
New York: Doubleday, 1959.

Inspector Septimus Finch

On his way to visit friends of his aunt, Finch is caught in a snowstorm and made a captive audience to a murder, carried out to take advantage of the storm. Leaving this crime in the hands of the local police, Finch visits his aunt's friend, who is suggesting in her novels that her husband may murder her in order to marry another.

The Woman at Belguardo
London: Hodder, 1961.
New York: Doubleday, 1961.

Inspector Septimus Finch

Lisa Harcourt seems to always get whatever she covets; at least her success with men is obvious. On the night before her divorce is final, at least three men are in love with her and several more have been pushed aside. One bears a malice more intense than that for a love lost, and Lisa dies a particularly ugly death before her divorce is final.

The House in Belmont Square
London: Hodder, 1963.

No. 9 Belmont Square
New York: Doubleday, 1963.

Inspector Septimus Finch

A retired opera singer learns that a long-lost love may be alive and living in England in a seaside resort. Less interested in her than in a legendary jewel she owned, he sets out to find her. He settles in a boardinghouse populated by eccentric elderly men and women, one of whom he hopes is his old lover.

Take a Dark Journey
London: Hodder, 1965.

The Family at Tammerton
New York: Doubleday, 1966.

Inspector Septimus Finch

A young nurse accepts a job in the country but soon learns that someone in the large household does not want her there. Not recognizing anyone in the family or on the household staff, she probes discreetly until she uncovers secrets about her own past as well as about her employer's family.

Case with Three Husbands
London: Hodder, 1967.
New York: Doubleday, 1967.

Inspector Septimus Finch

Three generations of Bonners share the family estate, and something has
upset their equable if eccentric way of life. First, an aunt claims that one
of her dead husbands may not be dead; another member unexpectedly has a
heart attack; and a third may be illegitimate. Before any of this can be
sorted out, one of the family is murdered.

The Ewe Lamb
London: Hodder, 1968.
New York: Doubleday, 1968.

Inspector Septimus Finch

Victoria Digby discovers one day a secret of the family that owns Old House,
a home and museum where she works as a guide. On her way to make the
secret known, she is killed by a train. Her only living relative is a cousin,
who intends to find out why Victoria died and how.

The Case of Mary Fielding
London: Hodder, 1969.
New York: Doubleday, 1970.

Inspector Septimus Finch

Friends and relatives gather four years after the death of Mary Fielding,
still aware of their loss. On a whim they attend a demonstration by a psychic, giving him an article of clothing from the scene of the murder. The
psychic seems to know from this article more than the police could learn
four years ago.

The Brood of Folly
London: Hodder, 1971.
New York: Doubleday, 1971.

Inspector Septimus Finch

Passionately tied to her childhood home and her spendthrift brother, Paula Gilderoy finds a rich businessman glad to marry her and buy the estate for her. Paula then happily ignores her husband, but another concern crops up: a one-hundred-year-old curse on the family seems to be coming true.

Besides the Wench Is Dead
London: Hodder, 1973.
New York: Doubleday, 1973.

Inspector Septimus Finch

Delia Sumner lives solely for the moment, attracting men easily and disregarding her effect on other people's lives. After breaking up one marriage and airily describing the process in court, she is not at all disturbed by the ex-wife's threats against her. Instead, she sets off for a weekend on the coast, but never arrives.

Harriet Farewell
London: Hodder, 1975.
New York: Doubleday, 1975.

Inspector Septimus Finch

The wealthy Buckler family is recovering from one tragedy when another strikes. A daughter-in-law recently released from a mental hospital is skulking around the family estate with a gun when her mother-in-law is murdered. When the police start looking for a motive, however, several others in the family have good reason to want both women dead.

The House in Hook Street
London: Hale, 1978.
New York: Doubleday, 1977.

Inspector Septimus Finch

Louise Winter was never unloved, but when she receives a letter from her
dead mother's sister, she is eager to meet the woman and learn about the
mother she never knew. Leaving a brief message for her father and stepmother, Louise begins a visit into a world of eccentric relatives, long-dead
secrets, and bizarre dangers.

J. Jefferson Farjeon*

The 5.18 Mystery
London: Collins, 1929.
New York: Dial, 1929.

Freddy Reeve is off for his holiday, and in the twelve hours after his train
leaves London he has more excitement than most people have in a lifetime.
Into a first-class compartment climb a clergyman, an expansive gentleman, a
middle-aged woman, a fastidious man, a belligerent cockney, and the most
beautiful girl Reeve has ever seen. This is a train ride to Norfolk everyone
will remember.

Dead Man's Heath
London: Collins, 1933.

The Mystery of Dead Man's Heath
New York: Dodd, Mead, 1934.

Lionel North crashes his motorcycle on the heath late one night, stumbles
to a cottage, asks for help, and falls in love with the young woman who
assists him. He also notes her anxiety, and the reason for it: the body of
Sir Rufus Lunt, well-known financier. Then she escapes, leaving Lionel with
the body.

The Fancy Dress Ball
London: Collins, 1934.

Death in Fancy Dress
New York: Bobbs, 1939.

The annual event of the Chelsea Arts Ball attracts all sorts of people, and this year is no exception. In addition to the regulars, who come for a good time, there are those who come for a different purpose. A young clerk hoping to find the light of his life gets mixed up with a woman and her seedy partner, who have come to do a job on a munitions manufacturer.

Mystery in White
London: Collins, 1937.
New York: Bobbs, 1938.

The train to Manchester is stranded outside a village on Christmas Eve in a snowstorm. One by one the six passengers in a third-class compartment walk to the village, and each one ends up taking refuge in Valley House. The home is awaiting guests for tea, but there is no one at home.

E. X. Ferrars

Give a Corpse a Bad Name*
London: Hodder, 1940.

Toby Dyke

Remove the Bodies
London: Hodder, 1940.

Rehearsals for Murder
New York: Doubleday, 1941.

Toby Dyke

For some people, young Lou Capell is the ideal companion: generous, adoring, and compliant. So when she is found poisoned in a house in the country, no one considers her a reasonable murder victim. Yet she had been crying uncontrollably the day before, she had been desperate for money, and she left a letter confessing to a betrayal.

Death in Botanist's Bay*
London: Hodder, 1941.

Murder of a Suicide
New York: Doubleday, 1941.

Toby Dyke

Don't Monkey with Murder
London: Hodder, 1942.

The Shape of a Stain
New York: Doubleday, 1942.

Toby Dyke

A foreign scientist asks Toby to help him recover his beloved and kidnapped Irma, who turns out to be, not a dear relative, but a chimpanzee. Then Irma is found murdered, and not even her owner can think of a good reason for her death.

Your Neck in a Noose
London: Hodder, 1942.

Neck in a Noose
New York: Doubleday, 1943.

Toby Dyke

Toby arrives at a friend's country house to find it locked and dark. When he finally gets in, he meets a scene of chaos--overturned furniture, broken glass, a revolver. bullets in the wall, and a bloodstain on the floor. In the chair sits his host, dead from natural causes. As Toby tells the police inspector, this is a murder without a corpse, and a corpse without murder.

A Stranger and Afraid
London: Collins, 1971.
New York: Walker, 1971.

Superintendent Ditteridge

Holly Dunthorne arrives home from Europe unexpectedly and is greeted with reserve by her aunt and a family she has always been close to. She reasons they are distracted by a son's problems. When she returns to her aunt's home later, her aunt is dead.

Foot in the Grave
London: Collins, 1973.
New York: Doubleday, 1972.

Superintendent Ditteridge

Christine Findon is trying to adjust to the changes in her life: servants, two children living with her and her husband temporarily, and security. On the weekend of a friend's visit, she has more problems: a strange man in the house, the theft of all of her guest's left shoes, and a body in the cellar.

Last Will and Testament
London: Collins, 1978.
New York: Doubleday, 1978.

Virginia Freer

When Evelyn Arliss dies of natural causes, her relatives murmur their shock and regret and quickly descend on the family home for the division of her estate. They are unpleasantly surprised to learn that Mrs. Arliss had developed a love of racehorses, and the only remaining item of value in the home is a collection of miniatures.

In at the Kill
London: Collins, 1978.
New York: Doubleday, 1979.

Virginia Freer

Charlotte Cambrey is looking forward to a quiet vacation in the country, but on the night of her arrival in the village the man from whom she rented her cottage is found dead.

Frog in the Throat
London: Collins, 1980.
New York: Doubleday, 1980.

Virginia Freer

The village of Stillbeam has an abundance of working artists, and the competition is friendly until two writers become engaged. This surprises several of their friends, who had been waiting for a different woman to become engaged.

Thinner than Water
London: Collins, 1981.
New York: Doubleday, 1982.

Virginia Freer

Gavin Brownlow's wedding party should be happier than it is, but txe guests must struggle to make the event festive. Even at the reception, the guests seem to fall prey to mundane disagreements. Finally, the announcement of another marriage fails to cheer anyone at the reception.

Death of a Minor Character
London: Collins, 1983.
New York: Doubleday, 1983.

Virginia Freer

A going-away party for a woman returning to Australia brings together an odd mix of people, who manage to enjoy themselves for their hostess's benefit. The most interesting person might be the silversmith, whose work has been chosen as a gift for the hostess, but the most consequential guests are the least notable. Soon after the party, an antiques dealer is found dead in his shop and a retired social worker is found dead in her apartment.

I Met Murder
London: Collins, 1985.
New York: Doubleday, 1986.

Virginia Freer

Mrs. Brightwell invites her orphaned teenaged niece to live with her, but Mr. Brightwell doesn't take to the girl and the other villagers don't seem to know what to make of her. Then Felix Freer, masquerading as a secretary to Mr. Brightwell, recognizes two men in a pub who are of questionable background. When the niece disappears, no one knows if she has run off or been kidnapped.

Something Wicked
London: Collins, 1983.
New York: Doubleday, 1984.

Professor Andrew Basnett

Godlingham is a village with everything a village should have, including its own murderess. Though never convicted of the murder of her husband, Mrs. Hewison is much discussed and her character the most popular topic in town. Then on a night like the evening when her husband died, her brother-in-law is found murdered.

The Root of All Evil
London: Collins, 1984.
New York: Doubleday, 1984.

Professor Andrew Basnett

Felicity Silvester is eighty-five and still going strong, enjoying her money and the power it gives her over people. She suddenly gets a view of herself as others might see her when a woman is found dead in the village. The woman is thought to be the victim of a hit-and-run driver until the police find a letter in her purse. In the letter, she confesses to murdering Felicity and then taking her own life.

The Crime and the Crystal
London: Collins, 1985.
New York: Doubleday, 1985.

Professor Andrew Basnett

Professor Basnett is spending the Christmas holiday in Australia with a former student. Tony Gardiner has recently married a woman who was (and still is by some) suspected of murdering her first husband. Tony and Jan seem happy and unaffected by the gossip about Jan until Jan's sister is found dead after a holiday dinner, murdered in the same way as Jan's first husband.

I, Said the Fly
London: Hodder, 1945.
New York: Doubleday, 1945.

The residents of No. 10, Little Carberry Street, have learned to tolerate each other, despite their differences. Then workmen find a gun under the floorboards of a room, and the police link the gun to an unidentified corpse, a young woman who moved out of her room a week or so earlier. Now the residents look at each other for the murderer.

Murder among Friends
London: Collins, 1946.

Cheat the Hangman
New York: Doubleday, 1946.

Cecily Lightwood hosts a party, and nothing seems to go right. The guests are irritated by one another, and one is very late. An air-raid warden complains about a light showing through, and an American soldier blunders into the apartment above and finds Cecily's late guest dead. Then the police arrive to investigate and arrest one of Cecily's guests for murder.

With Murder in Mind*
London: Collins, 1948.

The March Hare Murders
London: Collins, 1949.
New York: Doubleday, 1949.

David Obeney is learning to live with the pain of having accidentally killed a man who jumped in front of his truck. During his convalescence, David decides to confront the one man he thinks deserves to die: Mark Verinder, who seems almost pleased to so upset people that they would like to kill him.

Milk of Human Kindness*
London: Collins, 1950.

Hunt the Tortoise
London: Collins, 1950.
New York: Doubleday, 1950.

After nine years and a world war, Celia Kent returns to a small hotel on
the French Riviera for a holiday, bracing herself for the many changes time
has brought. The hotel owners have passed on the hotel to their son, who
has almost bankrupted the business; foreign divers are looking desperately
for a treasure ship sunk long ago; a number of guests live in a private terror;
and a businessman has a lucky tortoise.

The Clock That Wouldn't Stop
London: Collins, 1952.
New York: Doubleday, 1952.

Alex Summerhill is used to receiving crank letters sent to her pseudonym as
an advice columnist, but on the morning she leaves for a country wedding
she receives a nasty and personal letter accusing her of blackmail. Arriving
for the wedding, she meets the other guests and the groom, and her suspicions about the anonymous letter grow.

Alibi for a Witch
London: Collins, 1952.
New York: Doubleday, 1952.

Ruth Seabright, governess to a teenaged boy, finds her employer dead in
the house and a neighbor finds her standing over the body. Before they
can decide what to do, two policemen come to the house to report that
Ruth's employer has been killed in a car accident.

Murder in Time
London: Collins, 1953.

Mark Auty, MP, invites a number of old friends to fly to Nice to meet his
fianée, inviting them to foregather at his Surrey home. A free trip sounds
wonderful, but each guest is suspicious: the mill owner who gave Mark his
first job and the owner's adopted son; a respectable middle-aged woman from
his hometown; a publican and his wife from Auty's army days; a man who
met Auty in a prisoner-of-war camp; and a nightclub owner.

The Lying Voices*
London: Collins, 1954.

Enough to Kill a Horse
London: Collins, 1955.
New York: Doubleday, 1955.

Fanny Lynam holds an engagement party for her half brother and his fiancée, and admits to wondering what the woman sees in her quiet if not outright deep brother. This worry is soon replaced by another: murder.

Always Say Die
London: Collins, 1956.

We Haven't Seen Her Lately
New York: Doubleday, 1956.

Aunt Violet inherits a house and legacy from her late employer, suddenly marries, settles her new husband in her new home, and continues to travel around the country, or so her postcards to her niece indicate. By the time Helen Gamlen, her niece, becomes suspicious, her aunt hasn't been seen in the village for a year and her home is falling apart, completely neglected by her husband and his sister, who is trying to contact the dead employer who left Violet all the money.

Murder Moves In
London: Collins, 1956.

Kill or Cure
New York: Doubleday, 1956.

Robina Mellanby, a remarried widow with two children, likes her new home, but admits to finding Burnham Priors a bit odd. The neighbors never seem to be at ease with each other. The problem escalates when Martha Birch asks Robina for protection from her husband, who, she says, has just tried to kill her.

Furnished for Murder*
London: Collins, 1957.

Unreasonable Doubt
London: Collins, 1958.

Count the Cost
New York: Doubleday, 1957.

Professor Alistair Dirke and his wife are looking forward to a summer vacation in Monte Carlo until a friend asks them to visit a coin collector who has agreed to sell his collection to the local museum, where he once worked, for a nominal sum. Dirke agrees, but when he visits the collector, the man is dead and the coins gone. This seems to be an end to the matter for Dirke until one of the coins turns up in Dirke's village in England.

A Tale of Two Murders
London: Collins, 1959.

Depart This Life
New York: Doubleday, 1958.

Stephen Gazeley's friends turn against him over time. This may explain why his daughter, Katherine, is in a hurry to marry her boyfriend before her father can do any harm to the relationship. Then Stephen is murdered, and the few who still cared for him await the surprising results of the police investigation.

Fear the Light
London: Collins, 1960.
New York: Doubleday, 1960.

During a quiet visit with his aunt, Charles Robertson returns from mailing a letter to find his aunt dead from a fall at the bottom of the stairs. It seems impossible that a woman who led such a quiet life could have been murdered. The only recent excitement in her life had been a request from an American scholar to meet her and view the papers of her ancestor, a famous Victorian scientist.

Sleeping Dogs
London: Collins, 1960.
New York: Doubleday, 1960.

Teresa Swale may have been acquitted of murder, but people around her treat
her as though she were guilty. When she disappears before she can be paid
for telling her story to a ghostwriter, the writer's sister-in-law sets out to
find her and in very little time discovers a few facts never revealed in court.

The Wandering Widows
London: Collins, 1962.
New York: Doubleday, 1962.

Four older women are taking their regular holiday together with only outward
geniality. The women continue their comfortable roles as foolish and harmless widows until one of them is found dead.

The Busy Body
London: Collins, 1962.

Seeing Double
New York: Doubleday, 1962.

Anne and Peter marry only three weeks after meeting, well aware that they
have a lot to learn about each other. Journeying to meet his mother, they
stop at a pub for lunch. When Anne enters the bar, she sees Peter drunk
and surly. Moments later she realizes it isn't Peter and remembers that he
was adopted. She tells Peter what she has seen, and he now admits to a new
curiosity about his background.

The Doubly Dead
London: Collins, 1963.
New York: Doubleday, 1963.

Margot Dalziel usually makes known her return to the cottage in the village
by taking in the milk and tidying up the garden. This time, however, her
relatives arrive and notice the signs of her return, but cannot find Margot
herself. Instead, they find bloodstains in the house.

A Legal Fiction
London: Collins, 1964.

The Decayed Gentlewoman
New York: Doubleday, 1963.

A phone call from a friend long forgotten leads Dr. Lockie to an auction
room where a painting stolen from his car a few years ago has recently re-
appeared. The painting is sold and he searches for the new owner, who refuses to return the stolen painting to its rightful owner, an acquaintance of
Dr. Lockie.

Ninth Life
London: Collins, 1965.

Caroline Dyer decides to visit her sister, Fenella, and her brother-in-law,
Harry Lyddon, a former journalist and now cook of the couple's guest house.
Harry is belligerent and sometimes cruel in speech; Fenella is scared, though
still self-centered and oblivious of the feelings of others. What Caroline is
most uncomfortable with is Harry's reckless courage and his suspicions about
the guests in the guest house.

No Peace for the Wicked
London: Collins, 1965.
New York: Harper, 1966.

Antonia Winfield notices a man in a brown suit following her as she goes
about doing errands. Her niece convinces her that she is imagining things.
Then the two women are off to Greece for a holiday, and so is the man in
the brown suit.

Zero at the Bone
London: Collins, 1967.
New York: Walker, 1968.

A python escapes from a farm outside a village. This is, of course, the main
topic of village gossip until the villagers searching for the snake find a woman's body instead.

The Swaying Pillars
London: Collins, 1968.
New York: Walker, 1969.

Helena Sebright accepts a job as a companion to Jean Forrest, a young girl
going to Africa to visit her grandparents, but the trip is not what Helena
expects. Jean prefers animals to people, and her relatives assume that Helena
has helped Jean's father kidnap her from her mother. Then Jean runs away
to a game preserve, and the country erupts in the sporadic violence of a
coup.

Skeleton Staff
London: Collins, 1969.
New York: Walker, 1969.

Roberta Ellison is used to commanding people around her, and as a
semi-invalid feels entitled to do so. When her younger sister decides to
leave her with a live-in companion, Roberta arranges to have the companion
look dishonest. But Roberta's schemes get out of hand, leading to theft and
murder.

The Seven Sleepers
London: Collins, 1970.
New York: Walker, 1970.

Luke Latimer's grandmother was murdered many years ago by a man whose
Christian name was Duncan. She was third in a series of four wives he murdered during approximately fifteen years. Then a woman who could well be
the fifth wife writes to Luke, asking him to visit her.

Breath of Suspicion
London: Collins, 1972.
New York: Doubleday, 1972.

Hazel Clyro is young, beautiful, and unsociable. Some of her friends think
she is paranoid, looking for a stranger following her; others think she has
never recovered from the loss of her husband, a government scientist who
may have died or defected. Hazel has her own ideas about this.

The Small World of Murder
London: Collins, 1973.
New York: Doubleday, 1973.

Nicola Foley is an unlucky woman. First her baby is snatched from its carriage, then her marriage starts to fall apart, and when she agrees to travel to recover from the loss of her child, she has one accident after another. Even her traveling companion can't seem to protect her.

Hanged Man's House
London: Collins, 1974.
New York: Doubleday, 1974.

Keyfield is the home of several research scientists, but life there is neither orderly nor rational. First, a wife who deserted her husband long ago keeps writing to him; second, the director of the research facility commits suicide just before a dinner party; and third, neighbors find a corpse in a cupboard.

Alive and Dead
London: Collins, 1974.
New York: Doubleday, 1975.

Amanda Hassall arrives at the National Guild for the Welfare of Unmarried Mothers, pregnant and alone. Unfortunately, she is also married. Since her husband left her some time ago, Martha Crayle in the guild office decides the guild can help her and takes the woman home with her. The next day the guild asks Martha to take in another applicant. When Amanda's parents and her boyfriend arrive, Martha has a full house. Then the police find a man dead in a hotel room, and Amanda insists it is her husband.

Drowned Rat
London: Collins, 1975.
New York: Doubleday, 1975.

During a summer party, there is a sharp cry, a slip, and Douglas Cable falls into his swimming pool. He recovers quickly from the accident, but later someone else falls into the pool and drowns.

The Cup and the Lip
London: Collins, 1975.
New York: Doubleday, 1976.

A prospective murder victim has an unusual response to his looming fate.
Daniel Braile is a successful novelist living in a large house with a number
of younger, adoring beginning writers, and someone is trying to poison him.
Braile refuses to call the police to trace the poisoner because the suspect
is a member of his household and he loves everyone there.

Blood Flies Upwards
London: Collins, 1976.
New York: Doubleday, 1977.

When Alison Goodrich's younger sister disappears from her job as a cook in
a country home, she decides to find her by taking her job. Settling into
her job, Alison meets a handyman with a history of mental illness and two
old ladies who visit their neighbors after midnight.

The Pretty Pink Shroud
London: Collins, 1977.
New York: Doubleday, 1977.

The Economy Centre is a small, volunteer-supported thrift shop that counts
on the extravagance of several women. When Lady Guest's donation arrives,
the volunteers expect and find several expensive outfits. They also find an
Edwardian ball dress with a bullet hole in it, the same dress that Lady Guest
wore the night before.

Murders Anonymous
London: Collins, 1977.
New York: Doubleday, 1978.

Professor Tierney has long been used to his wife's dark moods, but lately
they seem to have worsened. At first he suspects mental instability, and
then he wonders if there is another man. But just when he is ready to talk
openly with her, he finds her dead.

Witness before the Fact
London: Collins, 1979.
New York: Doubleday, 1980.

Peter Corey is successful with his children's books partly because of the work of his illustrator-collaborator, Clare. When Clare asks him, therefore, to see if her long-estranged husband is all right, Peter agrees. When Peter arrives in the small town on the island of Madeira, Clare's husband is dead, an apparent suicide.

Experiment with Death
London: Collins, 1981.
New York: Doubleday, 1981.

Guy Lampard presides over a research institute and its scientists with a well-developed skill of alienating people for the pleasure of it. His latest escapade is the appointment of a middle-aged scientist who has not been able to hold a position for longer than two years.

Skeleton in Search of a Cupboard
London: Collins, 1982.

Skeleton in Search of a Closet
New York: Doubleday, 1982.

Henrietta Cosgrove is eighty years old. Her five stepchildren and their families host a surprise party, at which she announces her decision to sell two of her paintings on the following day. No one seems to mind. Later that night, she and a stepdaughter are forced out of the house by a fire that destroys everything. The police find evidence of arson and a skeleton in a cupboard.

A. (or A. E.) Fielding*

The Mysterious Partner
London: Collins, 1929.
New York: Knopf, 1929.

Inspector Pointer

The Danford family has everything: a stately home, a long family line, money, a successful business, and a family omen. Throughout the family history, the laughter of a ghost has signaled the violent death of the owner of the estate, and the laughter has been recently heard. Ironically, the only one who takes the laughter seriously is the only one who doesn't believe in the occult.

The Wedding-Chest Mystery
London: Collins, 1930.
New York: Kinsey, 1932.

Inspector Pointer

Boyd Armstrong is an international financier whose every word can send stocks up or down, so when a private agent is summoned to meet him, the agent has great hopes. Ordered to wait for Armstrong by a Chinese wedding chest, a gift from Major Hardy to Mr. and Mrs. Armstrong, the agent watches a party in progress until the chest is opened, to reveal Mr. Armstrong, dead.

The Paper-Chase
London: Collins, 1934.

The Paper-Chase Mystery
New York: Kinsey, 1935.

Inspector Pointer

Hugh Winslow, a stockbroker, is vacationing in the Italian Alps when he suspects that another guest is passing forged British notes. He confronts the

other tourist in London after they both return home. Winslow returns to
his own rooms and is in turn confronted by a young woman he met in Italy.
The next day, servants find the woman dead and no sign of Winslow.

The Case of the Missing Diary
London: Collins, 1935.
New York: Kinsey, 1936.

Inspector Pointer

Charles Dawnay is a likable businessman who may be forgiven if he sometimes
feels besieged by his family. He doesn't mind coddling his wife, but he does
worry about a cousin whose business deals are always a hair too close to
the line, and now he must decide if another cousin he hasn't seen for years
is who he says he is.

Black Cats Are Lucky
London: Collins, 1937.
New York: Kinsey, 1938.

Inspector Pointer

Sir Henry Batchelor is a self-made man little concerned with the personal
side of life, or at least he seems oblivious to the undercurrents moving among
his various cousins and other relatives during a house party. He is especially
amicable to Mr. Farrant, a guest of loutish qualities.

Nigel FitzGerald

Midsummer Malice
London: Collins, 1953.
New York: Macmillan, 1959.

Superintendent Patrick Duffy and Alan Russell

The well-liked young daughter of an English baronet is strangled in the
woods near her home, shocking the small town. Everyone wants to help

the police, and they have several witnesses to related events. But despite the confidences of an elderly and shy gentleman and the help of an eccentric Lady Ballybroghill, the police cannot find someone with a motive for murder.

The Rosy Pastor*
London: Collins, 1954.

Superintendent Patrick Duffy and Alan Russell

The House Is Falling
London: Collins, 1955.

Superintendent Patrick Duffy

After twenty years, Major Hugh Barry is invited to visit the family estate, which his step-grandmother managed to pass on to her family rather than to him. He is glad to discover that he no longer cares about Cooline House. But if his passions have cooled, those of his distant relations have not.

Imagine a Man*
London: Collins, 1956.

Superintendent Patrick Duffy

Suffer a Witch
London: Collins, 1958.
New York: Garland, 1982.

Superintendent Patrick Duffy

Ireland had an intelligent response to the wave of witchcraft that swept over the English-speaking world centuries ago, but that doesn't help fifteen-year-old Vanessa, who thinks she is a witch. When a writer visits the Irish village to research a tale of a famous witch, he finds the subject of witches and witchcraft still very much on the villagers' minds.

The Student Body
London: Collins, 1958.

Superintendent Patrick Duffy

Two college students and their girlfriends come across a suspected assassin in a Dublin pub. Undecided about calling the police, the students decide to waylay the man and take him to their rooms, where they and their friends are treated to an unexpected view of the political underground.

Black Welcome
London: Collins, 1961.
New York: Macmillan, 1962.

Superintendent Patrick Duffy

For the first time since his early childhood, Hector O'Brien Moore is returning home to Ireland. He has some misgivings about the reason: a call for a family consultation from his aunt. At Shannon Airport he learns that his relatives have gone to Dublin to meet him, so he drives to Moore Court to await their return. While he waits he encounters a very drunk servant and a beautiful corpse.

The Day of the Adder
London: Collins, 1963.

Echo Answers Murder
New York: Macmillan, 1965.

Superintendent Patrick Duffy

After his mother dies, John O'Corram returns to Ireland to visit the village where he grew up and the castle from which his mother ruled. His return opens old wounds, especially for Nellie Davoren, the red-haired beauty he left behind, and complicates the already intricate schemes of others.

Affairs of Death*
London: Collins, 1967.

Superintendent Patrick Duffy

Ghost in the Making
London: Collins, 1960.

Alan Russell

Alan Russell meets an odd assortment of people at Hunter's Hall, an empty house rented for a party outside Dublin. He thinks little about their conflicts and jealousies until the next day. Nancy Finchly, a middle-aged woman and Alan's hostess, runs away from home on a bicycle; after that bicycles appear and disappear frequently and confusingly.

The Candles Are All Out
London: Collins, 1960.
New York: Macmillan, 1961.

Alan Russell

A theatrical touring company and the judges and lawyers for the Circuit Court converge on Invermore at the same time, leaving several on both sides without a place to stay. A householder invites three of the theater company to stay with him, and thus he gathers at a home on an island on a suitably windy night three actors, a judge, a young veterinarian, two strangers stranded by the weather, and an Irishwoman planning to marry the host. One is dead in the morning, and all reveal a private identity behind the public one.

This Won't Hurt You
London: Collins, 1959.
New York: Macmillan, 1960.

A burglar breaks into a dentist's office and steals the petty cash; since the office is in a building of important businessmen, Scotland Yard sends a superintendent to investigate. While Superintendent Laud questions two dentists, they go about their work, in this instance one tending to the teeth of his medical partner, who is taking the appointment of a patient who canceled. In front of the police and office staff, the dentist gives his patient an injection, and all watch in horror as the man cries out and falls unconscious.

J.S. Fletcher*

The Murder at Wrides Park
London: Harrap, 1931.
New York: Knopf, 1931.

Ronald Camberwell

In 1920 the wealthy owner of a large estate is confronted in his home by an arrogant acquaintance, who is later found dead on the estate. No one seems to doubt that Mr. Nicholas killed the man, apparently a blackmailer, but now people are confronted with another problem: who is Mr. Nicholas? Even his lawyer knows only that Nicholas is a wealthy country gentleman.

The Ebony Box
London: Butterworth, 1934.
New York: Knopf, 1934.

Ronald Camberwell

Ronald Camberwell accepts the position of steward for a large estate in Yorkshire, but soon after his arrival his employer is killed. A coroner's jury concludes that death was from accidental poisoning, and the family settles into a new life--until the dead man's lover insists that part of what was intended as a bequest to her was taken only days before his death.

The Middle Temple Murder
London: Ward, 1918.
New York: Knopf, 1919.

In 1912 a man is found murdered in an entryway in Middle Temple Lane, and the only clues to his identity are a new gray cap purchased from a fashionable West End shop and a slip of paper with the name and address of a prominent barrister. This is Fletcher's classic tale of detection among the law offices of London.

The Matheson Formula
London: Jenkins, 1930.
New York: Knopf, 1929.

Robert Matheson has quietly invented a new explosive so powerful as to make war impossible. Without telling anyone, he gives a copy of the formula to the War Office and another to his bank. Yet someone must know what he has invented, for he is kidnapped as he walks home after delivering the copies of the formula.

The Yorkshire Moorland Murder
London: Jenkins, 1930.
New York: Knopf, 1930.

A rich American book collector travels to England regularly to purchase books, disappearing from his London hotel occasionally to negotiate a purchase. When he fails to return to his hotel after several days, however, his nephew and private secretary become concerned and try to track him down.

The Dressing Room Murder
London: Jenkins, 1930.
New York: Knopf, 1931.

After more than twenty years on the stage, Sir John Riversley decides to play the theater in his hometown, the first time he has returned there since he left as a young man. Unfortunately, before he can give even one performance, he is stabbed to death in his dressing room in the theater.

Dick Francis

Odds Against
London: Joseph, 1965.
New York: Harper, 1966.

Sid Halley

After Sid Halley, a jockey, is permanently injured in a racing fall, he goes
to work for a detective agency, where he is given almost nothing to do.
Then a timid man in one of his cases shoots Halley, and this is the beginning
of his return to normal life: fighting for what he wants and maintaining the
integrity of horse racing.

Whip Hand
London: Joseph, 1979.
New York: Harper,1980.

Sid Halley

Sid Halley gets several job offers as a private investigator: to help his
ex-wife find the man who used her name to defraud by a mail-order business;
to investigate a syndicate of owners whose mounts ride under the name of
one of Halley's former racehorse owners; to verify or refute the suspicions
of the head of security about another member of the Jockey Club; and to
find out why certain horses suddenly stop performing.

Dead Cert
London: Joseph, 1962.
New York: Holt, 1962.

Bill Davidson is riding a dead cert, a horse that is certain to win, and win
easily, but instead the horse falls at a fence and crushes Bill. The next rider
sees Bill go down and notices something on the ground that should not be
there. When he returns later to verify what he has seen, it is gone.

Nerve
London: Joseph, 1964.
New York: Harper, 1964.

Rob Finn is an up-and-coming jockey, hoping for a chance to ride better horses and doing the best with whatever he gets. He is not without sympathy for other jockeys who seem to be having a hard time or even entering a final decline. Only later does he begin to wonder if too many jockeys are too often having difficulties.

For Kicks
London: Joseph, 1965.
New York: Harper, 1965.

A random number of second-rate horses are suddenly becoming winners, but an intensive drug-testing program has turned up nothing. Desperate, one of the members of the governing body of the National Hunt asks the owner of an Australian stud farm to go underground and find out what drug is being used.

Flying Finish
London: Joseph, 1966.
New York: Harper, 1967.

The earl of Creggan and his wife are dismayed when their only son, Henry, announces that he has taken a job as a traveling head groom. He is looking forward, moreover, to the laborer's job of loading and caring for horses on long plane trips. Though his family comes to accept this, some of his co-workers maintain the hostilities in the class war.

Blood Sport
London: Joseph, 1967.
New York: Harper, 1968.

In ten years three stallions of international status have disappeared, leaving the owners to collect the insurance. With the third incident, one of the owners decides to fight back, hiring a government agent to track down the third horse taken.

Forfeit
London: Joseph, 1969.
New York: Harper, 1969.

James Tyrone is asked to write a magazine article on the Lamplighter Gold
Cup, and decides to focus on the people in the background. The first information he gathers concerns another newspaperman, who kept telling Tyrone
before he died not to sell out his column.

Enquiry
London: Joseph, 1969.
New York: Harper, 1970.

To his surprise, Kelly Hughes rides a red-hot favorite to second place. This
seems so suspicious to the authorities that he loses his license in a hearing
before the Disciplinary Committee. The hearing is a parody of due process,
and the full enquiry later is no better, forcing Kelly to conclude that he
was framed.

Rat Race
London: Joseph, 1970.
New York: Harper, 1971.

Matt Shore began his flying career with BOAC and worked his way down
to a taxi service that flies jockeys, trainers, and owners to racecourses.
His first flight for the taxi service introduces Shore to greed and ambition
as well as skill. His second flight introduces him to the violence of the
racing world.

Bonecrack
London: Joseph, 1971.
New York: Harper, 1972.

Neil Griffon has taken over his father's training stables while his father
recovers from an accident, though he has seen little of the business since
he was a youngster. When Neil is forced to take on a young, inexperienced
jockey in order to protect the business, he decides to let the boy prove himself and make the boy's father trap himself.

Smokescreen
London: Joseph, 1972.
New York: Harper, 1973.

When Edward Lincoln's aunt asks him to investigate the state of her horses
in South Africa, he protests that he is only an actor but agrees to go. As
he investigates the world of racing in South Africa, the line between fantasy
and reality blurs and he is no longer safe as the star of adventure films.

Slayride
London: Joseph, 1973.
New York: Harper, 1974.

An English jockey invited to ride in a race in Norway absconds with all the
track money. Unable to locate him, the Norwegian Jockey Club invites an
investigator from its British counterpart to help find him.

Knockdown
London: Joseph, 1974.
New York: Harper, 1974.

Jonah Dereham helps a rich American woman buy a horse for the son of a
special friend. Before Jonah and his client can even leave the sales ground,
however, he is attacked and beaten and his client is forced to sign over
the horse. At first the American client seems to be the object of the assault,
but other attacks of a different sort suggest that someone else is the intended victim.

High Stakes
London: Joseph, 1975.
New York: Harper, 1976.

Steven Scott enjoys owning racehorses until he begins to sense that his
trainer has other goals than training his horses. When Scott decides to
change trainers, the trainer fights back, and Steven learns that he is an
outsider and few are willing to give him help or even the benefit of the
doubt.

In the Frame
London: Joseph, 1976.
New York: Harper, 1977.

Charles Todd, painter and lover of horse races, arrives at his cousin's home in time to watch the police take over the house after a burglary and the murder of his cousin's wife. A few weeks later he meets a woman who also lost everything of value in her home, this time through arson. The crimes are linked only by the kind of valuables in the two homes.

Risk
London: Joseph, 1977.
New York: Harper, 1978.

An amateur rider can hope for little more than a chance to ride in the Gold Cup, so when Roland Britten, an accountant, rides and wins, he is understandably overjoyed. His final reward, however, is to be kidnapped and held in a dark hole for several days.

Trial Run
London: Joseph, 1978.
New York: Harper, 1979.

A prince of the royal family is prepared to back his brother-in-law's interest in training for the Olympics if he can be assured that the young man will not fall into a scandal during the games. To investigate this possibility, the prince hires Randall Drew, a former jockey, to go to Moscow, site of the upcoming games, to learn what, if anything, the Soviets have planned for the prince's brother-in-law.

Reflex
London: Joseph, 1980.
New York: Putnam, 1981.

Philip Nore has reached a crisis in his life: he is wondering why he rides for a living and a grandmother who has refused to see him for thirty years suddenly summons him to her. Even worse, she promises to give him £100,000 if he will find his sister, a person he never knew existed. Philip doesn't want the money and he certainly doesn't want a grandmother, but news of a sister is a different matter.

Twice Shy
London: Joseph, 1981.
New York: Putnam, 1982.

While visiting friends in Norwich, a young physics teacher is given three
tapes of a computer program on horse racing. A few days later the pro-
grammer is dead and two men appear on the teacher's doorstep demanding
the tapes. The violence spreads quickly, with everyone who knows about the
program trying to find and claim it.

Banker
London: Joseph, 1982.
New York: Putnam, 1983.

After a checkered childhood with high-living parents, Tim Ekaterin has
settled into the staid life of a banker. But his life begins to change when
random events push him in a new direction. Tim rescues his boss from what
appears to be a breakdown and intervenes in a knife attack on a business
acquaintance. Then the bank grants a loan for the purchase of a racehorse
that is to be put out to stud.

The Danger
London: Joseph, 1983.
New York: Putnam, 1984.

The world of horse racing attracts many types of people, but perhaps the
least attractive and most dangerous is the kidnapper who preys on the
wealthy of the racing world. Andrew Douglas specializes in hunting down
these people, freeing the victim, and pursuing his quarry while others try
to forget what has happened.

Proof
London: Joseph, 1984.
New York: Putnam, 1985.

A young wine merchant agrees to help the police test the drinks served at
the Silver Moondance bar and restaurant. He needs only a few minutes to
discover that the whiskey inside the bottle does not match the name on the
label. This seems a fairly straightforward swindle until the police find a
few days later that the restaurant has been emptied of every single bottle.
Only an extraordinary corpse remains.

Antonia Fraser

Quiet as a Nun
London: Weidenfeld, 1977.
New York: Viking, 1977.

Jemima Shore

In a secluded tower attached to a convent, a nun takes her own life after recovering from a nervous breakdown. She leaves two notes, one insisting that her old school friend, Jemima Shore, will understand what is going on. Anxious to restore the tranquillity of the convent, the mother superior tries to persuade Jemima to find out why the nun died.

The Wild Island
London: Weidenfeld, 1978.
New York: Norton, 1978.

Jemima Shore

Jemima Shore goes to Inverness for a quiet vacation, but it is not to be. Her landlord has died suddenly and no one is expecting her. When she is finally on her way to her Highland retreat, she is drawn into her landlord's funeral and then into a dispute over his death and who the proper ruling (royal) family is in Scotland.

A Splash of Red
London: Weidenfeld, 1981.
New York: Norton, 1981.

Jemima Shore

Chloe Fontaine is a successful writer of carefully crafted, highly polished novels, which provide a striking contrast to her disordered, frenetic personal life. Escaping from her flat for a holiday, she leaves Jemima Shore with her cat, obscene phone calls, and physical threats from her long list of past and present admirers.

Cool Repentance
London: Weidenfeld, 1982.
New York: Norton, 1982.

Jemima Shore

Christabel Cartwright believes she can go back in time to an earlier way of life with husband and children she abandoned for a young musician several years ago. She even believes she can reclaim her position as a foremost actress, as though her life had never led to wild newspaper stories and shattered lives.

Oxford Blood
London: Weidenfeld, 1985.
New York: Norton, 1985.

Jemima Shore

Prompted by a television program, a dying nurse confesses to Jemima Shore that she switched two babies at birth twenty years ago. She dies at peace, comforted by her old friends. Not long afterward, a friend of one of the now-grown babies dies accidentally, apparently. Jemima decides to unravel the lineage of the youths even though she dislikes what she assumes will be the results.

James Fraser*

The Evergreen Death
London: Jenkins, 1968.
New York: Harcourt, 1969.

Inspector Bill Aveyard

Colonel Innes's gardener finds the corpse of a teenaged girl under the ever-
greens, her body carefully but gruesomely cut. After the police investigate
and take statements from the villagers, they count no fewer than five stories
about where Linda was on the evening of her death. When they look into
the background of the villagers, they find a perfect suspect.

A Cock-pit of Roses
London: Jenkins, 1969.
New York: Harcourt, 1970.

Inspector Bill Aveyard

Every year the Marchmonts host a party at the manor for all of the villagers,
giving them the very best in food and drink. This year is no different except that Inspector Aveyard gets drunk and passes out in the rose garden.
When he comes to in the morning, his pants are unzipped and there is a
dead woman at his feet, apparently raped and strangled. This is the first
of four deaths that confuse the police as well as the villagers.

Deadly Nightshade
London: Jenkins, 1970.
New York: Harcourt, 1970.

Inspector Bill Aveyard

During his nightly patrol, Constable Verney is joined by a dog, which follows
him home. Not until he is at home does the constable see what the dog is
carrying--a human jawbone. It isn't long before the police find a matching

corpse, but they have more trouble figuring out who the corpse once was. The next evidence the police find points to another crime, one for which they have no body.

R. Austin Freeman*

The Red Thumb Mark
London: Collingwood, 1907.
New York: Newton, 1911.

Dr. John Thorndyke

A dealer in precious metals leaves a consignment of diamonds in his safe and in the morning the stones are gone. Left on a piece of paper is a thumb print in blood that matches the print of one of the dealer's nephews. The nephew is promptly arrested and charged. Only Dr. Thorndyke is not convinced of the man's guilt and ultimately reveals the flaws in a foregone conclusion based on fingerprints.

The Mystery of 31, New Inn
London: Hodder, 1912.
Philadelphia: Winston, 1913.

Dr. John Thorndyke

Called to attend a man who has a strong aversion to doctors, Dr. Jervis must agree to visit his patient at an unknown location and use a pseudonym. "Mr. Graves," the patient, appears to be suffering from morphine poisoning, but his staff seem convinced the disease is sleeping sickness. After another visit, Dr. Jervis loses contact with his patient. Some time later he learns that a respected figure has died of morphine poisoning.

A Silent Witness
London: Hodder, 1914.
Philadelphia: Winston, 1915.

Dr. John Thorndyke

Dr. Humphrey Jardine, only recently qualified, trips from one strange experience to another. First, he finds a body in a lane near his home, but the body is gone when he returns with the police. Then he attends a viewing of the body while a physician fills out a death certificate for the family. Not long after this, Jardine realizes his life is in danger.

Mr. Pottermack's Oversight
London: Hodder, 1930.
New York: Dodd, Mead, 1930.

Dr. John Thorndyke

Mr. Pottermack is a quiet, industrious, and well-liked member of his small community, but he becomes one day a tormented man when a figure from his past reenters his life. Mr. Pottermack cannot afford repeated blackmail and so sets in motion a train of events whose outcome no one could anticipate.

Dr. Thorndyke Intervenes
London: Hodder, 1933.
New York: Dodd, Mead, 1933.

Dr. John Thorndyke

Two men have come to claim their luggage in a train station and witness a startling mystery: a man claims a suitcase, suspects tampering, opens the case and finds a head inside, and runs off. The two men lose interest after the police arrive, for they have a mystery of their own: how is a rich young American going to prove to a court that he has a legitimate claim to the title and estate of the earl of Winsborough?

The Penrose Mystery
London: Hodder, 1936.
New York: Dodd, Mead, 1936.

Dr. John Thorndyke

Daniel Penrose has built a remarkable collection of antiques, but he is different from other collectors: he is not an expert or an enthusiast. He is primarily a collector and a secretive man, unwilling to talk openly and proudly of his collection yet willing to show his pieces occasionally to others.

The Stoneware Monkey
London: Hodder, 1938.
New York: Dodd, Mead, 1939.

Dr. John Thorndyke

Young Dr. Oldfield is called to attend a new patient, an artist of modern pottery. The patient complains of gastrointestinal pain, but after several days of medical attention he is getting worse, not better. When the problem is diagnosed as arsenic poisoning, the patient rapidly improves. Not long after this, he disappears.

The Jacob Street Mystery
London: Hodder, 1942.

The Unconscious Witness
New York: Dodd, Mead, 1942.

Dr. John Thorndyke

Tom Pedley is distracted from his painting in a village wood when three people walk by, two men followed by a woman, who appears to be eavesdropping. The woman and one of the men return, and Tom forgets about them after fitting them into his composition. Only several days later does he realize that he must have watched the beginnings of a murder.

Jonathan Gash

The Judas Pair
London: Collins, 1977.
New York: Harper, 1977.

Lovejoy

Lovejoy, an antiques dealer, thinks he has a promising buyer until the man asks to buy the Judas pair, a mythical pair of flintlock dueling pistols. The buyer acknowledges the myth, but insists he has seen the pair and is willing to pay whatever it costs to get them. His interest is more than that of a collector, and his determination persuades Lovejoy to search for a pair of pistols that may be the legendary set.

Gold from Gemini
London: Collins, 1978.

Gold by Gemini
New York: Harper, 1979.

Lovejoy

The local museum is robbed of its collection of Roman coins, bringing to light a fact about them much debated. The donor, recently dead, insisted that he had found the coins on the Isle of Man and that they be so described. The only other thing Lovejoy knows about the late donor is that he may have been a good forger.

The Grail Tree
London: Collins, 1979.
New York: Harper, 1980.

Lovejoy

Among the many scrupulous and unscrupulous dealers in antiques in East Anglia, Lovejoy is blessed with a gift for spotting forgeries as well as the true article. When a would-be client insists he has the Holy Grail, Lovejoy is understandably skeptical, but soon afterward the man is killed in an explosion and Lovejoy is curious.

Spend Game
London: Collins, 1980.
New Haven, Conn.: Ticknor, 1981.

Lovejoy

A debonair antiques dealer is murdered in a car accident, but not before disposing of his recent valuable purchases and leaving a cryptic message for help for his friend Lovejoy. The problem is that Lovejoy knows what Leckie bought and it can't be worth dying for. If it is, however, Lovejoy will have to find it, and that proves to be much more difficult than figuring out who murdered Leckie.

The Vatican Rip
London: Collins, 1981.
New Haven, Conn.: Ticknor, 1982.

Lovejoy

Down on his luck, as usual, Lovejoy is offered a commission by a collector. Step by step, Lovejoy is locked into the dangerous job: stealing a Chippendale table from the Vatican. Accepting the inevitable, Lovejoy studies Italian and flies to Rome.

Firefly Gadroon
London: Collins, 1982.
New York: St. Martin, 1984.

Lovejoy

Lovejoy stands in for an assistant auctioneer and watches a woman buy a Chinese firefly cage he had hoped to get for a small sum. The woman doesn't seem to know what it is, but she is still willing to pay well for it. Later she presents Lovejoy with an almost exact duplicate--and a request. Lovejoy is soon tracking down stolen antiques.

The Sleepers of Erin
London: Collins, 1983.
New York: Dutton, 1983.

Lovejoy

Lovejoy is lingering in church when he sees two men he knows begin a robbery. When he interrupts them, one throws a knife at him. Wounded, he flees and winds up in the hospital, where he is charged with the robbery. The charge is dropped when a woman he has never seen before appears and declares herself a witness to his innocence.

The Gondola Scam
London: Collins, 1984.
New York: St. Martin, 1984.

Lovejoy

Mr. Pinder owns a superb collection of art and antiques, but he is tormented over the condition of Venice. Every year the old city loses a large number of artworks to the rising waters, with little or nothing being done to save the art. Mr. Pinder has decided, therefore, to save the art by stealing it and replacing individual pieces with fakes. He asks Lovejoy to help him.

Pearlhanger
London: Collins, 1985.
New York: St. Martin, 1985.

Lovejoy

A medium tells the American wife of a British antiques dealer to search out her husband, who is somewhere in East Anglia, with Lovejoy. Lovejoy considers this nonsense, but he goes along until he realizes that the woman is deadly serious about finding her husband, and her husband cannot be a dealer or collector.

Michael Gilbert

Close Quarters
London: Hodder, 1947.
New York: Walker, 1963.

Inspector Hazlerigg

The insulated world of Melchester Cathedral close hardly seems the place
for the darker side of human nature, but the residents are getting poison-pen
letters and a canon dies unexpectedly. Thinking the unpleasantness a small
if troubling matter, the dean invites a nephew from Scotland Yard to investigate, just in time for an unambiguous murder.

They Never Looked Inside
London: Hodder, 1948.

He Didn't Mind Danger
New York: Harper, 1949.

Inspector Hazlerigg

Things are always different after a war, but the London police are struggling
with a change in crime that has them especially worried: there are now sometimes as many as three burglaries a night, each following a carefully
worked-out plan. Yet the burglars are often first-timers who have no experience in crime and have only recently been discharged from the army.

The Doors Open
London: Hodder, 1949.
New York: Walker, 1962.

Inspector Hazlerigg

Young Paddy Carter chances to see a neighbor about to commit suicide,
chases after him, and finds the man has thought better of it. Taking him
off to a pub for a drink, Carter listens to his story of having been fired

for a fault he discovered in his firm's bookkeeping. The next day the man is dead, an apparent suicide.

Smallbone Deceased
London: Hodder, 1950.
New York: Harper, 1950.

Inspector Hazlerigg

The respected old law firm of Horniman, Birley, and Craine has its minor personnel problems, but nothing serious. Even the death of the senior partner, Mr. Horniman, and the arrival of his well-meaning but inept son does not ruffle the office. The disruption comes with the discovery of the corpse of a man the office has been looking for for several days. And the location of the corpse casts grave doubts on the character of the late senior partner.

Death Has Deep Roots
London: Hodder, 1951.
New York: Harper, 1951.

Inspector Hazlerigg

In her short life Mademoiselle Lamartine has worked in the French Resistance during the war, borne and lost a child, and emigrated to England. When she is arrested for the murder of a Briton who served in her area during the war, both her counsel and the police believe her guilty though deserving of compassion.

Fear to Tread
London: Hodder, 1953.
New York: Harper, 1953.

Superintendent Hazlerigg

The intelligent and kind headmaster of a boys' school in southwest London is used to encountering the hardness of the slums in the lives of his students and their families. But when the corruption on the railways begins to infect his private life and that of others he knows, the kindly headmaster decides to fight back.

Blood and Judgment
London: Hodder, 1958.
New York: Harper, 1959.

Sergeant Patrick Petrella

A woman's body is found partly buried near a reservoir, and she turns out to be the wife of a criminal who has recently escaped from prison. The police at first can't imagine a motive for her murder. (Petrella reappears in several of Gilbert's short stories.)

Death in Captivity
London: Hodder, 1952.

The Danger Within
New York: Harper, 1952.

The Italian command of Campo 127 likes to think it has full control over the British prisoners of war, but its control is not complete. Many of the prisoners suspect that one of the prisoners is an informer, and the suspect is found dead in the only escape tunnel the Italians haven't discovered.

Sky High
London: Hodder, 1955.

The Country-House Burglar
New York: Harper, 1955.

The village of Brimberley has settled down after World War II, but many of the residents think things have changed. And soon they are proved right: the church poorbox is robbed, a retired military man receives threatening letters, and an explosion shakes the village.

Be Shot for Sixpence
London: Hodder, 1956.
New York: Harper, 1956.

Only one man could understand an advertisement placed in the personal columns of the Times: Philip recognizes a message from an old friend, Colin, now in the secret service. Philip pursues this and two other messages until he arrives at a palace on the Austrian-Hungarian-Yugoslavian border, enmeshed in a secret mission that takes him back to his war service.

After the Fine Weather
London: Hodder, 1963.
New York: Harper, 1963.

Laura Hart and her brother, a vice consul in Lienz, are fond of each other, but her willingness to speak openly and freely, even to the point of describing unpleasant events she has seen in Lienz, does not endear her to her brother or other members of the diplomatic corps. Nevertheless, Laura continues to be an observant, sometimes thoughtful guest.

The Crack in the Teacup
London: Hodder, 1966.
New York: Harper, 1966.

A young solicitor sees two teenaged boys being violently thrown out of a recreation-dance hall. Fired by outrage and idealism, the lawyer defends them in court and challenges the owner of the hall. Though no one in the quiet coastal town seems to care, the young lawyer pursues the defense of his clients, uncovering a web of corruption throughout the town government.

The Dust and the Heat
London: Hodder, 1967.

Overdrive
New York: Harper, 1968.

Oliver Nugent commanded tanks during the war and afterward set out to succeed in business with the same intention of riding over every opponent and obstacle. He has no reservations about methods that will get him what he wants, and he uses his keen observation and tactical mind to defeat his competitors.

The Etruscan Net
London: Hodder, 1969.

The Family Tomb
New York: Harper, 1969.

Professor Bronzini is immersed in the world of the Etruscans, hoarding their artifacts and imitating their way of life. As a result, his reputation as a collector has grown and attracted attention from both art connoisseurs and criminals.

The Body of a Girl
London: Hodder, 1972.
New York: Harper, 1972.

Just as Inspector Mercer arrives at his new posting, two boys discover the bones of a recently buried corpse. It is not long before Mercer is faced with a list of crimes and the problem of getting to the powers behind some of them.

The 92nd Tiger
London: Hodder, 1973.
New York: Harper, 1973.

Hugo Greest, known as Tiger to his fans, has rescued 91 damsels and defeated 91 villains when he learns, first, that his television series has been canceled and, second, that the ruler of a Middle East country wants him to serve as a military adviser. Hugo insists that television fantasy and reality are entirely different, but the sheikh also insists and Hugo agrees to give the new job a try.

Flash Point
London: Hodder, 1974.
New York: Harper, 1974.

A young lawyer known for his tenacity approaches the Law Society with evidence that an MP may be guilty of a criminal act, and thereby sets in motion discreet efforts to persuade the young man to back off. Nevertheless, word of the MP's wrongdoing quickly spreads, and soon the press, union officials, and other branches of government are involved.

The Night of the Twelfth
London: Hodder, 1976.
New York: Harper, 1976.

The southern Home Counties have been the scene of at least three brutal murders of young boys, the last one close to a boarding school for boys. The police can only scour the countryside for clues, looking for just one witness to something that might help.

The Empty House
London: Hodder, 1978.
New York: Harper, 1979.

During a storm along the Devon coast, a man sees a car drive over a cliff and disappear into the sea. The accident at first seems only tragic, but then unsettling. The dead man was a genetic scientist working at a government research center and had recently taken out a large insurance policy. The tire tracks leading to the cliff showed no signs of braking, and the local people insist that no one could survive a fall over the cliff.

Death of a Favourite Girl
London: Hodder, 1980.

The Killing of Katie Steelstock
New York: Harper, 1980.

A summer dance in a country town draws old and young, high and low, including Katie Steelstock, a local girl who has become a television star. Admired and envied by many, Katie seems to have everything, but before the evening is over she is brutally murdered. When the police investigate, they find far more to her life than that of a television personality known throughout the country.

The Final Throw
London: Hodder, 1982.

End-Game
New York: Harper, 1982.

A derelict who speaks the language of an educated man introduces the reader to the world of high finance in which ambitious men and women rise and fall according to their wits and their character. Knowing that some will do anything to get ahead, Scotland Yard pursues its own plan to trap those who want more than they can earn honestly.

The Black Seraphim
London: Hodder, 1983.
New York: Harper, 1984.

Dr. James Scotland moves into Melchester Cathedral close for a much-needed rest and is immediately caught in the politics of cathedral management. The archdeacon believes in running the cathedral like a business, and some of the local businessmen seem to expect to make a fortune by managing a piece of cathedral land.

The Long Journey Home
London: Hodder, 1985.
New York: Harper, 1985.

When John Benedict decides not to reboard in Rome his flight from London to New Zealand, he makes a decision that will alter the lives of hundreds of people. Benedict tours the villages in southern Italy, fixing farm equipment and staying with farmers. He soon becomes involved in what he thinks is a local battle between farmers and the Mafia. As he listens and questions, however, he sees connections to corporate power that reach back to London.

Kenneth Giles

Some Beasts No More
London: Gollancz, 1965.
New York: Walker, 1968.

Sergeant Harry James

Scotland Yard keeps a list of suspected but unconvicted murderers, and every year a few die or disappear. Recently a higher than usual number have been found dead, strongly suggesting that someone has found the list and is systematically shortening it.

A Provenance of Death
London: Gollancz, 1966.
New York: Simon, 1967.

Picture of Death
Chicago: Panther, 1970.

Inspector Harry James

Crime has struck another segment of the London population: sidewalk artists. The number of dead and missing among this group of artists is disturbing; then an art expert is found dead and the crime wave in the art world spreads.

Death in Diamonds
London: Gollancz, 1967.
New York: Simon, 1968.

Inspector Harry James

Miss Olga Hodden, a young American tourist, deposits her luggage in a borrowed flat, goes out for provisions, and returns to find the flat occupied by a Major Lupins and her luggage gone. When the police finally find the correct flat and her luggage, they also find a headless corpse. The police have to join the stream of tourists to Spain before they can solve the riddle of the missing flat.

Death and Mr. Prettyman
London: Gollancz, 1967.
New York: Walker, 1969.

Inspector Harry James

Mr. Prettyman is a shrewd and conservative solicitor with a modest but sufficient county practice. He seems the least likely candidate to end his days with a knife in his back. But as the police discover, he is capable of other surprises, at least in his professional life.

Death among the Stars
London: Gollancz, 1968.
New York: Walker, 1969.

Inspector Harry James

The Daily Bulletin, one of the less important newspapers in London, has an unexpected scoop: the murder of its own astrologer in his office. Although no one in the office ever thought the man capable of arousing dangerous passions, the police search his lodgings and find a box of the sort they have seen before.

Death Cracks a Bottle
London: Gollancz, 1969.
New York: Walker, 1970.

Inspector Harry James

When Cristobal Botling is found in a dumbwaiter with his head smashed in, no one is terribly unhappy at his death. Indeed, with the death of the chairman of the board, three other members of the board of the old firm of wine importers and bottlers rescind their recent resignations. While these three are reorganizing the board, their wives, who are sisters and descendants of the original owners, are contemplating other financial arrangements.

Murder Pluperfect
London: Gollancz, 1970.
New York: Walker, 1970.

Inspector Harry James

The wife of a rich industrialist wants to rehabilitate her husband's great aunt, who was suspected but not charged in the death of her fiancé in 1874. Armed with diaries and other documents, Inspector James resigns himself to a superficial review, perhaps a whitewash, of an independent Victorian woman.

A Death in the Church
London: Gollancz, 1970.

Inspector Harry James

Inspector James and his wife are watching their second twin receive baptism when the vicar wobbles and falls, dead from a bullet wound. Along with other members of Scotland Yard, guests at the baptism, James rushes to the street, to be met by four stagecoaches, each harnessed with three horses, and a man riding away on a bicycle. While Mrs. James and her aunt debate whether or not either of the twins was baptized, the police look for a reason for someone to kill a parson recently returned from South Africa.

A File on Death
London: Gollancz, 1973.
New York: Walker, 1973.

Inspector Harry James

Old secret files are stolen from the Foreign Office and traced to the estate of Sir Hugh Palabras, an opponent of most advances made since the eighteenth century. Surrounded by a menagerie of tenants, ranging from a singer to a leader of the Girl Guides, Sir Hugh is planning how best to use the documents to embarrass or defeat the current government.

The Big Greed
London: Gollancz, 1966.

Five Americans whose lives of failure have slowly faded into the mist of
the underworld are brought together to deliver a cache of stolen money for
organized crime. The payment of a substantial sum prompts each of the
five to dream of a future starkly different from the present.

Martha Grimes

The Man with a Load of Mischief
Boston: Little, Brown, 1981.

Inspector Richard Jury

In a quiet village in December, villagers find a number of murder victims,
and where they are found raises as many questions as why they were murdered. One man is found hung on a pub's mechanical clock, and another is found
in a beer keg. The villagers are alternately thrilled by the excitement and
scared of the unknown murderer.

The Old Fox Deceiv'd
Boston: Little, Brown, 1982.

Superintendent Richard Jury

A woman shows up at the home of a wealthy landowner claiming to be the
ward who disappeared fifteen years ago. Soon afterward she is murdered,
on the night of a costume party. Her death leaves the police with two questions: who was she, and why was she murdered?

The Anodyne Necklace
Boston: Little, Brown, 1983.

Superintendent Richard Jury

The village of Littlebourne has more than its share of problems: a villager was mugged in London, another found a corpse while out bird watching, and several have received poison-pen letters, written in crayon. The solution to these crimes turns out to be child's play.

The Dirty Duck
London: O'Mara, 1986.
Boston: Little, Brown, 1984.

Superintendent Richard Jury

Stratford in July might be crowded and hot, but at least it is predictable. Even the tourist writing a book on Marlowe and carrying around a personal computer with him is not an extreme. The surprises come with the murder of an American tourist and the disappearance of an American boy.

Jerusalem Inn
Boston: Little, Brown, 1984.

Superintendent Richard Jury

An attractive woman with no known relatives and no enemies is murdered. She was known for her charity work and her interest in family histories, but when police trace her recent travels around the countryside they follow a trail to the world of art, wealth, and titles.

Help the Poor Struggler
Boston: Little, Brown, 1985.

Superintendent Richard Jury

A convicted murderer is released after twenty years in prison and a child is murdered in the next county. Then another child is murdered. The police must go back twenty years to prove a convicted man innocent while finding a murderer who has remained hidden for all those years.

The Deer Leap
Boston: Little, Brown, 1985.

Superintendent Richard Jury

The quaint village of Ashdown Dean harbors at least one animal killer and at least one animal lover, a young girl who habitually saves pets from mistreatment and abuse. Unfortunately, there is no one to save their owners, who are in equally serious danger.

Cyril Hare

Tenant for Death
London: Faber, 1937.
New York: Dodd, Mead, 1937.

Inspector Mallett

In a neighborhood of retired professionals, one person stands out for his employment and aloofness. When he disappears, leaving behind a corpse, the trail of the murderer leads to the City and the complex arrangements of well-known financial firms that can bankrupt some and enrich others.

Death Is No Sportsman
London: Faber, 1938.
New York: Perennial, 1981.

Inspector Mallett

Every weekend, four men devoted to fly fishing gather at a resort to enjoy their favorite sport. Though not friends, the men have learned to get along in order to share fishing rights to an especially desirable section of the River Didder. Beneath the surface of courtesy shown by the men, there are unexpected currents that flow inexorably to murder along the riverbank.

Suicide Excepted
London: Faber, 1939.
New York: Macmillan, 1954.

Inspector Mallett

Disappointed with his hotel, the meals, and the service, Inspector Mallett is looking forward to the end of his holiday. He must endure only one more trial: the hotel boor, whose family once owned the country house, sits down at Mallett's table and unburdens himself. The next day the man is dead, an apparent suicide.

Tragedy at Law
London: Faber, 1942.
New York: Harcourt, 1943.

Inspector Mallett and Francis Pettigrew

The judges, lawyers, and others traveling the Southern Circuit are being overtaken by gloom, worry, and fear. Judge Barber disregards anonymous threatening letters and then is jolted by a car accident. The letters continue and the threats become real, touching others on the circuit, including the judge's wife and her old friend, Francis Pettigrew.

With a Bare Bodkin
London: Faber, 1946.
New York: Perennial, 1980.

Inspector Mallett and Francis Pettigrew

As his contribution to the war effort, Francis Pettigrew joins the Ministry of Pin Control and is sent to an old mansion in a remote part of Britain. Pettigrew thinks his coworkers decent sorts, but he is discomfited when they decide to plot the perfect murder to pass the time at work. This game seems to bring out the best and the worst in everyone, and soon there is a real murder to contend with.

When the Wind Blows
London: Faber, 1949.

The Wind Blows Death
Boston: Little, Brown, 1950.

Francis Pettigrew

The Markshire Orchestral Society survives as an amateur orchestra only because its various members overlook their differences in favor of their shared love of music. Indeed, they need all their goodwill to make it through the first concert, for members are missing, new ones appear, and one performer is murdered.

The Yew Tree's Shade
London: Faber, 1954.

Death Walks the Woods
Boston: Little, Brown, 1954.

Francis Pettigrew

Francis Pettigrew settles into a quiet country life and finds a niche in the area by taking over the local judge's duties. Just as he begins to understand and appreciate the complexities in village relationships, there is a new twist: a criminal just released from prison comes to live in the village.

He Should Have Died Hereafter
London: Faber, 1957.

Untimely Death
New York: Macmillan, 1958.

Francis Pettigrew and Inspector Mallett

Eleanor Pettigrew takes her husband on a vacation to Exmoor, where Francis spent vacations as a child. On an impulse, he decides to confront a ghost from his past and sets out to walk across the moor. Past and present merge when Pettigrew comes to the spot he remembers with discomfort: just where he saw a body fifty years ago, there he sees one again. When he returns with help, the body is gone.

An English Murder
London: Faber, 1951.
Boston: Little, Brown, 1951.

The Christmas Murder
New York: Mercury, 1953.

Lord Warbeck is dying and has set his heart on a traditional Christmas that will bring together his few remaining relatives and dear ones: his cousin, who is chancellor of the exchequer; his son, who leads a fascist group; his dead son's godmother, who is now married to an ambitious politician; and a young woman who was long a friend of Lord Warbeck's son. Antagonistic and ambitious, the guests come for an English Christmas and witness an English murder.

S.T. Haymon

Death and the Pregnant Virgin
London: Constable, 1980.
New York: St. Martin, 1980.

Inspector Benjamin Jurnet

The rediscovery of the image from a medieval shrine transforms a Norfolk village and many of its residents, inspiring some to saintliness and others to cynical opportunism. On the fifth anniversary of the rediscovery, the procession to the shrine leads to murder, bringing the harsh light of the police to shine on the work of the devotees.

Ritual Murder
London: Constable, 1982.
New York: St. Martin, 1982.

Inspector Benjamin Jurnet

The quiet religious life inside Angleby Cathedral close continues beside the world of the tourists until someone crosses the boundary between the two. First, there is the graffiti. Then there is the body, found at the site of an archaeological dig inside the close to explore the burial place of Little St. Ulf. The wounds on the body imitate those said to have been made on the body of the child saint by Jews in 1144.

Stately Homicide
London: Constable, 1984.
New York: St. Martin, 1984.

Inspector Benjamin Jurnet

Behind the rich, historic façade of Bullen Hall is a staff of curators, tour guides, and others who struggle to make the stately home profitable. When a new curator announces some of the changes he foresees, he is only adding to the list of grievances: the outgoing curator is denied access to the historically important letters he discovered; the craftspeople may lose their rent-free quarters; and many members of the staff want a more conservative management of the stately home.

Georgette Heyer

Death in the Stocks
London: Longmans, 1935.

Merely Murder
New York: Doubleday, 1935.

Superintendent Hannasyde and Sergeant Hemingway

The police find a corpse in evening clothes in the stocks on the village green. It is obviously a case of murder, and the man's relatives, eccentric or offensive, are convinced that one or more of them will be arrested for the deed. And everyone makes a point of how intolerable the victim was.

Behold, Here's Poison
London: Hodder, 1936.
New York: Doubleday, 1936.

Superintendent Hannasyde and Sergeant Hemingway

Gregory Matthews may be generous enough to offer a roof to his many relatives, but he certainly expects to enjoy their discomfort if they accept his charity. It is little wonder, then, that one of his eccentric relatives or friends should murder him. Certainly no one regrets his death, though the murder investigation is sometimes awkward.

They Found Him Dead
London: Hodder, 1937.
New York: Doubleday, 1937.

Superintendent Hannasyde and Sergeant Hemingway

Three generations gather for Silas Kane's birthday party, and the old man is his usual grouchy self. He is adamant in his opposition to a proposition from his business partner and contemptuous of some of his younger relatives, but overall is well liked by many in his family. When he is found dead at the bottom of a cliff the morning after the party, his relatives assume it must be an accidental death. Only one is hoping for murder: young Tim Harte, half brother of Jim Kane, a cousin of Silas, fan of gangster movies, and volunteer apprentice to the police.

A Blunt Instrument
London: Hodder, 1938.
New York: Doubleday, 1938.

Superintendent Hannasyde and Sergeant Hemingway

Ernest Fletcher is utterly charming to women and very good to his sister, but he is murdered just the same. After the police carefully piece together all the evidence, they conclude that the murder was impossible. Again, it doesn't help having a prankster among the suspects.

No Wind of Blame
London: Hodder, 1939.
New York: Doubleday, 1939.

Inspector Hemingway

Ermyntrude Carter, a spunky, goodhearted, and rich woman, can forgive almost anything, but the infidelities of her worthless second husband are a challenge. Amid weekend plans to entertain a bankrupt Russian prince, county society that disdains Ermy's money, and neighbors who adore her for her generosity of spirit, Ermy must contend with a daughter who switches stage roles every few hours, attempted blackmail, and a murder.

Envious Casca
London: Hodder, 1941.
New York: Doubleday, 1941.

Inspector Hemingway

Joseph Herriard has talked his older, wealthy brother into having their scattered relatives for an old-fashioned Christmas and is now going about with intolerable cheerfulness. Despite Joseph's holiday spirit, the guests grow grumpier, nurturing their grievances; the servants disapprove of much of the household; Maud Herriard, Joseph's wife, goes on playing cards; and the host is found stabbed to death in his bedroom.

Duplicate Death
London: Heinemann, 1951.
New York: Dutton, 1969.

Inspector Hemingway

Mrs. Haddington is determined to see her beautiful if brainless daughter married well and therefore hosts parties to introduce her to eligible young men. Despite her mother's efforts, the young woman continues her acquaintance with some men whom others would clearly avoid. When a man is murdered at one of her bridge parties, Mrs. Haddington has a serious social misstep to deal with. Once again in the thick of things and ready to help the police is the now-grown Tim Harte.

Detection Unlimited
London: Heinemann, 1953.
New York: Dutton, 1969.

Inspector Hemingway

The exclusive village of Thornden enjoys a major entertainment: Sampson Warrenby, a successful lawyer, is found shot to death in his garden by his niece, who is returning from an afternoon party at a nearby house. Although she hears the shot, she is too flustered on her arrival to do anything but run for help. And so the culprit appears to have escaped, and the villagers are free to speculate on murderer and motive.

Footsteps in the Dark
London: Longmans, 1932.
New York: Berkley, 1986.

When two sisters and a brother inherit an old priory that had been turned into a house, they think they have found the ideal weekend retreat. Warned by the villagers about a ghost in the priory, the new owners laugh off the warnings and move in. Soon they hear groans and other noises, find the bones of a murder victim, and see a cloaked figure on the grounds at night. Their hunt for the ghost becomes serious, as does his hunt for them.

Why Shoot a Butler?
London: Longmans, 1933.
New York: Doubleday, 1936.

On his way to his uncle's country home, a young barrister stops to ask directions of a young woman standing beside a car. As he draws closer he sees a man inside the car, dead from a gunshot wound in the chest. The woman insists she had nothing to do with the murder and sends the barrister on his way.

The Unfinished Clue
London: Longmans, 1934.
New York: Doubleday, 1937.

Sir Arthur is looking forward to spending the weekend with his guests, a young couple he met in southern France, until the house party grows to include his son and his fiancée, a nephew, a sister-in-law, and other assorted people. By the end of the weekend, Sir Arthur has done his best to offend everyone his wife let into the house.

Penhallow
London: Heinemann, 1943.
New York: Doubleday, 1943.

Adam Penhallow may be confined to his bed, but that does not dampen his spirit. He keeps his grown sons and daughters in line, enjoying their efforts to fight back and their discomfort at having his illegitimate son on the household staff. While the legitimate heirs are fuming upstairs, the illegitimate one is smoldering downstairs.

Reginald Hill

A Clubbable Woman
London: Collins, 1970.
Woodstock, Vt.: Foul Play Press, 1984.

Superintendent Andrew Dalziel and Sergeant Peter Pascoe

Sam Connon has a rough rugby game on Saturday afternoon and barely makes it home in time to pass out for several hours. When he awakens, he discovers his wife dead in the living room.

An Advancement of Learning
London: Collins, 1971.
Woodstock, Vt.: Foul Play Press, 1985.

Superintendent Andrew Dalziel and Sergeant Peter Pascoe

The students and faculty of a women's teacher-training school are still trying to adjust to their new incarnation as a coed college. These academic groves resonate with accusations of sexual harassment, political maneuvering, and murder. Beneath the veneer of educated men and women lie rabble-rousers, voyeurs, and a murderer.

Ruling Passion
London: Collins, 1973.
New York: Harper, 1977.

Superintendent Andrew Dalziel and Sergeant Peter Pascoe

Sergeant Pascoe hasn't seen the friends of his youth for five years and is looking forward to a visit with them in a village in Oxfordshire. When he arrives, however, he finds three of his friends dead and a fourth missing. Unable to accept his surviving friend as a suspect, Pascoe searches for the real murderer, though he has no official standing in the investigation.

An April Shroud
London: Collins, 1975.
Woodstock, Vt.: Foul Play Press, 1986.

Superintendent Andrew Dalziel and Inspector Peter Pascoe

Dalziel's vacation in the countryside is cut short by a flood. Stranded on a
back road, he gets a ride in a punt that is ferrying a funeral party back
home. Dalziel goes with them, listening to their conflicting stories about
how the man of the house died.

A Pinch of Snuff
London: Collins, 1978.
New York: Harper, 1978.

Superintendent Andrew Dalziel and Inspector Peter Pascoe

A dentist who belongs to a private club that shows porno movies is convinced
that the beating he saw on the movie screen was real. When the police
investigate, however, they can find no evidence that the actress was injured.
They are ready to drop the case when the club owner is attacked and beaten
and the club almost destroyed by fire.

A Killing Kindness
London: Collins, 1980.
New York: Pantheon, 1981.

Superintendent Andrew Dalziel and Inspector Peter Pascoe

Three women are murdered by a man who explains his acts by calling the
police and quoting Shakespeare. The women are from different parts of the
country and have nothing in common. Even the psychics among the Gypsies
have no suggestions for solving the murders.

Deadheads
London: Collins, 1983.

Dead-Heads
New York: Macmillan, 1984.

Superintendent Andrew Dalziel and Inspector Peter Pascoe

A young accountant develops a passion for roses, and all other interests in life come second to his garden. Yet his career seems as carefully controlled as his garden, and people on the rung above him on the career ladder seem to die just when he is ready to take the next step up. Only one man in the firm wonders if the accountant is pruning more than roses.

Exit Lines
London: Collins, 1984.
New York: Macmillan, 1985.

Superintendent Andrew Dalziel and Inspector Peter Pascoe

On a stormy November night, three old men die unexpectedly in different ways and different areas, but each dies saying a last word that makes no sense. None of the deaths is considered remarkable until a young doctor loudly insists that the apparent driver of the car involved in the last death take a breathalyzer test. The man is Superintendent Dalziel, and he says a friend was driving his car.

Fell of Dark
London: Collins, 1971.

Henry Bentink is taking a hiking trip in the Lake District with his friend Peter to help him recover from an illness. The holiday turns into a nightmare when the two men are arrested for the murder of two young women hikers. Henry escapes from the local authorities and begins an odyssey of flight in the mountains to prove his innocence.

A Fairly Dangerous Thing
London: Collins, 1972.
Woodstock, Vt.: Foul Play Press, 1983.

Schoolteacher Joe Askern relieves the tedium of his life with fantasy, but
his wandering imagination leads him into conflict with the father of one of
his students. Although Joe would rather have nothing to do with father
and son, the father begins to imagine a use for Joe.

A Very Good Hater: A Tale of Revenge
London: Collins, 1974.
Woodstock, Vt.: Foul Play Press, 1982.

Two army buddies who have met for a reunion in London think they have
seen a former German military officer. Intrigued, one of the men follows
the suspect until the suspect corners him and demands to know what he is
up to. The ex-soldier has his revenge, but the consequences are beyond anything he could have anticipated.

Another Death in Venice*
London: Collins, 1976.

The Spy's Wife
London: Collins, 1980.
New York: Pantheon, 1980.

On an ordinary morning, Molly Keatley's husband rushes out of the house
with a small suitcase. A few minutes later a man claiming to be a kind of
policeman arrives and searches the house. Then another man arrives and
informs Molly that her husband was a Russian spy who has now fled the
country. Questioned by government agents and badgered by the press, Molly
tries to sort out the myth and reality of her life.

Who Guards a Prince?
London: Collins, 1982.

Who Guards the Prince?
New York: Pantheon, 1982.

A British journalist dies in a fire in his cottage, and a doctor finds evidence of a ritual murder on a beach not far away. Both obviously call for further investigation, but the police find themselves blocked at every step. Persevering, the police follow the clues to the seats of power in Britain and the United States.

Traitor's Blood
London: Collins, 1983.
Woodstock, Vt.: Foul Play Press, 1986.

Lem Swift is given six months to live, and must finish his life in exile, never seeing his daughter again. Knowing that a return to England can cost him what little of life and freedom he has left, he returns anyway to see his daughter, is captured by the Special Branch, and offered a deal: assassinate a designated target and then see his daughter, or spend his remaining time in prison. The target is Lem's father, who is also returning to England from exile in the USSR.

John Buxton Hilton

The Quiet Stranger
London: Collins, 1985.
New York: St. Martin, 1985.

Constable Thomas Brunt

George Ludlam looks like any other successful artisan, but his arrival in Litton village in 1872 distresses old men and worries the constable. And rightly so, for George has returned to the village where he worked as a child and where he almost died from the beatings he received at the hands of the overseers at the mill. George's return reminds the villagers of the cruelty and injustice that was always a part of their lives many years ago.

Gamekeeper's Gallows
London: Macmillan, 1976.
New York: St. Martin, 1977.

Sergeant Thomas Brunt

Amy Harrington has disappeared from the mansion where she worked as a maid, and her employer claims she left with some of his property. Her parents are certain something has happened to her. Amy disappeared somewhere in the High Peak area, a collection of villages, farms, and mines untouched by the modern Victorian thought of 1875, isolated from the rest of the country by choice as much as by circumstance.

Dead-Nettle
London: Macmillan, 1977.
New York: St. Martin, 1977.

Inspector Thomas Brunt

In late 1904 Frank Lomas comes to the mining village of Margreave with only one purpose: to mine Dead-Nettle Drift, despite the skepticism of some and the outright hostility of others. Gradually the villagers come to tolerate if not respect him. Then the major figures of his past appear: a former fellow soldier and Hetty Wilson. Before long, Hetty is dead.

Rescue from the Rose
London: Macmillan, 1976.
New York: St. Martin, 1976.

Inspector Thomas Brunt

In the 1910s Miriam Bennett could have almost any man she wantet. After making her choice, she grows bored with married life and returns to the Rose, where she once worked as a barmaid. Sued for divorce and alimony, her husband refuses to pay and is sent to prison, where he dies. Later, on that day, Miriam is murdered.

Mr Fred
London: Collins, 1983.
New York: St. Martin, 1983.

Inspector Thomas Brunt

Kathy Hollinshead looks back on her childhood on a poor farm before World
War I to unravel a mystery that plagued her family for years. Aware that
the local police inspector, Thomas Brunt, had not caught the guilty party
he originally pursued, Kathy and her husband finally find a reason for her
family's sadness.

Some Run Crooked
London: Macmillan, 1978.
New York: St. Martin, 1978.

Inspector Simon Kenworthy

In 1977 Peak Forest is the site of a church with special privileges: couples
can marry in the church after they establish a fifteen-day residency. The
Church has fought this and now the practice, though legal, is almost
forgotten--until Julie Wimpole arrives to stay for fifteen days. Near the
end of her stay she is murdered in a manner that copies a murder committed
there almost twenty years earlier and another committed almost two hundred
years earlier. The solution to all three lies in 1957.

Death in Midwinter
London: Cassell, 1969.
New York: Walker, 1969.

Inspector Simon Kenworthy

When old Thomas John dies, his death is expected and his relatives gather
quickly. Two days later, the old man's heir is murdered and the money he
left is gone. The police look first to the heirs and then to a land development program undertaken fifty years ago.

Death of an Alderman
London: Cassell, 1968.
New York: Walker, 1968.

Superintendent Simon Kenworthy

Alderman Barson has risen from his working-class roots to a prominent position in his community, and his murder late one evening shocks the city. The official remembrance of him is kind, but underneath people scramble to limit the impact of his death and quietly sneer at the published eulogies.

Hangman's Tide
London: Macmillan, 1975.
New York: St. Martin, 1975.

Superintendent Simon Kenworthy

Cynthia Merridew has spent most of her adult life tracking down the legends and superstitions of Norfolk, but now she has touched on an old tale too sensitive for those who remember the original participants. She is found hanged according to the form of a local execution held more than three hundred years ago. The key to her murder, however, lies in a romance of the 1920s.

No Birds Sang
London: Macmillan, 1975.
New York: St. Martin, 1976.

Superintendent Simon Kenworthy

The first time Edward Milner came back to look at the deserted village, the army merely kicked him out. But this time he interrupts shooting practice and a soldier dies. No one can explain why a hard-working man would want to haunt two old hamlets taken over by the army during the war. The police finally conclude that he is looking for someone but he does not know who that person is.

The Anathema Stone
London: Collins, 1980.
New York: St. Martin, 1980.

Superintendent Simon Kenworthy

Kenworthy and his wife choose the village of Spentlow for their vacation, arriving just in time to participate in the preparations for the centenary celebration for the work of the Reverend Mr. Grabbitas. For some of the villagers this is the time to heat up family feuds and settle old scores according to folk traditions.

Playground of Death
London: Collins, 1981.
New York: St. Martin, 1981.

Superintendent Simon Kenworthy

The former mayor of a Lancashire mill town is found holding a gun and standing over his wife's dead body. He is charged and held in jail, where he begins to write his autobiography. While on his way to a court hearing, he is shot and killed, leaving the police only his memoirs to point to the murderer.

Surrender Value
London: Collins, 1981.
New York: St. Martin, 1981.

Simon Kenworthy

On a quiet morning of an ordinary day, teacher John Everard disappears, having put his papers in order for his wife. On the same day, Susan Shires, a student at Everard's college, also disappears, and many assume they have run away together. The cold Mrs. Everard wants her husband back, though she seems ample reason for his flight.

The Green Frontier
London: Collins, 1981.
New York: St. Martin, 1981.

Simon Kenworthy

A German Lutheran minister brought to Britain to appear on a television
show about World War II is arrested for shoplifting in the West End of
London. He pleads guilty, asks that a certain inspector take the case, and
is soon released. Some time later he is found dead in the English countryside.

The Sunset Law
London: Collins, 1982.
New York: St. Martin, 1982.

Simon Kenworthy

Kenworthy agrees to visit his daughter and her husband in the United States
to help him get over his forced retirement from Scotland Yard. The visit
goes badly, however; there is tension between the young people. Then the
son-in-law is forced to resign from the Florida State Police, and Kenworthy
gives way to his dislike of Peter. Later, he reconsiders Peter's position.

The Asking Price
London: Collins, 1983.
New York: St. Martin, 1983.

Simon Kenworthy

On a brisk March morning, armed men enter a village shop and kidnap everyone inside. A strange demand is made, and some time later all of the victims
are released, except one. Then the parish council of a Norfolk village is
kidnapped, and again the price is surprising. By the time the criminals kidnap a group of women from Lancashire, the police suspect what is going
on.

Corridors of Guilt
London: Collins, 1984.
New York: St. Martin, 1984.

Simon Kenworthy

Several civil servants have set up an administrative unit in Northern
Lincolnshire, called the Duchy of Axholme, to deal with lingering questions
of land title. Then the duchy takes on a life of its own. The perfect dump-
ing ground for slack, recalcitrant, rebellious, incompetent bureaucrats, the
duchy is inordinately interested in civil unrest and anarchic behavior, even
going so far as to develop a strategy in case of civil crisis.

The Hobbema Prospect
London: Collins, 1984.
New York: St. Martin, 1984.

Simon Kenworthy

Anne Cassey's mother commits suicide during Anne's honeymoon, but Anne
refuses to believe her mother would do this. As she delves into her mother's
life she is stumped by the lack of a birth certificate. Searching for this
leads her to discoveries about her childhood, during which her mother
changed the family name every time they moved.

Passion in the Peak
London: Collins, 1985.
New York: St. Martin, 1985.

Simon Kenworthy

Lord Furnival has gambled that Peak Low can be promoted as the festival
center of England, by backing a large performance in every way necessary.
Someone else, however, disagrees, and plagues the troupe with cruel practical
jokes; these culminate in a murder presented as a commentary on the nature
of the festival.

Kenneth Hopkins*

The Girl Who Died
London: Macdonald, 1955.

Gerald Lee

Just before Ringwood Castle is to open for the tourist season, Gerry Lee, a newspaper reporter, finds the body of a nude woman in the library, dead apparently less than an hour. She holds in her hand a ring, which Gerry had purchased only days earlier but not for her. The more Gerry tries to help the police, the more he uncovers incriminating evidence.

She Died Because...
London: Macdonald, 1957.
New York: Holt, 1964.

Dr. William Blow and Prof. Gideon Manciple

Dr. Blow stops working because he is hungry, and this is confusing because his housekeeper, Mrs. Sollihull, is so very reliable. Unfortunately, Mrs. Sollihull is lying dead in her room, and Dr. Blow, after rousing Professor Manciple to make him a sandwich, informs the police and prepares to help them in their investigation.

Dead against My Principles
London: Macdonald, 1960.
New York: Holt, 1962.

Dr. William Blow and Prof. Gideon Manciple

A recluse and former London financier dies and the police call in Dr. Blow to make the identification. Dr. Blow is ready to do so with alacrity, but, as he points out, his late friend had an appendix scar and this man has none. This problem sends Blow and Manciple to a tattooist, who proudly displays photos of sample scars, and then to a castle on the Isle of Wight, home of the dead recluse.

Body Blow
London: Macdonald, 1962.
New York: Holt, 1962.

Dr. William Blow and Prof. Gideon Manciple

Dr. Blow responds calmly and thoughtfully to the discovery of a woman's body in a case he thought would contain a large number of books he recently bought. With the help of Professor Manciple, Blow sets out to recover his books and return the woman's body.

S.B. Hough*

Dear Daughter Dead
London: Gollancz, 1965.
New York: Walker, 1966.

Inspector John Brentford

A young girl is found strangled on the beach, and the police turn to nearby homes to identify her. They have little trouble finding out who she is, but in the process they uncover a web of relationships among the four families on an enclosed private estate near the beach.

Sweet Sister Seduced
London: Gollancz, 1968.
New York: Perennial, 1983.

Inspector John Brentford

A woman drowns in a river and her death is considered an accident until a minister comes forward and insists she was drowned by her husband. Forced to investigate with no real evidence, Inspector Brentford listens to the husband narrate the story of his life, including his marriage. At the end Brentford must decide if the husband did in fact murder his wife.

The Primitives
London: Hodder, 1954.

In 1916 Helen Rudge cannot foresee what her twins, Elizabeth and Percy, will become, and that is a blessing. For the boy and girl grow up in the pleasant town of Longbarrow to commit a crime that shocks everyone.

Mission in Guemo
London: Hodder, 1953.
New York: Walker, 1964.

There were many casualties of World War II, and among the Nazis several went to Guemo to work on that country's science program, or so is the rumor. The British diplomats take the rumor seriously when a British singer decides to go to a utopia in the interior with her boyfriend. She writes to a contact that all is well and lovely, but the envelope tells a different story.

The Bronze Perseus
London: Secker, 1959.
New York: Walker, 1962.

The Tender Killer
New York: Avon, 1963.

Harold Clemens is an intelligent, solitary, and industrious young man traveling for his employer when he is arrested and charged with the rape of a school-teacher. Though innocent, he is convicted and sentenced. When he is released five years later, he has a plan to secure a reasonable if not luxurious future, which he carries out after meticulous planning. In the final stage of his plan he encounters the only factor he forgot to consider--the woman who accused him--and modifies his plan accordingly.

Fear Fortune, Father
London: Gollancz, 1974.

Dalby Pearson has struggled for a year to maintain his self-respect while he searches for work and lives on the meager sums the government gives him and his wife. Trapped by his own weakness, he lies to his wife, telling her he has found a job. Now he must go out in the evening; so he begins a new line of work during those hours: burglary.

P.M. Hubbard

Flush as May
London: Joseph, 1963.
New York: London House, 1963.

An Oxford student takes an early morning walk through village fields during her vacation and comes upon a neatly dressed corpse. She quite naturally informs the village constable and brings him back to the field, but the corpse is gone. Even worse, the constable does not seem at all interested. The student sets out to find someone who is.

Picture of Millie
London: Joseph, 1964.
New York: London House, 1964.

Everyone seems to have a different picture of Millie, the middle-aged woman who easily attracts men and happily goes off with them, leaving her husband to his own interests. When she is found floating in the ocean, the resort town is shaken, and people must come to grips with her death. To the surprise of many, the most innocent liked her best and the oldest knew her best.

A Hive of Glass
London: Joseph, 1965.
New York: Atheneum, 1965.

The antiques world is shaken by the discovery of a sixteenth-century tazza, but the collector who announces his discovery dies of natural causes, leaving the antiques world ignorant and curious. Johnnie Slade, who finds Mr. Levinson dead in his home, decides to trace the tazza and ends up in a small West Country town. But he is not the only one hoping to find Levinson's discovery.

The Holm Oaks
London: Joseph, 1965.
New York: Atheneum, 1966.

Jake Haddon's uncle leaves him a house on an isolated road along the coast, and he and his wife, Elizabeth, decide to give it a try for a few months. Elizabeth instantly loves it for the birds nearby; Jake is entranced by their only neighbor, Carol Wainwright, though put off by her husband; and Jake's sister-in-law warns him that in six months he'll be trapped there.

The Tower
London: Bles, 1968.
New York: Atheneum, 1967.

Making an unexpected stopover in the village of Coyle, John Smith is intrigued by a young woman who perches on tree stumps and fixes cars. There is also the man who moves discreetly through the woods. Coyle has other oddities: a vicar who wins the loyalty of some and the enmity of others in his devotion to the church bells, a beautiful widow of the squire now married to his land agent, and a retired gentleman cast in the role of Antichrist by the vicar.

The Custom of the Country
London: Bles, 1969.

The Country of Again
New York: Atheneum, 1968.

Jim Gilruth, formerly of the Indian civil service and now a novelist, accepts an assignment to research the attitudes of a community to industrial development in an area of Pakistan. The journey takes him back twenty years to an old murder case and the consequences of his own decisions.

Cold Waters
London: Bles, 1970.
New York: Atheneum, 1969.

On an impulse, Mr. Giffard, an official of a trade association, accepts an offer to escape his stifling job and serve as a handyman-sailor to a middle-aged couple living on an island. By taking this job, he finally turns his back on the advice of an old friend: take the safe road.

High Tide
London: Macmillan, 1971.
New York: Atheneum, 1970.

Released from prison after serving four years, Peter Curtis is enjoying his
freedom by driving through southern England to the coast. He soon realizes
he is not traveling alone, however. When he confronts the follower, Curtis
learns that not everyone is willing to let the past die and he must go back
four years to unravel a mystery he has only now discovered.

The Dancing Man
London: Macmillan, 1971.
New York: Atheneum, 1971.

Mark Hawkins, engineer, doesn't learn about the death of his brother, Dick,
a prehistory archaeologist, until he returns from an extended trip abroad.
His brother's death in a climbing accident doesn't disturb him until he travels
to Wales to collect Dick's things, left with the people he was visiting. They
are a strange family: an austere medievalist-archaeologist and his sister and
the man's wife, who is nervous, frightened, and ignored by her husband.

The Whisper in the Glen
London: Macmillan, 1972.
New York: Atheneum, 1972.

A new job in a school in Scotland brings hope to Richard Wychett and worry
to his wife, Kate, who remembers her father's tale of life in the Highlands.
Unwittingly, Kate becomes the catalyst among a small group of people who
need to confront old wounds and old wrongs.

A Rooted Sorrow
London: Macmillan, 1973.
New York: Atheneum, 1973.

Michael Hurst returns after five years to a small cottage to confront himself
and his past, but this is harder than he expects, for his past is gone. The
woman who drove him away is now married to the parson, the adolescent girl
is a poised secretary, her distraught mother now pleasant and unworried.
But no one has forgotten the old passions, and Michael finds again the unfinished questions of five years ago.

A Thirsty Evil
London: Macmillan, 1974.
New York: Atheneum, 1974.

Ian Mackellar is not so prosaic as to believe in love at first sight, but he
is so entranced by a woman he meets at a party given by his publisher that
he traces her to a farm in the country. Gradually he becomes entangled in
her life managing the family farm and caring for her younger brother and
sister. This seems normal enough until the brother's disturbing mental illness
makes itself known.

The Graveyard
London: Macmillan, 1975.
New York: Atheneum, 1975.

In the harsh and empty world of the Highlands, where few people means
few secrets, there is one secret known to only two or three. When a solitary
resident of the glen sees a strange young woman purposefully examining an
old graveyard and then two men doing the same, he becomes part of a dangerous quest in a now dangerous land.

The Causeway
London: Macmillan, 1976.
New York: Doubleday, 1978.

A sailing accident leaves Peter Grant stranded on a deserted island off the
coast of Scotland until he is found a few hours later by a man who has
walked across the causeway from the mainland. Barlow offers Grant shelter
and help with his boat in the morning, but keeps a close eye on his guest
in his home. When Grant leaves and returns to his own home, his thoughts
keep returning to the enigmatic Mrs. Barlow and the wind-swept coast.

The Quiet River
London: Macmillan, 1978.
New York: Doubleday, 1978.

Helen Anderson sets aside her own reservations when her husband decides
to rent a house in the country. Steve feels this is just the spot for a successful historical novelist, but Helen looks to the silent river, the silent vil-

lagers, and the long-empty house. The challenge of the river ultimately transforms both Helen and her husband.

Kill Claudio
London: Macmillan, 1979.
New York: Doubleday, 1979.

Ben Selby chases a wounded rabbit into the brush and finds a corpse, which he duly reports to the police. Only after some time passes does he realize he knew the dead man, Peter Gaston, a man Ben worked with many years ago on secret missions. For Selby, this changes everything. Gaston came out of a quiet retirement to reach Selby, also in retirement, and now he must find the person to whom this is a threat.

Fergus Hume*

The Mystery of a Hansom Cab
Melbourne: Kemp, 1886.
London: Hansom Cab Company, 1886.
New York: Munro, 1888.
Rev. ed. London: Jarrolds, 1896.

A man in evening dress who appears to be drunk is helped into a cab late one night by a friend. The friend rides a short distance, then alights, and directs the driver to continue with the other man. When the driver seeks further directions, he finds the remaining passenger dead, reeking of chloroform. This was the first international best-selling crime novel.

Alan Hunter

Gently Does It
London: Cassell, 1955.
New York: Rinehart, 1955.

Inspector George Gently

A successful timber merchant is found stabbed to death in front of an empty safe in his home, less than an hour after an argument with the son he disowned two years ago. The police are convinced that the son is the murderer and his motive money, though he has known for two years he would get nothing from his father's estate.

Gently by the Shore
London: Cassell, 1956.
New York: Rinehart, 1956.

Inspector George Gently

A simple-minded village boy finds a naked body on the beach, stabbed to death and covered with other wounds. There are no clothes and no one comes forward to identify the man. The police are ready to give up when Inspector Gently listens again, very carefully, to what the boy has to say.

Landed Gently
London: Cassell, 1957.
New York: British Book Service, 1957.

Inspector George Gently

A peer of the realm has retired from public life to nurture a school of tapestry weaving on his family estate. All seems to run smoothly until a loud young American begins to take classes. Though likable, the boy is clearly an outsider and determined to get what he wants.

Gently down the Stream
London: Cassell, 1957.
New York: Roy, 1960.

Inspector George Gently

The holiday peace of the Norfolk Broads is broken by the discovery of a rented yacht burned to the water line. The man on board is clearly dead, but not from the fire. The police have plenty of clues, far too many in fact to make a coherent case against a single person.

Gently through the Mill
London: Cassell, 1958.

In: **Gently in an Omnibus**
New York: St. Martin, 1971.

Inspector George Gently

Easter Sunday is a busy time for the baker in Lynton because he likes his Easter buns to be fresh. This year he has an even more trying experience than usual when he finds a corpse in a flour hopper. To make matters even more confusing, the dead man is a petty criminal who hangs around race tracks, and there are no race courses near and no crime in Lynton.

Gently in the Sun
London: Cassell, 1959.
New York: Berkley, 1964.

Inspector George Gently

Rachel Campion is a beautiful woman, even in death when a poacher finds her on the beach when he is returning from his night's work. She is beautiful enough to upset most of the wives in Hiverton, but she is not careless enough to offend her lover and boss, a London businessman, according to those who watched her--and there were many who did.

Gently with the Painters
London: Cassell, 1960.
New York: Macmillan, 1976.

Superintendent George Gently

A young woman is stabbed to death in a parking lot after leaving the monthly meeting of the Palette Group, a society of local artists. When the police begin to investigate, they find an odd assortment of artists but no one who can be linked to her death or who could even be said to care about the victim one way or the other.

Gently Go Man
London: Cassell, 1961.
New York: Berkley, 1964.

Superintendent George Gently

On a road known for its abruptly ending straightaway, a motorcycle crashes, killing the driver and injuring the rider. This is no accident, though it might be, and the police enter the world of the beat generation in provincial England, looking for a killer with a purpose.

Gently to the Summit
London: Cassell, 1961.
New York: Berkley, 1965.

Superintendent George Gently

The plans for the next expedition of the Everest Club are interrupted by the appearance of a man who was lost on Mt. Everest twenty-two years ago. Finally able to return from Tibet, Reginald Kincaid searches for his wife. Other climbers who knew Kincaid those many years ago insist that the man is an impostor. Then the man who climbed with Kincaid in 1937 falls to his death during a climb in Wales after filing a lawsuit against the man claiming to be Kincaid.

Gently Where the Roads Go
London: Cassell, 1962.

In: **Gently in Another Omnibus**
New York: St. Martin, 1972.

Superintendent George Gently

A Polish refugee decides to go silently and quickly to America, but before he can do so his body is found riddled with bullets in a van on a major highway. The police begin to hunt the murderer on the assumption that the Pole was killed for a crime committed during the war or for refusing to take orders from his superiors in a spy network.

Gently Floating
London: Cassell, 1963.
New York: Berkley, 1964.

Superintendent George Gently

Harry French has built his boatyard into a thriving concern, catering primarily to seasonal sailors, but the cost has been high. His son despises him, his employees don't care for him, and the owners of the only other boatyard in the area resent him. When he is drowned in the river, the police have a large number of suspects.

Gently Sahib
London: Cassell, 1964.

Superintendent George Gently

The bustle of a Saturday morning turns into chaos when a tiger is seen roaming through Abbotsham. The police finally shoot it, in the men's public lavatory, and the event passes into folklore--until a year later when the police find a body mauled by a tiger. The body is neatly buried in a garden.

Gently with the Ladies
London: Cassell, 1965.
New York: Macmillan, 1974.

Superintendent George Gently

Clytie Fazakerly, rich and in love with a woman friend, threatens to cut
off her husband's allowance if he continues to see his girlfriend. Not long
after the argument Clytie is found dead and the husband is gone. He is
the obvious suspect, but the women connected to the case would seem to
have equally strong motives. John Fazakerly's defense, when caught, is
that he certainly is a social parasite and lived on his wife, and that type
of man is definitely not a murderer.

Gently Continental*
London: Cassell, 1967.

Superintendent George Gently

Gently North-West
London: Cassell, 1967.

Gently in the Highlands
New York: Macmillan, 1975.

Superintendent George Gently

Donnie Dunglass buys an old Scottish estate and settles down to the life of
a laird, even joining the lairds' organization for Home Rule. Then he is
found dead on a mountain, stabbed by a traditional Scottish dagger not long
after he had refused to vote with his fellow lairds to train young men in
guerrilla warfare.

Gently Coloured*
London: Cassell, 1969.

Superintendent George Gently

Gently with the Innocents
London: Cassell, 1970.
New York: Macmillan, 1970.

Superintendent George Gently

An old recluse dies from a fall down a flight of stairs, leaving nothing for
his nephew but a dilapidated Elizabethan mansion. The police are reluctant
to accept this as an accidental death but can find no motive for murder.
The nephew, on the other hand, is certain his uncle was murdered for a
hoard of gold coins hidden in the old house.

Gently at a Gallop*
London: Cassell, 1971.

Superintendent George Gently

Vivienne--Gently Where She Lay*
London: Cassell, 1972.

Superintendent George Gently

Gently French*
London: Cassell, 1973.

Superintendent George Gently

Gently in Trees
London: Cassell, 1974.

Gently through the Woods
New York: Macmillan, 1975.

Superintendent George Gently

Success hasn't brought director Adrian Stoll much to be happy about: his live-in girlfriend is supporting him; his new actress-lover is using him to get ahead; her father has swindled him of a large sum of money; and his ex-wife and son are far away in America. When the police find his body, they wonder if he was murdered or committed suicide.

Gently with Love
London: Cassell, 1975.

Superintendent George Gently

The daughter of a dead policeman runs away on the evening before her wedding, telling no one where she is going. Her fiancé takes it hard and learns only months later that she has sought refuge in Scotland with her paternal grandparents. When he learns that she may be about to marry another man, he rushes to her and is soon charged with assault, which may be upgraded to murder.

Gently Where the Birds Are
London: Cassell, 1976.

Superintendent George Gently

A civic-minded person sends the police the photograph of a dead body in a wood, leaving the police to figure out where it is. When they do locate the spot, the body is gone. Now they must find the evidence of the crime as well as the criminal.

Gently Instrumental
London: Cassell, 1977.

Superintendent George Gently

The amateur Shinglebourne art and music festival is becoming known because of the work of a local composer, Walt Hozeley, but all this may be lost. Walt's live-in lover, Terence Virtue, also a musician, has taken a new lover and threatens to disrupt the performance by walking out on the quartet.

Gently to a Sleep*
London: Cassell, 1978.

Superintendent George Gently

The Honfleur Decision
London: Constable, 1980.
New York: Walker, 1981.

Superintendent George Gently

Gently's vacation is off to a messy start when a man dumps him into the harbor. While he is drying off in a pub, a man tries to shoot him and escapes. The police want to dismiss both incidents as coincidence until there is a third attempt on Gently's life. Yet, as Gently explains, it is improbable that an English criminal would follow him to France in order to get revenge.

The Scottish Decision
London: Constable, 1980.
New York: Walker, 1981.

Superintendent George Gently

Gently has just completed an important case in France, protecting in part a French businessman, but to no avail, for the man has just been kidnapped by terrorists. The French and British authorities have traced the terrorists to Scotland, and although they have no hope of saving Mr. Barentin, they have high hopes of wiping out the terrorists when they finally track them down in the Highlands.

Death on the Heath
London: Constable, 1981.
New York: Walker, 1982.

Superintendent George Gently

On the heath near a placid coastal village a successful businessman is found dead, wearing yachting clothes and murdered by an unidentified weapon. The only clue points directly to the man's wife and her lover, but the police can't help noticing a daughter who acts strangely and a business partner who has made unusual gains in the last year.

Gently between Tides
London: Constable, 1982.
New York: Walker, 1983.

Superintendent George Gently

From out of the mist comes a dinghy carrying Hannah Stoven, strangled and left to drift on the river. As the police look into the life of the aloof Czech-born daughter of a famous violinist, they find a list of friends who were drawn to her though, they insist, they were not close to her.

Amorous Leander
London: Constable, 1983.

Death on the Broadlands
New York: Walker, 1984.

Superintendent George Gently

Stella Rushton, a writer, falls passionately in love and is then jilted. Moving to a cottage on a lake in Norfolk, she tries to recover and reorder her life. Her landlord, Simon, a successful writer, includes her in his house party of theater people, suggesting that she become one of their group. Included in the group is Simon's nephew, a college student who is smitten with Stella and follows her around.

The Unhung Man
London: Constable, 1984.

The Unhanged Man
New York: Walker, 1984.

Superintendent George Gently

Arthur Pewsey, a former judge known for his harsh sentences, dies from a gunshot wound. The police arrest a poacher as the most likely suspect, but their easy case is lost when a police expert finds a fingerprint at the scene that belongs to a man whom the judge sentenced to hang eighteen years ago.

Francis Iles

Malice Aforethought
London: Gollancz, 1931.
New York: Harper, 1931.

Once he decides to murder his wife, Dr. Bickleigh takes a new and firmer hold on life and what he wants out of it. Murder becomes merely the solution to a problem, and he plans his wife's murder meticulously. The interest lies, not in figuring out who did it, but in watching the murderer and then the closing in of the law.

Before the Fact
London: Gollancz, 1932.
Rev. ed. London: Pan, 1958.
New York: Doubleday, 1932.

Lina Aysgarth gradually comes to the realization that she is married to a murderer and that she has already made the choices that will determine her fate. This is the classic study of the character of a murderer as it evolves and becomes manifest.

As for the Woman*
London: Jarrolds, 1939.
New York: Doubleday, 1939.

Michael Innes

Death at the President's Lodging
London: Gollancz, 1936.

Seven Suspects
New York: Dodd, Mead, 1937.

Inspector John Appleby

In an old English university, someone murders the president. Murder by itself would be bad enough, but the murderer decorated the room of the murder with skulls and bones and then escaped from a locked quadrangle, to which only the fellows had keys. Somewhere among the erudite but eccentric dons is a murderer with a sense of theater.

Hamlet, Revenge!
London: Gollancz, 1937.
New York: Dodd, Mead, 1937.

Inspector John Appleby

The duchess of Horton is known for her grand events, but this time she may have outdone herself: a complete amateur production of Hamlet as the heart of a house party. The guests come prepared to learn their parts, but one member of the party keeps dropping notes with lines from other plays by the Bard. The party and play go completely off track when one of the players is murdered.

Lament for a Maker
London: Gollancz, 1938.
New York: Dodd, Mead, 1938.

Inspector John Appleby

Ranald Guthrie is a laird in the Highlands who has lingered on from another time. When he dies suddenly on Christmas Eve, no one in the village nearby mourns him. Finding the murderer requires penetrating the wiles and ways of Highland folk and unexpected guests from America.

Stop Press
London: Gollancz, 1939.

The Spider Strikes
New York: Dodd, Mead, 1939.

Inspector John Appleby

Authors often come to loathe their creations, but Mr. Richard Eliot, creator of the Spider, has an even greater problem. The rogue-turned-detective seems to have stepped out of fiction and into reality, burgling a neighbor's home, sending clues to the police, and calling his creator. On top of that, Eliot's manuscripts seem to be rewriting themselves in the files over night.

There Came Both Mist and Snow
London: Gollancz, 1940.

A Comedy of Terrors
New York: Dodd, Mead, 1940.

Inspector John Appleby

The various cousins of the Roper family gather at the family home for Christmas and surprises: the end of a quarrel between uncle and nephew, a surprise guest for a young niece, unexpected houseguests, and murder. There is far too much opportunity for murder, since several cousins wander about with pistols in preparation for a new pastime--target shooting.

The Weight of the Evidence
London: Gollancz, 1944.
New York: Dodd, Mead, 1943.

Inspector John Appleby

Professor Pluckrose is struck and killed by a meteorite while sitting in the courtyard in a deck chair. The meteorite did not fall from the heavens, however; it fell from the roof of a nearby building. This unlikely mode of murder prompts the pompous colleagues of the late professor to speculate endlessly on motives for and methods of murder.

Appleby's End
London: Gollancz, 1945.
New York: Dodd, Mead, 1945.

Inspector John Appleby

A misstep in travel plans casts John Appleby into the company of the Ravens for the night. A coach ride with Judith Raven turns into a sail down a river, an interlude in a haystack, and a scramble through the snow before they come upon a corpse and Long Dream Manor. This death comes disconcertingly soon after two other tragedies that appear to have been predicted in the novels of a Raven long dead. Judith Raven, of course, becomes Mrs. Appleby ultimately.

The Secret Vanguard
London: Gollancz, 1940.
New York: Dodd, Mead, 1941.

Inspector John Appleby

In 1939 a retiring middle-aged poet is found shot to death in his garden, having spent his last days as quietly as all his others. A young woman disappears at a train station in Scotland. The only element comparable in these events is that both people corrected the poetic recitation of fellow travelers just before their respective calamities.

Appleby on Ararat
London: Gollancz, 1941.
New York: Dodd, Mead, 1945.

Inspector John Appleby

The tourists in the café of a cruise ship are suddenly drifting on open sea after their ship is torpedoed. When they land on an apparently deserted island, they await rescuers from the sea. Then one of their number is murdered, and another of them comes upon other inhabitants of the island, who are not at all what the castaways expected.

The Daffodil Affair
London: Gollancz, 1942.
New York: Dodd, Mead, 1942.

Inspector John Appleby

Scotland Yard has an unusual problem: someone has stolen a half-witted horse. In another part of the country someone has abducted a half-witted girl, and now a crazy house is missing. The pursuit of the criminals leads Appleby to an island for scientific experiments in South America.

A Night of Errors
London: Gollancz, 1948.
New York: Dodd, Mead, 1947.

Inspector John Appleby

Sir Romeo Dromio decides to end the curse on his family fortunes brought on by the birth of triplets in every generation by killing two of the three boys born to him. He soon dies insane, and forty years later the only son in his family is burned to death in his library. Left are his mother, who has drifted through her life, and an adopted sister, meant to fill the void in Lady Dromio's life after she got a good look at her son's emerging character.

Operation Pax
London: Gollancz, 1951.

The Paper Thunderbolt
New York: Dodd, Mead, 1951.

Sir John Appleby

Routh is a small-time con artist who finally discovers his limits: he accosts a woman who beats him up, and he is tricked into a private clinic where he is almost murdered. Fleeing, he escapes with the help of strangers met during his flight, and finally lands in Oxford. He is not yet safe, but at least he gains an ally in his fight to escape the scientists at Milton Manor in Milton Porcorum.

A Private View
London: Gollancz, 1952.

One-Man Show
New York: Dodd, Mead, 1952.

Murder Is an Art
Avon, 1959.

Sir John Appleby and Inspector Thomas Cadover

Sir John Appleby is persuaded by his wife to attend a gallery show of the work of a promising young painter. Unfortunately, the artist was murdered only a few days earlier and the police have no idea who did it. To make matters worse, one of the paintings is stolen from the exhibition only moments after Sir John inspects it.

Appleby Plays Chicken
London: Gollancz, 1957.

Death on a Quiet Day
New York: Dodd, Mead, 1957.

Sir John Appleby

A group of Oxford students and their tutor are staying at a pub at Dartmoor. On a solitary hike through the hills, one of them finds a man just shot. What follows is more adventure than the young man wants, but soon he and his friends have eagerly thrown themselves into the role of Appleby's assistants.

The Long Farewell
London: Gollancz, 1958.
New York: Dodd, Mead, 1958.

Sir John Appleby

Sir John spends a delightful evening in Italy with a scholar-friend known for his brilliance and zest in all he does. Sir John is therefore surprised to hear of the man's suicide in England a short time later. There are more surprises still: the dead man's solicitor insists it wasn't suicide and the scholar had another, secret life.

Hare Sitting Up
London: Gollancz, 1959.
New York: Dodd, Mead, 1959.

Sir John Appleby

A theoretical discussion among students on the fate of the world at the hands of mad scientists and old men gives way to a real fear when a government scientist disappears. Afraid of a panic, the government attempts to find him before anyone knows he is missing, but no one in the government knows where to look for him.

Silence Observed
London: Gollancz, 1961.
New York: Dodd, Mead, 1961.

Sir John Appleby

The world of fine paintings and good literature has a dark side, that of
forgery and the hoax. Yet even an established forger can become respectable
and command high prices for his work. In an ironic twist, a collector's discovery that he has purchased a forged forgery threatens a number of re-
putable members of the art world.

A Connoisseur's Case
London: Gollancz, 1962.

The Crabtree Affair
New York: Dodd, Mead, 1962.

Sir John Appleby

During a pleasant ramble through the countryside, the Applebys stop at an
inn and strike up a conversation with an old rustic only recently returned
from America. Though they both enjoy the old man's tale of his earlier
days, Sir John senses more to the man's talk than nostalgia. Not long afterward, the Applebys find the rustic dead in a canal, obviously murdered.

The Bloody Wood
London: Gollancz, 1966.
New York: Dodd, Mead, 1966.

Sir John Appleby

Grace Martineau is dying and she knows it. After a long and rewarding
life, she has left little undone, but that little she intends to take care of
in her final days. Gathering friends and relations around her, Grace prods
her pawns into her chosen direction, but she is not the only one with plans
for this gathering.

Appleby at Allington
London: Gollancz, 1968.

Death by Water
New York: Dodd, Mead, 1968.

Sir John Appleby

Appleby takes a tour of the control set of a sound and light show set up at a nearby estate. He and his host flick the switches on various scenes, failing to notice the body of a man lying in the corner under a pile of rags. When the body is discovered, Appleby guesses that there is more here than a tragic accident.

A Family Affair
London: Gollancz, 1969.

Picture of Guilt
New York: Dodd, Mead, 1969.

Sir John Appleby

A gang of thieves has been removing artwork from the homes of aristocrats, each removal carried out in the form of an elaborate practical joke or fraud that leaves the owner too embarrassed to complain. The frauds have added up over twenty years to a sizable amount of money and the exercise of considerable intelligence. This alone makes Appleby curious.

Death at the Chase
London: Gollancz, 1970.
New York: Dodd, Mead, 1970.

Sir John Appleby

While out walking one day, Appleby jumps over a wall and comes face to face with a man who accuses him of trying to murder him. The accuser is Martyn Ashmore, who insists that once a year an attempt is made on his life. And sure enough, a few minutes later, Appleby witnesses an attempt on Ashmore's life.

An Awkward Lie
London: Gollancz, 1971.
New York: Dodd, Mead, 1971.

Sir John Appleby

Bobby Appleby is having an early round of golf when he comes upon a corpse in a bunker. He is then startled by the arrival of a beautiful young woman, who agrees to watch the corpse until he returns with the police. When he returns, both corpse and girl are gone and Bobby seems to be caught in an awkward lie. Recalling that there was something familiar about the corpse, Bobby decides to solve the mystery himself.

The Open House
London: Gollancz, 1972.
New York: Dodd, Mead, 1974.

Sir John Appleby

Appleby's car breaks down on a country road late at night and he seeks help at a large estate. The mansion is dark until he approaches, when it is flooded with light. Every window is lit and the door is open. Inside, he finds a table set for dinner, a host to greet him, and an elusive woman in white.

Appleby's Answer
London: Gollancz, 1973.
New York: Dodd, Mead, 1973.

Sir John Appleby

Priscilla Pringle is gratified to see fellow travelers reading her mystery books on trains until one day a passenger asks her about planning a foolproof murder. Another writer has an almost identical experience. Then Priscilla arrives in the village of the curious traveling companion and learns that his home is the site of an unsolved murder, much to her delight and literary prospects.

Appleby's Other Story
London: Gollancz, 1974.
New York: Dodd, Mead, 1974.

Sir John Appleby

Sir John is persuaded by Colonel Pride to visit the nearby home of a wealthy art collector. When the two men arrive there, the driveway is packed with police cars, the owner of the mansion is dead, and his son has recently, and secretly, returned from Argentina. Also in the house is an art dealer known for his success on the other side of the law.

The Gay Phoenix
London: Gollancz, 1976.
New York: Dodd, Mead, 1977.

Sir John Appleby

Rich Charles Povey is killed in a sailing accident off the coast of Australia. His poor look-alike brother, Arthur, is only injured and decides to take over his brother's life. Impersonating Charles turns out to be harder than Arthur expected; he runs into a former servant and a former mistress, both of whom see through the deception at once.

The Ampersand Papers
London: Gollancz, 1978.
New York: Dodd, Mead, 1979.

Sir John Appleby

Lord Ampersand has managed to dampen the interests of inquiring scholars by collecting all the family papers and placing them in a nearly inaccessible room. Then Agatha, Lady Ampersand's sister, points out that at least one of their ancestors knew famous names of the time, and this in turn could mean valuable papers. Now the family rethinks the treatment given thus far to the family papers.

Sheiks and Adders
London: Gollancz, 1982.
New York: Dodd, Mead, 1982.

Sir John Appleby

Intrigued by a crying girl in a forest, Appleby decides to attend a fête in a nearby village the girl has told him about. Dressed as Robin Hood, he encounters the local police, who have been assigned to guard against an unknown enemy. Appleby joins them and patrols in costume among an ever-increasing number of guests dressed as sheikhs.

Appleby and Honeybath
London: Gollancz, 1983.
New York: Dodd, Mead, 1983.

Sir John Appleby and Charles Honeybath

Terence Grinton is famous for his love of fox hunting and his dislike of books and things intellectual, so when guest Charles Honeybath decides to explore the library, he does not expect to find much of interest. There he discovers a corpse sitting in a chair. Keeping his wits about him, Honeybath locks the library and goes in search of Appleby, also a guest. When they return, the corpse is gone.

Carson's Conspiracy
London: Gollancz, 1984.
New York: Dodd, Mead, 1984.

Sir John Appleby

Carl Carson has climbed almost to the top financially and socially. Now he is saddled with neighbors he doesn't care for and a wife who is clearly batty. For instance, Mrs. Carson has invented a son, much to Mr. Carson's embarrassment. But when Mr. Carson decides he must escape, he takes a kinder view of his mythical son, Robin.

What Happened at Hazelwood?
London: Gollancz, 1946.
New York: Dodd, Mead, 1946.

Inspector Thomas Cadover

Hazelwood Hall, the home of Sir George Simney, is full of relatives from near and far when Sir George is found dead in his library at midnight while snow falls outside. And almost no one, from the Australian cousins to Lady Simney's former lover, to the anthropologist, to the servants, among others, has an alibi.

The Journeying Boy
London: Gollancz, 1949.

The Case of the Journeying Boy
New York: Dodd, Mead, 1949.

Inspector Thomas Cadover

A brilliant physicist decides to send his unruly and imaginative son to Ireland for a holiday and engages a tutor to accompany him. Even before man and boy can leave London, the spies and villains of the boy's imagination become all too real, following the youngster and his mild-mannered tutor on their journey to Ireland. (Inspector Cadover also appears with Sir John Appleby in A Private View.)

The Mysterious Commission
London: Gollancz, 1974.
New York: Dodd, Mead, 1975.

Charles Honeybath

Honeybath is presented with a challenge and an opportunity; he is offered a large fee to paint in a locale to remain unnamed the portrait of a man who must remain unidentified. Honeybath agrees, already imagining several explanations for this curious affair. None is correct, as he ultimately learns.

Honeybath's Haven
London: Gollancz, 1977.
New York: Dodd, Mead, 1978.

Charles Honeybath

A visit to an old friend and fellow artist, Edwin Lightfoot, so distresses Honeybath that he decides to reinvestigate the home he has chosen for his final years. Disturbed by Edwin's senility or madness or play (Charles is uncertain what behavior he is seeing), Charles wants to ensure his freedom and comfort at Hanwell Court. What he finds, however, only upsets him more.

Lord Mullion's Secret
London: Gollancz, 1981.
New York: Dodd, Mead, 1981.

Charles Honeybath

Honeybath is looking forward to painting the portrait of Lady Mullion at Mullion Castle. He is intrigued by the relations and staff but does not begin to wonder seriously about them until he takes a closer look at some of the family treasures. In the stately home, a Hilliard miniature has been replaced by a photograph, and no one else seems to have noticed.

From "London" Far
London: Gollancz, 1946.

The Unsuspected Chasm
New York: Dodd, Mead, 1946.

Richard Meredith is on the verge of an important scholarly discovery when he absent-mindedly quotes poetry in a tobacconist's shop, is shown a concealed flight of stairs, and descends to an entirely different world. Carrying a valuable manuscript, Meredith meanders into the storehouse of the International Society for the Diffusion of Cultural Objects, a vast if illegal organization. When it dawns on Meredith that he has been mistaken for an important member of the gang, he adopts the role in order to learn more about them.

Christmas at Candleshoe
London: Gollancz, 1953.
New York: Dodd, Mead, 1953.

Candleshoe
London: Penguin, 1978.

Mrs. Feather, an American, and her son, Grant, a student at Oxford, are touring the countryside when Mrs. Feather spots an old castle that is exactly what she has been longing for. The owner is a Miss Candleshoe, of impeccable lineage, who is well over ninety and living in the last century. Even so, the rich American and the impoverished gentlewoman come to a meeting of minds.

The Man from the Sea
London: Gollancz, 1955.
New York: Dodd, Mead, 1955.

Death by Moonlight
New York: Avon, 1957.

An early morning assignation brings a man to a secluded cove where he waits for his lover. From the sea comes a man fleeing a ship out in the cove and a smaller boat coming toward shore. Richard Cranston in a second chooses to help the man and is thus caught in a net of hunters and hunted on a frantic journey to London.

Old Hall, New Hall
London: Gollancz, 1956.

A Question of Queens
New York: Dodd, Mead, 1956.

Four young people set out to verify an old story. A university is located on an estate once owned by Sir Joscelyn Jory, who collected tombs. Younger brother Edward collected something else. The brothers challenged each other to bring back in one year the best example of their respective collections. Joscelyn, smitten by Edward's addition to his collection, offered his own best item, worth a fortune, in exchange. Apparently, the brothers did not complete the swap, and a descendant of Edward's line is looking for the treasure on the estate.

The New Sonia Wayward
London: Gollancz, 1960.

The Case of Sonia Wayward
New York: Dodd, Mead, 1960.

During a holiday sail, Colonel Petticate faces a dismal prospect: the death by natural causes of his famous novelist-wife, on whom he has long been dependent financially. After drinking most of a bottle of whiskey, he decides to dump her body overboard and pretend to everyone that she has gone on a trip. He will write her romantic novels himself.

Money from Holme
London: Gollancz, 1964.
New York: Dodd, Mead, 1965.

Failed artist and critic Mervyn Cheel attends a gallery exhibit of the paintings of Sebastian Holme, who died in an African revolution. Cheel is hoping for a free meal and a few contacts, but instead trips over a golden opportunity. As he wanders through the crowd he recognizes the dead artist wearing a disguise.

A Change of Heir
London: Gollancz, 1966.
New York: Dodd, Mead, 1966.

George Gadberry barely manages to make a living as an actor, but he is not eager for the different opportunity that presents itself. John Smith expects to inherit a large fortune from his great-aunt, Prudence, but she wants him to live with her during her last years. Smith wants to live in France with Lulu, free to enjoy life. Smith persuades Gadberry to pose as the heir and live with Aunt Pru until she dies.

Going It Alone
London: Gollancz, 1980.
New York: Dodd, Mead, 1980.

Gilbert Averell lives in France for most of the year to avoid taxation in England, and he often laments the limited amount of time he can spend in England. When his close friend Prince de Silistrie points out that they are almost twins and then invites him to swap passports for a week, Gilbert at first refuses and then agrees after a phone call from his sister. No sooner is Gilbert on his way as the prince, however, than he enters a world of lurking spies, fleeing relatives, and criminal gangs.

P.D. James

Cover Her Face
London: Faber, 1962.
New York: Scribner, 1966.

Inspector Adam Dalgliesh

Mrs. Maxie hires Sally Jupp, a young girl from the village home for unwed mothers, as household help, allowing the new mother to bring her baby with her. This seems to be the ideal solution to finding staff for the large house and the several adults living there, until someone points out that Sally's presence has already prompted several arguments in her first week.

A Mind to Murder
London: Faber, 1963.
New York: Scribner, 1967.

Superintendent Adam Dalgliesh

The Steen Psychiatric Clinic caters to a select clientele, only the very best neurotics. So it is especially unseemly when the administrative secretary of the clinic is stabbed to death with the porter's chisel. The staff and patients are eager to offer interpretations of the crime and a psychological profile of the murderer.

Unnatural Causes
London: Faber, 1967.
New York: Scribner, 1967.

Superintendent Adam Dalgliesh

Monksmere village is home to several writers, each specializing in a different genre and not always tolerant of each other. When Maurice Seton, author of detective novels, disappears, his colleagues assume this is a prank to promote his work. Then his immaculately suited body floats ashore in a dinghy; his hands have been cut off.

Shroud for a Nightingale
London: Faber, 1971.
New York: Scribner, 1971.

Superintendent Adam Dalgliesh

At a demonstration of nursing techniques presented for a visiting inspector of nursing schools, the patient is a student nurse receiving intragastric feeding. Suddenly she jumps from the table and writhes on the floor. Soon dead from poison, she is only the first of several victims murdered in what seems like plain sight of numerous witnesses.

An Unsuitable Job for a Woman
London: Faber, 1972.
New York: Scribner, 1973.

Superintendent Adam Dalgliesh and Cordelia Gray

On the morning that Bernie Pryde commits suicide, his detective agency finally gets a break. The scientist who heads a research lab in Cambridge hires Pryde's partner, Cordelia Gray, to determine why his son dropped out of college, took a job as a gardener, and then committed suicide.

The Black Tower
London: Faber, 1975.
New York: Scribner, 1975.

Superintendent Adam Dalgliesh

Dalgliesh is invited to stay at a home for disabled young people, and although
Father Baddeley assures Dalgliesh that it isn't urgent, Dalgliesh soon goes
down. When he arrives he finds the chaplain dead from a weak heart. As
he paces around his friend's cottage, he wonders about a missing diary. He
later learns that the chaplain left a considerable sum of money to the home.

Death of an Expert Witness
London: Faber, 1977.
New York: Scribner, 1977.

Superintendent Adam Dalgliesh

Dr. Lorrimer is the disturbing factor in so many lives at Hoggatt's Forensic
Science Laboratory that it is not surprising when he is found murdered. Identifying the murderer means sorting through several motives and resolving
issues that many would prefer to leave hidden.

The Skull beneath the Skin
London: Faber, 1982.
New York: Scribner, 1982.

Cordelia Gray

A actress who has been receiving notes warning of death is scheduled to
appear in The Duchess of Malfi, to be presented on an island in the Channel.
Although the actress takes steps to protect herself, she arrives on an island
whose owner avidly collects Victorian artifacts of death and mourning.

Innocent Blood
London: Faber, 1980.
New York: Scribner, 1980.

Philippa Palfrey is an adopted child who wants to trace her natural parents.
She is prepared for surprises, but her investigations lead her to a past she
could not have anticipated even in her wildest fantasies.

Roderic Jeffries*

Troubled Deaths
London: Collins, 1977.
New York: St. Martin, 1978.

Inspector Enrique Alvarez

Drawn to Majorca for its sailing and the climate, the British expatriates
have learned to coexist with the locals and the tourists. The only seriously
discordant note is sounded by a young and ambitious Englishman, who manages to offend everyone with his callousness and shallowness.

Murder Begets Murder
London: Collins, 1979.
New York: St. Martin, 1979.

Inspector Enrique Alvarez

William Heron has come to Majorca to die, a rich recluse with a beautiful
young wife. When the European community suspects she is having an affair
while her older lover lies upstairs dying, they are shocked. When Heron
finally dies, they are relieved at the prospect of being rid of Betty. Then
she is found dead, from food poisoning.

Just Desserts
London: Collins, 1980.

Just Deserts
New York: St. Martin, 1980.

Inspector Enrique Alvarez

The British expatriates are having their usual string of troubles: an obscure novelist must raise several hundred thousand pesetas, a playboy is confronted by his pregnant lover, a greedy woman wants control of the last parcel of developable land on Majorca. Yet the one who dies is a plain, middle-aged secretary who inexplicably became engaged to the novelist.

Unseemly End
London: Collins, 1981.
New York: St. Martin, 1981.

Inspector Enrique Alvarez

Dolly Lund cannot control the passage of time and its effects on her looks, but she has enough money to keep many people under her thumb, or wherever else she may want them: a younger lover, financial partners, and other expatriates. She also has so little feeling for others that she can enjoy their troubles, including those of her daughter, who wrote asking for help and was scorned. When dolly is found dead, Inspector Alvarez half-wishes she was killed for moral reasons.

Deadly Petard
London: Collins, 1983.
New York: St. Martin, 1983.

Inspector Enrique Alvarez

Gertrude Dean has escaped to the solitude of Majorca after giving an alibi for a man accused of his wife's murder. Though the man is acquitted, the police refuse to quit, following Gertrude to her new home. Then the man for whom she lied shows up.

Three and One Make Five
London: Collins, 1984.
New York: St. Martin, 1984.

Inspector Enrique Alvarez

Roger Clarke, a Britisher, dies in a tragic car accident, apparently drunk while driving, but his live-in girlfriend insists that he hasn't been drinking for years, and certainly not before the accident. Then a friend of the dead man drowns in a swimming accident, and Inspector Alvarez becomes curious about the two men and a friendship that was little known, even to Clarke's girlfriend.

Layers of Deceit
London: Collins, 1985.
New York: St. Martin, 1985.

Inspector Enrique Alvarez

The comforting warmth of Majorca turns hot when a series of accidents befalls the British residents. A retired British couple narrowly escapes a car accident, a young girl tries to kill herself, and a man dies in a drunken accident.

Evidence of the Accused
London: Collins, 1961.
New York: London House, 1963.

Mark and Lindy Cheesman are a beautiful young couple with everything going for them. Then Lindy dies from a fall while her husband and a friend are out shooting. The police decide this is no accident and soon make an arrest. The accused uses the trial to do more than defend himself and to confound the police.

The Benefits of Death
London: Collins, 1963.
New York: Dodd, Mead, 1964.

Charles Leithan is neither upset nor wary when his wife fails to return from
a trip to London. As he tells the police, he assumes she will reappear when
she wants to. But the police suspect foul play and continue to prowl around
the farm and kennel buildings and search through the forests.

An Embarrassing Death
London: Collins, 1964.
New York: Dodd, Mead, 1965.

Bill Stemple is willing to admit that he is sometimes foolish, perhaps even
stupid. It was pointless to send a photograph of a new car to a French
motor magazine. But now he has to explain that escapade to his superiors
at the motor company and show that he is not the kind of man to murder
his secretary.

Dead against the Lawyers
London: Collins, 1965.
New York: Dodd, Mead, 1966.

Radwick Holter is a rich and successful barrister and believes in showing it,
even though doing so creates enemies among his colleagues. He is nonplussed
but still a fighter when the corpse of a colleague is found in his office.
He needs all his training to defend himself against the charge of murder,
but nothing can prepare him for the discovery of the real murderer.

Death in the Coverts
London: Collins, 1966.

The Decker family has managed to hold on to the family estate by selling
places in the pheasant shoot to outsiders. Then there is an accident and
one of the guests is shot and killed. Mrs. Decker isn't unhappy about the
death of this man, but his death is followed by others and her son is arrested
for murder. Insisting on his innocence, Julian Decker saves himself by a clever legal maneuver, forcing the police and legal experts to begin again.

Romilly and Katherine John

Death by Request
London: Faber, 1933.

The Reverend Joseph Colchester narrates the story of a country house visit
during which lovers quarrel, the scion of the house hunts moths late at night,
and a guest is murdered. The police are incompetent, the private detective
is charming, and the servants have their own mysteries.

H.R.F. Keating

The Murder of the Maharajah
London: Collins, 1980.
New York: Doubleday, 1980.

Superintendent Howard

In 1930 the maharajah of Bhopore invites a number of Americans and Euro-
peans to be his guests at the opening of a new dam and treats them to the
pleasures and customs of his kingdom. But beneath the ruler's ostentation
and the veneer of British civility and Western sophistication lie forces that
erupt in first one murder and then another.

The Perfect Murder
London: Collins, 1964.
New York: Dutton, 1965.

Inspector Ganesh Ghote

Inspector Ghote, in India, has a full load of number-one priority cases: Mr.
Perfect, the Parsi secretary to a rich businessman, has been assaulted but
not quite murdered, and money has been stolen from the desk of the minister
of police affairs and arts. The sum stolen is Rs. 1.00 (one rupee). To make
matters worse, Ghote is also expected to assist Axel Svensson, a well-meaning
but tactless Swede who is on a tour sponsored by Unesco to write a book
about police procedures in the third world.

Inspector Ghote's Good Crusade
London: Collins, 1966.
New York: Dutton, 1966.

Inspector Ganesh Ghote

Few care to help the many beggars of India, but those who do are venerated by the people. And this is why the murder of Frank Masters, an American who helps child beggars, is the more confounding. Surrounded by beggars and intimidated by the Westerners associated with the Masters Foundation, Inspector Ghote must find a motive for murder and then a murderer.

Inspector Ghote Caught in Meshes
London: Collins, 1967.
New York: Dutton, 1968.

Inspector Ganesh Ghote

An American professor is killed in the countryside on the road to Poona, a deplorable highway robbery according to the local constable. But on closer examination, it appears to be murder, planned in detail well in advance. The professor's brother, a famous scientist, insists the death was murder throughout and presses Ghote for news of his progress.

Inspector Ghote Hunts the Peacock
London: Collins, 1968.
New York: Dutton, 1968.

Inspector Ganesh Ghote

Inspector Ghote is fulfilling an old dream of finally seeing England. He arrives in London to deliver a paper to a conference and is unexpectedly met by Vidur Datta, his wife's cousin's husband. Datta implores Ghote to help him find a niece who is missing. Reluctantly, Ghote agrees and explores two different worlds in London.

Inspector Ghote Plays a Joker
London: Collins, 1969.
New York: Dutton, 1969.

Inspector Ganesh Ghote

Inspector Ghote is assigned to prevent a murder--of the fourth and last of
a group of flamingos given by the U.S. consul. Unfortunately, Ghote arrives
in time to witness the murder. Now he must decide if this is an an-
ti-American act or a practical joke. His investigations lead him into the
richer levels of Bombay life, both spiritual and financial.

Inspector Ghote Breaks an Egg
London: Collins, 1970.
New York: Doubleday, 1971.

Inspector Ganesh Ghote

An Eminent Figure in public life orders Inspector Ghote to investigate a
death that occurred fifteen years ago in a small town far from Bombay. A
young wife died, and through a judicious second marriage, her husband rose
to prominence and now controls the town and its district. But since he has
broken with the main political party, he is now vulnerable to police investigation.

Inspector Ghote Goes by Train
London: Collins, 1971.
New York: Doubleday, 1972.

Inspector Ganesh Ghote

Inspector Ghote must bring from Calcutta to Bombay the noted figure in
several antiques frauds, A.K. Bhattacharya. As Ghote settles down for the
long train ride, he wonders about the man sharing his compartment and soon
finds himself wondering if Bhattacharya is indeed waiting for him in Calcutta.
He gains three more traveling companions, two hippies and a wandering holy
man. And so begins a journey Ghote will long remember.

Inspector Ghote Trusts the Heart
London: Collins, 1972.
New York: Doubleday, 1973.

Inspector Ganesh Ghote

Criminals pose a serious threat to the businessman Mr. Desai, but at the moment they are only a threat because they kidnapped, not Mr. Desai's son, but a playmate, the tailor's son. Inspector Ghote is left with the dilemma of counseling Mr. Desai in dealing with the criminals and somehow persuading police, criminals, and Mr. Desai that the son of a lowly tailor is also important.

Bats Fly Up for Inspector Ghote
London: Collins, 1974.
New York: Doubleday, 1974.

Inspector Ganesh Ghote

Inspector Ghote, assigned to the antipickpocket squad and failing to make any arrests, assumes that his days with the police are numbered. He is surprised when he is transferred to the Black-Money and Allied Transactions Squad, and given a special assignment--to identify the squad member who has been compromising the work of the squad.

Filmi, Filmi, Inspector Ghote
London: Collins, 1976.
New York: Doubleday, 1977.

Inspector Ganesh Ghote

Inspector Ghote is cast into the flamboyant world of Indian films when an actor who is famous for his portrayal of villains is murdered in a film studio. The obvious suspects are also the best actors, and Ghote has much trouble maintaining his perspective as a police investigator.

Inspector Ghote Draws a Line
London: Collins, 1979.
New York: Doubleday, 1979.

Inspector Ganesh Ghote

A judge long retired from the Madras High Court is unmoved by threats
against his life, and Inspector Ghote is sent to a remote part of South India
to prevent the promised murder. It isn't long before he concludes that the
threat comes from within the judge's household, but the judge still refuses
to take any action.

Go West, Inspector Ghote
London: Collins, 1981.
New York: Doubleday, 1981.

Inspector Ganesh Ghote

A fabulously rich Indian businessman sends his daughter to college in California, where she joins an ashram and refuses to leave. Inspector Ghote is
sent to bring her home, but first he must cope with huge Americans, Los
Angeles, a murder, and the Los Angeles Police Department.

The Sheriff of Bombay
London: Collins, 1984.
New York: Doubleday, 1984.

Inspector Ganesh Ghote

Inspector Ghote faces an evening of disillusionment, embarrassment, and worse
when he is assigned to escort a famous British film star through Bombay's
red-light district. Reluctantly, Ghote chooses one of the better brothels,
and as the two men enter, Ghote sees the sheriff of Bombay slipping down
a hallway. Moments later, Ghote discovers a dead prostitute.

Death of a Fat God
London: Collins, 1963.
New York: Dutton, 1966.

Mrs. Craggs

The opera company performing at the Flinwich Festival has the usual tensions
between artists, but the singer playing Scarpia in <u>Tosca</u> adds a new one when
he refuses to remain dead, shocking the audience and upsetting the company.
Indeed, Jean-Aitaban seems intent on upsetting everyone, and the other performers take a quiet pleasure in his discomfort at appearing in a machine
that descends to the stage, required for the performance of <u>Death of a Fat
God</u>. One of the commentators on the action is Mrs. Craggs, the astute
and sensible cleaning lady. (Mrs. Craggs also appears in several short stories.)

The Underside
London: Macmillan, 1974.
Godfrey Mann, artist in the 1860s, is always welcome at the balls and parties
of the Season, but he is less enthusiastic than the young ladies and their
mothers about these events. When he meets Elizabeth Hills, a doctor from
the United States, he is nonchalant but gradually his attraction for her
and his growing passion for the prostitute he patronizes force him into a
double life.

A Remarkable Case of Burglary
London: Collins, 1975.
New York: Doubleday, 1976.

In 1871 Val Leary walks the streets of London looking for work. One early
morning he chances upon a maid scrubbing the steps of her employer's home
in a fashionable neighborhood. He returns several times, and plans in his
mind a burglary of all that the maid shyly describes within.

Death and the Visiting Firemen
London: Gollancz, 1959.
New York: Doubleday, 1973.

Members of the American Institute for the Investigation of Incendiarism,
Inc., mean to see England in style. A travel agent meets the group in a

coach with horses, giving the tourists a view of travel in Old England. The agent has also hired a number of performers for the journey, and even included a robbery by a highwayman. As the travelers ride through the countryside the agent directs the actors with threats, insults, and near violence.

Zen There Was Murder
London: Gollancz, 1960.

Mr. Utamaro leads a week-long seminar on Japanese Zen Buddhism at Mulcheaten Manor, attracting a heterogeneous group of adults. Before the students can answer even their first question (What is the sound of one hand clapping?), an antique sword is stolen, and circumstances soon add murder to the list of knotty problems for the students.

A Rush on the Ultimate
London: Gollancz, 1961.
New York: Doubleday, 1982.

Humphrey Boddershaw has planned a private croquet party at his school, but his guests are turning on him, one insisting that he is violent and dangerous and another threatening to kill him. In addition, a convict with a grudge against Humphrey escapes from prison, and the school maid is the convict's girlfriend. All in all, Humphrey's house party does not look good.

The Dog It Was That Died
London: Gollancz, 1962.

In an academic tale with a twist, two research scholars move to Dublin to build a new life for themselves, but colleagues from their earlier work with the British government are reluctant to let them go. When one researcher finds the other dead, he knows he must face what he has run from and master it.

Is Skin Deep, Is Fatal
London: Collins, 1965.
New York: Dutton, 1965.

The owner of a seedy bar is found dead only hours after she writes a letter to the owner of a nearby ballroom that is the site for a coming beauty contest. Soon after the letter arrives, police find another body, in the ballroom

offices. With a guard on the door and only beauty contestants practicing
for their big night, the police seem to have few suspects and fewer clues.

The Strong Man
Heinemann, 1971.

Michael Quine, a Dublin journalist, returns to his island nation to write about
the dictator Mr. Mylchraine. He finds his brother and everyone else more
subservient than on his last visit--and is shocked at the reason behind this.
Because he is impressed by a convict's dignity, he impulsively helps him escapes from a chain gang and is thereby drawn into a revolution by a man
of strong ethics.

C. H. B. Kitchin

Death of My Aunt
London: Hogarth, 1929.
New York: Harcourt, 1929.

Malcolm Warren

Malcolm Warren is a young stockbroker from a good family with little money,
so he is pleased to receive an invitation to work on his aunt's stock portfolio. Knowing that she is the only rich member of a large extended family,
he settles down to discuss her investments with her but instead is dismayed
to see her die suddenly before his eyes. Even worse, he turns out to be
the most likely suspect in her murder.

Crime at Christmas
London: Woolf, 1934.
New York: Harcourt, 1935.

Malcolm Warren

On Christmas morning, one of several houseguests is found dead: Mrs. Harley,
the elderly mother of the host's secretary. She seems to have died from
natural causes after walking in her sleep onto a balcony. Even though she

cannot have been murdered, her death points up the oddness of this Christmas gathering.

Death of His Uncle
London: Constable, 1939.
New York: Perennial, 1984.

Malcolm Warren

Malcolm is persuaded to help an old college friend whose uncle has mysteriously disappeared. A man of regular and economical habits, the uncle altered his regular vacation plans at the last moment, making instead a trip to Cornwall.

The Cornish Fox*
London: Secker, 1949.

Malcolm Warren

Ronald A. Knox

The Three Taps*
London: Methuen, 1927.
New York: Simon, 1927.

Miles Bredon

The Footsteps at the Lock
London: Methuen, 1928.
New York: Dover, 1983.

Miles Bredon

Two cousins who are known for their lack of friendship with each other decide to take a canoe trip up the Thames. The younger one must return briefly to Oxford for exams, but when he returns to meet his cousin on the river, there is no sign of him or his canoe. The insurance company, represented by Miles Bredon, is suspicious because the mishap occurs just days before one of the cousins was to receive a large inheritance.

The Body in the Silo
London: Hodder, 1933.

Settled Out of Court
New York: Dutton, 1934.

Miles Bredon

Mrs. Halliford likes to organize entertainments for her guests during a party, but her recent efforts have upset the neighborhood. Farmers disliked the treasure hunt and teachers disliked the scavenger party, since both games disrupted the property of others. This time Mrs. Halliford has settled on an eloping party, which involves a late-night car chase after the would-be couple.

Still Dead
London: Hodder, 1934.
New York: Dutton, 1934.

Miles Bredon

The Reivers of the Dorn estate in Scotland are used to living out their family curses: the estate never passes directly and branches of the family are regularly estranged. Then Donald Reiver decides to take advantage of fate and insure his son's life, expecting Colin to predecease him, in accord with family curses. Colin is true to his family tradition and is found dead--twice.

Double Cross Purposes*
London: Hodder, 1937.

Miles Bredon

The Viaduct Murder
London: Methuen, 1925.
New York: Simon, 1926.

Four long-time partners in golf come upon a body during a game. Intrigued by the prospect of a real crime in their midst, they set about detecting and sleuthing with confusing and sometimes unpredictable results. Not the least entertaining are the various theories devised to explain a body on the ground under a viaduct.

Elizabeth Lemarchand

Death of an Old Girl
London: Hart-Davis, 1967.
New York: Walker, 1985.

Inspector Tom Pollard

The Meldon School for Girls has undergone many changes in the last several years, and all of them deplored by Beatrice Baynes, now retired but still living near the school and disrupting it and the lives of its staff whenever possible. She is found dead after the annual reunion; although no one mourns her, no one will admit to how strongly disliked she was.

The Affacombe Affair
London: Hart-Davis, 1968.
New York: Walker, 1985.

Inspector Tom Pollard

Village life has settled into the easy pace of late fall when a gardener's wife suddenly leaves him, a young servant girl quits her job and returns to London, and a well-off woman is suddenly taken ill. Soon afterward, the nurse at a local boys' school is found dead in the river and her room yields what appears to be evidence of blackmail. She also had more than three victims.

Alibi for a Corpse
London: Hart-Davis, 1969.
New York: Walker, 1986.

Superintendent Tom Pollard

Derek Wainwright has just ·nherited an isolated mansion on the moors, and his two children are happily exploring the area when they find a skeleton in the trunk of a car. A neighbor who is in contact with the Beyond claims to have had special sightings on the most important night at the general time of the death.

Death on Doomsday
London: Hart-Davis, 1971.
New York: Walker, 1975.

Superintendent Tom Pollard

The family of the eighth earl of Seton has adjusted remarkably well to opening the mansion to the public, and the tourists have come in droves. For three years the Tirles have led tours, served tea, and sold souvenirs, but the family faces a sudden closing after one of the guests discovers a body in a priest's hole.

Cyanide with Compliments
London: MacGibbon, 1972.
New York: Walker, 1973.

Superintendent Tom Pollard

Audrey Vickers has no qualms about making life miserable for people who fail to cater to her. So having taken her niece and nephew-in-law on a trip to the Mediterranean without receiving the proper gratitude from them, she promptly turns nasty as soon as she returns home, ordering her solicitor to leave her niece out of her will. Fortunately for the niece, before Audrey can sign the new will she is dead from a box of poisoned chocolates sent by the cruise line.

Let or Hindrance
London: Hart-Davis, 1973.

No Vacation from Murder
New York: Walker, 1974.

Superintendent Tom Pollard

The summer season brings busloads of tourists to the coastal village of Kittitoe, and prosperity to the local travel agencies. It also brings a quiet teenager, Wendy Shaw, anxious to earn some money of her own and enjoy her independence. When she suddenly disappears and is later found dead, the police have almost a hundred suspects, both tourists and locals, but no motives.

Buried in the Past
London: Hart-Davis, 1974.
New York: Walker, 1975.

Superintendent Tom Pollard

The small town of Corbury is proud of its history and plans to celebrate its millenary, but Bernard Lister remembers the town only as the place of his unhappy childhood. First, he is drawn to return after twenty years to debunk the town's supposedly medieval charter; then he is drawn by the death of the only person he remembers kindly from his childhood.

Step in the Dark
London: Hart-Davis, 1976.
New York: Walker, 1977.

Superintendent Tom Pollard

The staid library of the Ramsden Literary and Scientific Society hardly seems the site for burglary and murder, but library employees find a corpse on the library floor the morning after the library's centenary celebration. When police look for the murderer, they uncover secrets about the most respectable members, but no motives for murder.

Unhappy Returns
London: Hart-Davis, 1977.
New York: Walker, 1978.

Superintendent Tom Pollard

Change in the conduct of local affairs comes hard for some, but Ethel Ridd is determined more than most to stand her ground. Housekeeper to the late vicar of Ambercombe, she alone remembers him kindly, just as she alone attended his many services in his efforts to restore monastic worship. More important, she alone remembers a third chalice used by the vicar, one of greater antiquity and value than the remaining two.

Suddenly While Gardening
London: Hart-Davis, 1978.
New York: Walker, 1978.

Superintendent Tom Pollard

In one year community workers have secured all rights for a walk across the Cattesmoor, opened Possel Way, and beaten back threats of developers. Now they have another challenge: students on a walking tour have found a skeleton in a Bronze Age grave. The skeleton is only about a year old and does not fit any of the descriptions of persons missing in the area.

Change for the Worse
Loughton, Engl.: Piatkus, 1980.
New York: Walker, 1981.

Superintendent Tom Pollard

The beautiful gardens and well-appointed rooms of Fairlynch Manor, a property of the Heritage of Britain Trust, shelter a recurring turmoil. Just as Katharine Ridley believes she has secured a sound future for the manor she loves and her granddaughter, a figure from the past appears and a burglar breaks into the manor. Once again, Katharine's life begins to fall apart.

Nothing to Do with the Case
Loughton, Engl.: Piatkus, 1981.
New York: Walker, 1981.

Superintendent Tom Pollard

Virginia Gould, a quiet and shy young woman, receives a large bequest on the death of a relative. Other relatives suggest, not always discreetly, that she did not come by her inheritance fairly. Eager to leave this unpleasantness behind, Virginia moves to another county and begins a new life. But her relatives are not willing to let her go so easily.

Troubled Waters
Loughton, Engl.: Piatkus, 1982.
New York: Walker, 1982.

Superintendent Tom Pollard

A young American returns to England to trace his ancestors, but before he can do more than engage a genealogist he dies in an accident. Several weeks later, a series of anonymous letters persuades the police to look again at the man's death, agreeing in part with the genealogist's rule that most people have a skeleton in their closets.

The Wheel Turns
Loughton, Engl.: Piatkus, 1983.
New York: Walker, 1984.

Superintendent Tom Pollard

Everything is going well for Basil Railsdon, a young politician who has successfully managed both his career and his personal life, until he accidentally kills a small child while driving. Coldly, he weighs the child's life against his own ambitions and decides to hide the child's body.

Light through Glass
Loughton, Engl.: Piatkus, 1984.
New York: Walker, 1986.

Superintendent Tom Pollard

Dr. John Paterson is thoroughly despicable beneath his charming exterior as a successful and independently wealthy scientist-scholar. He torments his assistant, uses his relatives, manipulates his colleagues, and insults whomever he pleases. It is little wonder he is found dead.

E.C.R. Lorac*

Fire in the Thatch
London: Collins, 1946.
New York: Mystery House, 1946.

Inspector Macdonald

Colonel St. Cyres has several applications from prospective tenants for the old cottage on his land, and he chooses a hard-working northerner, believing that he will now have peace and quiet with a stolid farmer as a tenant. Instead, the hamlet attracts London businessmen and sudden death.

Policemen in the Precinct
London: Collins, 1949.

And Then Put out the Light
New York: Doubleday, 1950.

Inspector Macdonald

The middle-aged daughter of a former canon dies of heart failure, much to the gratification of the other residents of the Abbey precinct. So disliked and malicious in her gossip was she that after her death her neighbors wonder aloud how she could have lived so long without being murdered.

Let Well Alone
London: Collins, 1954.

Superintendent Macdonald

Two young couples, writers and artists, rent a house in Devon so they can concentrate more on their work and less on bare survival. When they arrive to begin work on the house, everyone they meet tries to discourage them from moving into the old house, claiming that it's unlucky and haunted. Not long after they move in, they learn part of the truth behind the warnings.

Peter Lovesey

Wobble to Death
London: Macmillan, 1970.
New York: Dodd, Mead, 1970.

Sergeant Cribb

The newest event in the Victorian sporting world in 1879 is the "Go As You Please" pedestrian races, and competition is fierce for the title and prize money. One of the pedestrians dies from poison, and the police must solve the murder before the race, covering several days in an indoor arena, is over and the participants disperse.

The Detective Wore Silk Drawers
London: Macmillan, 1971.
New York: Dodd, Mead, 1971.

Sergeant Cribb

Pugilism, or bare-knuckle fighting, may be illegal in 1880, but it is still attractive to a certain clientele. When Sergeant Cribb finds a corpse that points to pugilism, he sets a trap for one of the gangs engaged in this activity. The bait is another policeman who can box and agrees to train as a pugilist.

Abracadaver
London: Macmillan, 1972.
New York: Dodd, Mead, 1972.

Sergeant Cribb

Performers in music halls in 1881 are having an unusual number of accidents: the sword swallower discovers mustard on his sword, a singer says his music has been tampered with, two trapeze artists report their equipment has been damaged. The accidents become progressively serious for the performers, though they at first seem to be pranks.

Mad Hatter's Holiday
London: Macmillan, 1973.
New York: Dodd, Mead, 1973.

Sergeant Cribb

Strolling along the promenade in Brighton in 1882, Albert Moscrop is entranced by a woman on the beach and pursues a meeting with her. Drawn into her world and that of her family, he discovers less beauty and more mystery than he anticipated. When she disappears, he is more concerned than her husband and sons.

Invitation to a Dynamite Party
London: Macmillan, 1974.

The Tick of Death
New York: Dodd, Mead, 1974.

Sergeant Cribb

In 1884 several different groups set off bombs in London, and Scotland Yard suspects one of its own constables of complicity with the guilty parties. To investigate the constable and infiltrate a group of dynamiters, Sergeant Cribb studies the workings of "infernal machines" and joins a group of Irish revolutionaries.

A Case of Spirits
London: Macmillan, 1975.
New York: Dodd, Mead, 1975.

Sergeant Cribb

A new kind of burglar appears in the London area in 1885, one who steals only one valuable object and then departs. Miss Cross lost a vase and Dr. Probert a week later lost a painting. The burglar in both instances over-looked more valuable items. Even stranger, the two victims had only just met--at a seance being investigated from a scientific point of view.

Waxwork
London: Macmillan, 1978.
New York: Pantheon, 1978.

Sergeant Cribb

In 1888 Miriam Cromer is convicted of murdering her husband's photography assistant after confessing to the crime. Now she awaits her execution in Newgate Prison, but two things bother the police. First, she is entirely com-posed and self-possessed. Second, the police have received a photograph that casts doubts on Miriam's guilt.

Swing, Swing Together
London: Macmillan, 1976.
New York: Dodd, Mead, 1976.

Sergeant Cribb

A student at a women's college is the only witness to a late-night incident: three men throwing a corpse into the Thames. Since the three men have disguised themselves as tourists who are following the trip up the Thames described in the current best-seller of the year 1888, <u>Three Men in a Boat</u>, Sergeant Cribb decides to follow them also disguised as a tourist, taking along the student to identify the men.

Keystone
London: Macmillan, 1983.
New York: Pantheon, 1983.

In 1915 an out-of-work British vaudeville performer finds work as a Keystone Cop in the movie industry in California. He soon learns that the life of an actor can be dangerous after he survives reckless stunts and other mishaps. Others in the movie company are not as lucky.

The False Inspector Dew
London: Macmillan, 1982.
New York: Pantheon, 1982.

In 1921 Walter Brown decides it is time to end his marriage and run away with the woman he loves. He plans to murder his wife on an ocean liner sailing to America, but his plans change when he is mistaken on the ship for a famous retired policeman and asked to investigate the death of a woman passenger.

Philip MacDonald

The Wraith
London: Collins, 1931.
New York: Doubleday, 1931.

Colonel Anthony Gethryn

Gethryn recalls a dinner party in 1920 that initiated his interest in crime.
A dinner party at a country home limps to a close when the guests finish
their bridge game before the return of their host and hostess. When found,
Mr. Manx is dead and Mrs. Manx is unconscious. The obvious suspect is
Mr. Höst, a local eccentric who has complained bitterly that Mr. Manx was
using Höst's cats for experiments.

The Rasp
London: Collins, 1924.
New York: Dial, 1925.

Colonel Anthony Gethryn

A cabinet minister is brutally murdered, apparently after a violent struggle,
in the late evening in his home. None of the several guests or servants
heard a sound even though heavy furniture was overturned. Gethryn works
with his partner in the newspaper business to scoop the other papers and
find the murderer.

The White Crow*
London: Collins, 1928.
New York: Dial, 1928.

Colonel Anthony Gethryn

The Noose
London: Collins, 1930.
New York: Dial, 1930.

Colonel Anthony Gethryn and Inspector Arnold Pike

Stunned by the magnificence of Mrs. Bronson's beauty, Colonel Gethryn agrees to help her prove that her husband is innocent of murder. He has five days before Bronson, a publican convicted of a brutal, sneaky murder, is hanged, having been convicted on evidence extensive and persuasive.

The Link
London: Collins, 1930.
New York: Doubleday, 1930.

Colonel Anthony Gethryn

A young vet is smitten by Lady Grenville, whereas the lady in question is coping with an unlikable husband and her own ambivalent feelings. Conveniently, someone shoots Lord Grenville and, inconveniently, the young vet is a likely suspect, since he admits he was wandering around the murder scene with a rifle not long before the body was found.

The Crime Conductor
London: Collins, 1932.
New York: Doubleday, 1931.

Colonel Anthony Gethryn and Superintendent Arnold Pike

Theatrical producer Willington Sigsbee is murdered in his bath just after he has offered the highest salary in the history of the theater to Lars Kristania. No one thinks Lars deserves the money.

The Choice
London: Collins, 1931.

The Polferry Mystery
London: Collins, 1932.

The Polferry Riddle
New York: Doubleday, 1931.

Colonel Anthony Gethryn and Superintendent Arnold Pike

On a rainy and windy evening along an isolated part of the coast, Dr.
Hale-Storford welcomes two men whose ketch has gone down in the bad
weather. One turns out to be an old friend, and the other an old friend of
his wife of six months. Also confined to the house on this night are Mrs.
Hale-Storford's sister and a friend. When the host accompanies his unexpected guests to bed, he turns to his own room and finds his wife dead.
This is a locked-room mystery with a twist.

The Maze
London: Collins, 1932.

Persons Unknown
New York: Doubleday, 1931.

Colonel Anthony Gethryn

Maxwell Brunton, businessman, is found dead in his study by his private secretary late one evening. Solely through the testimony of family, friends,
and servants in the house that evening given to the coroner's court, Colonel
Gethryn identifies the murderer.

Rope to Spare
London: Collins, 1932.
New York: Doubleday, 1932.

Colonel Anthony Gethryn

Colonel Gethryn is convalescing in a hamlet for three weeks when he receives
a threatening letter and a warning telephone call, and hears a strange tale
from a terrified boy. Wondering how he could have missed so much malevolence under his very nose, Gethryn sets out to identify the woman described in the letter, a snake who does not deserve any help and whose beauty
is only the mask of evil.

Death on My Left
London: Collins, 1933.
New York: Doubleday, 1933.

Colonel Anthony Gethryn

Watching a street brawl, Leo Petrass, master of the art of self-defense, discovers a youngster with the potential to be great, and so begins the career
of Kim Kinnaird. It ends more than ten years later when Kinnaird, after
years of training and fighting and winning, and now the British hope for
the world heavyweight title, is found dead in the ring in Petrass's gymnasium.
Isolated in the countryside, Kinnaird can have been killed only by one of
those closest to him.

The Nursemaid Who Disappeared
London: Collins, 1938.

Warrant for X
New York: Doubleday, 1938.

Colonel Anthony Gethryn and Superintendent Arnold Pike

A visiting American playwright overhears two women in a tea shop planning
a crime. None of his friends is interested in his tale and Scotland Yard

refuses to take him seriously. Determined to prevent the crime, he and
Gethryn begin to trace the women through a glove and a shopping list.

The List of Adrian Messenger
London: Jenkins, 1960.
New York: Doubleday, 1959.

Colonel Anthony Gethryn

Adrian Messenger turns over to Scotland Yard a list of ten names, asking
his friend to learn if the men listed are still living at their given addresses.
The next day he dies in a plane crash, and the police look closely at the
list of names, which are tied, in Messenger's words, to a "far older sin than
any politics."

Murder Gone Mad
London: Collins, 1931.
New York: Doubleday, 1931.

Superintendent Arnold Pike

Pleasant little Holmdale is shocked by the murder of Lionel Colby, a school-
boy both well behaved and popular. The murder is brutal and senseless, and
the murderer brags of success in letters sent to prominent persons in the
town. More murders follow, along with more letters from the Butcher.

Rynox
London: Collins, 1930.

The Rynox Murder Mystery
New York: Doubleday, 1931.

The Rynox Mystery
London: Collins, 1933.

The Rynox Murder
New York: Avon, 1965.

Boswell Marsh, a detestable and reclusive old man, makes an uncharacteristic trip to London for the day, antagonizing everyone he meets. After his last appointment in the evening, a man is found dead and the police search frantically for the recluse.

R.I.P.
London: Collins, 1933.

Menace
New York: Doubleday, 1933.

For six years Lady Verity has received a letter to commemorate an incident on August 21, 1918, an incident the lady would rather forget. She is not alone, however; the letter writer blames her and two of her friends for the death of seven hundred men, and this year the letter was postmarked in a nearby town. Then on the night of the anniversary, Lady Verity and her two friends find evidence that the letter writer is among her guests or servants.

The Dark Wheel
London: Collins, 1948.
New York: Morrow, 1948.

Sweet and Deadly
New York: Zenith, 1959.

Every night Cornelius Van Toller arrives at the New York theater with his
manservant to watch a second-rate play, to relive for a moment his love
for an actress now dead. The new actress is a stranger to him, an aid to
his fantasy, until she meets him at his home. Her smile transforms him,
erasing the memory of his earlier love. Van Toller now has a new obsession.
(Written with A. Boyd Correll.)

Guest in the House
London: Jenkins, 1956.
New York: Doubleday, 1955.

No Time for Terror
New York: Bestseller, 1956.

Living on his wits and his friends since he left the army, St. George impresses his hosts with his manners, his plans, and his Alfa Romeo. When he
moves in with an old army pal and his wife and stepdaughter, St. George
quickly senses that all is not well in golden California. The problem is the
ex-husband, an unsavory fellow who once made the law work for him in a
manner that can still frighten his ex-wife. This dilemma offers St. George
the kind of opportunity he hasn't had since the war.

Jessica Mann

The Only Security
London: Macmillan, 1973.

Troublecross
New York: McKay, 1973.

Professor Thea Crawford

Professor Thea Crawford comes to her new position at the University of Buriton determined to take charge without stepping on her colleagues' toes. This does not sway her colleagues, who are jealous of her academic standing and success. Thea, however, is not the only newcomer who must win over the hearts of the locals.

Captive Audience
London: Macmillan, 1975.
New York: McKay, 1975.

Professor Thea Crawford

A spring protest at the University of Buriton takes a predictable course, with a march of straggling students, speeches, and chanting outside the registrar's building. After that comes the unpredicted. The building catches fire and is gutted. Inside the police find the body of a student. Closely observing the goings-on is Thea's husband, a television interviewer temporarily bedridden.

No Man's Island
London: Macmillan, 1983.
New York: Doubleday, 1983.

Tamara Hoyland

Oil is discovered on the remote island of Forway and the British government plans to evacuate the islanders and use the island as the site of an oil rig.

The islanders, however, have a different idea and are prepared to fight for their homes.

Grave Goods
London: Macmillan, 1984.
New York: Doubleday, 1985.

Tamara Hoyland

Margot Ellice's pastime is writing the biography of an obscure Englishwoman who married a German prince. The completion of her manuscript coincides with the exhibition in London of a treasure of royal jewels, including those of the prince in her book. This is not cause for celebration, for Margot has found evidence that the Germans hold only fakes, the real ones having been removed in the last century.

A Charitable End
London: Collins, 1971.
New York: McKay, 1971.

The women members of a charitable organization rarely look deeper than the obvious results of their efforts: money raised and spent. And many seem to prefer to avoid any more involvement with the other members. Indeed, the author of several poison-pen letters knows exactly how much these women have withheld of themselves.

Mrs. Knox's Profession
London: Macmillan, 1972.
New York: McKay, 1972.

Generally dissatisfied with middle-class life in a small city, Sarah Foster becomes involved with the politician Victor Nightingale. Her pleasant adventure backfires, however, when the baby she is minding one day is kidnapped during a visit with Vic. Unable to turn to her husband, she turns to Vic, who wants nothing to do with her problem.

The Sticking Place
London: Macmillan, 1974.
New York: McKay, 1974.

On a March afternoon Rachel Seton listens to charges of sedition against
her husband, Gus. Gus is being challenged for the directorship of the Centre
for Self-Determination by Edward Leary, who insists that Gus is a supporter
of Scottish nationalism and is using the center for this end. After the meeting, Rachel's best friend hints that Gus is seeing another woman. In one
day Rachel's life begins to unravel.

The Eighth Deadly Sin*
London: Macmillan, 1976.

The Sting of Death
London: Macmillan, 1978.
New York: Doubleday, 1983.

A young man who has inherited his grandmother's farm rents part of it to
young campers who, in the eyes of the owner's cousin, are desecrating the
land. The breach between the two young men grows, and the townspeople
are caught between the two sides, the artist-conservationists and the rich
but careless campers.

Funeral Sites
London: Macmillan, 1981.
New York: Doubleday, 1982.

Rosamond Sholto does not like her sister's husband, and now that Phoebe is
dead after a frightening decline, Rosamond likes him even less. As a deputy
PM, however, Aidan Britton has many resources at his command and can
squelch anything Rosamond can come up with. Only through her own courage
and the help of old friends can Rosamond avoid the fate of her sister and
expose the up-and-coming politician.

Ngaio Marsh

A Man Lay Dead
London: Bles, 1934.
New York: Sheridan, 1942.

Inspector Roderick Alleyn

Sir Hubert is known for his original and fascinating house parties, and his
plans for his current group of guests include a game called Murder. His
plans go awry, however, when a member of a secret society decides to use
the weekend for other purposes.

The Nursing Home Murder
London: Bles, 1935.
New York: Sheridan, 1941.

Inspector Roderick Alleyn

During a speech in the House, the home secretary faints and is taken to
the hospital, where he immediately undergoes an operation. When he dies
soon afterward, his wife insists he was murdered by anarchists. When the
police investigate, they identify several suspects, including his wife, his doctor, his lover, and several colleagues. (Written with Dr. H. Jellett.)

Enter a Murderer
London: Bles, 1935.
New York: Pocket Books, 1941.

Inspector Roderick Alleyn

The actors performing <u>The Rat and the Beaver</u> have in their roles variations
on their roles in life, and perhaps this is what makes the play so successful,
for there is love and hate, passion, fear, and deception. There is also mur-
der--in the plot of the play and in the acting of it. An entire audience
witnesses an actor murder another.

Death in Ecstasy
London: Bles, 1936.
New York: Sheridan, 1941.

Inspector Roderick Alleyn

To prevent any disruption of the service, a guard closes and locks the door to the House of the Sacred Flame once the priest has entered and begun the service. And there, locked away from the world on a windy, rainy evening, the congregation watches as a woman possessed receives the sacred cup and drops dead from cyanide poisoning.

Vintage Murder
London: Bles, 1937.
New York: Sheridan, 1940.

Inspector Roderick Alleyn

The members of the Carolyn Dacres Comedy Company have the usual petty arguments and tifts during their travels, as well as the perhaps inevitable petty thievery. But it is a murder that demonstrates creativity and planning among the members of the theater group.

Artists in Crime
London: Bles, 1938.
New York: Furman, 1938.

Inspector Roderick Alleyn

The autumn teaching schedule of Agatha Troy, the well-known painter, gets off to an inauspicious start. Sonia Gluck, the model, is assigned a pose from a murder scene, and the artists debate whether or not the murder as described is possible. They decide that it is, and Sonia later offers the ultimate proof.

Death in a White Tie
London: Bles, 1938.
New York: Furman, 1938.

Inspector Roderick Alleyn

Someone in the small circle of high society knows intimate details of the lives of several wealthy and respectable women. Several women in society receive blackmailing letters instructing them to make their payments at the grandest parties of the London Season.

Overture to Death
London: Collins, 1939.
New York: Furman, 1939.

Inspector Roderick Alleyn

Parishioners in the vale of Pen Cuckoo decide to raise funds for their church by staging a play. Despite personal animosities and unexpected volunteers, the group manages to be ready for opening night and a full house. Then they lose one of the members of their production.

Death at the Bar
London: Collins, 1940.
Boston: Little, Brown, 1940.

Inspector Roderick Alleyn

On his way to a village where he will spend a holiday with friends, Mr. Watchman has an accident with another car. Later he meets the other driver, Mr. Legge, in a pub, but the man is not interested in conversation with Mr. Watchman. Miffed, Mr. Watchman makes a point of trying to learn more about Mr. Legge and what sort of man he is.

Surfeit of Lampreys
London: Collins, 1941.

Death of a Peer
Boston: Little, Brown, 1940.

Inspector Roderick Alleyn

The Lampreys are a charming, eccentric, if financially careless, family, occasionally desperate enough to call on Uncle Gabriel to bail them out of debt. With a "bum" in the house (a bill collector who stays until paid) and bills piling up, the Lampreys again ask Uncle Gabriel and his wife, who has just taken up witchcraft, for help, but the uncle refuses. And to the astonishment of all, he is almost killed before he can leave the building.

Death and the Dancing Footman
London: Collins, 1942.
Boston: Little, Brown, 1941.

Inspector Roderick Alleyn

Jonathan Royal adds a twist to the plans for his house party: to ensure that it will be dramatic he will invite only those who bear a deep and abiding hatred for one of the other guests. The twist comes with another guest, a playwright, who will have the opportunity to watch his new play unfold before his eyes.

Colour Scheme
London: Collins, 1943.
Boston: Little, Brown, 1943.

Inspector Roderick Alleyn

A family of British colonials from India runs a rapidly decaying resort with hot springs in the north of New Zealand, catering to an occasional guest and an unpleasant relative. To this failing resort with neighboring Maori tribesmen come an offensive salesman, an actor and his attendants, and a few tourists. One of these has a strong interest in the remote areas reserved for the Maori.

Died in the Wool
London: Collins, 1945.
Boston: Little, Brown, 1945.

Inspector Roderick Alleyn

In 1942 in New Zealand a prominent businesswoman, rancher, and parliamentarian disappears; her body is later found compressed in a bale of wool. By that time, the wool business has moved on to another season, ensuring that all physical clues have been destroyed.

Final Curtain
London: Collins, 1947.
Boston: Little, Brown, 1947.

Inspector Roderick Alleyn

Agatha Troy agrees to paint the portrait of an elderly, well-known actor in his role for <u>Macbeth</u>. While staying at his estate, she decides the family must all be slightly mad. How else can she account for the casual and repeated vandalism of her work?

Swing, Brother, Swing,
London: Collins, 1949.

A Wreath for Rivera
Boston: Little, Brown, 1949.

Swing, Brother, Swing
New York: Pocket Books, 1951.

Inspector Roderick Alleyn

A marquis has adjusted to the postwar world by taking up dance music and practicing with a nightclub band. On the night of his first performance for the public, he performs as planned only to discover later that one of the musicians died on stage, and the marquis appears to have killed him.

Opening Night
London: Collins, 1951.

Night at the Vulcan
Boston: Little, Brown, 1951.

Inspector Roderick Alleyn

The usual tensions that build during rehearsals for a new play are aggravated when a young woman is hired as a dresser for the leading lady. The unknown woman bears an uncanny resemblance to the leading man and is undeniably a better choice for one part in the play than the actress cast for it. By opening night, even the most placid member of the cast is on edge.

Spinsters in Jeopardy
London: Collins, 1954.
Boston: Little, Brown, 1953.

The Bride of Death
New York: Mercury, 1955.

Inspector Roderick Alleyn

On a secret assignment in France to investigate drug dealing in a remote fortress, Inspector Alleyn is interrupted at the outset of his plan by the sudden illness of another traveler. Desperate for medical help, Alleyn must take the sick woman into the suspected dealer's home.

Scales of Justice
London: Collins, 1955.
Boston: Little, Brown, 1955.

Inspector Roderick Alleyn

Sir Harold Lacklander dies peacefully in his bed, surrounded by his family, but the aftermath is anything but peaceful. Sir Harold gave his memoirs to a neighbor, and one chapter in them could ruin the family, or at least some members of it. Colonel Cartarette feels bound by his word to publish the book.

Off with His Head
London: Collins, 1957.

Death of a Fool
Boston: Little, Brown, 1956.

Superintendent Roderick Alleyn

Mardian village has managed to remain unattractive and unknown to tourists, but the arrival of Mrs. Bünz may change that. Mrs. Bünz is a folklorist on the trail of a dance performed after the winter solstice in Mardian. The participants and other villagers try to drive Mrs. Bünz off, and one among them is especially averse to having outsiders present this year.

Singing in the Shrouds
London: Collins, 1959.
Boston: Little, Brown, 1958.

Superintendent Roderick Alleyn

Someone is strangling beautiful young women in London. When a policeman discovers another victim on the docks, clutching an embarkation card for a ship that has just weighed anchor, the police think they have a murderer isolated on the ship. Now they only need to identify the murderer before he can kill again.

False Scent
London: Collins, 1960.
Boston: Little, Brown, 1959.

Superintendent Roderick Alleyn

Actress Mary Bellamy is looking forward to all the attention she expects to receive on her fiftieth birthday from her family and friends, but one after the other lets her down. Her supporting actress has accepted a leading role, and Mary's costume designer has offered to do the woman's wardrobe. The young writer she and her husband raised has written an excellent serious play with no role for Mary. Mary yells at her dresser, her old nurse, and her husband, and before the party is over, Mary is dead.

Hand in Glove
London: Collins, 1962.
Boston: Little, Brown, 1962.

Superintendent Roderick Alleyn

The various members of the Cartell family don't usually have to see much of each other, but a party draws them all together, giving added scope to their animosities. There is open hostility by some for an adopted niece, and contained disapproval by others for other relatives. By the time of the treasure hunt, the murderer is ready to act.

Dead Water
London: Collins, 1964.
Boston: Little, Brown, 1963.

Superintendent Roderick Alleyn

In a small fishing village, a young boy is cured of his warts by a Green Lady who tells him to put his hands in a waterfall. News of this brings others seeking miraculous cures. When an old woman inherits the island and the waterfall, she decides to put a stop to the profiteering that has grown up around the site of the original cure, despite the protests and threats of the islanders.

Death at the Dolphin
London: Collins, 1967.

Killer Dolphin
Boston: Little, Brown, 1966.

Superintendent Roderick Alleyn

A Greek millionaire restores an old theater, prompting a director to write a play around an old glove that may have belonged to Shakespeare's family. The play and the theater are a success, and after several months the backer decides to sell out--both theater and glove.

Clutch of Constables
London: Collins, 1968.
Boston: Little, Brown, 1969.

Superintendent Roderick Alleyn

On an impulse Troy Alleyn takes a five-day cruise on the inland waterways.
She soon regrets her decision when she finds herself among a group of bickering passengers. Then she reads an announcement of the death of a passenger who canceled at the last minute. Before long there is murder and
suspicion on board.

When in Rome
London: Collins, 1970.
Boston: Little, Brown, 1971.

Superintendent Roderick Alleyn

A British novelist in Rome loses the manuscript of his most recent work,
only to recover it a few days later when it is returned by another Britisher.
Grateful and relieved, the novelist wants to repay his benefactor, who certainly wants to be repaid, but on his own terms.

Tied up in Tinsel
London: Collins, 1972.
Boston: Little, Brown, 1972.

Superintendent Roderick Alleyn

Hilary Bill-Tasman has worked hard to rebuild the family fortunes and buy
back the ancestral home. Now he is ready to announce his engagement at
a Christmas house party. As the guests arrive, all seems picturesque and
traditional, except perhaps the staff, all of whom are convicted murderers
released to work for Bill-Tasman.

Black as He's Painted
London: Collins, 1974.
Boston: Little, Brown, 1973.

Superintendent Roderick Alleyn

When the president of an African nation plans a visit to England, his penchant for moving in crowds without adequate security prompts the Special Branch to ask old friends of the president to appeal to him to accept greater security. One of these friends is currently engaged in attending to his new home and new cat, which turns out to be excellent preparation for his task.

Last Ditch
London: Collins, 1977.
Boston: Little, Brown, 1977.

Superintendent Roderick Alleyn

Having decided to become a writer, young Ricky Alleyn rents rooms on an island and begins his novel. He is distracted from his work by a lovely neighbor and then by the death of a young woman who had recently announced she was pregnant but would not name the father. Ricky examines the accident scene and realizes that he is thinking like his father. Soon he is facing the kinds of dangers his father faces.

Grave Mistake
London: Collins, 1978.
Boston: Little, Brown, 1978.

Superintendent Roderick Alleyn

Losing a gardener in a small village can be a major calamity, but finding a good one can make up for all the shabby nephews, smooth in-laws, and rich outsiders. In Upper Quintern, gardens bloom while friendships turn sour and the unsuspecting die.

Photo Finish
London: Collins, 1980.
Boston: Little, Brown, 1980.

Superintendent Roderick Alleyn

Troy Alleyn is invited to visit a retreat in New Zealand in order to paint the portrait of a popular opera singer while she is on holiday. Roderick Alleyn is asked to accompany his wife in order to advise the singer's associates on how to deal with a photographer who is harassing her wherever she sings.

Light Thickens
London: Collins, 1982.
Boston: Little, Brown, 1982.

Superintendent Roderick Alleyn

The Scottish play, Shakespeare's <u>Macbeth</u>, has its own reputation among theater folk, so when a director finds rehearsals for the play going well, he is relieved. But the reputation of the play wins out as cast and crew face unsettling experiences as opening night approaches.

J.C. Masterman

An Oxford Tragedy
London: Gollancz, 1933.
New York: Dover, 1981.

Ernst Brendel

St. Thomas's College has invited Ernst Brendel, a Viennese lawyer, to lecture, and on his first evening at the college he and his new colleagues immerse themselves in a discussion on the nature of the crime of murder. Before the evening is out, however, the least-liked don is found shot to death in the dean's office, and the academic discussion turns practical.

The Case of the Four Friends*
London: Hodder, 1956.

Ernst Brendel

A.A. Milne

The Red House Mystery
London: Methuen, 1922.
New York: Dutton, 1922.

Mark Ablett receives a letter informing him that a brother he has not seen for fifteen years is returning from Australia. The brother arrives and is soon afterward found dead in a locked room. Antony Gillingham, a young man of independent means casting about for a career, also arrives at Ablett's home and decides to become a private detective, in light of the given opportunity.

Four Days' Wonder
London: Methuen, 1933.
New York: Dutton, 1933.

Miss Jenny Windell stumbles over the body of her aunt, the flamboyant actress Jane Latour, in a place where neither should be. Afraid she will be arrested for the murder, Jenny plots her escape with the help of her friend Nancy, secretary to a famous novelist, and heads for the countryside, where various characters aid her on her journey.

Gladys Mitchell*

The Saltmarsh Murders
London: Gollancz, 1932.
Philadelphia: Macrae-Smith, 1933.

Mrs. Beatrice Adela Lestrange Bradley

Saltmarsh village is a quiet place with the usual number of scandals and ec-
centrics, but when the vicar's wife discovers that the housemaid is pregnant,
the delicate balance between public propriety and private sin begins to wobble. Soon there is a rash of strange incidents: a villager locked in a crypt,
footsteps on a roof, signals in the night, and an infant unseen.

Tom Brown's Body
London: Joseph, 1949.

Mrs. Beatrice Adela Lestrange Bradley

The Spey School for Boys harbors the difficult or eccentric boys and masters
spawned by the close environment of a boys' school. These types and the
various animosities of a school are taken for granted until two masters find
a headless black cock. The masters are right in thinking that things are getting out of hand.

Spotted Hemlock
London: Joseph, 1958.
New York: British Book Centre, 1958.

Dame Beatrice Adela Lestrange Bradley

A women's agricultural college, located only twenty-five miles from a school
for gentlemen farmers, is the site of several pranks, which the headmistress
sagely attributes to the men's college. When one of the women sees a headless horseman and another disappears, the headmistress decides things have
gone too far.

Death of a Delft Blue
London: Joseph, 1964.
New York: London House, 1965.

Dame Beatrice Adela Lestrange Bradley

Traveling in the Netherlands, Dame Beatrice and her secretary, Laura Gavin, meet a family of bulb growers and diamond merchants. The family histories have left members living in Scotland, England, and Holland, gathering in one place on occasion to bicker and argue over their respective interests.

Gwen Moffat*

Miss Pink at the Edge of the World
London: Gollancz, 1975.
New York: Scribner, 1975.

Melinda Pink

In a remote Highland hamlet the hard but secure life of farmers and fishermen is interrupted by rock climbers making a movie. Stark, the lead climber, savors a cruel pleasure in putting people down, baiting even his climbing partner and the villagers. Even more threatening are the tourists his film could attract, which would destroy the warm, trusting community of Highlanders.

Over the Sea to Death
London: Gollancz, 1976.
New York: Scribner, 1976.

Melinda Pink

In the beautiful mountains of the Isle of Skye, skillful climbers and their guides face the challenges of sheer cliffs and personal animosity. The wife of one climber is bitterly jealous of her husband; one of the guides is growing careless and surly; and an alluring teenaged girl arrives unannounced, upsetting the relationships among the climbers and hotel owners.

Persons Unknown
London: Gollancz, 1978.

Melinda Pink

Roderick Bowen is celebrating his eighty-seventh birthday and his defeat of the Atomic Energy Authority, which wanted to build a fast breeder reactor on his property. He falls down the granary steps and insists he was pushed, but no one believes him. While he grumbles about this, the villagers grumble about the person who is trying to scare away the tourists by throwing rocks at them.

Die Like a Dog
London: Gollancz, 1983.

Melinda Pink

The Welsh village of Dinas is being torn apart by the provocative behavior of Mr. Judson and his two Alsatians. Judson enjoys damaging the trails in the nature preserve, land he leased to the government, and letting his dogs run free. When the dogs escape from him, threatening the lives of the villagers, a search is begun. Then Judson disappears.

Last Chance Country
London: Gollancz, 1983.

Melinda Pink

Miss Pink is invited to spend a vacation with an American millionaire on his mountain ranch. The days are filled with riding and swimming, and the separate lives of the ranch hands and other employees are rarely noticed. The problems of the larger world come with the report of the death of two women who had been staying at a nearby motel in the desert, a lost place for lost souls.

Grizzly Trail
London: Gollancz, 1984.

Melinda Pink

Exploring the Rocky Mountains, Miss Pink meets four young people on a hiking expedition. The encounter leaves Miss Pink concerned, for the young people were not dressed for hiking. Later she learns that they have not returned as expected, and she joins the search party. Adding to her worries is her introduction to the grizzly bear and its habits.

Deviant Death
London: Gollancz, 1973.

Ruth Stanton, a crime novelist, is glad to get back to her village and her family and lover. But village life quickly palls when she notices that almost everyone she meets is in some sort of trouble. The greatest interest of the villagers is in the disappearance of Olive Lynch, who caught her husband with Judy Scroop. Then Judy Scroop disappears, leaving behind her six illegitimate children.

Anne Morice

Death in the Grand Manor
London: Macmillan, 1970.

Tessa Crichton

The residents of Roakes Common are delighted to have a family moving into the manor house, but the Cornfords are determined to change that. The parents and two children seem set on alienating everyone with a variety of cruel or petty tricks--blinding a dog, tormenting a cat, ruining a view with an ugly shed, starting bonfires. The villagers have every reason for turning on the newcomers, but little recourse against their harassments.

Death of a Gay Dog*
London: Macmillan, 1971.

Tessa Crichton

Murder in Married Life
London: Macmillan, 1971.

Tessa Crichton

Tessa is maneuvered into meeting an owner of a large department store and finds he is an old childhood acquaintance. She agrees to read an unpublished diary and is appalled to find page after page devoted to the hero's efforts to get even with people who slighted or injured him. This hardly seems more than unpleasant until Tessa learns that he is seeking revenge against a former store employee who has disappeared.

Murder on French Leave*
London: Macmillan, 1972.

Tessa Crichton

Death and the Dutiful Daughter
London: Macmillan, 1973.
New York: St. Martin, 1974.

Tessa Crichton

The death of opera singer Maud Stirling at age eighty-two precipitates some interesting choices: the chauffeur's wife runs off with another man; Maud's second daughter throws away many of her mother's trinkets; and several comment on how unlikable the old woman was. Then the family learns that Maud changed her will only hours before she died, remembering generously only one of her many heirs.

Death of a Heavenly Twin*
London: Macmillan, 1974.
New York: St. Martin, 1974.

Tessa Crichton

Killing with Kindness
London: Macmillan, 1974.
New York: St. Martin, 1975.

Tessa Crichton

Mike Parsons easily wins the admiration of people he works with by his sim-
ple qcts of kindness, and his friends in turn sympathize with his devotion
to an alcoholic wife. Then one day Mike disappears, and day by day his
wife learns more about what kind of man her long-suffering husband really
was.

Nursery Tea and Poison
London: Macmillan, 1975.
New York: St. Martin, 1975.

Tessa Crichton

Serena Hargrave has lived most of her adult life in West Lodge, moving there
with her young daughter after the death of her husband. Her brother-in-law
has been generous, giving her a stipend and employing her as a caretaker
for the tenants of the main house. Now he has returned from America with
a young wife to visit his old home, his old nanny, and his sister-in-law.

Death of a Wedding Guest
London: Macmillan, 1976.
New York: St. Martin, 1976.

Tessa Crichton

After a brief courtship, Ellen Crichton, Tessa's cousin, becomes engaged to a rich, charming, well-educated, and apparently responsible young man. Tessa, for reasons of her own, takes an instant dislike to him. Her reservations about Ellen's choice for a husband are forgotten at the wedding when one of the guests drops dead.

Murder in Mimicry
London: Macmillan, 1977.
New York: St. Martin, 1977.

Tessa Crichton

The cast of Host of Pleasures has been together for some time, and when the play is scheduled for an American run, the continuation of most of the cast seems to augur well for the success of the play. Unfortunately, the lead is given to Gilbert Mann, a master manipulator beloved by no one. Indeed, rehearsals in Washington are tense, and one of the actors is actually mugged and killed on the city streets.

Scared to Death
London: Macmillan, 1977.
New York: St. Martin, 1979.

Tessa Crichton

Rich and autocratic Edna Mortimer has long loved horse racing, though her bets are miserly. But one day racing loses its appeal when she sees herself a few feet ahead in the betting line and then a few feet away in the crowd. When she sees herself walking in her garden at home, Edna's health begins to deteriorate.

Murder by Proxy
London: Macmillan, 1978.
New York: St. Martin, 1978.

Tessa Crichton

Anne Monk has an awkward living arrangement. Because she lives with Harry Purveyance and their two-year-old daughter, with another child on the way, she calls herself Mrs. Purveyance. But Henry's wife and their daughter, from whom he has been separated for many years, live nearby. Anne is convinced that someone dislikes her way of life to the point of trying to murder her. The three attempts on her life so far, however, sound like minor accidents.

Murder in Outline
London: Macmillan, 1979.
New York: St. Martin, 1979.

Tessa Crichton

Tessa is delighted to be invited to serve as a judge for a competition at her alma mater and to look over her old school. She notices many changes she had not expected, particularly in the head of the school. Most surprising is a student caught stealing and another found dead.

Death in the Round
London: Macmillan, 1980.
New York: St. Martin, 1980.

Tessa Crichton

The patron of the Rotunda Theatre has found a new pleasure in life to complement her lifelong love of the theater: her friendship with a teenaged orphan. When the girl suddenly disappears with the petty cash, her benefactor refuses to believe what seems obvious to everyone else on the cast and crew.

The Men in Her Death
London: Macmillan, 1981.
New York: St. Martin, 1981.

Tessa Crichton

A young American heiress disappears in London, leaving no clues to her
whereabouts. Her aunt comes to look for her, and she and Tessa hire a
detective to help them. Still, there is no evidence of foul play, and the
girl's family fears she has fallen in with the wrong crowd. Then a ransom
note arrives from France.

Hollow Vengeance
London: Macmillan, 1982.
New York: St. Martin, 1982.

Tessa Crichton

Mrs. Trelawney, a rich widow from Australia, is set on turning her large
estate into a ranch, and to that end razes walls, bulldozes hills and shrubs,
and warns off the neighbors. She cuts down trees, sets traps, and harasses
her tenants. Many are grateful for her death.

Sleep of Death
London: Macmillan, 1982.
New York: St. Martin, 1983.

Tessa Crichton

The West End production of Elders and Betters is plagued with bad luck,
and the company is beginning to wonder if they will make it through opening
night. Two actors have been lost to illness and the financing is shaky. Then
members of the cast receive anonymous letters, further depressing their morale.

Murder Post-Dated
London: Macmillan, 1983.
New York: St. Martin, 1984.

Tessa Crichton

At an elegant dinner party, Tessa Crichton finds herself sitting next to a boor and across from a beautiful girl. The day after the party Tessa learns that the man's wife ran off with another man and the beautiful girl thinks her stepmother is trying to kill her.

Getting Away with Murder?
London: Macmillan, 1984.
New York: St. Martin, 1984.

Tessa Crichton

Tessa agrees to a vacation at a luxury hotel in the countryside before she discerns the ulterior motive: two years earlier her husband had been called in on the murder of a young woman at a nearby racecourse and had failed to find the murderer. Now he wants a second look, but his return visit unsettles the guests and upsets the hotel staff.

Dead on Cue
London: Macmillan, 1985.
New York: St. Martin, 1985.

Tessa Crichton

The death of crime novelist William Montgomerie could not be entirely a surprise for a man of his years, but the event prompts other surprises. A fellow writer is convinced that her writing led to his death, and a manuscript produced by his widow may have been stolen.

Patricia Moyes

Dead Men Don't Ski
London: Collins, 1959.
New York: Rinehart, 1960.

Inspector Henry Tibbett

The presence of young people at an Italian ski resort promises the older guests a lighthearted vacation, but the youths' exuberance in ski classes and zest for dancing in the evening cannot conceal an undercurrent of fear. While the villagers stoically conceal their own tragedies, the tourists react in surprising ways to the death of a fellow guest.

The Sunken Sailor
London: Collins, 1961.

Down among the Dead Men
New York: Holt, 1961.

Inspector Henry Tibbett

Several weekend sailors are stopped by fog, with one getting caught on a sandbank as well. The fog lifts and the boats sail on, returning when the boat on the bank is expected to be free. But it is still there, riding at anchor, the captain dead. The police accept the man's death as an accident, the result of an unexpected change in the weather, until Henry Tibbett, on his first sail, points out the logical impossibility of a man being killed by a boom in a fog with no wind.

Death on the Agenda
London: Collins, 1962.
New York: Holt, 1962.

Inspector Henry Tibbett

Henry Tibbett is sent to Geneva for a high-level conference on drug smuggling. Just before the conference begins, Tibbett learns that someone has leaked information on government countermeasures under discussion and the agenda for Tibbett's subcommittee. This means that one of the six high-level police officials, two interpreters, one   reporter, and a secretary is tied to drug smuggling.

Murder à la Mode
London: Collins, 1963.
New York: Holt, 1963.

Inspector Henry Tibbett

Putting together the special issue of a fashion magazine means quick decisions, tight deadlines, and frequent arguments, with little time for soothing bruised egos.   The staff at Style magazine seems to have worked out a good system for working on special issues until a key member of the staff is murdered only a few hours before the final deadline.

Falling Star
London: Collins, 1964.
New York: Holt, 1964.

Inspector Henry Tibbett

The wealthy son of an old family founds a movie company with a group of professionals in the business and soon finds the life of a budget director frustrating and unglamorous. The real problems, however, come with the actors. The leading man in a movie makes his entrance, runs down a flight of stairs, trips, and falls under a train.

Johnny under Ground
London: Collins, 1965.
New York: Holt, 1966.

Inspector Henry Tibbett

Emmy Tibbett goes back twenty years when she attends a reunion of officers who served at Dymfield during 1943. For her there are bittersweet memories, but for others there are lives still linked to the tragedies of the war. Pulled by her memories, Emmy agrees to write a history of that period, and this has a purpose she can't even imagine.

Murder Fantastical
London: Collins, 1967.
New York: Holt, 1967.

Inspector Henry Tibbett

The directed chaos of the Manciple family is mildly redirected when Raymond Mason, a neighbor, is shot in the driveway. The family members are persuaded to turn from their normal pursuits in the sciences or religion to attend to the mundane matter, in an effort to help their brother George Manciple. Though intelligent and inventive, poor George is not a genius like the rest of his family.

Death and the Dutch Uncle
London: Collins, 1968.
New York: Holt, 1968.

Superintendent Henry Tibbett

A small-time gambler is killed in a seedy pub in a manner that suggests professional planning. This seems at first like just another eruption of the criminal world until the police look into the victim's personal life. At the same time Tibbett is trying to figure out if the members of an international committee for border disputes are dying of old age or are being helped to their graves.

Who Saw Her Die?
London: Collins, 1970.

Many Deadly Returns
New York: Holt, 1970.

Superintendent Henry Tibbett

Lady Balaclava is convinced that someone will try to murder her, and Tibbett is therefore sent to allay her fears during a family reunion at her home. At the reunion-birthday party, Tibbett courteously tastes the birthday cake, sips the champagne, and smells the roses to reassure Lady Balaclava. But all in vain. Lady Balaclava enjoys these delights in the same order, and promptly drops dead.

Season of Snows and Sins
London: Collins, 1971.
New York: Holt, 1971.

Superintendent Henry Tibbett

In the Swiss ski resort, the lives of villagers and tourists rarely intersect for more than a moment, but for one village couple the world of the tourists promises opportunity and a future. Step by step, the young couple become enmeshed in a world of values they cannot understand, with tragic results.

The Curious Affair of the Third Dog
London: Collins, 1973.
New York: Holt, 1973.

Superintendent Henry Tibbett

Emmy Tibbett has gone to visit her sister Jane in the country, and Henry is looking forward to joining Emmy for a quiet weekend. As he listens to the sisters talk about Jane's work as the local representative for the RSPCA, a missing dog, and the recent conviction of a drunken driver for manslaughter, he begins to see connections between village life and London crime.

Black Widower
London: Collins, 1975.
New York: Holt, 1975.

Superintendent Henry Tibbett

Mavis Ironmonger, wife of the ambassador of the new nation of Tampica, is
the kind of woman who makes diplomats cringe: she is young, beautiful, sometimes indiscriminate in her attentions, and loud when she's drunk. Most of
the diplomats are used to her, though still easily embarrassed around her.
Then she is found dead, an apparent suicide who makes people just as uncomfortable when she is dead.

To Kill a Coconut
London: Collins, 1977.

The Coconut Killings
New York: Holt, 1977.

Superintendent Henry Tibbett

A U.S. senator is found dead on an exclusive golf course on a Caribbean
island. The death is attributed to local unrest, and the police arrest a man
employed by a small hotel. The hotel is owned by a British couple, who
insist that their barman would never have murdered a tourist or anyone else.

Who Is Simon Warwick?
London: Collins, 1978.
New York: Holt, 1979.

Superintendent Henry Tibbett

When Lord Charlton learns he has only a few months to live, he decides to
change his will. Instead of leaving his fortune to charity, he will leave it
to his nephew. The child was presumed dead in the war, but was in truth
adopted by a couple moving to the United States. Charlton's lawyer must
now find the heir to a fortune and break the news to those who were disin-
herited.

Angel Death
London: Collins, 1980.
New York: Holt, 1981.

Superintendent Henry Tibbett

The elderly miss Betsy Sprague enjoys visiting old friends and students scattered around the world. On a visit to the Caribbean she spots a young woman who was thought to have been lost at sea. Miss Sprague reports this odd occurrence to her friends before she goes off to confront the woman, moments later disappearing from the island.

A Six-Letter Word for Death
London: Collins, 1983.
New York: Holt, 1983.

Superintendent Henry Tibbett

Henry receives an ingenious crossword puzzle in the mail and later an invitation to address a club of mystery writers. When he gives his talk, revealing the solution to the puzzle, not all the members of the audience are pleased, and one is noticeably changed by Tibbett's information.

Night Ferry to Death
London: Collins, 1985.
New York: Holt, 1985.

Superintendent Henry Tibbett

The Harwich Hook night ferry is a popular way of traveling to Europe, and cabins are sometimes hard to get. On a return journey a British traveler is frantic for a cabin but must make do with the sleeping salon. In the morning he is dead, the police are waiting at the dock, and a fortune in stolen diamonds, thought to have been carried by the dead man, is gone. The police search the passengers and ship but find neither diamonds nor a murderer.

Simon Nash

Dead of a Counterplot
London: Bles, 1962.
New York: Perennial, 1985.

Adam Ludlow and Inspector Montero

The leader of the "small but vocal" Communist group at North London College is found murdered in a room in a men's residence hall. Unfortunately, the room belongs to one of the best third-year students in the school, a young man who seems an unlikely suspect in the murder of a woman student.

Killed by Scandal
London: Bles, 1962.
New York: Roy, 1964.

Adam Ludlow and Inspector Montero

During rehearsals for a play, cast and crew expect tempers to run high, but members of the theater group of Hareham Green are losing their perspective entirely. By the evening of dress rehearsal, members have broken down in tears, been threatened, or been publicly humiliated.

Death over Deep Water
London: Bles, 1963.
New York: Roy, 1965.

Adam Ludlow and Inspector Montero

A beautiful young woman traveling with her family is the natural focus of attention of her fellow passengers, but one by one they come to dislike her, leaving an air of hostility lingering over the cruise ship. This doesn't seem to bother the beauty, who chooses the least likely people to get along with.

Dead Woman's Ditch
London: Bles, 1964.
New York: Roy, 1966.

Adam Ludlow and Inspector Montero

Late in September, after the holiday season is almost over, a small inn in
Somerset is filled with guests who are noticeably lacking in holiday spirit.
Though some try to befriend or at least acknowledge the other guests, most
remain distant and uncomfortable with each other.

Unhallowed Murder
London: Bles, 1966.
New York: Roy, 1966.

Adam Ludlow and Inspector Montero

A North London church is beset with difficulties: an elderly vicar who repeatedly gets the church into embarrassing positions; dissension within the
church committee; and vandalism inside the church, apparently by Satanists.
On top of all this, the newspapers are eager for a scandal and someone considers the vicar dangerous, not the harmless and charitable soul he is known
to be.

Anthony Oliver

The Pew Group
London: Heinemann, 1980.
New York: Doubleday, 1981.

Lizzie Thomas and John Webber

Bored with her husband and her life, Doreen Corder trips him as he is going
downstairs, leaving him very dead. Widowhood, however, presents her with
other problems. Settling down to learn her husband's antiques business, she
falls into the arms of a supplier and is later robbed of the most valuable
item in the shop. Watching over Doreen with an increasingly suspicious eye

is her mother, Lizzie Thomas, and Lizzie's new friend, John Webber, a retired police detective.

The Property of a Lady
London: Heinemann, 1983.
New York: Doubleday, 1983.

Lizzie Thomas and John Webber

Margaret Garland, young and financially independent, picks up a hitchhiker on an impulse. When she learns he is sick, she takes him home with her and nurses him according to her doctor's instructions and to her neighbors' dismay.

The Elberg Collection
London: Heinemann, 1985.
New York: Doubleday, 1985.

Lizzie Thomas and John Webber

A middle-aged couple vacationing in France dies in an accident while walking on the beach. Although the manner of death seems improbable, the police can find nothing in the lives of the husband and wife, who ran a successful pottery business in Staffordshire, to justify suspicion or investigation.

Emma Page*

Every Second Thursday
London: Collins, 1981.
New York: Walker, 1981.

Inspector Kelsey

For many years Vera Foster was regarded as a lonely, self-pitying neurotic who let her sciatica keep her from living a full life and getting over the death of her father nine years earlier. When she is found dead, the coroner is quick to rule her death a suicide, and Inspector Kelsey agrees until he sees Vera's husband and her nurse-companion after the inquest.

Last Walk Home
London: Collins, 1982.
New York: Walker, 1983.

Inspector Kelsey

When her younger sister suddenly marries, a schoolteacher decides to move to another village and live her own life. Her new life, however, may involve less work, since she no longer has anyone to take care of, but it is no less solitary, despite her many kind and outgoing neighbors.

Cold Light of Day
London: Collins, 1983.
New York: Walker, 1984.

Inspector Kelsey

Gavin Elliot is likable as well as prosperous, getting along with his co-workers and even making amends with his half brother. His neighbor, Leonard Picton, is annoyed when Gavin's neighborly investment advice costs him money, but there is nothing in Gavin's life to justify his murder.

Scent of Death
London: Collins, 1985.
New York: Doubleday, 1986.

Inspector Kelsey

Joanne Mowbray will inherit a modest sum of money if she and her sister present themselves to the executor of their aunt's estate. The problem is that Helen left home four years ago, so Joanne must now find her. Refusing the help of the police in locating her sister, Joanne sets out to find Helen and promptly disappears.

Family and Friends
London: Collins, 1972.

The once beautiful Zena Yorke is now a petulant, diabetic, wasted middle-aged woman. She has alienated her husband, Owen, manipulated her brother, Neil, and rejected his second wife. She is famous for her rudeness to servants and her demands for attention from doctors. She even uses an old lover's confidence to torment a man, and she enjoys keeping wages low in the family business. The question is, who will be the first to attempt to murder this woman?

A Fortnight by the Sea
London: Collins, 1973.

Add a Pinch of Cyanide
New York: Walker, 1973.

A mansion turned into a hotel on the coast is an ideal spot for a holiday, even for relatives who have little to say to each other. When they do start talking, however, the motives for murder almost equal the number of guests. Nevertheless, the guests manage to enjoy some of the activities of the hotel, up to a lovely picnic on the golf course.

Frank Parrish

Fire in the Barley
London: Constable, 1977.
New York: Dodd, Mead, 1977.

Dan Mallett

The fields and lanes in Dorset farmland are deserted in the early morning hours, as Dan Mallett and other poachers well know. But on this night Dan is not alone; first he sees a car moving slowly along a lane, then he hears the driver and another man talking. Dan knows they must be up to something illegal, but he goes about his own business, poaching. The next day he gets a better sense of what is happening in his corner of Dorset when he comes upon a trout pond in which every trout has been killed. To Dan, this is truly murder.

Sting of the Honeybee
London: Constable, 1978.
New York: Dodd, Mead, 1978.

Dan Mallett

A man returns with his two children to the village of his birth, determined
to buy back the land where he was born. His devotion to recovering his
ancestral land impresses the villagers and farmers, except two old spinsters,
who refuse to sell even after he makes an outrageously generous offer. It
is some time before anyone in the village knows the results of the old ladies'
refusal.

Snare in the Dark
London: Constable, 1982.
New York: Dodd, Mead, 1981.

Dan Mallett

Poacher Dan Mallett has carried on his private war with groundskeeper Edgar
Bland for years, usually getting the best of the humorless man. But Bland
unwittingly puts Mallett in an almost perfect trap when Bland catches Mallett
poaching and is suddenly killed in the dark by an unseen third party.

Bait on the Hook
London: Constable, 1983.
New York: Dodd, Mead, 1983.

Dan Mallett

Dan is enjoying a quiet romantic interlude with the daughter of the local
bobby while her baby-sitting charge, Anna, sleeps. A shotgun blast alerts
them all, and they discover the estranged father of Anna dead in the front
hall. Anna insists she saw the killer and will turn in Dan to the police unless he takes her with him on his hunt for the killer.

Face at the Window
London: Constable, 1984.

Death in the Rain
New York: Dodd, Mead, 1984.

Dan Mallett

The villages around Milchester are the locale of numerous crimes: some legal, some illegal; some sophisticated, some heavy-handed. Several were in progress on the night of a brutal murder, and the main suspects of this crime are, understandably, loath to present their alibis.

John Penn

A Will to Kill
London: Collins, 1983.
New York: Scribner, 1984.

Superintendent George Thorne

The Derwent family has a deep love for the family home, willingly living in near poverty to remain there. When mild Peter Derwent is shot in the back on a rainy afternoon, the family faces the loss of Broadfields. There is nothing to be gained by Peter's death, leaving the police at a loss for a motive.

Mortal Term
London: Collins, 1984.
New York: Scribner, 1985.

Superintendent George Thorne

Middle-aged and just married, Hugh Roystone is truly contented. He settles his new wife into the school for which he is headmaster, looking forward to the coming term. Then a series of accidents damage the school and students, and finally Roystone is suspected of murder.

A Deadly Sickness
London: Collins, 1985.
New York: Scribner, 1985.

Superintendent George Thorne

Sir Oliver Poston, frail and bedridden, lingers alone in his manor, tended by his servant of forty years while his son, Alan, and Alan's wife, Diana, party in the lodge nearby. An accident during his fortieth birthday party changes Alan, subduing his wildness and driving away his friends and guests. When Sir Oliver dies a few months later, Alan's friends and relatives return.

Notice of Death
London: Collins, 1982.

An Ad for Murder
New York: Scribner, 1982.

A retired major opens his newspaper one morning to see a notice of a new book whose title heralds his own death. Annoyed but not worried, he goes about his business until a series of accidents, each more dangerous than the last, convinces him that the book title is a genuine threat, not a prank or coincidence.

Deceitful Death
London: Collins, 1983.

Stag Dinner Death
New York: Scribner, 1983.

Gerald Hinton is willing to attend a stag party only because it brings his wedding day closer, but this party seems designed to do the opposite. Just as the party gets going a beautiful and obviously pregnant woman bursts in, declaring Hinton the father of her unborn child. Later the guests discover another woman--dead.

Anne Perry

The Cater Street Hangman
London: Hale, 1979.
New York: St. Martin, 1980.

Inspector Thomas Pitt

In 1881 in London, someone is strangling young women in a comfortable, middle-class neighborhood. Much as the residents want the murderer caught, they are not entirely convinced of the need for the police to ask questions of the men and women who live in the area. Intrigued, Charlotte Ellison asks a few questions of her own, drawing the attention of the police inspector.

Callander Square
London: Hale, 1980.
New York: St. Martin, 1980.

Inspector Thomas Pitt

Two gardeners uncover the bodies of two children buried in the square of a fashionable Victorian neighborhood. The residents assume that the bodies are the misbegotten children of a servant girl. Charlotte Pitt, now married to her inspector, returns to her old neighborhood to learn discreetly what some will never tell the police.

Paragon Walk
London: Hale, 1981.
New York: St. Martin, 1981.

Inspector Thomas Pitt

The upper-class world of Paragon Walk is shocked in 1885 by the death of Fanny Nash. Young and innocent, Fanny comes home one evening, collapses in her sister-in-law's arms, and dies. She has been raped and stabbed to death. Since Charlotte Pitt's sister married up and now lives in Paragon Walk, Charlotte decides it is time to visit Emily and meet her neighbors.

Resurrection Row
London: Hale, 1981.
New York: St. Martin, 1981.

Inspector Thomas Pitt

In 1886 two theater patrons are waiting for a cab and try to take the first one to come along, but the cab doesn't stop immediately. When it does, the patron is appalled to see that the cabby is a corpse and has been for some time. The corpse is Lord Augustus Fitzroy-Hammond, who was buried two weeks ago. The police bury him again, but he is disinterred again. Inspector Pitt suggests to the family that this unpleasantness may be directed at one of them.

Rutland Place
New York: St. Martin, 1983.

Inspector Thomas Pitt

In March 1886 several trinkets are stolen from the mansions in Rutland Place; no one wants to disturb the well-ordered surface of their society over such minor articles, but everyone remains uncomfortable about the thefts. At her mother's request, Charlotte searches discreetly for her mother's stolen locket, until the thefts are overshadowed by murder.

Bluegate Fields
New York: St. Martin, 1984.

Inspector Thomas Pitt

In the sewers of Bluegate Fields, one of the roughest areas of London in 1886, the police find the unclothed body of a boy. Bodies have been found before in the sewers, but this one is of a well-cared-for boy who was drowned in bath water. When the boy is identified, the family refuses to believe he was murdered. When they are finally convinced, suspicion is conveniently fastened on the boy's tutor.

Death in the Devil's Acre
New York: St. Martin, 1985.

Inspector Thomas Pitt

In 1887 a grotesque murder in a slum called the Devil's Acre leads Inspector
Pitt to the wealthy neighborhoods of earlier investigations. The murderer
is vicious but appears to select his victims at random.

Ellis Peters

A Morbid Taste for Bones
London: Macmillan, 1977.
New York: Morrow, 1978.

Brother Cadfael

In the year 1137 Prior Robert is determined to find the relics of a suitable
saint for the abbey at Shrewsbury and settles on the Welsh Saint Winifred.
The prior and a small delegation travel to the saint's burial place in Wales
in the hope of bringing back the relics. Prior Robert is arrogant and force-
ful, and the villagers are not ready to give up their saint. Before the Welsh
folk can be persuaded, one of their number is murdered, and the murderer
must be found before the question of the relics can be resolved.

One Corpse Too Many: A Medieval Whodunit
London: Macmillan, 1979.

One Corpse Too Many: A Medieval Novel of Suspense
New York: Morrow, 1980.

Brother Cadfael

By 1138, King Stephen has brought Shrewsbury to his side and the Castle
Foregate has fallen; the nobles and vassal lords who opposed Stephen have
been sentenced to death. The townspeople and others hope the king will
now move on, and Abbot Heribert hopes he will allow the executed to have
a Christian burial. The abbot sends Brother Cadfael to attend to the 94

men ordered to death, but Cadfael counts 95, and the extra man was not executed like the others.

Monk's-Hood: The Third Chronicle of Brother Cadfael
London: Macmillan, 1980.
New York: Morrow, 1981.

Brother Cadfael

It is not unusual for a man of some wealth to give all to an abbey in exchange for a residence and care for him and his family for the rest of his life. Even so, the great wealth of Master Bonel raises questions about his motives. And a motive he has: angry with his stepson, Bonel decides to disinherit him and so has moved to the abbey with his wife and two servants, there to wait for a contrite stepson or a charter sealed by the abbot.

Saint Peter's Fair: The Fourth Chronicle of Brother Cadfael
London: Macmillan, 1981.
New York: Morrow, 1981.

Brother Cadfael

The wars of King Stephen have been settled, but the people of Shrewsbury are still living with the damage. At the approach of St. Peter's Fair, a delegation of townsmen from the guilds seeks a payment from the abbey from the fees paid by the merchants. The abbot refuses. Later, young men from the town make an impassioned plea to the arriving merchants, a brawl ensues, and the rich merchant who struck the first blow is later found murdered.

The Leper of Saint Giles: The Fifth Chronicle of Brother Cadfael
London: Macmillan, 1981.
New York: Morrow, 1982.

Brother Cadfael

The granddaughter of a crusader, barely eighteen years old and rich, is to be married to a sixty-year-old nobleman who regards the marriage as a profitable business arrangement for himself and the girl's guardians, an aunt and uncle. Many sense the wrong in this marriage, from the lepers who watch the parties pass by to the monks who note the mute acquiescence of the bride.

The Virgin in the Ice: The Sixth Chronicle of Brother Cadfael
London: Macmillan, 1982.
New York: Morrow, 1983.

Brother Cadfael

The war between King Stephen and Empress Maud reaches again into the west when the people of Worcester flee the city, seeking safety in the next county. Ironically, two of those fleeing are the kin of a knight returning from the Crusades and taking the side of Maud, whose forces raided Worcester. The two in flight left the care of the monastery and are now lost in the winter landscape.

The Sanctuary Sparrow:
The Seventh Chronicle of Brother Cadfael
London: Macmillan, 1983.
New York: Morrow, 1983.

Brother Cadfael

Just after Easter in 1140, the goldsmith's son prepares to marry. The goldsmith's wedding party for his son is interrupted when the son discovers his father beaten and his strongbox empty. The wedding guests turn into a mob, and chase after a young juggler, who was earlier thrown out of the party for breaking a jug. The juggler, Liliwin, seeks sanctuary in the abbey, and this is granted, giving Brother Cadfael and the deputy sheriff time to uncover the truth of the attack and robbery.

The Devil's Novice: The Eighth Chronicle of Brother Cadfael
London: Macmillan, 1983.
New York: Morrow, 1984.

Brother Cadfael

By 1140 the civil war throughout England has hurt the church as well as the countryside, with young men taking arms instead of church vows. The Shrewsbury abbey is therefore pleased to have as a novice a young man, Meriet Aspley, who is educated and of good family. The monks' welcome cools, however, after a few weeks with the novice. Then a canon arrives to question the novice about an incident at Aspley Manor.

Dead Man's Ransom: The Ninth Chronicle of Brother Cadfael
London: Macmillan, 1984.
New York: Morrow, 1985.

Brother Cadfael

The civil war between King Stephen and Empress Maud again moves close to Shrewsbury when the Shropshire sheriff is captured at the Battle of Lincoln and a young Welsh nobleman is captured by the nuns at Godric's Ford. Both sides consider the men a fair exchange, but one of the captives does not want to leave his confinement and a death disrupts the plans on the other side.

The Pilgrim of Hate: The Tenth Chronicle of Brother Cadfael
London: Macmillan, 1984.
New York: Morrow, 1984.

Brother Cadfael

News of the relics of Saint Winifred has drawn many pilgrims to Shrewsbury abbey. Most who come hope for a cure, like Alice Weaver and her nephew, who is lame, but some are doing penance by their journey and the pain it causes them. At the same time the abbot is praying for the soul of a knight who died trying to defend a supporter of the empress; the knight was attacked while he was traveling on a safe passage.

An Excellent Mystery:
The Eleventh Chronicle of Brother Cadfael
London: Macmillan, 1985.
New York: Morrow, 1985.

Brother Cadfael

By 1141, the intrigues among the followers of King Stephen and Empress Maud have brought about the destruction of Winchester and other cities, driving townspeople and churchmen north. Brother Humilis, old and dying, and Brother Fidelis, young and mute, seek rest at the Shrewsbury abbey; a knight betrayed by his wife takes the cowl; and a squire comes with a request for Brother Humilis.

Death and the Joyful Woman
London: Collins, 1961.
New York: Doubleday, 1961.

Sergeant George Felse

Alfred Armiger, owner of a brewery and a string of pubs, is ambitious and ruthless and no one is surprised when he rejects his son after the young man marries a woman of his own choice and sets out to become a painter. But people are surprised when Alfred pursues Leslie with a single-minded malevolence. The most recent episode is Alfred's purchase of a rundown former pub that Leslie and a friend expected to buy.

Flight of a Witch
London: Collins, 1964.

Inspector George Felse

Annet Beck's beauty takes the breath away, but she is singularly unprepossessing. She is content to live quietly with her parents, except for an aborted attempt to run away with a teenaged boy. Then one day she walks up Hallowmount, subject of local superstitions, and disappears for five days. When she returns, she insists she has been gone for only a few hours.

A Nice Derangement of Epitaphs
London: Collins, 1965.

Who Lies Here?
New York: Morrow, 1965.

Inspector George Felse

The Cornish coast was once famous for its smugglers, who operated at night.
Tourists may think this has ended, but the observant visitor might wonder.
When a group of tourists and locals decide to investigate an old family tomb
near the beach, they find a corpse only a few hours old.

The Piper on the Mountain
London: Collins, 1966.
New York: Morrow, 1966.

Dominic Felse

Herbert Terrell, an accomplished climber and head of security at a scientific
institute, dies in a fall while on holiday in Czechoslovakia> A member of
the British embassy there later visits the director of the institute and insists
that Terrell's death was not an accident. He repeats his view to Terrell's
stepdaughter, who arranges to travel there with her fellow students.

Black Is the Colour of My True-Love's Heart
London: Collins, 1967.
New York: Morrow, 1967.

Inspector George Felse

Several dozen people have come to Follymead College for a weekend seminar
on folk music, many drawn by the name musicians and the disc jockey Dickie
Meurice. Meurice enjoys the adulation of the students and the opportunity
to bait the performers, but he gets a bonus when Liri Palmer shows up.
Although Palmer says she came only as a student, Meurice persuades her to
perform, and she does, pointedly challenging another performer.

The Grass-Widow's Tale
London: Collins, 1968.
New York: Morrow, 1968.

Bunty Felse

Inspector Felse's wife, Bunty, is forty-one years old and the realization depresses her; worse, her husband is off to London on a case and her son has forgotten her birthday. To shake off her depression, Bunty takes a long walk, stops for a drink, and gets into a conversation with a sad young man. She accepts a ride from him and they stop to talk and eat. After he falls asleep Bunty opens the trunk to find a blanket for him but instead finds a body.

The House of Green Turf
London: Collins, 1969.
New York: Morrow, 1969.

Inspector George Felse

Maggie Tressider, an opera singer, has everything, but she almost loses it all in a car accident. When she is recovering, she admits that the accident has brought back the uncomfortable recollection of having caused someone's death. Obsessed with this dim memory, Maggie hires a private detective to find the corpse. He goes back thirteen years and as far as Austria before he begins to believe her story.

Mourning Raga
London: Macmillan, 1969.
New York: Morrow, 1970.

Dominic Felse

Dominic and his girlfriend, Tossa Barber, agree to accompany a teenaged girl to India. Anjli Kumar, aged fourteen, is going to India to see her father after almost ten years in the United States with her American mother, an actress. When the trio arrives at Mr. Kumar's house, however, they are told that the father disappeared one night a year ago, and Anjli's grandmother has been waiting patiently for her son's return ever since.

The Knocker on Death's Door
London: Macmillan, 1970.
New York: Morrow, 1971.

Inspector George Felse

When the last members of the Macsen-Martel family clean up their home to attract the interest of the National Trust, they also return a huge old door to the church, bringing in the bishop to preside over the installation. The locals take this opportunity to josh the newspaper reporters and tourists with tales of family curses pronounced by the monks turned out by Henry VIII and reprisals from the devil. It's all good fun until a photographer is found dead at the foot of the door.

Death to the Landlords
London: Macmillan, 1972.
New York: Morrow, 1972.

Dominic Felse

An idyllic boat ride on Periyar Lake in India ends abruptly when the young Western and Indian tourists come upon a boat just destroyed by a bomb. The boatman is still alive, but the rich landowner is dead, a victim of the Naxalites, a terrorist group determined to end the hold of landowners and empower laborers and tenants.

City of Gold and Shadows
London: Macmillan, 1973.
New York: Morrow, 1974.

Inspector George Felse

Dr. Morris, a renowned archaeologist, is known for his long absences from home, but his solicitor begins to worry when the scholar is unheard from after a year. His only heir is a young musician who has never met her famous great-uncle. Informed of his absence, Charlotte wonders what the man is like and reads his latest book, about a Roman site near the Welsh border. Curious, she visits the site and meets a guide who is as interested in her as she is in the site.

Rainbow's End
London: Macmillan, 1978.
New York: Morrow, 1979.

Superintendent George Felse

Arthur Everard Rainbow is an expert in several fields, most notably music
and antiques, and he uses this expertise to command people's attention.
When he and his wife move into the village of Middlehope, Rainbow joins
every society he can find and lays plans to co-opt every leadership position.
No one is happy about it when he takes over the choir, and one of the
choirboys sets out to make Rainbow look foolish and discredit him in the
village.

Death Mask
London: Collins, 1959.
New York: Doubleday, 1960.

After being separated from her husband for twelve years, Dorothy Almond
becomes a widow and responsible for her teenaged son. Collecting her son
from an archaeological dig in Greece where Bruce Almond died, Dorothy
brings young Crispin home to England, where he fights her at every turn.
He finally comes to trust his tutor, telling him a tale of a practical joke
that may have led to his father's death and the theft of a valuable artifact.

The Will and the Deed
London: Collins, 1960.

Where There's a Will
New York: Doubleday, 1960.

The Will and the Deed
New York: Avon, 1966.

When Antonia Byrne realizes she is dying, she decides to leave the money
from her successful operatic career to the people she cares for, regardless
of what people expect of her. Her doctor, manager, assistant, lawyer, and
relations learn this only after her death and are openly angry at the provisions of the will.

Funeral of Figaro
London: Collins, 1962.
New York: Morrow, 1964.

After his service in the war and his later work in shipping, Johnny Truscott turned to opera with the same passion and determination that kept him and his crew alive during the war. Indeed, many of his old crew are still with him, as members of the theater crew. It all starts to go wrong when Johnny hires a famous baritone to sing Figaro. Cast and crew dislike the newcomer, all except Johnny's daughter, who finds him charming.

The Horn of Roland
London: Macmillan, 1974.
New York: Morrow, 1974.

After twenty-eight years, Lucas Corinth is returning to his hometown in Austria, which he has not seen since he escaped from the Nazis in 1944. To this town he gives the honor of the first performance of his new work, "The Horn of Roland." But to someone else in the town, this is an opportunity for revenge twenty-eight years overdue.

Never Pick up Hitch-Hikers
London: Macmillan, 1976.
New York: Morrow, 1976.

Willie Banks is goodhearted and intelligent, but not shrewd or savvy. He accepts a ride from a truck driver and in exchange agrees to deliver a parcel to a flat, where, Alf tells him, he can spend the night. Later, Willie can't find the address, which is the best luck he has ever had. By getting lost he meets a lovely woman and saves his own life.

Stella Phillips*

The Hidden Wrath
London: Hale, 1968.
New York: Walker, 1982.

Inspector Matthew Furnival

Four librarians volunteer to catalogue the library of a new college and take advantage of the pleasant holidaylike atmosphere between terms. The work goes along well until one of them makes known that she has uncovered secrets about each of them and the college faculty as well. She is, of course, without blemish in her own past.

Death in Sheep's Clothing
London: Hale, 1971.
New York: Walker, 1983.

Inspector Matthew Furnival

Convinced that his aunt will leave him a modest fortune, George Shannon moves his wife and children to Elmbridge, his aunt's village. Here he has the opportunity to observe how hard and selfish his aunt really is. Soon both George and his wife are wishing Aunt Grace would die.

Martin Porlock

Mystery at Friar's Pardon*
London: Collins, 1931.
New York: Doubleday, 1932.

The Porlock novels were published in the United States under the name Philip MacDonald.

Mystery in Kensington Gore
London: Collins, 1932.

Escape
New York: Doubleday, 1932.

A young man who has fallen on hard times--out of work, out of money, and
out on the streets--breaks into a home in a fashionable London neighborhood.
He helps himself to a meal and a nap. When he is discovered by a young
woman, he apologizes for intruding. She asks for his help and shows him
a corpse in the library. Naturally, he agrees to help and carries off the
corpse into the night.

X v. Rex
London: Collins, 1933.

Mystery of the Dead Police
New York: Doubleday, 1933.

The Mystery of Mr. X
London: Literary Press, 1934.

In a quiet Surrey village a policeman is shot to death in the police station.
Less than a month later another policeman is strangled in London. Before
Scotland Yard can discern a pattern, yet more policemen, apparently chosen
at random, have been murdered.

Sheila Radley

Death and the Maiden
London: Hamilton, 1978.

Death in the Morning
New York: Scribner, 1979.

Inspector Douglas Quantrill

Mary Gedge's body is found near a bridge in a shallow river. On first sight she appears to have slipped, fallen, and drowned, but the river is too shallow for an adult to drown in and there is no sign that she had fallen and hit her head. Moreover, she appears to have been gathering flowers, wearing a long dress and going barefoot. Reluctantly, the police suspect murder.

The Chief Inspector's Daughter
London: Constable, 1981.
New York: Scribner, 1980.

Inspector Douglas Quantrill

Jasmine Woods is the author of several best-selling romantic novels, a fact not lost on her less-successful friends and other writers. She collects art and lives peacefully in the countryside, making no pretense about the reasons for her success. When she is found brutally murdered and her art collection gone, police proceed on the assumption that she was murdered during the burglary.

A Talent for Destruction
London: Constable, 1982.
New York: Scribner, 1982.

Inspector Douglas Quantrill

Two children find a skeleton under the snow in the rector's field, but no one from the area is missing. When the police try to get the villagers to remember a strange young man from the previous summer, they recall only a pretty young woman who visited the rector and his wife.

Blood on the Happy Highway
London: Constable, 1983.

The Quiet Road to Death
New York: Scribner, 1984.

Inspector Douglas Quantrill

A killer leaves a decapitated body of a woman on a major highway, and the police are baffled until someone decapitates a cat as part of a warning to a village housewife. Once again, the motive lies in the woman's past.

Fate Worse Than Death
London: Constable, 1985.
New York: Scribner, 1986.

Inspector Douglas Quantrill

Sandra Websdell disappeared two days before her wedding, but since most people thought she had changed her mind about marriage, no one notified the police for several days. They begin a search, but the days drag into weeks and Sandra remains a captive in a cellar. There is no ransom note and no threats to guide the police.

Ruth Rendell

From Doon with Death
London: Hutchinson, 1964.
New York: Doubleday, 1965.

Inspector Reginald Wexford

When Ronald Parsons arrives home one evening, his wife is gone, the first time his wife has not been there to greet him. When they find Margaret's body, Ronald insists she could not have gone to meet another man. Nevertheless, the police find books inscribed many years ago from another would-be lover. After many years away, Margaret had come back to live in the village of her teen years and an ardent friend.

A New Lease of Death
London: Long, 1967.
New York: Doubleday, 1967.

Sins of the Fathers
New York: Ballantine, 1970.

Inspector Reginald Wexford

Mr. Archery, an Anglican clergyman, is researching a sixteen-year-old murder, seeking evidence that might suggest the innocence of the man convicted of and executed for the murder of his elderly employee. The handyman on an estate was convicted of murdering an old woman, and now his daughter, engaged to marry the clergyman's son, is convinced that her father was innocent.

Wolf to the Slaughter
London: Long, 1967.
New York: Doubleday, 1968.

Inspector Reginald Wexford

The police receive an anonymous letter describing a murder and giving the first name of the victim, Ann. Since no one has complained of a missing or dead relative, the police can do nothing. When Rupert Margolis, a famous painter, arrives at the police station looking for a charwoman because his sister, Ann, seems to have left him for a while, the police think they have the beginning of a case.

The Best Man to Die
London: Long, 1969.
New York: Doubleday, 1970.

Inspector Reginald Wexford

Charlie Hatton and Jack Pertwee have been close since they were children, though their personalities have led them in different directions. Thanks to Charlie, Jack can begin married life with more than his pay as an electrician can buy. Indeed, so close are they that Jack cancels the wedding on his wedding day when he learns that his best man, Charlie, was murdered the night before.

A Guilty Thing Surprised
London: Hutchinson, 1970.
New York: Doubleday, 1970.

Inspector Reginald Wexford

Behind the façade of wealth, beauty, and generosity, the Nightingales live a sterile life, Quentin Nightingale deriving his pleasure from his brother-in-law's writings on Whitman and Elizabeth deriving her pleasure from her beauty. The façade crumbles when Elizabeth is murdered for no apparent reason.

No More Dying Then
London: Hutchinson, 1971.
New York: Doubleday, 1972.

Inspector Reginald Wexford

A young boy doesn't come home to tea, making him the second child to disappear in recent months. That fact, however, is all the two cases have in common as police probe the background of the mother, an artist from London very much out of place in her Sussex neighborhood.

Murder Being Once Done
London: Hutchinson, 1972.
New York: Doubleday, 1972.

Inspector Reginald Wexford

A young woman is strangled with a silk scarf in a neglected burial vault in a cemetery in a run-down section of London. The police have no trouble identifying her, but they can learn nothing about her beyond the last few months of her life.

Some Lie and Some Die
London: Hutchinson, 1973.
New York: Doubleday, 1973.

Inspector Reginald Wexford

Kingsmarkham is invaded by thousands of rock music fans, who camp in the parkland of a local estate and listen to their favorite musicians. When the festival is ending, the police are just about ready to congratulate themselves on the orderliness of the kids when a young couple announces the discovery of a body of a woman in a nearby quarry.

Shake Hands Forever
London: Hutchinson, 1975.
New York: Doubleday, 1975.

Inspector Reginald Wexford

Mrs. Hathall is looking forward to staying with her son and his wife, for the old woman is certain that in no way will the young woman compare with her son's first wife. The visit is not quite what she expects, however. True, the garden is full of weeds, but the house is immaculate. But worst of all, Mrs. Hathall walks into the master bedroom and finds her daughter-in-law dead.

A Sleeping Life
London: Hutchinson, 1978.
New York: Doubleday, 1978.

Inspector Reginald Wexford

Rhoda Comfrey was making one of her rare visits to her father when she was murdered. Convinced that the reason for her death lies in her life in London, the police set out to explore her life there, but no one who knew Rhoda has an address for her in London. When the police find where she lived, they also know the motive for her murder.

Put On by Cunning
London: Hutchinson, 1981.

Death Notes
New York: Pantheon, 1981.

Inspector Reginald Wexford

Only days before his wedding to a woman almost fifty years his junior, a famous concert flautist drowns in a pond near his home, leaving his considerable estate to a daughter he has seen only once in almost twenty years.

Speaker of Mandarin
London: Hutchinson, 1983.
New York: Pantheon, 1983.

Inspector Reginald Wexford

Wexford fulfills a lifelong dream during a two-week trip to China. He sees
many of the sites he had expected never to see and others he had expected
to be gone in time: old women with bound feet, who appear to follow him
about, and groups of foreign tourists whose concentrated time together provokes tempers. When he returns to England, Wexford's first problem is solving the murder of another tourist directly back from the East.

An Unkindness of Ravens
London: Hutchinson, 1985.
New York: Pantheon, 1985.

Inspector Reginald Wexford

Rodney Williams has traveled for the same company for a number of years,
so when he fails to return home, the police don't worry. But when he fails
to appear after several more days, they begin to look for him, and uncover
a number of clues that are contradictory.

To Fear a Painted Devil
London: Long, 1965.
New York: Doubleday, 1965.

Most people are awed by the wealth and style of families living in The Green
in Linchester, and few would recognize the signs of jealousy, anger, fear,
and ambition that the residents carefully conceal. But those among the residents who are honest would admit that many were glad when Patrick Selby
was found dead: his wife, friends, business colleagues, almost anyone who
knew him.

Vanity Dies Hard
London: Long, 1966.

In Sickness and in Health
New York: Doubleday, 1966.

Vanity Dies Hard
New York: Beagle, 1970.

Alice Fielding has always been plain, which is perhaps why she treasures
her friendship with the beautiful Nesta Drage, and appreciates her husband,
who married her after she had expected never to marry. When Alice decides
to pay a surprise visit to Nesta, she finds there is no address to match the
one she has been using for correspondence. Alice is determined to find
Nesta.

The Secret House of Death
London: Long, 1968.
New York: Doubleday, 1969.

The residents of Orchard Drive keep a casual eye on each other's comings
and goings, until their attention is fastened on Louise North, who has a male
visitor fairly regularly. Louise says he's preparing the installation of central
heating; her husband says they can't afford it. Susan Townsend is the only
neighbor who doesn't want to hear about the Norths' troubles, and she is
the one to find Louise and her boyfriend dead.

One Across, Two Down
London: Hutchinson, 1971.
New York: Doubleday, 1971.

Stanley Manning is longing for the day when his wife's mother dies, for Maud
has been living with them for four intolerable years. Maud is hoping Vera
will leave Stanley, and Vera is hoping for a little peace and quiet after working all day to support them both. They get what they want, but it is not
at all what they expect.

The Face of Trespass
London: Hutchinson, 1974.
New York: Doubleday, 1974.

A struggling writer becomes involved with the young wife of a middle-aged businessman, but when she begins to toy with the idea of murdering her husband for his money, the writer breaks off the relationship. For almost a year he struggles with his ruined career and his desire for his old lover.

A Demon in My View
London: Hutchinson, 1976.
New York: Doubleday, 1977.

For twenty years Arthur Johnson has lived secure in the routine of his drab controlled existence. Now he faces changes in the world around him that threaten to undermine the security he has created and maintained for so many years.

A Judgement in Stone
London: Hutchinson, 1977.
New York: Doubleday, 1978.

Two worlds collide in this tale of the literate and the illiterate. The Coverdales are sophisticated, cultured, and well-off financially. They hire as a housekeeper Eunice Parchman, lower class, stolid and plain, and illiterate. Eunice ultimately murders her employers because she cannot read or write, and throughout that is her deepest shame.

Make Death Love Me
London: Hutchinson, 1979.
New York: Doubleday, 1979.

Alan Groombridge is resigned to his lot in life: a wife who really doesn't care for him, two children who are at best distant, a dead-end job, and no money. To compensate he spends his lunch hour holding £3,000 at the bank where he works; this is the amount of money he would need to live a real life for a year. Then one day two young men rob the bank.

The Lake of Darkness
London: Hutchinson, 1980.
New York: Doubleday, 1980.

Many people dream of enjoying the luxury of enormous charity, but Martin Urban plans to make it a reality after he wins almost £105,000. He selects four worthy recipients, not knowing that one of the four regularly receives large sums for special services. Now this one must figure out who Martin Urban wants killed for his money.

Master of the Moor
London: Hutchinson, 1982.
New York: Pantheon, 1982.

Vangmoor is a forbidding place of closed mines, desolate stretches, and dolmen, but for Stephen Whalby it is a retreat and a world beyond all others. All this begins to change for Stephen when he finds the body of a woman, whose hair has been cropped off at death.

The Tree of Hands
London: Hutchinson, 1984.
New York: Pantheon, 1984.

Benet Archdale had long ago learned to live with her mother's eccentricities, even when they came to include threats with a knife. Now she must manage life with her young son and a visit from her mother, who insists she is now perfectly well.

The Killing Doll
London: Hutchinson, 1984.
New York: Pantheon, 1984.

A teenaged boy sells his soul to the devil in return for whatever will make him happy. His sister hopes the science he studies will help him advance in life. And a young Irishman discovers a railway tunnel, where he can sit happily and safely during the day and watch the big people go by.

John Rhode*

The Claverton Mystery
London: Collins, 1933.

The Claverton Affair
New York: Dodd, Mead, 1933.

Dr. Lancelot Priestley

Dr. Priestley receives an invitation from an old friend he has not seen for some time. When he arrives, he finds his friend, Mr. Claverton, sick and three strangers in the drawing room. Dr. Oldland arrives, tends to his patient, and takes Dr. Priestley away with him, to explain that the old recluse may have been poisoned a week ago. Though Dr. Oldland insists all is now well, Claverton is dead within a week.

Death in Harley Street
London: Bles, 1946.
New York: Dodd, Mead, 1947.

Dr. Lancelot Priestley

Mr. Mawsley, a successful Harley Street doctor, is not well liked by those who know him, but he is smugly happy with his life. At the end of a busy day, he has even more reason to smile when a lawyer brings him documents showing that he will inherit a substantial sum of money from a greatful patient. Yet not an hour later the doctor is found writhing on his dispensary floor from a self-administered injection of strychnine.

Nothing But the Truth
London: Bles, 1947.

Experiment in Crime
New York: Dodd, Mead, 1947.

Dr. Lancelot Priestley

Henry Watlington is a successful, hard-nosed manufacturer who demands the
best service from everyone. When his chauffeur arrives drunk to pick him
up after dinner at his solicitor's house, Watlington, less than sober himself,
is furious. Fortuitously, a policeman also appears, on another matter, and
offers to drive Watlington home. That is the last anyone knows of the businessman until his body falls out of a locked telephone booth in another
county.

Death of an Author
London: Bles, 1947.
New York: Dodd, Mead, 1948.

Dr. Lancelot Priestley

At the age of fifty-seven, Nigel Ebbfleet, a writer of second-rate novels,
has a best-seller. Free of financial worries for the first time in his life,
he retires to a cottage, finishes one more book, and vows never to write
again. So determined is he to begin a new life that he tells no one except
his agent where he is going. Nevertheless, old friends and distant relations
find him.

Robert Robinson

Landscape with Dead Dons
London: Gollancz, 1956.
New York: Rinehart, 1956.

When a scholar discovers that pages have been torn from an autograph edition of <u>Paradise Lost</u>, Scotland Yard concludes that this is part of a larger

plan to "create a climate" that will undermine the sense of security of citizens of the free world. But before an inspector can even begin his investigation, a body is found in a most undignified position.

The Conspiracy*
London: Hodder, 1968.

Jonathan Ross

The Blood Running Cold*
London: Casell, 1968.

Inspector George Rogers

Diminished by Death
London: Cassell, 1968.
New York: Bantam, 1984.

Inspector George Rogers

When a young couple returns their rented boat after a row on the river, the owner finds a blood-stained knife in the bottom and calls the police. When the police finally trace the knife and murder victim, the body they find was definitely not killed by the knife.

Dead at First Hand*
London: Cassell, 1969.

Inspector George Rogers

The Deadest Thing You Ever Saw
London: Cassell, 1969.
New York: McCall, 1970.

Inspector George Rogers

Attractive and middle-aged, Mrs. Bowker died during an assault and rape.
Her three attackers served three years and were released, but found they
were not free. One is hanged, and that is enough to convince the other
two that death is near. Spiteli is scared but also angry at his wife, who
has run off with another man, and Sconlar joins a religious group, a chapel
run by the Reverend Mr. Bowker, the dead woman's son.

Here Lies Nancy Frail
London: Constable, 1972.
New York: Saturday Review Press, 1972.

Inspector George Rogers

Nancy Frail is a high-class prostitute, selective in her clientele and private
life. When she ends one business relationship, she adopts a cat. On the
night she is found dead in a car accident, she was the owner of seven cats,
each named after a departing lover. Her most recent lover does not appear
to be named among them: a young policeman who had hoped to marry her.

The Burning of Billy Toober
London: Constable, 1974.
New York: Walker, 1976.

Superintendent George Rogers

Billy Toober informed on a local criminal, who was convicted on Billy's information. Now Billy is being threatened by the man's brother. When a body
is found burned beyond recognition but apparently Billy's, the police vow to
get the obvious suspects.

I Know What It's Like to Die
London: Constable, 1976.
New York: Walker, 1978.

Superintendent George Rogers

Four men are arrested and sentenced after a botched bank robbery, but the money is never found. The most probable explanation is that Deirdre Quimby, wife of one of the robbers, ran off with it. When the men are released from prison, the police wait for one to give away the secret of the money's location. Then one of the robbers is killed by a hit-and-run driver, and the police are stumped until a psychic comes forward to help.

A Rattling of Old Bones
London: Constable, 1979.
New York: Scribner, 1982.

Superintendent George Rogers

A burglar finds a mummified body in a cupboard in a house that has been empty for some time. The body is taken to be that of a woman of some social standing who was disliked by many and whose husband left her when he became fed up with her many casual affairs, including one with a police detective.

Dark Blue and Dangerous
London: Constable, 1981.
New York: Scribner, 1981.

Superintendent George Rogers

Police Sergeant Christopher Proctor is an up-and-coming officer whose career comes to an abrupt halt when he is drowned in a canal. Unhappy at the idea of investigating one of their own, the police soon find other factors that might have stopped his career. His private life included a maze of affairs with married women and small lies to promote his career.

Death's Head
London: Constable, 1982.
New York: St. Martin, 1982.

Superintendent George Rogers

Mr. Lockersbie is an amiable, educated man who is now the town drunk. His tale one evening of having seen a dead man on the church porch, where he usually sleeps, is too lucid to ignore. The corpse is gone when the police arrive. They consider the matter, but the only missing person is a lepidopterist whose wife reported him missing almost two days earlier and no longer seems interested in finding him.

Dead Eye
London: Constable, 1983.
New York: St. Martin, 1984.

Superintendent George Rogers

A man surges out of the dark in a quiet lane, lunging and falling to the ground. Miss Birkin thinks she is being attacked, but the man is dying. A private detective, the man had been standing alone in the lane, watching the house of a woman who had hired him to trail her husband.

Dropped Dead
London: Constable, 1984.
New York: St. Martin, 1985.

Superintendent George Rogers

A gameskeeper finds a body in the woods, apparently that of a woman who has fallen from the sky. This seems to the police to be an unlikely accident, and they turn to two local flying clubs. The club members immediately recognize the woman, telling the police that she has just left for Europe.

Burial Deferred
London: Constable, 1985.
New York: St. Martin, 1986.

Superintendent George Rogers

Rogers wakes up in a hospital with no recollection of how he got there.
The police at first think he is simply the victim of a car accident until the
doctors find bits of tree bark mixed in with the auto glass in his hair. When
the police locate the spot where Rogers must have been hit, they find a
grave but no body. The closest dwelling in the area, moreover, is a Victorian
guest house owned by a blind woman.

Patrick Ruell

The Castle of the Demon
London: Long, 1971.
New York: Hawthorn, 1973.

At her husband's request, Emily Salter agrees to spend two weeks in a cottage on the Solway, to give herself time before she decides to leave him
for good. The idyllic coast she knew as a child is gone, however, and in its
place she finds a sinister undercurrent hard to define. Her cottage is searched carefully, a face appears at a window, a tourist disappears while out walking, and two archaeologists are digging a trench in bushes.

Red Christmas
London: Long, 1972.
New York: Hawthorn, 1972.

Guests gather at Dingley Dell, an inn that attempts to recreate a Dickensian
Christmas. The jovial if sometimes inaccurate recreation is marred by increasingly bizarre developments: a footman is badly injured, guests fail to
arrive, and Mr. Boswell takes a more than close interest in the guests, even
keeping files on them.

Death Takes the Low Road
London: Hutchinson, 1974.

A university administrator is suddenly reminded that twenty years earlier he had agreed to work for the Communists. Now called upon to do so, he is shocked and flees to Scotland, hoping to elude his former comrades. His American girlfriend, worried by his peripatetic behavior, decides to go after him.

Urn Burial
London: Hutchinson, 1975.

In a desolate region of Cumberland, neglected by business and now the site of an abandoned research center, a young archaeologist uncovers a set of bones, which then disappear and later reappear. While she is looking for the bones, her guardian, a senior archaeologist, also disappears, sending her notes that he is visiting friends in the area.

Dorothy L. Sayers

Whose Body?
London: Unwin, 1923.
New York: Boni, 1923.

Lord Peter Wimsey

A timid architect returns from a business trip to find the body of a middle-aged man in his bathtub. The man's hair has been neatly cut and his face well shaven, but no one seems to recognize him.

Clouds of Witness
London: Unwin, 1926.
New York: Dial, 1927.

Lord Peter Wimsey

Murder becomes a family affair for Lord Peter when his brother, the duke of Denver, is arrested for the murder of his future brother-in-law. The Dowager Duchess maintains the family standards while two of her children mislead and misinform the police.

The Unpleasantness at the Bellona Club
London: Benn, 1928.
New York: Payson, 1928.

Lord Peter Wimsey

Every day General Fentiman arrives at his club and settles into a chair with his newspaper, until one evening another member notices that he is dead. Discomforting but not unexpected, his death is hardly remarked upon until the Fentiman family solicitor points out that the exact time of death is of crucial importance for his heirs.

Unnatural Death
London: Benn, 1927.

The Dawson Pedigree
New York: Dial, 1928.

Lord Peter Wimsey

An old woman who is given only a few more months to live in her battle against cancer dies suddenly one evening, and her doctor can find no reason for her early death. Still, he cannot simply forget it, especially after recalling the old woman's fear that a nurse was trying to kill her.

Strong Poison
London: Gollancz, 1930.
New York: Brewer, 1930.

Lord Peter Wimsey

Mystery writer Harriet Vane is on trial for the murder of her lover, Philip Boyes, but the jurors cannot agree on a verdict. The juror with the strongest reservation about Vane's guilt is a Miss Climpson, who happens to know Lord Peter Wimsey. Lord Peter, like Miss Climpson, is convinced of the young woman's innocence and demands of the defense counsel the opportunity to prove it.

The Five Red Herrings
London: Gollancz, 1931.

Suspicious Characters
New York: Brewer, 1931.

Lord Peter Wimsey

In a corner of Scotland the residents have combined the agreeable arts of painting and fishing to produce an idyllic community. A recent arrival, however, has brought only discord and is soon dead from a fall.

Have His Carcase
London: Gollancz, 1932.
New York: Brewer, 1932.

Lord Peter Wimsey

On a walking tour after being acquitted of murder and before beginning her next mystery novel, Harriet Vane stops to eat lunch on a quiet beach. When she awakens from a short nap, she sees a man lying on the rocks, his throat cut and the tide rising. Once again, Harriet is a suspect in a murder case.

Murder Must Advertise
London: Gollancz, 1933.
New York: Harcourt, 1933.

Lord Peter Wimsey

The cynical world of Pym's Publicity, an advertising agency, is disrupted by
the death of a young copy writer, who dies in a fall down the stairs. He is
quickly replaced by a new writer, who spoofs and spies as he tries to figure
out the advertising game and the copy writer's death.

The Nine Tailors
London: Gollancz, 1934.
New York: Harcourt, 1934.

Lord Peter Wimsey

Winter in East Anglia can be harsh. First, two change-ringers are stricken
with the flu, disrupting the vicar's plans for ringing the bells during the
holiday season; then Sir Henry Thorpe dies, and when the grave diggers open
the family grave, they find another corpse, this one buried without cere-
mony.

Gaudy Night
London: Gollancz, 1935.
New York: Harcourt, 1936.

Lord Peter Wimsey

Harriet Vane returns to her college at Oxford for a Gaudy, steeling herself
for the tactless remarks and probing questions that are inevitable when old
friends meet one of their own who has been accused of murder. She is
therefore not prepared for what she does encounter: a campaign of poison-
pen letters directed against others at the college.

Busman's Honeymoon
London: Gollancz, 1937.
New York: Harcourt, 1937.

Lord Peter Wimsey

Lord Peter and Harriet Vane slip away after their wedding to a house in the country, only to find it locked and no sign of preparations for their arrival. Nevertheless, they settle in for a honeymoon until Bunter, the butler, finds a corpse in the cellar.

The Documents in the Case
London: Benn, 1930.
New York: Brewer, 1930.

Two artists, a writer and a painter, share a flat in the home of a middle-aged couple. One artist draws close to the couple and the other grows distant, and one of the tenants is intimate with the wife. (Written with Robert Eustace.)

John Sherwood*

Green Trigger Fingers
London: Gollancz, 1984.
New York: Scribner, 1984.

Celia Grant

The village of Westfield is slowly recovering from the shock of finding two residents murdered at their back door. The gossips have settled on the most likely suspect and are busy analyzing the crimes. Then Celia Grant, the owner of a gardening business, notices that the flowers planted in a garden the year before are not coming up where she expected them to.

A Botanist at Bay
London: Gollancz, 1985.
New York: Scribner, 1985.

Celia Grant

Uncle Bertie has disappeared somewhere in New Zealand, and the duke and duchess can't sell any family treasures to pay their bills until Bertie is found. The only clue to Bertie's whereabouts are three photos of a nude redhead and some rare New Zealand flowers. Celia Grant, a botanist on her way to visit her daughter and soon-to-arrive first grandchild, agrees to look for Bertie. Celia's first big surprise is finding out who the redhead is.

A Shot in the Arm
London: Gollancz, 1982.

Death at the BBC
New York: Scribner, 1983.

Angie Chatham threatens to divorce her husband, which wouldn't matter except that in 1937 the BBC, Tony Chatham's employer, has a strict rule about the moral behavior of its staff. Angie thinks Tony is trying to poison her, but only moments after she makes this accusation Tony is shot in the arm while standing on the sidewalk. At first Tony thinks Angie is trying to kill him, which would be a quicker end to their marriage than divorce. Then he begins to wonder. Things at work aren't going well either.

Dorothy Simpson

Harbingers of Fear*
London: Macdonald, 1977.

Inspector Luke Thanet

The Night She Died
London: Joseph, 1981.
New York: Scribner, 1981.

Inspector Luke Thanet

Mr. Holmes arrives home with a friend after an evening class and finds his wife stabbed to death in the front hall. She is dressed to go out, with a lovely pin on her coat but no purse. She and her husband have lived in the neighborhood for only six weeks, and Julie was a quiet young woman. As the police investigate, they come to know a woman without love for her husband or passion for her lover, a woman with a secret about another death.

Six Feet Under
London: Joseph, 1982.
New York: Scribner, 1982.

Inspector Luke Thanet

Someone murders a middle-aged spinster who has spent most of her life caring for her invalid mother and doing occasional jobs for her neighbors. The victim's nondescript life is mirrored in her clothing and her drab, austere bedroom. Then the police find almost a thousand pounds under her mattress.

Puppet for a Corpse
London: Joseph, 1983.
New York: Scribner, 1983.

Inspector Luke Thanet

A doctor who appears to have everything--a good practice, a loving wife, an accomplished son--commits suicide. His family and friends refuse to believe it, and then the police find a receipt for two tickets for a cruise in three weeks, meant to be a gift from the dead man to his wife.

Close Her Eyes
London: Joseph, 1984.
New York: Scribner, 1984.

Inspector Luke Thanet

Charity Pritchard and her family belong to a religious group that requires strict obedience in all areas of life. When Charity cannot travel to a weekend retreat because her friend is sick, that seems to be the end of it. But when her parents return home from an emergency trip to the home of relatives, Charity is gone. No one knows where she went. When the police finally find her, she appears to have been returning from a weekend trip, just as originally planned.

Last Seen Alive
London: Joseph, 1985.
New York: Scribner, 1985.

Inspector Luke Thanet

Alicia Parnell is a face from the past, come back to her hometown after twenty years to hear a concert by a now-famous performer who also is returning to his hometown after a long absence. Though she was well liked when she was a teenager, no one seems glad to see Alicia again after so many years.

Jeremy Sturrock

The Village of Rogues
London: Macmillan, 1972.

The Thieftaker
New York: Walker, 1972.

Jeremy Sturrock

In 1798, Jeremy Sturrock of the Bow Street Runners is dispatched to the hamlet of Roehampton to apprehend a highway robber who stole Lady Hartingfield's jewels from her while she was traveling in her carriage. Along the way, Sturrock picks up a young chimney sweep named Maggsy and trains him as an assistant. (The series of Sturrock novels was published in the United States under the name J.G. Jeffreys.)

A Wicked Way to Die
London: Macmillan, 1973.
New York: Walker, 1973.

Jeremy Sturrock

During a performance in the Theatre Royal, Drury Lane, a man is found dead in the ladies' common dressing room, apparently after locking himself in and then shooting himself with a gun. The dead man is the son of a wealthy banker, and the reason for his death is a mystery to his family.

The Wilful Lady
London: Macmillan, 1975.
New York: Walker, 1975.

Jeremy Sturrock

In 1802 a sea captain and his friend rescue a young lad from a press gang, but the lad is a young lady with sores from leg irons. She is soon delirious, calling out names and amounts of money. A Scots doctor attends her and falls in love with her, determined to protect her from all parties and to restore her to her rightful place in the world.

A Conspiracy of Poisons
London: Hale, 1977.
New York: Walker, 1977.

Jeremy Sturrock

Jeremy Sturrock receives a letter from a Frenchwoman asking him to meet her. When he arrives, she is dead; moments later her old servant is murdered. The Frenchwoman was a prostitute who fled the Terror in 1793, but Sturrock suspects there is more to her death than an angry client or robbery, for in 1804 the English are warily watching the goings-on in France.

Suicide Most Foul
London: Hale, 1981.
New York: Walker, 1981.

Jeremy Sturrock

In the days before Wellington and Bonaparte meet, London is filled with rumors, plans, predictions. While soldiers at a salon announce their intentions to meet Bonaparte, in the next room a French soldier who has deserted to the English commits suicide. There is no explanation for his presence there, his suicide, or the lines of a nursery rhyme scribbled on a piece of paper nearby.

Captain Bolton's Corpse
London: Hale, 1982.
New York: Walker, 1982.

Jeremy Sturrock

A sea captain finds a corpse hanging from the yardarm of his ship, only the most blatant evidence of something sorely wrong along the docks of Wapping. Tied to the crime in some way is an American captain and other highly regarded merchants and American visitors.

The Pangersbourne Murders
London: Hale, 1983.
New York: Walker, 1984.

Jeremy Sturrock

Sturrock has rescued from the streets a Miss Amelia Pangersbourne, who ran off with Gypsies a year ago after her grandfather died. The unacknowledged child of an only, unmarried son, Amelia has nothing to claim as her own. Nevertheless, Sturrock sets out to identify her inheritance from among her unacknowledging relatives and find her a proper place in the world.

Julian Symons

Bland Beginning
London: Gollancz, 1949.
New York: Harper, 1949.

Mr. Bland

Anthony Shelton is a dearheart and a cricketer, but when he falls in love in 1924 with Victoria Rawlings, the granddaughter of a minor Victorian poet, he gives up cricket for literature, or tries to. His first foray into the world of books leaves him with what may be a master forgery of a rare first edition. Although his father tells him that the book is probably not worth much, Anthony has several offers for it.

The Immaterial Murder Case
London: Gollancz, 1945.
New York: Macmillan, 1957.

Inspector Bland

Critics, artists, and hangers-on gather for a party to celebrate an exhibit of Immaterialist art, a new movement stressing the value of what is not there. The egg is the supreme symbol of Immaterialism. Even though their art is advanced, the participants in the movement are still bound by the baser passions--love, hate, jealousy. And before the party is over, there is a material body among the Immaterial art.

A Man Called Jones
London: Gollancz, 1947.

Inspector Bland

Edward Hargreaves built up his advertising agency by pushing everyone and keeping control, and the party he holds for the twenty-fifth anniversary of the agency is typical of him. Edward plans this party to announce the decision to take his older son, Lionel, into the business, but after Edward's speech, Lionel is missing. Edward finally finds him--dead in the library. The only clue is a pair of yellow gloves left on the steps outside.

The Narrowing Circle
London: Gollancz, 1954.
New York: Harper, 1955.

Inspector Crambo

David Nelson, executive editor for crime novels at Gross Enterprises, which churns out about three hundred titles a year in romance, crime, westerns, and science fiction, didn't get the promotion he had been all but promised; that went to his hated rival. Later he gets picked up by a prostitute, a slap at his manly judgment. His marriage is falling apart. Then his rival is murdered, and David learns that his wife was the man's lover.

The Gigantic Shadow
London: Collins, 1958.

The Pipe Dream
New York: Harper, 1959.

Inspector Crambo

Bill Hunter has managed to remain anonymous while achieving success as a television investigator-interviewer, but he finally meets someone equally ruthless. Prepared to push hard into the sordid deals of Nicholas Mekles, Hunter can only listen as Mekles reveals on the air Hunter's real name and his past. The police are also interested in this exchange and how Hunter comes by some of his information.

Sweet Adelaide
London: Collins, 1980.
New York: Harper, 1980.

Adelaide Bartlett has always meant to live out her destiny. Raised alone with a nurse in the 1860s, she only gradually learned that she is the illegitimate daughter of an English gentleman and a Frenchwoman. She sets her heart on an education, though others try to discourage her. Finally she is married to a grocer, and that is supposed to be the end of her struggle to change her destiny. It is not. Her husband dies of poison, and she is charged with his murder.

The Blackheath Poisonings
London: Collins, 1978.
New York: Harper, 1978.

By the 1890s Harriett Collard has ruled her family and the family business for almost fifty years, and the consequences are evident. Beatrice conveniently married a cousin who would join the business; George married Isabel, as his mother wanted; and Charlotte stayed at home. They have gotten along well for years, but Harriett's control is slipping. Beatrice's husband is the first to die.

The Detling Murders
London: Macmillan, 1982.

The Detling Secret
New York: Viking, 1983.

In the 1890s Sir Arthur finds the ways of the modern world closing in on him: his son marries the daughter of a financier, his elder daughter insists on marrying an MP with no family and no background, and his younger daughter wants to go to art school. Sir Arthur manages as best he can, but the ways of the new generation involve the family in murder and deceit.

The Thirty-first of February
London: Gollancz, 1950.
New York: Harper, 1951.

By 1949 Mr. and Mrs. Anderson are no longer close, but they live quietly together until Mrs. Anderson dies from a fall down the cellar stairs. Mr. Anderson is quiet about her death, not dwelling on it in the office or among his friends. He has been in a slump at work for some time, and his business colleagues suggest he take a holiday. Anderson is suspicious of this; he is also suspicious about someone turning back his calendar to the date of his wife's death every time he is out of his office.

The Broken Penny
London: Gollancz, 1953.
New York: Harper, 1953.

Charles Garden fought in the Spanish civil war and World War II and then withdrew from government service, disillusioned with governments and politics. His old contacts in the British government persuade him to topple an already teetering government behind the Iron Curtain. But even before he can begin his assignment, his partner is killed and Charles no longer knows who he can trust.

The Paper Chase
London: Collins, 1956.

Bogue's Fortune
New York: Harper, 1957.

After his parents die, Charles Applegate drops out of college and writes a successful detective novel. He settles on a prep school as the setting for his second novel, and accepts a teaching position at a progressive school for juvenile delinquents to get atmosphere. Fate accommodates him with students who carry knives, a murdered teacher, and letters naming Charles as an agent of a secret conspiracy.

The Colour of Murder
London: Collins, 1957.

The Color of Murder
New York: Harper, 1958.

The world of silent denial and aching need is closing in on John Wilkins. The blackouts he only occasionally had growing up are more frequent now. The only bright spot in his life is Sheila, the young librarian who smiles at him and seems to enjoy his company. When Sheila is murdered on a night when Wilkins has a blackout, he becomes the obvious suspect.

The Progress of a Crime
London: Collins, 1960.
New York: Harper, 1960.

Hugh Bennett is assigned to cover village news and a Guy Fawkes celebration, neither one very exciting until a gang of motorcycle riders arrives. The gang has come to get even with a man who threw them out of a local dance a few days earlier. To Hugh's surprise he witnesses a brawl and a murder, and later meets a sister of one of the suspects. This, he thinks, is his big break.

The Killing of Francie Lake
London: Collins, 1962.

The Plain Man
New York: Harper, 1962.

The editor of the Plain Man is used to digging out news, of various sorts, from resisting bureaucrats and politicians. When a member of his staff is murdered, he must turn his hard-hitting investigative skills to his own staff and the backers of the paper.

The End of Solomon Grundy
London: Collins, 1964.
New York: Harper, 1964.

At the monthly cocktail party for the residents of The Dell, a woman guest
screams and comes down the stairs angry, her dress torn. Solomon Grundy
follows her, holding his handkerchief to the scratches on his cheek. To
the neighbors this is delicious gossip; to Grundy, it is the first stitch dropped
in his fast unraveling life.

The Belting Inheritance
London: Collins, 1965.
New York: Harper, 1965.

Lady Wainwright accepted the death of her two oldest sons in the war, but
she never saw much promise in her remaining two sons and let them know
it. So it is with ambivalence that the household receives the news that the
oldest son, and Lady Wainwright's favorite, is alive and ready to come home.
When he arrives, only his mother accepts him as who he says he is. The
next day, the only servant who knew him years ago is dead.

The Man Who Killed Himself
London: Collins, 1967.
New York: Harper, 1967.

Arthur Brownjohn chose badly when he married Clare Slattery, though he
had his reasons. His solution to a poor marriage is to start another life,
this time as the man he has always wanted to be, and so the debonair major
is born. But even this is not enough to make Arthur happy when, as the
major, he meets Patricia Parker, who, he thinks, would make an ideal wife.
Perhaps now it is time to get rid of Clare and start a new life, again.

The Man Whose Dreams Came True
London: Collins, 1968.
New York: Harper, 1969.

Tony has big plans; unfortunately, his petty crimes keep tripping him up.
He lands a job with a retired general and meets the daughter of a millionaire,
but this ideal setup falls apart. All Tony wants is lots of easy money and
the freedom to live as he chooses, and he has no intention of giving up on
his dream.

The Man Who Lost His Wife
London: Collins, 1970.
New York: Harper, 1971.

Gilbert Welton inherited a successful publishing business that went into decline. A new partner brought in capital, and another associate brought in
authors. Still, Gilbert was unhappy--until his wife said she was leaving him.
Gilbert suspected his wife was having an affair with his partner, so when
his partner went to Europe on business and his wife went to Yugoslavia for
a holiday, Gilbert decided to go, too.

The Players and the Game
London: Collins, 1972.
New York: Harper, 1972.

The town of Rawley is home to Paul Vane's boss and other important people
he should get along with. Alice is not convinced of this, but agrees to move
there, and so these two join a town about to be enveloped in a special horror. One of the residents finds his only pleasure in life as Dracula, and he
meets a woman who understands him, who sees life as Bonnie Parker. To
keep their fantasy alive, they need a third.

The Plot against Roger Rider
London: Collins, 1973.
New York: Harper, 1973.

Roger Rider had enough drive to climb out of the London slum of his childhood and enough sentimentality to stay in touch with his childhood friend
Geoffrey Paradine. And they stayed friends even after Geoffrey found Roger
in bed with his wife, even after she killed herself, and even after Geoffrey
had an affair with Roger's wife.

A Three-Pipe Problem
London: Collins, 1975.
New York: Harper, 1975.

A nondescript man living a nondescript life is killed by a karate chop on
New Year's Eve. A week later a flamboyant MP is murdered in the same
way. Sheridan Haynes, an actor playing Sherlock Holmes in a television series,

is certain that Holmes could solve the killings, and Haynes, whose character seems to have merged with Sherlock's, sets out to find the solution.

The Name of Annabel Lee
London: Macmillan, 1983.
New York: Viking, 1983.

Dudley Potter has arranged a satisfactory life for himself as a professor in the United States, and it is all upset when he meets an actress named Annabel Lee. When she suddenly leaves him to return to England, he follows her, now willing to face the pain that drove him from England in the first place.

The Criminal Comedy of the Contented Couple
London: Macmillan, 1985.

A Criminal Comedy
New York: Viking, 1986.

Derek and Sandy Crowley are considered the perfect couple--until they and their friends receive anonymous letters stating that Derek is having an affair with his partner's wife, Gerda Porson. Derek says this is ridiculous. At the rehearsal of a village drama society, Charles Porson is almost shot by a prop gun, and on the following evening his drink is drugged. Now it seems that someone is out to get Charles.

Josephine Tey

The Man in the Queue
London: Macmillan, 1953.

Killer in the Crowd
New York: Mercury, 1954.

Inspector Alan Grant

The book was first published under the name Gordon Daviot.

A Shilling for Candles
London: Methuen, 1936.
New York: Macmillan, 1954.

Inspector Alan Grant

The body of a famous movie actress washes up on a beach on the Channel, sending shock waves through the movie industry. Living apart though not estranged from her husband, Christine had escaped to a small cottage with a stranger she picked up on the way. The police identify several obvious suspects, but none seems to have had motive or opportunity.

The Franchise Affair
London: Davies, 1948.
New York: Macmillan, 1948.

Inspector Alan Grant

Elizabeth Kane, a fifteen-year-old schoolgirl, disappears for four weeks. When she reappears, she tells her foster parents that she was kidnapped by two older women and held in their home as a servant. Her description of the women and the house matches precisely a home and its owners not far away.

To Love and Be Wise
London: Davies, 1950.
New York: Macmillan, 1951.

Inspector Alan Grant

A beautiful young man insinuates himself into the home of Lavinia Fitch,
successful writer, and her family. Leslie, who seems to be all things to all
people, charms just about everyone but turns subtly, insidiously, on others.

The Daughter of Time
London: Davies, 1951.
New York: Macmillan, 1952.

Inspector Alan Grant

Confined to a hospital bed, Inspector Grant peruses a collection of books
and photos from well-wishers until he is drawn into the controversy of the
reign of Richard III. By approaching the historical case much as he would
a contemporary murder, Grant identifies another explanation for the deaths
of the two princes in the Tower long attributed to Richard's command.

The Singing Sands
London: Davies, 1952.
New York: Macmillan, 1953.

Inspector Alan Grant

When the London Mail arrives in northern Scotland, one of the passengers
is dead, after penciling the beginnings of a poem on a newspaper. In Scotland for a much-needed rest, Inspector Grant recalls the lines, learning that
the details of the description of paradise fit the western islands of Scotland.

Miss Pym Disposes
London: Davies, 1946.
New York: Macmillan, 1948.

After reading thirty-seven books on psychology, every one a disappointment,
Miss Lucy Pym writes her own and finds herself a best-selling author. As

an expert on psychology she is invited to lecture at a small girls' college. Here she ultimately learns that she is not very perceptive about people, especially young women.

Brat Farrar
London: Davies, 1949.
New York: Macmillan, 1950.

Come and Kill Me
New York: Pocket Books, 1951.

Brat Farrar, a young man without family or connections in Britain, could pass as the twin of Simon Ashby, and this is precisely what Alec Loding wants him to do--present himself as the twin who committed suicide eight years ago.

Leslie Thomas*

Ormerod's Landing
London: Eyre, 1978.
New York: St. Martin, 1979.

In 1940 Sergeant Ormerod becomes obsessed with the brutal rape and murder of a young woman. When he thinks he has finally identified the murderer, the man is shipped to France. After Dunkirk, Ormerod traces the suspect to a hospital in France and persuades the military to let him go after the man.

Dangerous Davies: The Last Detective
London: Eyre, 1976.
New York: Dell, 1982.

Dangerous Davies, so called because he is considered harmless, discovers new information about an old crime and discreetly appropriates the old murder case. Proudly, Davies stumbles through his murder investigation and learns that others involved in the case have not forgotten it.

June Thomson

Not One of Us
London: Constable, 1972.
New York: Harper, 1971.

Inspector Finch

The villagers in Frayling are tolerant and glad to accept the man called John Smith, who chooses to live a mile from anyone in an old, run-down cottage. They even accept his laconic ways. Then a farmer finds the body of a young shopgirl, one never well regarded in the village, and the villagers quickly become less tolerant of strangers in their midst.

Death Cap
London: Constable, 1973.

Inspector Finch

New York: Doubleday, 1977.

Inspector Rudd

Mrs. King is a pleasant widow whose modest clothing shop is a welcome addition to the small village. Since she has been readily assimilated into village life, the police are puzzled when told that her death was murder. The means appears to be something she ate, and the murderer one of the modest, easygoing villagers.

The Long Revenge
London: Constable, 1974.

Inspector Finch

New York: Doubleday, 1975.

Inspector Rudd

A secret service agent is planning to retire to the countryside when he receives threats against his life. Someone has waited thirty years to seek vengeance in the Suffolk countryside for something that happened in France during the war.

Case Closed
London: Constable, 1977.

Inspector Finch

New York: Doubleday, 1977.

Inspector Rudd

Inspector Finch is being followed, and he is curious rather than concerned. Then an old pickpocket comes to him with a story of a conversation overheard, and Finch recognizes a reference to a four-year-old unsolved murder of a teenaged girl. The chance to solve this crime supersedes all other interests for Finch.

A Question of Identity
London: Constable, 1978.

Inspector Finch

New York: Doubleday, 1977.

Inspector Rudd

Grateful to a farmer for letting them dig in his field, the members of a local archaeological society are carefully uncovering Saxon artifacts. Among them they find a corpse, but this is definitely not from Saxon times. A neighbor mistrusted by other farmers for his coolness toward them becomes the prime suspect, and it is some time before Inspector Finch understands what is behind the farmer's reserve.

Deadly Relations
London: Constable, 1978.

Inspector Finch

The Habit of Loving
New York: Doubleday, 1979.

Inspector Rudd

The loneliness and hard work of farming can push farmers to extremes, but even the extremes can be borne until an outsider enters the delicately balanced farm community. A young man passing through a village sparks a final explosion of passions that lead to murder and fear.

Alibi in Time
London: Constable, 1980.

Inspector Finch

New York: Doubleday, 1980.

Inspector Rudd

A writer from London seems the perfect tenant for a vacant estate cottage, but within months many of the villagers openly dislike him. At first this seems no more than a natural response to the man's obvious malice toward others. Then the writer is killed, and the police take a closer look at his relationships with the villagers.

Shadow of a Doubt
London: Constable,   1981.

Inspector Finch

New York: Doubleday, 1982.

Inspector Rudd

Hawton Hall Clinic accepts only the wealthy, famous, or important as
patients, thereby ensuring prestige for the psychiatrists and other doctors
who work there. Maintaining this standing is important to Dr. Jordan, who
keeps a close eye on all who have any connection with the clinic. His wife,
a woman who is easily flustered, is only a mild threat to the clinic's reputation until she disappears. Then she is a serious threat to the clinic staff
as well as her husband.

To Make a Killing
London: Constable, 1982.

Inspector Finch

Portrait of Lilith
New York: Doubleday, 1982.

Inspector Rudd

The artist Max Gifford is now an old man, bedridden with arthritis, his dying
fame resting on two portraits of an unknown nude. When an art dealer from
London expresses an interest in mounting a retrospective of Max's work,
Max's second wife, Nina, begins to hope there will be an end to their poverty. As she arranges for the Londoner's visit, she must also deal with her
sponging brother and Max's first wife.

Sound Evidence
London: Constable, 1984.

Inspector Finch

New York: Doubleday, 1985.

Inspector Rudd

Against his better judgment, Hugo Bannister helps out a friend who wants to remain hidden for a while. He gradually regrets it, however, for Ray has a habit of drawing others into his problems. He angers his friends and lovers until someone finally murders him. His forays into crime and his dallyings with respectable civil servants like Hugo mean a long list of suspects for the police.

Dying Fall
London: Constable, 1985.

Inspector Finch

New York: Doubleday, 1986.

Inspector Rudd

Rex Holt has achieved his ambitions of wealth, but he is estranged from his son, Martin, and his mistress refuses to marry him. Unwilling to relinquish his control over others, he arranges a lunch at which his son will meet his mistress, who has just moved into the village. At the lunch, Martin also meets an American scholar who is photographing unpublished poems sent to Martin's mother by an admirer before her marriage. Martin is thus doubly betrayed by his father, but he is not the only one.

Leonard Tourney

The Players' Boy Is Dead
London: Hale, 1982.
New York: Harper, 1980.

Matthew Stock

In 1601 a troupe of actors comes to Chelmsford to perform at the hall at the request of Sir Henry Saltmarsh and his wife. Before they can do so, however, the boy who takes the woman's role is murdered. His shocking death is the first sign that the manner of living of Sir Henry and his wife must come to an end.

Low Treason
New York: Dutton, 1983.

Matthew Stock

In 1602, Thomas Ingram, apprenticed to one of the best jewelers in London, decides he must leave city life and return home to Chelmsford. Before he can arrive safely, he is stopped and beaten by a group of men who followed him from London. Left for dead, Thomas recovers just in time to avoid a burial, but not before others have gone in search of him in London.

Familiar Spirits
New York: St. Martin, 1984.

Matthew Stock

A young servant girl is hanged for witchcraft despite her employer's defense of her. Less than two months later, in late 1602, one of those who testified against her claims to see her face in a window, and then dies. So begins the time of fear that prompted more accusations of witchcraft and more strange sights, all testifying to the power of the young Ursula, the hanged witch.

Glen Trevor

Murder at School
London: Benn, 1931.

Was It Murder?
New York: Harper, 1933.
New York: Perennial, 1980.

When a young boy dies accidentally at school, the headmaster asks Colin Revell, a former student, to investigate. Revell finds nothing amiss and returns home. Months later the older brother of the dead student also dies accidentally. This time Revell is certain something is wrong. His instincts are good, but his detecting is terrible. (The 1980 edition was published under the name James Hilton.)

Michael Underwood*

Murder on Trial
London: Hammond, 1954.
New York: Washburn, 1958.

Inspector Simon Manton

William Edgar Tarrant was a charming rogue who persuaded rich women to pass on money to him, though they might think better of it later. Yet here he was on trial for shooting a policeman. Tarrant is about to explain this contradiction when he is shot in the heart as he steps to the witness box.

Murder Made Absolute
London: Hammond, 1955.
New York: Washburn, 1957.

Superintendent Simon Manton

Christopher Henham, London barrister, finds himself in an awkward position when his wife is arrested for a hit-and-run accident involving her car but driven by him. When he realizes he must tell the truth, his decision provokes sharp criticism from the one person who can corroborate his story and equally sharp reactions from others. Before Henham can do anything, however, he is poisoned in a courtroom during a divorce trial.

False Witness
London: Hammond, 1957.
New York: Walker, 1961.

Superintendent Simon Manton

Jeremy Harper, a young barrister, arrives in Seahaven intending to defeat his rival for the hand of Jennie Rawlins. Instead, Harper almost trips over his rival, Derek Yates, in a park. The cashier of Jennie's father's company, Yates has been attacked and the company payroll stolen. Even after the police settle on a culprit and the court tries and sentences him, others are still searching for the stolen money.

Lawful Pursuit
London: Hammond, 1958.
New York: Doubleday, 1958.

Superintendent Simon Manton

In six months, six petty criminals have jumped bail, all but one writing to a brother and reporting a safe arrival in Algeria. When Scotland Yard plants an officer among the petty criminals, he too jumps bail and writes from Algeria. The man's sister-in-law also agrees to help by dating a club owner thought to have connections with the criminal underground, but so far all the police have is a letter from Algeria.

Cause of Death
London: Hammond, 1960.

Superintendent Simon Manton

When Mrs. Sophie Easterberg is found dead on her bedroom floor, the police do not take long to identify a suspect--the most obvious and vulnerable person in the case. Dave Lucas, an ex-convict given a job by Mrs. Easterberg, was fired only ten days before and seems to have a perfect motive. But then motives seem to abound as soon as the police look more closely.

Adam's Case
London: Hammond, 1961.
New York: Doubleday, 1961.

Superintendent Simon Manton

Adam Cape is elated when he finally gets what he considers a real case: a prosecution for Scotland Yard. Carole Young has charged her husband with stabbing her during an argument. Despite his best efforts, Adam cannot convince the jury that Carole's husband is guilty; the jury finds him innocent and Adam is dejected. He thinks the case is over, but his trouble with this case is just beginning.

The Crime of Colin Wise
London: Macdonald, 1964.
New York: Doubleday, 1964.

Superintendent Simon Manton

Colin Wise wants to be rich, for he has expensive tastes in cars and art, and he methodically sets about defrauding his boss's customers. Though only a television repairman, Colin thinks big, and after defrauding a customer of £6,000 Colin murders him. He has worked out every detail of the fraud and murder and is annoyed when the police keep questioning him about small details.

The Anxious Conspirator
London: Macdonald, 1965.
New York: Doubleday, 1965.

Superintendent Simon Manton

The efficiency of the police has its limitations: after promising an informant that he will be allowed to escape a raid, the police capture him along with his fellow criminals. The police expected five and arrested five, but a sixth escaped. While the police prepare their case against the five counterfeiters, they also wonder how they will get rid of one of them, the informer, without arousing suspicion.

The Unprofessional Spy
London: Macdonald, 1964.
New York: Doubleday, 1964.

Martin Ainsworth

The comfortable life of a barrister is put on hold when Martin Ainsworth agrees to visit Berlin for security reasons. A woman he fell in love with in the 1930s is now an agent for East Germany and the British want Martin to rekindle the affair and find out her other contacts in the network of spies. Martin knows only that Elli remembers him, displaying in a silver frame a photograph he gave her twenty-five years ago.

A Trout in the Milk
London: Macmillan, 1971.
New York: Walker, 1972.

Martin Ainsworth

Robin Appleman has managed to rise above his beginnings to the level of a barrister, though he is still only a pupil. He is likable, well meaning, and competent, and it is therefore all the more surprising when he is found dead in chambers one morning. Even more puzzling is the early realization that the murderer had to be someone in the legal profession.

Reward for a Defector
London: Macmillan, 1973.
New York: St. Martin, 1973.

Martin Ainsworth

Charles Ashmore is an upper-class solicitor whose clients rarely do more than get a traffic ticket, so he is uncomfortable to find himself dealing with the defense of a client's son charged with espionage. Not long after the trial begins, his old college friend, now living in East Germany, appears in England and defects, seeking help from Charles. Even staid old Charles begins to wonder if there is more here than meets the eye.

A Pinch of Snuff
London: Macmillan, 1974.
New York: St. Martin, 1974.

Martin Ainsworth and Rosa Epton

Brian Tanner has just settled into his new job as assistant wine steward at the Blackstone Club when he is persuaded to take part in a burglary of the club's collection of snuff boxes. Unfortunately, this is followed by a murder, and Brian is charged with this crime instead of the one he knows about.

The Juror
London: Macmillan, 1975.
New York: St. Martin, 1975.

Sergeant Nick Attwell

On trial for pornography and a host of other offenses, Bernie Mastyn and his backers are determined to persuade the jury to his point of view one way or another. One juror receives a threatening telephone call, one is pushed off the sidewalk, and one is murdered. All this puts a damper on the camaraderie some of the jurors are trying to generate.

Menaces, Menaces
London: Macmillan, 1976.
New York: St. Martin, 1976.

Sergeant Nick Attwell

Herbert Sipson is on trial for blackmail against a bingo parlor, defending himself by psychology and charm. The police are convinced they have the right man even after another business is blackmailed in precisely the same manner as that allegedly used by Sipson. While police search for likely suspects in this case, Sipson remains under tight security, apparently fully absorbed by the business of the trial.

The Fatal Trip
London: Macmillan, 1977.
New York: St. Martin, 1977.

Sergeant Nick Attwell

After providing the court with the necessary evidence to convict, Sergeant Attwell doubts Stephen Burley's conviction for burglary from his employer's offices. Everything hangs on the testimony of the owner's assistant, and Attwell decides to reinvestigate the entire case.

Murder with Malice
London: Macmillan, 1977.
New York: St. Martin, 1977.

Sergeant Nick Attwell

An old woman is found murdered shortly after a violent quarrel with a tenant and another argument with a young gardener. Incensed by the questioning of his son, the gardener's father, a noted television personality, levels an attack against the police, leading to an internal investigation along with the murder inquiry.

Crooked Wood
London: Macmillan, 1978.
New York: St. Martin, 1978.

Sergeant Nick Attwell

An informant has led the police to the contract killer of the senior lawyer of a large law firm. The same informant now reports that there will be an attempt to bribe the jury. While the lawyers keep a close eye on the jurors, trying to keep anyone from derailing their trial, the police try to find the man behind the threats.

Crime upon Crime
London: Macmillan, 1980.
New York: St. Martin, 1981.

Rosa Epton

Arthur Kedby is a small-time crook who believes in keeping up appearances and cultivating a select clientele. At his club one day he recognizes a guest he has seen somewhere else, in circumstances the guest would not want publicized. And so Arthur prepares a blackmail scheme that destroys two men before almost destroying Arthur.

Double Jeopardy
London: Macmillan, 1981.
New York: St. Martin, 1981.

Rosa Epton

Toby Nash's New Year gets off to a wild start when his New Year's Eve date argues with him while making love and then demands to be driven to a police station, where she charges him with rape while he waits outside in the car. Although she later regrets her actions, she can't seem to bring herself to tell the police to drop the charges.

Goddess of Death
London: Macmillan, 1982.
New York: St. Martin, 1982.

Rosa Epton

An early morning call from a man she remembers as likable sends Rosa Epton
to the defense of his younger brother, who has been arrested for tampering
with cars and is an example of the surly youth with a chip on his shoulder.
Rosa tries several times to let the older brother know the state of the case,
but he never has the time to talk whenever Rosa calls him. Then the newspapers report his death, and Rosa wonders who was answering the phone
for him and pretending to be him.

A Party to Murder
London: Macmillan, 1983.
New York: St. Martin, 1983.

Rosa Epton and Martin Ainsworth

The lawyers in the chief prosecuting solicitor's office know they are in for
a change when the director retires, but no one is ready for the man chosen
to replace him: a solicitor who is charming but hard, and remembered for
his shabby treatment of another member of the firm with whom he once
had an affair. All of this is carefully analyzed by the staff, and by the time
of their annual Christmas party, there is little goodwill in the office.

Death in Camera
London: Macmillan, 1984.
New York: St. Martin, 1984.

Rosa Epton

The official opening of the new Runnymede Crown Court is a tedious affair
of polite speeches and even politer applause. The etiquette is breached, however, when the judges and counselors gather for a photo session. Suddenly
one of the judges is startled, falls out of a window into the Thames, and
drowns. Murder hardly seems possible in the company in question, but murder
it is.

The Hidden Man
London: Macmillan, 1985.
New York: St. Martin, 1985.

Rosa Epton

Jonathan Cool is the idol of millions, and Cheryl Peterson, his girlfriend,
the envy of them all, according to her parents. Then one night he is struck
and killed on a country road and Cheryl's version of the accident disagrees
with that of the driver of the other car. As the driver, Sarah Atkins, tries
to cope with the coming trial, her husband disappears at odd moments,
smoothing over his bizarre behavior with contradictory explanations.

The Silent Liars
London: Macmillan, 1970.
New York: Doubleday, 1970.

Christopher Laker lives what he considers an intelligent life: he works when
he needs money, lives with a series of girlfriends, and studies guitar and
topics of interest to him. None of these features of his life will endear
him to the jury charged with deciding if he murdered a Hungarian businessman Chris insists he never met.

Anything But the Truth
London: Macmillan, 1978.
New York: St. Martin, 1978.

Ian Tanner is charged with killing a pedestrian with a car he has stolen for
a joyride. He doesn't deny this, but he doesn't explain why the victim, whom
he knew, was in the remote area in the first place, why he stole a car, and
why he stole the car of the owner of the pub he frequents. In addition,
one of the main witnesses against him is a member of a rival gang who has
a pretty lame reason for being at the site of the accident.

Smooth Justice
London: Macmillan, 1979.
New York: St. Martin, 1979.

Mr. Justice Ferney is called the kindly magistrate by the newspapers, but
he is anything but kind to the lawyers and court officers he works with.
He fails to realize just how insufferable he is until he receives anonymous
threatening letters. Even then he continues to harass his officers and lawyers, a sign he has succumbed completely to "judgitis," according to one barrister.

Victim of Circumstance
London: Macmillan, 1979.
New York: St. Martin, 1980.

John Farndon made a mistake when he married the Frenchwoman Monique,
but he lived with it for four years. The arrival of Belinda Dow at the boys'
school where John teaches changes everything, for she touches in him an
old longing. Carefully and deliberately, John plans his wife's murder.

A Clear Case of Suicide
London: Macmillan, 1980.
New York: St. Martin, 1980.

After a brilliant success in court, Laurence Deegan returns to his chambers
and later commits suicide. Before his death, this had been an ordinary day
for Laurence, except for two incidents. For the first time, he sent back a
brief that had been accepted, to defend a man charged under the Official
Secrets Act. He also showed no interest in defending the son of a millionaire
charged with murder.

Hand of Fate
London: Macmillan, 1981.
New York: St. Martin, 1982.

Frank Wimble is accustomed to getting his way, in business as well as in
his personal life. When he falls for Maureen Yates, she makes it clear it is
marriage or nothing. Frank's wife refuses to divorce him, so he decides he
must simply get rid of her. One day in September, therefore, Elspeth Wimble
disappears. When a severed hand with her wedding band is found several

months later, Frank is charged with her murder. Throughout a long trial, Frank steadfastly maintains his innocence of dismembering his wife's body.

Roy Vickers*

Murdering Mr Velfrage
London: Faber, 1950.

Maid to Murder
New York: Mill, 1950.

Inspector Kyle

Bruce Habershon, the newest member in the family firm of shipping agents and well liked on many counts, leaves his office early for the day after coming down with a fever. After taking quinine to steady himself on his drive home, he encounters a lawyer, Mr. Velfrage, and blunders into a fight between assorted nefarious characters, all viewed through the haze of fever and medication.

"The Sole Survivor" and "The Kynsard Affair"
London: Gollancz, 1952.
New York: Detective Book Club, 1951.

The Sole Survivor. Sailing from the Cape to London, the <u>Marigonda</u> goes down in heavy seas, and seven men make it to a deserted island. Once ashore they find a hut that has been abandoned, perhaps years ago, perhaps days ago. The story opens with the beginning of the inquiry into the fate of the survivors. When a rescue ship reaches the island, only one man is still alive, Clovering, a history don, who tells in detail a story of the deaths of his fellow men.

The Kynsard Affair. On the day the convicted murderer Gibbern is executed, the police find a body in a car near the prison. The body is that of a woman who has been murdered in the manner considered to be Gibbern's style. The police have no trouble identifying the body; in fact, they have two identities to choose from: Miss Elizabeth Trotwood or Mrs. Kynsard, the wife of a barrister.

Henry Wade

The Duke of York's Steps
London: Constable, 1929.
New York: Grosset, 1929.

Inspector John Poole

Sir Garth Fratten, a noted London financier, is at odds with his stepson and in declining health, but he determines to carry on as he always has. Just when he has decided to join the board of a new company, against the advice of his doctor and a close friend, his health gives out. He dies crossing through a small park in London.

No Friendly Drop
London: Constable, 1931.
New York: Brewer, 1932.

Inspector John Poole and Major Faide

Everything in life has come easily for Lord Grayle, depriving him of the opportunities for achievement that would have strengthened his character. Still, he is not unhappy, and Lady Grayle is happy with her riding and the occasional London Season. Their son, Charles, shows signs of success in government, and this is generally attributed to the ambition and perseverance of his wife. When Lord Grayle dies unexpectedly in his sleep, the police take a close look at his family.

Constable, Guard Thyself!
London: Constable, 1934.
Boston: Houghton, 1935.

Inspector John Poole

In October 1933 Albert Hinde, a poacher convicted of killing a keeper in 1912, is released from prison and disappears from view. He then makes himself known to Captain Scole, the chief constable whose testimony sent him to prison. Scole's men set out to protect him from Hinde's revenge.

Bury Him Darkly*
London: Constable, 1936.

Inspector John Poole

Lonely Magdalen
London: Constable, 1940.
Rev. ed. London: Constable, 1946.

Inspector John Poole

Police find the body of a prostitute who has been murdered, and they are surprised at the difficulty they have in identifying her. They learn only that her name was Bella Knox and that she spoke like a lady. This and a scar are the only clues the police have. To find her murderer, they must go back to another era and another way of life to find the woman who became Bella.

Too Soon to Die
London: Constable, 1953.
New York: Macmillan, 1954.

Inspector John Poole

John Jerrod took great pride in his family and their home, Brackton Manor, even going so far as to make over the property to his son in order to avoid the crippling death duties. Now John learns that he is dying and will be dead three months before the gift to his son, Grant, is final. Grant immediately grasps the problem and devises a solution.

Gold Was Our Grave
London: Constable, 1954.
New York: Macmillan, 1954.

Inspector John Poole

Hector Berrenton has a car accident but dismisses it until he receives a note reminding him of a Bolivian gold mine and his partner. Both men were ac quitted three years earlier of defrauding the public, but someone remembers and means to have revenge. Then Berrenton's partner is found dead with a note promising that Berrenton will be next.

The Dying Alderman
London: Constable, 1930.
New York: Brewer, 1930.

Inspector Henry Lott

The Borough Council is accustomed to long-winded but obviously directed debates, but a personal attack against one of the members by another member is shocking. First, Mr. Garrett charges that a member is leaking secret information; then Mr. Trant charges that the council's affairs are being handled by men of leisure who have no right by experience to hold their positions. Needless to say, Mr. Trant is later found murdered.

The Hanging Captain
London: Constable, 1933.
New York: Harcourt, 1933.

Inspector Henry Lott

When Herbert Sterron married Griselda, society envied the perfection of their lives. Then the couple withdrew to live in the country, and they grew old in different ways during fifteen years of marriage. When Herbert is found hanging in his study, the police have little trouble finding reasons for suicide. Then they find equally good reasons for murder.

The High Sheriff
London: Constable, 1937.

Major Faide

For almost twenty years Sir Robert D'Arcy has lived with a secret that at times seemed painful enough to destroy him. In the year that he is appointed high sheriff of Brackenshire County he also comes to grips with his shame,

until a stranger steps into his life and recounts to Sir Robert every detail
of his well-kept secret.

Released for Death
London: Constable, 1938.

Constable John Bragg

Toddy Shaw's optimism and pleasant nature make prison bearable for him
and win the respect of the warders. But loyalty in prison is everything
among the prisoners, and when Toddy's partner, Jacko Carson, takes a dislike
to Toddy, all of Toddy's efforts to straighten out his life after his release
are wasted. Not until the police step in does Toddy have a chance of staying
free. (Constable John Bragg appears in several short stories.)

The Verdict of You All
London: Constable, 1926.
New York: Payson, 1927.

Sir John Smethurst is murdered in his study late at night, and the police
identify the likely suspects. The more evidence they collect, however, the
clearer it becomes that two men fit the description of the most likely suspect. Inspector Dobson and Superintendent Fraser, therefore, pick their favorite suspects, and each pursues that one.

The Missing Partners*
London: Constable, 1928.
New York: Payson, 1928.

Mist on the Saltings
London: Constable, 1933.
New York: Perennial, 1985.

After World War I, Hilary married John Pansel, and together they set off to
live the life of a struggling artist and his wife; of course, the artist would
soon be a great success and his wife would be especially appreciated for
her support. After ten years of scraping by, Hilary knows the dream is dead,

and she and John have settled into the ordinary sadness of failure. Then a successful novelist moves to the village and, looking for occasional amusement, casts his eye on Hilary.

Heir Presumptive
London: Constable, 1935.
New York: Macmillan, 1953.

Eustace Hendel had never thought much about his rich cousins, but when two die unexpectedly, he recognizes the dearth of male heirs in the other family line. As he renews his acquaintance with his distant relations during the funeral, he calculates the probability of the failure of one family line.

New Graves at Great Norne
London: Constable, 1947.
New York: Perennial, 1986.

Great Norne is a quiet fishing village, its only scandal the suicide of a young wife several years ago. The harsh demeanor of the husband has kept the memory alive, however, until there is another unexpected death for the villagers to think about, and then another.

Diplomat's Folly
London: Constable, 1951.
New York: Macmillan, 1952.

Major General Sir Vane Tabbard gathers family and friends for dinner one evening in 1947, and on that weekend they learn how much the war has changed them all. Major Gray Tabbard must break with his past if he is to have a future, and Aylwin Hundrych, a diplomat, must confront his past.

Be Kind to the Killer
London: Constable, 1952.

The police struggle with the rise in crime after World War II. When there is a burglary of violence in Beckenham, the police mobilize and search the area night after night for the criminals. One night two young policemen are successful, but one of them dies. So begins a relentless search for the men responsible for his death.

A Dying Fall
London: Constable, 1955.
New York: Macmillan, 1955.

Charles Rathlyn, who has devoted his life to horse racing, watches his entire business fall away when his prize horse comes in second. But instead of losing everything, he is offered a job as a racing manager by the owner of the winning horse. The owner is a pleasant, rich widow.

The Litmore Snatch
London: Constable, 1957.
New York: Macmillan, 1957.

The most important issue in the town of Harborough is who will attend the Yacht Club parties. The community is jolted out of its complacency when the editor of a powerful newspaper is threatened and then his son is kidnapped.

Colin Watson

Coffin Scarcely Used
London: Eyre, 1958.
New York: Putnam, 1967.

Inspector Walter Purbright

The professional population of Flaxborough loses two of its members in six months, which by itself is not shocking. But when a housekeeper insists she has seen one return from the grave and the second is found in an embarrassing condition, the police fear a clever criminal beyond the scope of the regular Flaxborough police.

Bump in the Night
London: Eyre, 1960.
New York: Walker, 1961.

Inspector Walter Purbright

The people of Chalmsbury do not scale intellectual heights or plumb emotional
depths in life. They are therefore more puzzled than anything else when a
series of explosions disrupts the quiet town. First, the public fountain is
blown up; then the head of a statue is blown off, and then the sign of an
occultist is shattered. No one is sure if the bombs are a social statement,
a practical joke, or an inept attempt at murder.

Hopjoy Was Here
London: Eyre, 1962.
New York: Walker, 1963.

Inspector Walter Purbright

When the police receive a series of anonymous letters about the goings-on
in Beatrice Avenue, the police investigate the named house, finding evidence
that one of the two men who lived there was probably murdered. The central
government is also interested, particularly in locating the second man.

Lonelyheart 4122
London: Eyre, 1967.
New York: Putnam, 1967.

Inspector Walter Purbright

A middle-aged spinster disappears and some weeks later a middle-aged widow
disappears after leaving instructions for her house to be sold. The police
trace the women to Handclasp House, a matrimonial bureau. A third woman,
Miss Lucilla Teatime, is warned about the police suspicions but she is notably
unconcerned. Miss Teatime demonstrates that she can take care of herself.

Charity Ends at Home
London: Eyre, 1968.
New York: Putnam, 1968.

Inspector Walter Purbright

A woman sends a letter to three officials--the coroner, the chief constable, and the editor of the local newspaper--asking them to help her and saying that the person to whom she has been a constant and loyal companion now plans to murder her. For obvious reasons, she says, she cannot sign her name; instead she encloses a photograph. There is no photograph, and the police can make nothing of the letter. Reluctantly they turn to the main problem in Flaxborough at the moment: the current state of war between the forty-three local charities.

The Flaxborough Crab
London: Eyre, 1969.

Just What the Doctor Ordered
New York: Putnam, 1969.

Inspector Walter Purbright

Three women are attacked at night, and each escapes serious harm, reporting the scary incident to the police. Unfortunately, the clearest detail of each incident is the manner in which the attacker ran away--sideways, like a crab.

Broomsticks over Flaxborough
London: Eyre, 1972.

Kissing Covens
New York: Putnam, 1972.

Inspector Walter Purbright

A local folklore society gathers for one of its regular meetings, holding a dance in the woods. This society is different, however, for the dancers are nude or partly nude and pray to non-Christian gods. The next day, the members go about their business, but one is missing. The police find her car and her clothes abandoned in the woods.

The Naked Nuns
London: Eyre, 1975.

Six Nuns and a Shotgun
New York: Putnam, 1975.

Inspector Walter Purbright

A telephone receptionist intercepts a cryptic telegram about two naked nuns in Philadelphia and dutifully reports the matter to the police. The police, for their part, would be glad to help, but they can't make out what the message is about.

One Man's Meat
London: Eyre, 1977.

It Shouldn't Happen to a Dog
New York: Putnam, 1977.

Inspector Walter Purbright

Julia Harton wants a divorce, and Mortimer Rothermere, of Happy Endings, Inc., promises to get it for her; furthermore, he will get her a divorce that will not in any way affect her social position or reputation. Mr. Rothermere proposes to force Mr. Harton to pay a generous divorce settlement by having Julia disappear in a manner that suggests to the police that she has been murdered--by Mr. Harton.

Blue Murder*
London: Eyre, 1979.

Inspector Walter Purbright

Plaster Sinners
London: Eyre, 1980.
New York: Doubleday, 1981.

Inspector Walter Purbright

A box of odds and ends, lot 34, draws unusual attention at a regular auction. A police sergeant is knocked out while examining one of the items, and several people bid aggressively for the lot. When the police impound the lot, the buyer faints. The auctioneer is mystified by all this interest in a lot of junk.

Whatever's Been Going on at Mumblesby?
London: Methuen, 1982.
New York: Doubleday, 1983.

Inspector Walter Purbright

The well-to-do village of Mumblesby is the site of several odd incidents. A prominent lawyer dies, and his common-law wife is locked in the bathroom during the funeral. She is found just before the house is seriously damaged by fire. Next, a farmer's wife commits suicide in the church, and her family dismisses her as a religious fanatic.

The Puritan
London: Eyre, 1966.

The Evening Telegram usually gets a nice column from each day's quota of inquiry letters, readers asking for help in locating an old friend or relative. A letter from Elizabeth Hailes seems ordinary enough until one of the news writers recognizes the name and connects it to a famous case six years earlier. Fifteen-year-old Margaret Lawson was raped and her friend murdered. On the day of her attacker's execution a London doctor, Sir Wilfrid Hailes, offered to abort the child resulting from the rape. Margaret declined the offer and moved away from the area. Now Sir Wilfrid wants to find her.

Patricia Wentworth*

The Catherine Wheel
London: Hodder, 1951.
Philadelphia: Lippincott, 1949.

Maud Silver

Jacob Taverner, millionaire grandson of an old smuggler, decides to meet
the many cousins he has never seen. Though ostensibly he is seeking heirs
for his vast estate, his penchant for malicious mischief prompts him to hold
a family reunion at the old smuggler's inn.

Ladies' Bane
London: Hodder, 1954.
Philadelphia: Lippincott, 1952.

Maud Silver

Caught in a London fog, Ione Muir hears but cannot see two men talking,
one of them using language that seems to promise a crime. Not long afterward, she hears the voice again, in a country town near her sister's home.

Out of the Past
London: Hodder, 1955.
Philadelphia: Lippincott, 1953.

Maud Silver

Carmona and James Hardwick are spending the summer in their seaside home
with friends when a man who was once engaged to Carmona arrives for a
visit. A figure from the past with a murky present, the handsome newcomer
unsettles the other guests, prompting others to deal with their own uncomfortable memories.

The Listening Eye
London: Hodder, 1957.
Philadelphia: Lippincott, 1955.

Maud Silver

Paulina Paine uses her eyes better than most people and therefore is one of
the more attentive guests at an art show. In addition to the paintings, she
observes the guests, including two men talking on the other side of the room.
Deaf for many years, Paulina is a skilled lip-reader, and what she reads sends
her quickly out of the gallery.

R. J. White

The Smartest Grave
London: Collins, 1961.
New York: Harper, 1961.

Inspector David Brock

The hearty Mr. Dugdale and his petite wife arrive in a Suffolk village to
take up residence on a large farm. The landlady of the inn has growing
reservations about Mr. Dugdale but takes a liking to his wife, who is half
French and determined to be a good country wife now that she has married
late in life. Beneath the veneer of a gentleman and his lady, however, less
than proper behavior is occasionally glimpsed. In 1901 villagers have clear
ideas about what is right and what is not, and they are uncomfortable with,
puzzled by, or hostile to some of what they see. Based on a true case.

The Women of Peasenhall
London: Macmillan, 1969.
New York: Harper, 1969.

Inspector David Brock

In 1902 a remote village in Suffolk is home to a large number of so-called
Bible thumpers, who take their morality and their religion seriously. Accused
by two boys of improper involvement with a maid, Rose Harsent, William
Gardiner, carpenter and Bible teacher, rigorously defends himself before his

fellow members of chapel. When Rose is later found strangled, he faces
another trial. Based on a true case.

A Secondhand Tomb
London: Macmillan, 1971.
New York: Harper, 1971.

Professor Peck is leading one of his regular tours through various sites in
Yorkshire, but this group is different. Mrs. Peck is highly suspicious of
two German tourists, and the assistant, Iris Armstrong, is worried about Mrs.
Peck's safety.

David Williams

Unholy Writ
London: Collins, 1976.
New York: St. Martin, 1977.

Mark Treasure

The quaint, quiet village of Mitchell Stoke is getting a new image. In the
manor house is a new owner, leader of the Forward Britain movement; in
the vicarage is a young vicar who believes in a literal interpretation of the
Bible and the "overt practice" of Christian principles; and in the cemetery
is a woman who dropped dead from shock.

Treasure by Degrees
London: Collins, 1977.
New York: St. Martin, 1977.

Mark Treasure

An American self-made millionaire leaves his considerable fortune to any
agricultural school that agrees to meet certain conditions. This seems like
a godsend for University College in Hampshire, but someone disagrees. The
spunky American widow is getting threatening messages and being warned
to stay away.

Treasure up in Smoke
London: Collins, 1978.
New York: St. Martin, 1978.

Mark Treasure

King Charles Island, a crown colony in the West Indies, has emerged in the late twentieth century as the home of contented people who have avoided the catastrophes and crises visited upon their neighbors. All this may come to an end, however, if the current head of the founding family goes through with his decision to accept the development of tourist facilities.

Murder for Treasure
London: Collins, 1980.
New York: St. Martin, 1981.

Mark Treasure

An American company has almost completed negotiations to buy a British company that produces foot deodorant, and Mark Treasure is sent to west Wales to work out the details with one of the shareholders. On Mark's train ride out, a clergyman is attacked, leading to a wholesale mêlée in a train station. By the time Treasure arrives in Panty village, the plans of big business, murderers, and blackmailers have been seriously disrupted.

Copper, Gold and Treasure
London: Collins, 1982.
New York: St. Martin, 1982.

Mark Treasure

Roderick Copper, a retired schoolteacher, and Benjamin Gold, a retired cab driver, meet during an interview during which they are both told that their hoped-for retirement home is about to close because of bankruptcy. Seeing a last hope about to dissolve, Copper and Gold decide to find the funds needed to keep the home for retired officers and gentlemen open, by appealing to the heirs of the founder and other likely philanthropists.

Treasure Preserved
London: Collins, 1983.
New York: St. Martin, 1983.

Mark Treasure

The inevitable conflict between developers and preservationists escalates in the seacoast resort of Tophaven. A British construction company has invested most of its finances in the local project, and one of the town residents has invested most of her time in finding a way to stop the company. The townspeople and others who stand to make money through this development are not happy with the preservationist's tenacity, but she is soon killed in an explosion.

Advertise for Treasure
London: Collins, 1984.
New York: St. Martin, 1984.

Mark Treasure

Officers from an American advertising agency come to London to buy a British firm, a move unexpected by the company officers, bankers, and clients. Ostensibly a straight business deal, the takeover has hidden consequences for the negotiators. As the consequences become known, the negotiators change their tactics and even their goals, bringing to the discussions a new edge and an uneasiness.

Wedding Treasure
London: Macmillan, 1985.
New York: St. Martin, 1985.

Mark Treasure

A wedding at a country manor takes on the atmosphere of a business merger when the mother and stepfather of the bride prepare for the wedding of nineteen-year-old Fleur and the arrival of her father, Kit Jarvas, who opposes the marriage. By marrying before she is twenty-one without the consent of both parents, Fleur is sacrificing a large trust fund--until she is thirty. But Jarvas sees other opportunities in his daughter's early marriage and has no intention of passing them by.

Murder in Advent
London: Macmillan, 1985.
New York: St. Martin, 1986.

Mark Treasure

Litchester Cathedral is old, magnificent, and run-down, prompting some of
the cathedral officials to consider selling their rare 1225 copy of the Magna
Carta. Before there can be a final vote on the matter, there is a fire in
the cathedral library, killing the verger and destroying the Magna Carta.

Colin Wilson*

Ritual in the Dark
London: Gollancz, 1960.
Boston: Houghton, 1960.

A young writer makes friends with a man who is a murderer along the lines
of Jack the Ripper. Through examining his own life and seeking insights
from others, the young man tries to understand his friend's mind and reach
a moral decision for his own behavior.

The World of Violence
London: Gollancz, 1963.

The Violent World of Hugh Greene
Boston: Houghton, 1963.

Young Hugh Greene's mind is shaped by a mad uncle who discovers the child's
mathematical ability, another uncle who articulates the child's feelings of
dislike for human beings and his sensitivity to violence, and an aunt's forays
into the occult and spiritualism. Hugh also discovers as a boy the power of
violence to challenge violence, and he pursues the logic of his discovery.

Necessary Doubt
London: Barker, 1964.
New York: Trident, 1964.

The merest accident opens up the past again to Professor Karl Zweig when
he thinks he sees a former student and friend from Germany whom he knew
before he escaped from the Nazis. Zweig takes the story of his friend's
early years and philosophical discussions about the master criminal to another
friend and former policeman. To the professor's shock, the police officer
pieces together enough information to suggest that Zweig's friend may be
killing old men for their money.

The Glass Cage
London: Barker, 1966.
New York: Random, 1967.

The police are baffled by a series of nine murders, now known as the Thames
murders. The murderer dismembers the victim and writes, in chalk on a
nearby wall, lines taken from Blake's poetry. Daunted, the police seek out
a well-known Blake scholar for advice, who in turn applies his mind to the
task of identifying the murderer, perhaps from among his many scholarly
correspondents.

The Killer
London: New English Library, 1970.

Lingard
New York: Crown, 1970.

Dr. Samuel Kahn, prison psychiatrist, is drawn into the case of Arthur
Lingard, who is serving an eight-year sentence for second-degree murder.
As Kahn tries to win Lingard's trust, he pieces together information about
the prisoner's life history gleaned from various sources, discovering Lingard's
traumatic childhood as well as his role in other crimes. The author discusses
his criminal and psychological theories at length in a final note, "Note to
Lingard."

The Schoolgirl Murder Case
London: Hart-Davis, 1974.
New York: Crown, 1974.

In six months there have been eight attacks on schoolchildren in North London. The most recent, the ninth, however, is different: a teenaged girl is raped and murdered, strangled by a white cord. To solve this one, the police follow a trail into the world of magic and pornography.

Sara Woods

They Love Not Poison
London: Macmillan, 1972.
New York: Holt, 1972.

Antony Maitland

No one is surprised when old Mrs. Thornton dies in 1947 after a long illness, but the country people have their own explanation for her death. When the doctor refuses to sign the death certificate, the farmers wait for the investigation by the police to lead to the witches rumored to be in the area.

The Taste of Fears
London: Collins, 1963.

The Third Encounter
New York: Harper, 1963.

Antony Maitland

Dr. Martin is an easygoing retired doctor whose real passion in the 1950s is inventing bizarre gadgets. He also fills in for doctors on vacation and occasionally supports a younger cousin. A harmless and ordinary man, the doctor is strangled one afternoon just after calling Antony Maitland. The only thing not ordinary about Dr. Martin, other than his death, is the information he supplied during the war to military intelligence on contacts in France.

Bloody Instructions
London: Collins, 1962.
New York: Harper, 1962.

Antony Maitland

On an errand for his uncle, Sir Nicholas Harding, Antony Maitland is taking
tea with the secretary of a firm of solicitors while he waits for a report.
When another secretary goes in search of the senior partner, Mr. Winter,
she finds him dead at his desk, stabbed in the back. It seems hard to believe
that the murderer must be either a member of the office or a client.

Malice Domestic
London: Collins, 1962.
New York: Avon, 1986.

Antony Maitland

William Cassell returns home after eighteen years to see his brother and
the other members of his family, but on his first evening home he is shot
to death. His great-nephew Paul is found standing nearby, holding the rifle
that killed him. The family claims Paul must have been sleepwalking, Paul
claims he is innocent, and the police claim Paul is the murderer: after all,
Paul's father shot and killed his own wife and brother eighteen years ago.

Error of the Moon
London: Collins, 1963.

Antony Maitland

The General Aircraft Company has been quietly engaged in secret missile
work for the government until a civil servant discovers a leak of information.
Then a letter is missing for a brief period, an employee is hit and killed by
a car on a foggy night, and those who know something is amiss begin to
worry that they are also in danger.

The Windy Side of the Law
London: Collins, 1965.
New York: Harper, 1965.

Antony Maitland

The only clue Peter Hammond has to his identity is a letter bearing his name and a passport. Suffering from amnesia, Peter seeks out a man whose name appears in his diary, Antony Maitland, who confirms Peter's identity. But amnesia is only the beginning of Peter's problems: Scotland Yard wants to search his room, and a few days later the police are back again.

This Little Measure
London: Collins, 1964.
New York: Avon, 1986.

Antony Maitland

Members of the Gaskell family alternate between rogues and puritans, and in 1962 Roderick Gaskell has left one of his heirs a particularly vexing problem. To his son Andrew, Roderick left the problem of the Velasquez. This, when found, turns out to have been stolen in the 1940s from a museum. Then it is stolen from the Gaskells, and the question for Andrew seems to be answered.

Trusted Like the Fox
London: Collins, 1964.
New York: Harper, 1965.

Antony Maitland

Michael Godman, a photographer from a seaside resort, is accused of high treason during World War II. According to the government, he is really Guy Harland, who went to work for the Germans during the war. The defense must go back twenty years to an old house in Yorkshire, a biologist, and the strangers who came to work in a nearby plant.

Though I Know She Lies
London: Collins, 1965.
New York: Holt, 1965.

Antony Maitland

Barbara Wentworth is an extraordinarily beautiful model and a sound business-woman. Accused of murdering her sister, Barbara maintains both her dignity and her reserve as the trial opens, leaving her counsel at a loss for an effective defense. Hoping the clue to the sister's death lies in her character, Maitland delves into the background of the two women and at first thinks he has uncovered a motive for murder.

Let's Choose Executors
London: Collins, 1966.
New York: Harper, 1967.

Antony Maitland

In 1964 Frances Gifford, a young woman who was raised by her godmother, is arrested for the older woman's murder, which was committed only days after she changed her will in favor of Frances. Although she is a nice girl, Frances is definitely lying about certain details of the evening in question. Through this case Antony comes to know Vera Langhorne.

Enter Certain Murderers
London: Collins, 1966.
New York: Harper, 1966.

Antony Maitland

Roger Farrell knows he will be questioned closely by the police after he reports finding a man shot to death near a motorists' telephone on a country road. He can maintain his innocence, but the police have cause for suspicion. Roger's mother had committed suicide rather than pay blackmail, and Roger arranged a payment in order to identify the blackmailer.

The Law's Delay
London: Macmillan, 1977.
New York: St. Martin, 1977.

Antony Maitland

In 1965 Ellen Gray is arrested for the murder of John Wilcox, a friend of her father and an important witness at her father's trial twenty years before for the murder of his wife and her lover. Like her father, Ellen insists she is innocent, and now insists that her father was also innocent.

Tarry and Be Hanged
London: Collins, 1969.
New York: Holt, 1971.

Antony Maitland

In 1965 children uncover a body while playing in a doctor's garden. Though buried for some time, the body turns out to be that of a patient who testified a year ago that the doctor was attending her when his wife was killed. The doctor is charged with the woman's murder, and the doctor's counsel immediately stumbles on the question of who she is, since she was new in the area in 1964.

Knives Have Edges
London: Collins, 1968.
New York: Holt, 1970.

Antony Maitland

After many hard years, actor Jon Kellaway is enjoying some success, and it seems especially cruel that he should lose it through bad luck. His landlord is found dead and the police find what they think is a motive for murder: newspaper clippings about Jon's wife's death. But as Jon points out, twelve years ago, in 1953, Beth's suicide was public knowledge.

Past Praying For
London: Collins, 1968.
New York: Harper, 1968.

Antony Maitland

Camilla Barnard was convicted in 1957 of shooting her husband and served a prison sentence. After her release, she married her husband's cousin. When he died from poison in 1965, the police arrested her again for murdering her husband. To save her from a second conviction Maitland must prove her innocence twice.

Exit Murderer
London: Macmillan, 1978.
New York: St. Martin, 1978.

Antony Maitland

In 1965 the Northdean police meticulously put together a case against two diamond smugglers, identifying witnesses and verifying their statements. Then in court the entire case unravels, the two men walk away, and the senior police officer is charged with wrongful arrest. At the heart of the matter is an unknown man of power who intends to protect his illicit business at all costs.

And Shame the Devil
London: Collins, 1967.
New York: Holt, 1972.

Antony Maitland

Two policemen are charged with the wrongful arrest of two Pakistanis, who were acquitted of burglary. Both policemen seem decent and honest, and both plaintiffs are also considered decent and honest, though one is a fiery journalist. The general consensus is that all four men may be innocent, but it will take both sides working together to prove it.

The Case Is Altered
London: Collins, 1967.
New York: Harper, 1968.

Antony Maitland

Jo Marston, an eighteen-year-old movie actress, is determined to help her boyfriend, Roy Bromley, prove his innocence of stealing an emerald necklace. Since the necklace was found in his pocket only minutes after the robbery and he has already been convicted, the young woman has a formidable task ahead of her.

An Improbable Fiction
London: Collins, 1970.
New York: Holt, 1971.

Antony Maitland

At the end of her regular broadcast, television journalist Lynn Edison declares that her sister, an actress, did not commit suicide as the coroner concluded. Rather, she was murdered by Paul Grenville, the television personality. Lynn is charged with libel and asks her counsel to prove she was correct. Then Paul is shot and Lynn is charged with murder.

Serpent's Tooth
London: Collins, 1971.
New York: Holt, 1973.

Antony Maitland

In 1966 Mr. and Mrs. Alfred Baker are popular in the newspapers for the twelve foster children they care for. Their family is called the ideal of Christian charity and home life, with the older ones staying on and contributing part of their paychecks to the household expenses. Then one day in 1966, one of the boys murders Mr. Baker and is ready to plead guilty rather than say anything more about the incident.

The Knavish Crows*
London: Collins, 1971.
New York: Raven, 1980.

Antony Maitland

Done to Death
London: Macmillan, 1974.
New York: Holt, 1975.

Antony Maitland

Something has gone terribly wrong in the small village of Burton Cecil, but no one can put a finger on it. It might be the recent suicide, or it might be the unusual letters that appear regularly for women in the village. No one complains outright until the bank produces another problem: counterfeit coins.

A Show of Violence
London: Macmillan, 1975.
New York: McKay, 1975.

Antony Maitland

A boy known only as Tommy Smith is arrested for the murder of an old man with whom he was living on the edge of town. In addition, police suspect the boy of stealing three miniatures from a surgeon's home. The boy will say nothing, leaving the police to infer he has nothing to say in his defense.

Enter the Corpse
London: Macmillan, 1973.
New York: Holt, 1974.

Antony Maitland

Roger Farrell is persuaded to take in his godfather in 1968 after he is released from prison for robbery. Roger rationalizes that things are different now: the burglar is an old man and undoubtedly changed. Roger is wrong. The night before Uncle Hubert's release, Roger and his wife find a man stabbed to death in their front hall. When Uncle Hubert finally comes to them, he hasn't changed at all.

Yet She Must Die
London: Macmillan, 1973.
New York: Holt, 1974.

Antony Maitland

Several people have reasons for murdering Lydia Skelton, but the police arrest her husband, Jeremy, a writer. Jeremy is researching a murder case that was never solved, and the details of that case closely match the circumstances of his wife's death. The only important difference is in the mode of death.

My Life Is Done
London: Macmillan, 1976.
New York: St. Martin, 1976.

Antony Maitland

Graham Chadwick, MP, is proud of his record as an environmentalist, but he may soon lose it. A letter he wrote to his sister to explain his opposition to a development in his home constituency has been stolen. By taking his words out of context, a blackmailer threatens to use the letter to ruin Chadwick if he refuses to back the proposed development.

This Fatal Writ
London: Macmillan, 1979.
New York: St. Martin, 1979.

Antony Maitland

In 1971 an investigative journalist is charged under the Official Secrets Act with obtaining information about a secret project from a science laboratory and passing it to a Soviet agent. He insists he is innocent, but as Sir Nicholas Harding points out, if he is innocent, someone else is guilty and the Soviets won't like having the guilty party discovered.

Proceed to Judgement
London: Macmillan, 1979.
New York: St. Martin, 1980.

Antony Maitland

Douglas Johnstone made no secret of his diabetes. A successful stockbroker, he kept a tight rein on his health, his business, his wife, and his two children, though they were a disappointment to him, the boy frail and the girl a tomboy. When Johnstone is killed with an overdose of morphine taken instead of insulin, the police arrest his wife and Dr. Collingwood, who were close friends. Each insists the other is innocent and that the other possible suspects are too nice to commit murder.

Weep for Her
London: Macmillan, 1980.
New York: St. Martin, 1980.

Antony Maitland

Emily Walpole is distraught over her son's death during a skiing holiday and seeks solace from a psychic. After several seances, the medium receives a message from Michael Walpole asking that his mother join him. Three days later Mrs. Walpole commits suicide. Soon after, Mr. Walpole lodges a civil action against the medium, holding her responsible for his wife's death.

Cry Guilty
London: Macmillan, 1981.
New York: St. Martin, 1981.

Antony Maitland

In 1972 Antony Maitland accepts the brief of a young man charged with receiving stolen goods--a Rubens painting found in his closet. The case does
not seem especially complicated until another attorney advises him that a
woman client in another matter says that Maitland's client is innocent. The
woman is charged with killing her husband to prevent him from revealing
the name of the head of a ring of art thieves.

They Stay for Death
London: Macmillan, 1980.
New York: St. Martin, 1980.

Antony Maitland

In 1972, at the Restawhile Hotel, a nursing home and residence for the elderly, there have been three deaths in six months. This alone is enough to
set Chedcombe gossiping, but the deceased and the manner of death add to
the general interest. Then there is a fourth death--and it fits the pattern.

Dearest Enemy
London: Macmillan, 1981.
New York: St. Martin, 1981.

Antony Maitland

For forty-three years, Leonard and Victoria Buckley have played opposite
each other on the London stage to the delight of their fans. By 1973 the
marriage is dead, and now Leonard confides to a friend that Victoria is trying
to poison him. On opening night of their new play, however, it is Victoria
who is murdered, not Leonard.

Most Grievous Murder
London: Macmillan, 1982.
New York: St. Martin, 1982.

Antony Maitland

Antony and his wife, Jenny, are vacationing in New York City in 1973 when the British ambassador asks Antony to look into a delicate matter. The son of the president of an African nation was shot to death on the steps of the UN building, and the police have arrested the son of the ambassador of a neighboring African nation.

Enter a Gentleman
London: Macmillan, 1982.
New York: St. Martin, 1982.

Antony Maitland

English law does not allow divorce before the third year of marriage unless one partner can prove exceptional depravity. And this is the charge that Sir Nicholas Harding has agreed to defend for his client Elizabeth Coke. Her husband, an attorney fearing for his career, is charging his wife with libel and has sought Antony Maitland as his counsel.

Villains by Necessity
London: Macmillan, 1982.
New York: St. Martin, 1982.

Antony Maitland

By 1973 Jim Arnold has gone straight for seven years, thanks in part to help from Sir Nicholas Harding. Now Jim's arrest for burglary suggests that he has returned to his old way of life. Jim finally tells all: he had been running his newsstand and paying protection money. Then one day he decided to follow the two collectors. After several weeks, he thought he had traced the men to the head of the racket.

The Bloody Book of Law
London: Macmillan, 1984.
New York: St. Martin, 1984.

Antony Maitland

In 1974 a country gentleman is charged with the theft of jewelry from the home of friends, but he insists he is innocent. This is the second time the man has found himself in this predicament. Maitland agrees to defend him and then comes upon a coincidence that leads his investigation into an entirely different direction.

The Lie Direct
London: Macmillan, 1983.
New York: St. Martin, 1983.

Antony Maitland

Dr. Boris Gollnow defects in 1974 and names two Britishers as his contacts in order to prove his sincerity to the British. One of the two commits suicide; the other, John Ryder, is brought to trial. Ryder claims he has been mistaken for another man, but his second wife and Gollnow claim he is an agent. Ryder turns out to have another wife and to be both a bigamist and a traitor, according to the testimony.

Call Back Yesterday
London: Macmillan, 1983.
New York: St. Martin, 1983.

Antony Maitland

Harriet Carr is charged with contempt of court in 1974 for her persistence in trying to see Peter Wallace. Harriet is convinced she is married to Peter, but Peter says he has known her only six months and has been married for several years to another woman. Harriet agrees to see a psychiatrist, who hypnotizes her. This produces only more confusion, for Harriet regresses to 1940, when she was a young woman apparently married to Peter.

Where Should He Die?
London: Macmillan, 1983.
New York: St. Martin, 1983.

Antony Maitland

Samuel Keats is an old man and no one is surprised when he dies in 1974.
But everyone is nonplussed to learn that he had changed his will and left
everything to his nurse, a beautiful but tactless woman. Veronica sees no
reason why her claim to the family wealth should be held up, but there is
more than one delay. Distressed by the course of events, the police order
an autopsy and find that Mr. Keats died of poison.

Away with Them to Prison
London: Macmillan, 1985.
New York: St. Martin, 1985.

Antony Maitland

When Mr. Goodbody is beaten to death in 1975 after refusing to pay protection money, Mrs. Goodbody decides to tell all to the police. For their part
the police put together a solid case against two men, prepare for court, and
are stymied when the government witnesses deny everything they said earlier,
and instead accuse the police of corruption. Now the government must prose-
cute two policemen, and the authorities are no nearer to the truth of Goodbody's death.

Murder's out of Tune
London: Macmillan, 1984.
New York: St. Martin, 1984.

Antony Maitland

In 1975 a successful provincial actor is charged with the murder of his
estranged wife; the charge is ludicrous to all who know him. Laura and
Richard had parted amicably, and Richard had continued to be an attentive
father to their son. Change had come with Mr. Eardley, a fundamentalist
and Laura's new suitor, who declared Richard an evil influence on Laura's
son.

An Obscure Grave
London: Macmillan, 1985.
New York: St. Martin, 1985.

Antony Maitland

Oliver Linwood eschews material goods and lives in near-poverty, but he is also heir to a large estate. When his cousin dies suddenly in 1975 and the cousin's baby is murdered soon afterward, Oliver is the likely suspect. The police see no connection between this child's death and two others brought about by a young mother who recently had a stillborn child.

Defy the Devil
London: Macmillan, 1984.
New York: St. Martin, 1984.

Antony Maitland

Thomas Wilmot, a successful portrait painter, lived in solitude until he was murdered in 1975 by his grandson, Simon Winthrop, a struggling artist. Simon denies the charge, but the evidence against him is strong: three eyewitnesses. His solicitor's defense is that he suffers from multiple personality disorder. Again the evidence is strong: recent paintings completely unlike his earlier work, a dead lover he does not remember, and forgotten meetings with people he knows.

Put out the Light
London: Macmillan, 1985.
New York: St. Martin, 1985.

Antony Maitland

An actress believes she has found the first detective story, written as a drama by a Restoration playwright. Cast and crew are assembled and rehearsals begin for the 1975-1976 season, but from the outset the production is plagued by tasteless and then unpleasant practical jokes.

A Thief or Two
London: Macmillan, 1977.
New York: St. Martin, 1977.

Antony Maitland

Malcolm Harte, an assistant to a jeweler, is accused of murdering and robbing his employer on the night of a house party that was arranged to show guests some of the jeweler's best work. Maitland is given no clear direction by the instructing solicitor and must instead rely on developing leads during the trial. In addition, he must keep the attention of jurors whose minds easily wander to other concerns.

Margaret Yorke

Dead in the Morning
London: Bles, 1970.

Dr. Patrick Grant

After ten years as a widower, Gerald Ludlow marries an American and brings her home to meet his teenaged daughter, his mother, and other relatives. The visit goes well until Sunday morning, when Gerald's daughter finds the housekeeper dead. The assorted problems of the family recede as everyone tries to figure out why anyone would want to murder a trusted elderly housekeeper.

Silent Witness
London: Bles, 1972.
New York: Walker, 1975.

Dr. Patrick Grant

Tourists in a ski resort in the Austrian Alps are frustrated when heavy snow and avalanches prevent them from skiing. The skiers are soon back on the slopes, however, facing another problem: a British skier is missing. While they try to locate the skier, some of the guests begin to have doubts about the identities of the other guests.

Grave Matters
London: Bles, 1973.
New York: Bantam, 1983.

Dr. Patrick Grant

A retired headmistress dies from a fall while on vacation in Athens. Those who knew her well miss her, particularly her old friend. Then her friend dies in a fall down steps in the British Museum, just before she was to meet her friend's great-niece.

Mortal Remains
London: Bles, 1974.

Dr. Patrick Grant

Dr. Grant was looking forward to his vacation in Greece as a time for no plans and no schedules. Then his traveling companion dies just before the trip, leaving Grant with a last request--to find his godson in Crete. Dr. Grant agrees, but before he can do anything in Crete he comes across a drowned man during an early morning swim. The dead man is a colleague who was supposed to be lecturing on a cruise ship.

Cast for Death
London: Hutchinson, 1976.
New York: Walker, 1976.

Dr. Patrick Grant

Sam Irwin was making a slow but steady comeback on the stage when his body was found floating in the Thames. There is no reason to suspect suicide, and the police quickly realize that he did not die by drowning.

The China Doll
London: Hale, 1961.

Married only three months, Penelope Dereham hasn't quite settled down and
is eager to spend Christmas with her great-aunt and old friends. Her husband gives her a beautiful china doll that looks remarkably like her just
before they leave for the country for the holiday. The doll becomes an ominous presence until Penny sees it for what it is after Christmas. By then
she has faced death and a secret terror.

No Medals for the Major
London: Bles, 1974.

Major Johnson has planned his life carefully, including retirement in a small
village. Then random violence alters everything: two unemployed youths
leave a trail of petty crimes that mistakenly lead to the major, leaving him
to face the anger and suspicion of his new neighbors.

The Small Hours of the Morning
London: Bles, 1975.
New York: Walker, 1975.

The civilized life of Felsbury conceals more fundamental needs and passions
than anyone would want to admit. In the quiet evenings, the wife of the
deputy librarian meets her lover, a young man plans a series of robberies,
and a silent watcher sees them all and more.

The Cost of Silence
London: Hutchinson, 1977.
New York: Walker, 1977.

Norman Widnes cared for his invalid mother and then his invalid wife, remaining nevertheless a genuinely considerate man toward the people of
Bidbury. For his relatives and for other residents of the small town there is
a crisis of violence: for the invalid Emma, the shop assistant Madge, the
boy who is afraid of dogs, the girl starved for love and food, and the widow
who has lost her dog.

The Point of Murder
London: Hutchinson, 1978.

The Come-On
New York: Harper, 1979.

Controlled by her spiteful, manipulative mother, Kate Wilson has no pleasure in her life until her employer takes her to dinner after a conference. Dinner in a luxury hotel is the first step in a plan to have a life of her own, if only for an occasional weekend. And so Kate becomes Mrs. Havant, a widow, who one day sees a young man stop to help a young woman change a flat tire.

Death on Account*
London: Hutchinson, 1979.

The Scent of Fear
London: Hutchinson, 1980.
New York: St. Martin, 1981.

Mrs. Anderson has lived for years in her old Victorian house and is used to being alone. Young Kevin Timms understands this when he follows her home one day, later breaking into the house to explore and note the value of its contents. Kevin is content to return regularly, pilfering food and money. Muriel Dean, who is new in town and whose children are gone, is distressed that Mrs. Anderson should live alone so far away from everyone, and makes plans to rearrange the old woman's life.

The Hand of Death
London: Hutchinson, 1981.
New York: St. Martin, 1982.

Ronald Trimm is living the life his wife has set out for him with one exception: his fantasies about women. These remain alive only in magazines until he helps a young widow home one evening and discovers a world of sensual pleasure. After that he cannot go back to his old way of life, and he knows his wife won't change.

Devil's Work
London: Hutchinson, 1982.
New York: St. Martin, 1982.

When Alan Parker loses his job, he cannot tell his wife and so maintains
the appearance of being employed, leaving for work in the morning and then
driving aimlessly through strange neighborhoods. One afternoon he notices
a girl walking home alone, mustering her courage to cross the street. Alan
stops to help and becomes her protector, gradually becoming part of her and
her mother's life.

Find Me a Villain
London: Hutchinson, 1983.
New York: St. Martin, 1983.

Nina Crowther's life undergoes a sea change when she learns her husband is
divorcing her for another woman. In desperation she accepts a job as a
house-sitter from a stranger she meets at Fortnum and Mason's. This job
seems the ideal solution until she moves into the house. On her first night
she answers the telephone to silence and a shuddering sigh.

The Smooth Face of Evil
London: Hutchinson, 1984.
New York: St. Martin, 1984.

Alice Armitage struggles to make a new life for herself after the death of
her husband, but she is isolated and alone in her daughter-in-law's house.
When she does finally break out, she meets a charming young man who knows
exactly how to prey on women like Alice.

Intimate Kill
London: Hutchinson, 1985.
New York: St. Martin, 1985.

After serving ten years for the murder of his wife even though no body
was found, Stephen Dawes wants to know who killed her. He traces his
former mistress and her friends, who did nothing to help him during the
trial.

3

Characters and Creators

Martin Ainsworth	Michael Underwood
Superintendent Roderick Alleyn	Ngaio Marsh
Inspector Enrique Alvarez	Roderic Jeffries
Sir John Appleby	Michael Innes
Sergeant Nick Attwell	Michael Underwood
Inspector Bill Aveyard	James Fraser
Professor Andrew Basnett	E.X. Ferrars
Superintendent Battle	Agatha Christie
Sergeant William Beef	Leo Bruce
Tommy and Tuppence Beresford	Agatha Christie
Colonel Peter Blair	J.R.L. Anderson
Inspector Bland	Julian Symons
Dr. William Blow	Kenneth Hopkins
Inspector Salvador Borges	John and Emery Bonett
Dame Beatrice Bradley	Gladys Mitchell
Constable John Bragg	Henry Wade
Miles Bredon	Ronald A. Knox
Ernst Brendel	J.C. Masterman
Inspector John Brentford	S.B. Hough
Ronald Briercliffe	Francis Beeding
Inspector David Brock	R. J. White
Superintendent John Brock	John Bingham
Jane and Dagobert Brown	Delano Ames
Inspector Thomas Brunt	John Buxton Hilton
Inspector Burnivel	Edward Candy
Brother Cadfael	Ellis Peters
Inspector Thomas Cadover	Michael Innes

Ronald Camberwell — J.S. Fletcher
Albert Campion — Margery Allingham
Youngman Carter

John Carlyle — Henry Calvin
Superintendent Charlesworth — Christianna Brand
Ambrose Chitterwick — Anthony Berkeley
Joshua Clunk — H.C. Bailey
Inspector Cockrill — Christianna Brand
Mrs. Craggs — H.R.F. Keating
Inspector Crambo — Julian Symons
Professor Thea Crawford — Jessica Mann
Sergeant Cribb — Peter Lovesey
Tessa Crichton — Anne Morice
Superintendent Adam Dalgliesh — P.D. James
Professor Daly — Eilís Dillon
Superintendent Andrew Dalziel — Reginald Hill
Dr. R.V. Davie — V.C. Clinton-Baddeley
Carolus Deene — Leo Bruce
Inspector Piet Deventer — J.R.L. Anderson
Superintendent Ditteridge — E.X. Ferrars
Kenneth Ducane (Vandoren) — John Bingham
Superintendent Duffy — Nigel FitzGerald
Toby Dyke — E.X. Ferrars
Rosa Epton — Michael Underwood
Major Faide — Henry Wade
Bunty Felse — Ellis Peters
Dominic Felse — Ellis Peters
Superintendent George Felse — Ellis Peters
Gervase Fen — Edmund Crispin
Inspector Finch (Rudd) — June Thomson
Inspector Septimus Finch — Margaret Erskine
Reggie Fortune — H.C. Bailey
Superintendent Francis Foy — Lionel Black
Virginia Freer — E.X. Ferrars
Inspector Joseph French — Freeman Wills Crofts
Dr. Henry Frost — Josephine Bell
Inspector Matthew Furnival — Stella Phillips
Inspector Robert Fusil — Michael Alding
Superintendent George Gently — Alan Hunter
Colonel Anthony Gethryn — Philip MacDonald
Inspector Ganesh Ghote — H.R.F. Keating
Colonel Alistair Granby — Francis Beeding

Inspector Alan Grant	Gordon Daviot
	Josephine Tey
Celia Grant	John Sherwood
Dr. Patrick Grant	Margaret Yorke
Cordelia Gray	P.D. James
Emma Greaves	Lionel Black
Sid Halley	Dick Francis
Superintendent Hannasyde	Georgette Heyer
Paul Harris	Gavin Black
Jimmie Haswell	Herbert Adams
Inspector Hazlerigg	Michael Gilbert
Inspector Hemingway	Georgette Heyer
Charles Honeybath	Michael Innes
Tamara Hoyland	Jessica Mann
Inspector Harry James	Kenneth Giles
Inspector Benjamin Jurnet	S.T. Haymon
Superintendent Richard Jury	Martha Grimes
Inspector Kelsey	Emma Page
Inspector Mike Kenny	Eilís Dillon
Superintendent Simon Kenworthy	John Buxton Hilton
Inspector Don Kerry	Jeffrey Ashford
Inspector Kyle	Roy Vickers
Gerald Lee	Kenneth Hopkins
Corporal Juan Llorca	Delano Ames
Inspector Henry Lott	Henry Wade
Lovejoy	Jonathan Gash
Adam Ludlow	Simon Nash
Superintendent Macdonald	E.C.R. Lorac
Antony Maitland	Sara Woods
Dan Mallett	Frank Parrish
Inspector Mallett	Cyril Hare
Professor Gideon Manciple	Kenneth Hopkins
Professor Mandrake	John and Emery Bonett
Superintendent Simon Manton	Michael Underwood
Miss Jane Marple	Agatha Christie
Inspector George Martin	Francis Beeding
Superintendent George Masters	Douglas Clark
Superintendent Steven Mitchell	Josephine Bell
Inspector Montero	Simon Nash
Inspector Morse	Colin Dexter
Ariadne Oliver	Agatha Christie
Dai Owen	Henry Calvin

Charles Paris	Simon Brett
Inspector Peter Pascoe	Reginald Hill
Douglas Perkins	Marian Babson
Sergeant Patrick Petrella	Michael Gilbert
Mikael Petros	James Anderson
Francis Pettigrew	Cyril Hare
Superintendent James Pibble	Peter Dickinson
Superintendent Arnold Pike	Philip MacDonald
Miss Melinda Pink	Gwen Moffat
Charlotte E. Pitt	Anne Perry
Inspector Thomas Pitt	Anne Perry
Inspector Pointer	A. Fielding
Hercule Poirot	Agatha Christie
Superintendent Tom Pollard	Elizabeth Lemarchand
Inspector John Poole	Henry Wade
Thomas Preston	Francis Beeding
Dr. Lancelot Priestley	John Rhode
Inspector Walter Purbright	Colin Watson
Dr. Henry Pym	W. J. Burley
Inspector Douglas Quantrill	Sheila Radley
Colonel Race	Agatha Christie
Superintendent George Rogers	Jonathan Ross
Inspector Rudd (Finch)	June Thomson
Alan Russell	Nigel FitzGerald
Roger Sheringham	Anthony Berkeley
Jemima Shore	Antonia Fraser
Maud Silver	Patricia Wentworth
Inspector C. D. Sloan	Catherine Aird
Superintendent Ben Spence	Michael Allen
Matthew Stock	Leonard Tourney
Nigel Strangeways	Nicholas Blake
Jeremy Sturrock	Jeremy Sturrock
Professor Hilary Tamar	Sarah Caudwell
Inspector Luke Thanet	Dorothy Simpson
Kate Theobald	Lionel Black
Lizzie Thomas	Anthony Oliver
Dr. John Thorndyke	R. Austin Freeman
Superintendent George Thorne	John Penn
Emily Tibbett	Patricia Moyes
Superintendent Henry Tibbett	Patricia Moyes
Mark Treasure	David Williams
Philip Trent	E.C. Bentley

Superintendent Perry Trethowan	Robert Barnard
Miss Amy Tupper	Josephine Bell
Malcolm Warren	C.H.B. Kitchin
Claud Warrington-Reeve	Josephine Bell
John Webber	Anthony Oliver
Inspector Reginald Wexford	Ruth Rendell
Inspector Wilkins	James Anderson
Inspector Wilkins	Francis Beeding
Lord Peter Wimsey	Dorothy L. Sayers
Dr. David Wintringham	Josephine Bell
Superintendent Charles Wycliffe	W. J. Burley

4

Occupations of Series Characters

Academics

University/College

Ernst Brendel (J.C. Masterman)
Professor Thea Crawford (Jessica Mann)
Dr. R.V. Davie (V.C. Clinton-Baddeley)
Gervase Fen (Edmund Crispin)
Dr. Patrick Grant (Margaret Yorke)
Adam Ludlow (Simon Nash)
Professor Mandrake (John and Emery Bonett)
Dr. Henry Pym (W. J. Burley)
Professor Hilary Tamar (Sarah Caudwell)

Secondary School

Carolus Deene (Leo Bruce)

Retired

Professor Andrew Basnett (E.X. Ferrars)
Dr. William Blow (Kenneth Hopkins)
Professor Daly (Eilís Dillon)
Professor Gideon Manciple (Kenneth Hopkins)
Dr. Lancelot Priestley (John Rhode)

Actors/Actresses

> Tessa Crichton (Anne Morice)
> Charles Paris (Simon Brett)
> Alan Russell (Nigel FitzGerald)
> Miss Amy Tupper (Josephine Bell)

Artists

> Charles Honeybath (Michael Innes)
> Philip Trent (E.C. Bentley)

Business Men and Women

> Miles Bredon (Ronald A. Knox)
> Celia Grant (John Sherwood)
> Paul Harris (Gavin Black)
> Douglas Perkins (Marian Babson)
> Thomas Preston (Francis Beeding)
> Matthew Stock (Leonard Tourney)
> Mark Treasure (David Williams)
> Malcolm Warren (C.H.B. Kitchin)

Clergy

> Brother Cadfael (Ellis Peters)

Detectives

Amateur

> Tommy and Tuppence Beresford (Agatha Christie)
> Jane and Dagobert Brown (Delano Ames)
> Albert Campion (Margery Allingham, Youngman Carter)
> Ambrose Chitterwick (Anthony Berkeley)
> Colonel Anthony Gethryn (Philip MacDonald)
> Emma Greaves (Lionel Black)
> Jane Marple (Agatha Christie)
> Lord Peter Wimsey (Dorothy L. Sayers)

Private

    Sergeant William Beef (Leo Bruce)
    Ronald Camberwell (J.S. Fletcher)
    Cordelia Gray (P.D. James)
    Sid Halley (Dick Francis)
    Hercule Poirot (Agatha Christie)
    Maud Silver (Patricia Wentworth)
    Nigel Strangeways (Nicholas Blake)

Free-lance/Self-employed

    John Carlyle (Henry Calvin)
    Mrs. Craggs (H.R.F. Keating)
    Lovejoy (Jonathan Gash)
    Dan Mallett (Frank Parrish)
    Dai Owen (Henry Calvin)

Housewives

    Bunty Felse (Ellis Peters)
    Lizzie Thomas (Anthony Oliver)

Legal Professionals

    Martin Ainsworth (Michael Underwood)
    Joshua Clunk (H.C. Bailey)
    Rosa Epton (Michael Underwood)
    Jimmie Haswell (Herbert Adams)
    Antony Maitland (Sara Woods)
    Francis Pettigrew (Cyril Hare)
    Claud Warrington-Reeve (Josephine Bell)

Medical Professionals

    Dame Beatrice Bradley (Gladys Mitchell)
    Reggie Fortune (H.C. Bailey)
    Virginia Freer (E.X. Ferrars)
    Dr. Henry Frost (Josephine Bell)
    Dr. John Thorndyke (R. Austin Freeman)
    Dr. David Wintringham (Josephine Bell)

Newspaper/TV Journalists

Toby Dyke (E.X. Ferrars)
Gerald Lee (Kenneth Hopkins)
Professor Mandrake (John and Emery Bonett)
Jemima Shore (Antonia Fraser)
Kate Theobald (Lionel Black)

Novelists/Writers

Jane Brown (Delano Ames)
Ariadne Oliver (Agatha Christie)
Melinda Pink (Gwen Moffat)
Roger Sheringham (Anthony Berkeley)

Police

Metropolitan Police (Scotland Yard)

Superintendent Roderick Alleyn (Ngaio Marsh)
Sir John Appleby (Michael Innes)
Sergeant Nick Attwell (Michael Underwood)
Superintendent Battle (Agatha Christie)
Constable John Bragg (Henry Wade)
Superintendent John Brock (John Bingham)
Inspector Thomas Cadover (Michael Innes)
Superintendent Charlesworth (Christianna Brand)
Inspector Cockrill (Christianna Brand)
Inspector Crambo (Julian Symons)
Sergeant Cribb (Peter Lovesey)
Superintendent Adam Dalgliesh (P.D. James)
Inspector Septimus Finch (Margaret Erskine)
Superintendent Francis Foy (Lionel Black)
Inspector Joseph French (Freeman Wills Crofts)
Superintendent George Gently (Alan Hunter)
Inspector Alan Grant (Gordon Daviot, Josephine Tey)
Superintendent Hannasyde (Georgette Heyer)
Superintendent Hazlerigg (Michael Gilbert)
Inspector Hemingway (Georgette Heyer)
Inspector Harry James (Kenneth Giles)
Superintendent Richard Jury (Martha Grimes)
Superintendent Simon Kenworthy (John Buxton Hilton)

Inspector Kyle (Roy Vickers)
Inspector Henry Lott (Henry Wade)
Superintendent Macdonald (E.C.R. Lorac)
Inspector Mallett (Cyril Hare)
Superintendent Simon Manton (Michael Underwood)
Inspector George Martin (Francis Beeding)
Superintendent George Masters (Douglas Clark)
Superintendent Steven Mitchell (Josephine Bell)
Inspector Montero (Simon Nash)
Sergeant Patrick Petrella (Michael Gilbert)
Superintendent James Pibble (Peter Dickinson)
Superintendent Arnold Pike (Philip MacDonald)
Inspector Thomas Pitt (Anne Perry)
Inspector Pointer (A. Fielding)
Superintendent Tom Pollard (Elizabeth Lemarchand)
Inspector John Poole (Henry Wade)
Jeremy Sturrock (Jeremy Sturrock)
Superintendent Henry Tibbett (Patricia Moyes)
Superintendent Perry Trethowan (Robert Barnard)
Inspector Wilkins (Francis Beeding)

County/Borough/District Police

Inspector Bill Aveyard (James Fraser)
Inspector Brentford (S.B. Hough)
Inspector David Brock (R. J. White)
Inspector Thomas Brunt (John Buxton Hilton)
Superintendent Burnivel (Edward Candy)
Superintendent Andrew Dalziel (Reginald Hill)
Chief Constable Piet Deventer (J.R.L. Anderson)
Superintendent Ditteridge (E.X. Ferrars)
Superintendent George Felse (Ellis Peters)
Inspector Finch/Rudd (June Thomson)
Inspector Matthew Furnival (Stella Phillips)
Inspector Robert Fusil (Michael Alding)
Inspector Benjamin Jurnet (S.T. Haymon)
Inspector Kelsey (Emma Page)
Inspector Don Kerry (Jeffrey Ashford)
Inspector Morse (Colin Dexter)
Inspector Peter Pascoe (Reginald Hill)
Inspector Walter Purbright (Colin Watson)
Inspector Douglas Quantrill (Sheila Radley)

Superintendent George Rogers (Jonathan Ross)
Inspector C.D. Sloan (Catherine Aird)
Superintendent Ben Spence (Michael Allen)
Inspector Luke Thanet (Dorothy Simpson)
Superintendent George Thorne (John Penn)
Inspector Reginald Wexford (Ruth Rendell)
Superintendent Charles Wycliffe (W. J. Burley)

Retired Police

John Webber (Anthony Oliver)

Secret Service/British Intelligence

Colonel Peter Blair (J.R.L. Anderson)
Ronald Briercliffe (Francis Beeding)
Kenneth Ducane (John Bingham)
Major Faide (Henry Wade)
Colonel Alistair Granby (Francis Beeding)
Tamara Hoyland (Jessica Mann)
Colonel Race (Agatha Christie)

Police outside Great Britain

Inspector Enrique Alvarez (Roderic Jeffries)
Inspector Salvador Borges (John and Emery Bonett)
Superintendent Duffy (Nigel FitzGerald)
Inspector Ganesh Ghote (H.R.F. Keating)
Inspector Mike Kenny (Eilís Dillon)
Sergeant Juan Llorca (Delano Ames)

Secret Agents outside Great Britain

Mikael Petros (James Anderson)

5

Period of Story
(2000 B.C. to A.D. 1959)

2000 B.C.	Agatha Christie
	Death Comes as the End
A.D.	
1130-1139	Ellis Peters
	A Morbid Taste for Bones
	One Corpse Too Many
	Monk's-Head
	Saint Peter's Fair
	The Leper of Saint Giles
	The Virgin in the Ice
1140-1149	Ellis Peters
	The Sanctuary Sparrow
	The Devil's Novice
	Dead Man's Ransom
	The Pilgrim of Hate
	An Excellent Mystery
1480-1489	Josephine Tey
	The Daughter of Time
1600-1609	Leonard Tourney
	The Players' Boy Is Dead
	Low Treason
	Familiar Spirits

Anne Perry
The Cater Street Hangman
Callander Square
Paragon Walk
Resurrection Row
Rutland Place
Bluegate Fields
Death in the Devil's Acre

Julian Symons
Sweet Adelaide

1890-1899   Julian Symons
The Blackheath Poisonings
The Detling Murders

1900-1909   G.K. Chesterton
The Man Who Was Thursday

R. Austin Freeman
The Red Thumb Mark

John Buxton Hilton
Dead-Nettle

R. J. White
The Smartest Grave
The Women of Peasenhall

1910-1919   E.C. Bentley
Trent's Last Case

Agatha Christie
The Mysterious Affair at Styles
The Secret Adversary

Freeman Wills Crofts
The Cask

J.S. Fletcher
The Middle Temple Murder

R. Austin Freeman
The Mystery of 31, New Inn
A Silent Witness

John Buxton Hilton
Rescue from the Rose
Mr Fred

Peter Lovesey
Keystone

1920-1929   Herbert Adams
The Crooked Lip
The Golden Ape

Margery Allingham
The Crime at Black Dudley
Mystery Mile
The White Cottage Mystery

Francis Beeding
The Seven Sleepers
The Hidden Kingdom
The Six Proud Walkers
Pretty Sinister
The Five Flamboys
The League of Discontent
The Four Amourers
The Little White Hag
The House of Dr. Edwardes

Anthony Berkeley
The Poisoned Chocolates Case
The Piccadilly Murder

G.K. Chesterton
Four Faultless Felons

Agatha Christie
The Murder on the Links
The Murder of Roger Ackroyd
The Big Four

The Mystery of the Blue Train
Five Little Pigs
The Man in the Brown Suit
The Secret of Chimneys
The Seven Dials Mystery

Freeman Wills Crofts
Inspector French's Greatest Case
Inspector French and the Cheyne Mystery
Inspector French and the Starvel Tragedy
The Sea Mystery
The Box Office Murders
Sir John Magill's Last Journey
The Ponson Case
The Pit-Prop Syndicate
The Groote Park Murder

Gordon Daviot
The Man in the Queue

Peter Dickinson
A Summer in the Twenties

J. Jefferson Farjeon
The 5.18 Mystery

A. Fielding
The Mysterious Partner
The Wedding-Chest Mystery

J.S. Fletcher
The Murder at Wrides Park
The Matheson Formula
The Yorkshire Moorland Murder
The Dressing Room Murder

R. Austin Freeman
Mr. Pottermack's Oversight

Georgette Heyer
Footsteps in the Dark

Francis Iles
Malice Aforethought
Before the Fact

C.H.B. Kitchin
Death of My Aunt

Ronald A. Knox
The Three Taps
The Footsteps at the Lock
The Viaduct Murder

Peter Lovesey
The False Inspector Dew

Philip MacDonald
The Wraith
The Rasp
The White Crow
The Noose
Rynox

A.A. Milne
The Red House Mystery

Dorothy L. Sayers
Whose Body?
Clouds of Witness
The Unpleasantness at the Bellona Club
Unnatural Death
Strong Poison
The Documents in the Case

Julian Symons
Bland Beginning

Glen Trevor
Murder at School

Henry Wade
The Duke of York's Steps
No Friendly Drop

The Dying Alderman
The Verdict of You All
The Missing Partners

1930-1939   Herbert Adams
                The Woman in Black

                Margery Allingham
                Death of a Ghost
                Police at the Funeral
                Flowers for the Judge
                Look to the Lady
                Sweet Danger
                The Case of the Late Pig
                Dancers in Mourning
                The Fashion in Shrouds
                Black Plumes

                Delano Ames
                No Traveller Returns

                James Anderson
                The Affair of the Blood-stained Egg Cosy
                The Affair of the Mutilated Mink Coat

                H.C. Bailey
                Shadow on the Wall
                The Great Game
                The Bishop's Crime
                Clunk's Claimant
                The Veron Mystery
                The Little Captain

                Francis Beeding
                The Nine Waxed Faces
                The Ten Holy Horrors
                Death Walks in Eastrepps
                Murder Intended
                The Three Fishers
                No Fury
                The Emerald Clasp
                The Big Fish

Josephine Bell
Fall over Cliff
Death at Half-Term
The Port of London Murders

E.C. Bentley
Trent's Own Case

Anthony Berkeley
Panic Party
Trial and Error

Nicholas Blake
A Question of Proof
Thou Shell of Death
There's Trouble Brewing
The Beast Must Die
The Smiler with the Knife
Malice in Wonderland
The Private Wound

Christianna Brand
Death in High Heels

Leo Bruce
Case for Three Detectives
Case without a Corpse
Case with No Solution
Case with Four Clowns

Agatha Christie
Peril at End House
Lord Edgware Dies
Murder on the Orient Express
Three Act Tragedy
The ABC Murders
Death in the Clouds
Murder in Mesopotamia
Cards on the Table
Dumb Witness
Death on the Nile
Appointment with Death

Hercule Poirot's Christmas
Sad Cypress
One, Two, Buckle My Shoe
Evil under the Sun
Murder Is Easy
The Murder at the Vicarage
The Sittaford Mystery
Why Didn't They Ask Evans?
Ten Little Niggers

Edmund Crispin
The Moving Toyshop

Freeman Wills Crofts
Mystery in the Channel
Death on the Way
Sudden Death
The Hog's Back Mystery
The 12:30 from Croydon
Mystery on Southampton Water
Crime at Guildford
Man Overboard
The Loss of the Jane Vosper
Found Floating
The End of Andrew Harrison
Antidote to Venom
Fatal Venture
Golden Ashes
Fear Comes to Chalfont
The Affair at Little Wokeham
James Tarrant, Adventurer
The Losing Game

Detection Club
"The Scoop" and "Behind the Screen"
The Floating Admiral
Ask a Policeman
Double Death

Margaret Erskine
And Being Dead

J. Jefferson Farjeon
Dead Man's Heath
The Fancy Dress Ball
Mystery in White

E.X. Ferrars
Give a Corpse a Bad Name
Remove the Bodies
Death in Botanist's Bay
Don't Monkey with Murder

A. Fielding
The Paper-Chase
The Case of the Missing Diary
Black Cats Are Lucky

J.S. Fletcher
The Ebony Box

R. Austin Freeman
Dr. Thorndyke Intervenes
The Penrose Mystery
The Stoneware Monkey
The Jacob Street Mystery

Michael Gilbert
Close Quarters

Cyril Hare
Tenant for Death
Death Is No Sportsman
Suicide Excepted
Tragedy at Law

Georgette Heyer
Death in the Stocks
Behold, Here's Poison
They Found Him Dead
A Blunt Instrument
No Wind of Death
Why Shoot a Butler?
The Unfinished Clue

S.B Hough
The Primitives

Francis Iles
As for the Woman

Michael Innes
Death at the President's Lodging
Hamlet, Revenge!
Lament for a Maker
Stop Press
There Came Both Mist and Snow
The Weight of the Evidence
Appleby's End
The Secret Vanguard

Romilly and Katherine John
Death by Request

H.R.F. Keating
The Murder of the Maharajah

C.H.B. Kitchin
Crime at Christmas
Death of His Uncle

Ronald A. Knox
The Body in the Silo
Still Dead
Double Cross Purposes

Philip MacDonald
The Link
The Crime Conductor
The Choice
The Maze
Rope to Spare
Death on My Left
The Nursemaid Who Disappeared
Murder Gone Mad
R.I.P.

Nagio Marsh
A Man Lay Dead
The Nursing Home Murder
Enter a Murderer
Death in Ecstasy
Vintage Murder
Artists in Crime
Death in a White Tie
Overture to Death
Death at the Bar
Surfeit of Lampreys

J.C. Masterman
An Oxford Tragedy

A.A. Milne
Four Days' Wonder

Gladys Mitchell
The Saltmarsh Murders

Martin Porlock
Mystery at Friar's Pardon
Mystery in Kensington Gore
X v. Rex

John Rhode
The Claverton Affair

Dorothy L. Sayers
The Five Red Herrings
Have His Carcase
Murder Must Advertise
The Nine Tailors
Gaudy Night
Busman's Honeymoon

John Sherwood
A Shot in the Arm

Julian Symons
The Immaterial Murder Case

Josephine Tey
A Shilling for Candles

Henry Wade
Constable, Guard Thyself!
Bury Him Darkly
Lonely Magdalen
The Hanging Captain
The High Sheriff
Released for Death
Mist on the Saltings
Heir Presumptive
New Graves at Great Norne

1940-1949   Margery Allingham
Traitor's Purse
Coroner's Pidgin
More Work for the Undertaker
The Tiger in the Smoke
Take Two at Bedtime
No Love Lost (The Patient at Peacocks Hall)

Delano Ames
She Shall Have Murder
Murder Begins at Home
Corpse Diplomatique
Death of a Fellow Traveller

H.C. Bailey
Mr. Fortune Finds a Pig
Dead Man's Shoes
Slippery Ann
The Wrong Man

Robert Barnard
Out of the Blackout

Francis Beeding
The Twelve Disguises

Josephine Bell
Death at the Medical Board
Death in Clairvoyance
The Summer School Mystery

E.C. Bentley
Elephant's Work

Nicholas Blake
The Case of the Abominable Snowman
Minute for Murder
Head of a Traveler

John and Emery Bonett
Dead Lion
A Banner for Pegasus

Christianna Brand
Heads You Lose
Green for Danger
Suddenly at His Residence
Death of Jezebel

Leo Bruce
Case with Ropes and Rings
Case for Sergeant Beef

Agatha Christie
The Hollow
Taken at the Flood
Mrs. McGinty's Dead
N or M?
Sparkling Cyanide
Towards Zero
The Body in the Library
The Moving Finger
Crooked House

Edmund Crispin
The Case of the Gilded Fly
Holy Disorders
Swan Song

Love Lies Bleeding
Buried for Pleasure
Frequent Hearses

Freeman Wills Crofts
Death of a Train
Enemy Unseen
Silence for the Murderer
French Strikes Oil

Margaret Erskine
The Whispering House
I Knew MacBean
Give up the Ghost
The Disappearing Bridegroom

E.X. Ferrars
Your Neck in a Noose
I, Said the Fly
Murder among Friends
The March Hare Murders
Milk of Human Kindness
Hunt the Tortoise

Michael Gilbert
They Never Looked Inside
The Doors Open
Smallbone Deceased
Death Has Deep Roots

Cyril Hare
When the Wind Blows
With a Bare Bodkin
An English Murder

Georgette Heyer
Envious Casca
Penhallow

S.B. Hough
Moment of Decision
Mission in Guemo

Michael Innes
Appleby on Ararat
The Daffodil Affair
A Night of Errors
What Happened at Hazelwood?
The Journeying Boy
From "London" Far

C.H.B. Kitchin
The Cornish Fox

E.C.R. Lorac
Fire in the Thatch
Policemen in the Precinct

Philip MacDonald
The Dark Wheel

Ngaio Marsh
Death and the Dancing Footman
Colour Scheme
Died in the Wool
Final Curtain
Swing, Brother, Swing

Gladys Mitchell
Tom Brown's Body

John Rhode
Death in Harley Street
Nothing But the Truth
Death of an Author

Julian Symons
A Man Called Jones
The Thirty-first of February

Josephine Tey
The Franchise Affair
To Love and Be Wise

Miss Pym Disposes
Brat Farrar

Leslie Thomas
Ormerod's Landing

Roy Vickers
Murdering Mr Velfrage

Henry Wade
Too Soon to Die
Diplomat's Folly
Be Kind to the Killer

Patricia Wentworth
The Catherine Wheel

Colin Wilson
The World of Violence

Sara Woods
They Love Not Poison

1950-1959   Margery Allingham
The Beckoning Lady
Hide My Eyes
No Love Lost (Safer than Love)

Delano Ames
The Body on Page One
Murder, Maestro, Please
No Mourning for the Matador
Crime, Gentlemen, Please
Landscape with Corpse
Crime out of Mind
She Wouldn't Say Who
Lucky Jane
The Man in the Tricorn Hat

Josephine Bell
Bones in the Barrow
The China Roundabout

The Seeing Eye
Easy Prey
A Well-Known Face
The Upfold Witch
A Question of Inheritance
To Let: Furnished
Fires at Fairlawn
Death in Retirement
Double Doom
The House above the River
New People at the Hollies

John Bingham
My Name is Michael Sibley
Five Roundabouts to Heaven
The Third Skin
The Paton Street Case
Marion
Murder Plan Six

Nicholas Blake
The Dreadful Hollow
The Whisper in the Gloom
End of Chapter
The Widow's Cruise
A Tangled Web
A Penknife in My Heart
The Deadly Joker

John and Emery Bonett
No Grave for a Lady

Christianna Brand
London Particular
Tour de Force
Cat and Mouse

Leo Bruce
Neck and Neck
Cold Blood
Our Jubilee Is Death
Furious Old Women

Jack on the Gallows Tree
A Bone and a Hank of Hair

Edward Candy
Which Doctor?
Bones of Contention

Agatha Christie
After the Funeral
Hickory Dickory Dock
Dead Man's Folly
Cat among the Pigeons
A Murder Is Announced
They Do It with Mirrors
A Pocket Full of Rye
4:50 from Paddington
They Came to Baghdad
Destination Unknown
Ordeal by Innocence

Edmund Crispin
The Long Divorce

Freeman Wills Crofts
Anything to Declare

Eilís Dillon
Death at Crane's Court
Death in the Quadrangle
Sent to His Account

Margaret Erskine
Death of Our Dear One
Dead by Now
Fatal Relations
The Voice of Murder
Sleep No More
The House of the Enchantress

E.X. Ferrars
The Clock That Wouldn't Stop
Alibi for a Witch

Murder in Time
The Lying Voices
Enough to Kill a Horse
Always Say Die
Murder Moves On
Furnished for Murder
Unreasonable Doubt
A Tale of Two Murders
Fear the Light
Sleeping Dogs

Nigel FitzGerald
Midsummer Malice
The Rosy Pastor
The House Is Falling
Imagine a Man
Suffer a Witch
The Student Body
Ghost in the Making
The Candles Are All Out
This Won't Hurt You

Michael Gilbert
Fear to Tread
Blood and Judgment
Death in Captivity
Sky High
Be Shot for Sixpence

Cyril Hare
The Yew Tree's Shade
He Should Have Died Hereafter

Georgette Heyer
Duplicate Death
Detection Unlimited

John Buxton Hilton
Some Run Crooked

Kenneth Hopkins
The Girl Who Died

She Died Because . . .
Dead against My Principles

S.B. Hough
The Bronze Perseus

Alan Hunter
Gently Does It
Gently by the Shore
Landed Gently
Gently down the Stream
Gently through the Mill
Gently in the Sun
Gently with the Painters
Gently Go Man
Gently to the Summit

Michael Innes
Operation Pax
A Private View
Appleby Plays Chicken
The Long Farewell
Hare Sitting Up
Christmas at Candleshoe
The Man from the Sea
Old Hall, New Hall
The New Sonia Wayward

H.R.F. Keating
Death and the Visiting Firemen
Zen There Was Murder

E.C.R. Lorac
Let Well Alone

Philip MacDonald
The List of Adrian Messenger
Guest in the House

Ngaio Marsh
Opening Night
Spinsters in Jeopardy

Scales of Justice
Off with His Head
Singing in the Shrouds
False Scent

J.C. Masterman
The Case of Four Friends

Gladys Mitchell
Spotted Hemlock

Patricia Moyes
Dead Men Don't Ski

Simon Nash
Dead of a Counterplot
Killed by Scandal

Ellis Peters
Death Mask
The Will and the Deed

Robert Robinson
Landscape with Dead Dons

Julian Symons
The Narrowing Circle
The Gigantic Shadow
The Broken Penny
The Paper Chase
The Colour of Murder
The Progress of a Crime
The Belting Inheritance

Josephine Tey
The Singing Sands

Michael Underwood
Murder on Trial
Murder Made Absolute

False Witness
Lawful Pursuit
Case of Death

Roy Vickers
The Sole Survivor
The Kynsard Affair

Henry Wade
Gold Was Our Grave
A Dying Fall
The Litmore Snatch

Colin Watson
Coffin Scarcely Used
Bump in the Night

Patricia Wentworth
Ladies' Bane
Out of the Past
The Listening Eye

Colin Wilson
Ritual in the Dark
Necessary Doubt

Sara Woods
The Taste of Fears
Bloody Instructions

6

Locations outside England

The vast majority of British mysteries are set in England; I have listed here the novels in which all or a significant part of the action takes place outside England.

Africa (fictional countries)

J.R.L. Anderson
  Death in the Desert
  Death in the Greenhouse
E.X. Ferrars
  The Swaying Pillars
Ngaio Marsh
  Black as He's Painted

Algeria

Michael Underwood
  Lawful Pursuit

Arctic Circle

J.R.L. Anderson
  Death in a High Latitude

Australia

Robert Barnard
  Death of an Old Goat
E.X. Ferrars
  The Crime and the Crystal
  The Small World of Murder
Dick Francis
  For Kicks
Michael Innes
  The Gay Phoenix

Austria

Francis Beeding
  The Nine Waxed Faces
Michael Gilbert
  Be Shot for Sixpence
  After the Fine Weather
Ellis Peters
  The Will and the Deed
  The Horn of Roland
Michael Underwood
  The Anxious Conspirator
Margaret Yorke
  Silent Witness

China

Gavin Black
  A Dragon for Christmas

Czechoslovakia

Ellis Peters
  The Piper on the Mountain

Egypt

Agatha Christie
  Death on the Nile
  Death Comes as the End

Europe (fictional countries)

James Anderson
  Assassin
  The Abolition of Death
Henry Calvin
  The Chosen Instrument
G.K. Chesterton
  Four Faultless Felons (The Loyal Traitor)
H.R.F. Keating
  The Strong Man

France

Delano Ames
  Corpse Diplomatique
  Murder, Maestro, Please
  Crime, Gentlemen, Please
Francis Beeding
  The League of Discontent
  The Twelve Disguises
  The House of Dr. Edwardes
Josephine Bell
  The House above the River
John Bingham
  Five Roundabouts to Heaven
Henry Calvin
  It's Different Abroad
Agatha Christie
  The Murder on the Links
  The Mystery of the Blue Train
Freeman Wills Crofts
  The Cask
  The Pit-Prop Syndicate
E.X. Ferrars
  Hunt the Tortoise
Alan Hunter
  The Honfleur Decision
Michael Gilbert
  Death Has Deep Roots

Ngaio Marsh
    Spinsters in Jeopardy
    Last Ditch
Anthony Oliver
    The Elberg Collection
Leslie Thomas
    Ormerod's Landing
Sara Woods
    The Taste of Fears

Germany

Francis Beeding
    The Three Fishers
Agatha Christie
    Passenger to Frankfurt
Michael Underwood
    The Unprofessional Spy
    Reward for a Defector

Greece

Josephine Bell
    The Catalyst
John Bingham
    Vulture in the Sun
Peter Dickinson
    The Lizard in the Cup
E.X. Ferrars
    No Peace for the Wicked
Margaret Yorke
    Grave Matters
    Mortal Remains

Greenland

J.R.L. Anderson
    Reckoning in Ice

Hong Kong

Gavin Black
   The Eyes around Me
   The Golden Cockatrice
Detection Club
   The Floating Admiral

India

H.R.F. Keating
   The Murder of the Maharajah
   The Perfect Murder
   Inspector Ghote's Good Crusade
   Inspector Ghote Caught in Meshes
   Inspector Ghote Plays a Joker
   Inspector Ghote Breaks an Egg
   Inspector Ghote Goes by Train
   Inspector Ghote Trusts the Heart
   Bats Fly up for Inspector Ghote
   Filmi, Filmi, Inspector Ghote
   Inspector Ghote Draws a Line
   The Sheriff of Bombay
Ellis Peters
   Mourning Raga
   Death to the Landlords

Iraq

Agatha Christie
   Murder in Mesopotamia
   They Came to Baghdad

Ireland

Nicholas Blake
   Thou Shell of Death
   The Private Wound
Eilís Dillon
   Death at Crane's Court
   Death in the Quadrangle
   Sent to His Account

Nigel FitzGerald
  Midsummer Malice
  The Rosy Pastor
  The House Is Falling
  Suffer a Witch
  The Student Body
  Black Welcome
  The Day of the Adder
  Affairs of Death
  Ghost in the Making
  The Candles Are All Out
Jonathan Gash
  The Sleepers of Erin
Michael Innes
  The Journeying Boy
H.R.F. Keating
  The Dog It Was That Died

Italy

Francis Beeding
  The Six Proud Walkers
  The Emerald Clasp
Josephine Bell
  A Question of Inheritance
  A Pigeon among the Cats
John Bingham
  A Fragment of Fear
Christianna Brand
  Tour de Force
Sarah Caudwell
  Thus Was Adonis Murdered
E.X. Ferrars
  Alibi for a Witch
A. Fielding
  The Paper-Chase
Nigel FitzGerald
  Imagine a Man
Dick Francis
  The Danger

Jonathan Gash
    The Vatican Rip
    The Gondola Scam
Michael Gilbert
    Death in Captivity
    The Etruscan Net
    The Long Journey Home
Michael Innes
    The Long Farewell
Ngaio Marsh
    When in Rome
Patricia Moyes
    Dead Men Don't Ski

Japan

Gavin Black
    Dead Man Calling

Jordan

Lionel Black
    Arafat Is Next!
Agatha Christie
    Appointment with Death

Malaysia

Gavin Black
    You Want to Die, Johnny?
    A Wind of Death
    A Time for Pirates
    The Bitter Tea

Mexico

Kenneth Giles
    The Big Greed

Middle East (fictional countries)

G.K. Chesterton
  Four Faultless Felons (The Moderate Murderer)
Agatha Christie
  Cat among the Pigeons
Peter Dickinson
  The Poison Oracle
Michael Gilbert
  The 92nd Tiger

Morocco

Agatha Christie
  Destination Unknown

Netherlands

Gladys Mitchell
  Death of a Blue Delft
Patricia Moyes
  Death and the Dutch Uncle
  Who Saw Her Die?

New Zealand

Ngaio Marsh
  Vintage Murder
  Surfeit of Lampreys
  Colour Scheme
  Died in the Wool
  Photo Finish
John Sherwood
  A Botanist at Bay

Northern Ireland

Freeman Wills Crofts
  Sir John Magill's Last Journey
  Man Overboard

Norway

Robert Barnard
   Death in a Cold Climate
John Bingham
   Night's Black Agent
Dick Francis
   Slayride

Pakistan

P.M. Hubbard
   The Custom of the Country

Portugal

John Bingham
   God's Defector
E.X. Ferrars
   Skeleton Staff
   Breath of Suspicion
   Witness before the Fact

Rhodesia (Zimbabwe)

Agatha Christie
   The Secret of Chimneys

Scotland

Gavin Black
   The Cold Jungle
   A Big Wind for Summer
Simon Brett
   So Much Blood
Henry Calvin
   The Poison Chasers
Gordon Daviot
   The Man in the Queue

Gwen Moffat
  Miss Pink at the Edge of the World
  Over the Sea to Death
Patrick Ruell
  Death Takes the Low Road
Dorothy L. Sayers
  The Five Red Herrings
Josephine Tey
  The Singing Sands
Henry Wade
  Too Soon to Die

South Africa

Agatha Christie
  The Man in the Brown Suit
Freeman Wills Crofts
  The Groote Park Murder
Dick Francis
  Smokescreen

South America (fictional countries)

S.B. Hough
  Mission in Guemo
Michael Innes
  The Daffodil Affair

Spain

Delano Ames
  No Mourning for the Matador
  Landscape with Corpse
  The Man in the Tricorn Hat
  The Man with Three Chins
  The Man with Three Jaguars
Jeffrey Ashford
  A Sense of Loyalty
  Presumption of Guilt
Francis Beeding
  The Hidden Kingdom
  The Four Amourers

Josephine Bell
  Adventure with Crime
Nicholas Blake
  The Morning after Death
Simon Brett
  The Dead Side of the Mike
Dick Francis
  Blood Sport
  The Danger
Reginald Hill
  Who Guards a Prince?
John Buxton Hilton
  The Sunset Law
H.R.F. Keating
  Go West, Inspector Ghote
Peter Lovesey
  Keystone
Philip MacDonald
  The Dark Wheel
  Guest in the House
Gwen Moffat
  Last Chance Country
  Grizzly Trail
Anne Morice
  Murder in Mimicry
Patricia Moyes
  Black Widower
Julian Symons
  The Name of Annabel Lee
Sara Woods
  Most Grievous Murder

USSR

John Bingham
  The Double Agent
Dick Francis
  Trial Run

Venezuela

Reginald Hill
  Traitor's Blood

Wales

Herbert Adams
  The Crooked Lip
J.R.L. Anderson
  The Nine-spoked Wheel
H.C. Bailey
  Mr. Fortune Finds a Pig
Christianna Brand
  Cat and Mouse
Agatha Christie
  Why Didn't They Ask Evans?
Freeman Wills Crofts
  The Sea Mystery
Cyril Hare
  With a Bare Bodkin
P.M. Hubbard
  The Dancing Man
Alan Hunter
  Gently to the Summit
Gwen Moffat
  Persons Unknown
  Die Like a Dog
Ellis Peters
  A Morbid Taste for Bones
David Williams
  Murder for Treasure

West Indies

Delano Ames
  No Traveller Returns
J.R.L. Anderson
  Death in the Caribbean
Josephine Bell
  The Wilberforce Legacy
  The Fennister Affair

Agatha Christie
  <u>A Caribbean Mystery</u>
Peter Dickinson
  <u>Walking Dead</u>
Patricia Moyes
  <u>Black Widower</u>
  <u>To Kill a Coconut</u>
  <u>Angel Death</u>
David Williams
  <u>Treasure up in Smoke</u>

Yugoslavia

Brian Ball
  <u>Montenegrin Gold</u>
Agatha Christie
  <u>Murder on the Orient Express</u>
Julian Symons
  <u>The Man Who Lost His Wife</u>

7

Setting

The quintessential British mystery is set in a village, thereby defining the boundaries within which the detective must solve the crime. Within these limits, however, many writers unfold their tale in a distinctive setting or choose a distinct site for the crime. I have listed here novels with settings that add to or define the tale; the sites are usually the place of the crime or the principal locale of the criminal investigation.

Archaeological Dig

J.R.L. Anderson
  The Nine-spoked Wheel
Josephine Bell
  Bones in the Barrow
W. J. Burley
  Wycliffe and the Four Jacks
Youngman Carter
  Mr. Campion's Falcon
Agatha Christie
  Murder in Mesopotamia
Philip MacDonald
  The Noose
Ellis Peters
  City of Gold and Shadows
  Death Mask

Patrick Ruell
  Urn Burial
June Thomson
  A Question of Identity

Art Gallery/Exhibition Hall

Margery Allingham
  Death of a Ghost
  Black Plumes
Marian Babson
  Murder on Show
Josephine Bell
  The Seeing Eye
Christianna Brand
  Death of Jezebel
R. Austin Freeman
  The Stoneware Monkey
Michael Gilbert
  The Etruscan Net
Kenneth Giles
  A Provenance of Death
Michael Innes
  A Private View
  Silence Observed
  Money from Holme
Julian Symons
  The Immaterial Murder Case
Patricia Wentworth
  The Listening Eye

Bank

Jeffrey Ashford
  Hostage to Death
Ruth Rendell
  Make Death Love Me

Boardinghouse

Margery Allingham
  More Work for the Undertaker

Marian Babson
  The Twelve Deaths of Christmas
Josephine Bell
  The China Roundabout
Agatha Christie
  Hickory Dickory Dock
  N or M?
Peter Dickinson
  The Lively Dead
Margaret Erskine
  The House in Belmont Square
E.X. Ferrars
  I, Said the Fly
Cyril Hare
  With a Bare Bodkin
Ruth Rendell
  Murder Being Once Done
  A Demon in My View

Church/Chapel/Convent/Monastery

Catherine Aird
  The Religious Body
Delano Ames
  Landscape with Corpse
H.C. Bailey
  The Great Game
  The Bishop's Crime
Robert Barnard
  Blood Brotherhood
John Bingham
  God's Defector
Agatha Christie
  The Murder at the Vicarage
Douglas Clark
  Heberden's Seat
Edmund Crispin
  Holy Disorders
Colin Dexter
  Service of All the Dead
Peter Dickinson
  The Seventh Raven

Antonia Fraser
  Quiet as a Nun
Michael Gilbert
  Close Quarters
  Sky High
  The Black Seraphim
Kenneth Giles
  A Death in the Church
S.T. Haymon
  Death and the Pregnant Virgin
  Ritual Murder
H.R.F. Keating
  Go West, Inspector Ghote
Elizabeth Lemarchand
  Unhappy Returns
E.C.R. Lorac
  Policemen in the Precinct
Ngaio Marsh
  Death in Ecstasy
  Vintage Murder
Simon Nash
  Unhallowed Murder
Ellis Peters
  A Morbid Taste for Bones
  One Corpse Too Many
  Monk's-Hood
  Saint Peter's Fair
  The Leper of Saint Giles
  The Virgin in the Ice
  The Sanctuary Sparrow
  The Devil's Novice
  Dead Man's Ransom
  The Pilgrim of Hate
  An Excellent Mystery
  The Knocker on Death's Door
  Rainbow's End
Sheila Radley
  A Talent for Destruction
Dorothy L. Sayers
  The Nine Tailors
R. J. White
  The Women of Peasenhall

David Williams
  Unholy Writ
  Murder in Advent

Company Office/Business

Jeffrey Ashford
  A Sense of Loyalty
Marian Babson
  Death in Fashion
John Bingham
  A Case of Libel
Christianna Brand
  Death in High Heels
Douglas Clark
  Nobody's Perfect
Freeman Wills Crofts
  Mystery on Southampton Water
Michael Gilbert
  Smallbone Deceased
Roderic Jeffries
  An Embarrassing Death
Patricia Moyes
  Murder à la Mode
Dorothy L. Sayers
  Murder Must Advertise
John Sherwood
  A Shot in the Arm
Julian Symons
  The Narrowing Circle
  The Killing of Francie Lake

Cottage/Home

Margery Allingham
  Police at the Funeral
  The White Cottage Mystery
Delano Ames
  She Wouldn't Say Who
Jeffrey Ashford
  The Hands of Innocence
  A Man Will Be Kidnapped Tomorrow

Josephine Bell
　Death in Retirement
Leo Bruce
　Case for Three Detectives
Agatha Christie
　Endless Night
J. Jefferson Farjeon
　Dead Man's Heath
　Mystery in White
P.M. Hubbard
　The Holm Oaks
E.C.R. Lorac
　Fire in the Thatch
　Let Well Alone
Margaret Yorke
　The Scent of Fear

Courtroom

Jeffrey Ashford
　Forget What You Saw
Michael Gilbert
　Death Has Deep Roots
Cyril Hare
　Tragedy at Law
Roderic Jeffries
　Evidence of the Accused
　Dead against the Lawyers
　Death in the Coverts
Philip MacDonald
　The Maze
Julian Symons
　The Colour of Murder
Michael Underwood
　Murder on Trial
　Murder Made Absolute
　False Witness
　Lawful Pursuit
　Cause of Death
　Adam's Case
　A Trout in the Milk

Margaret Erskine
  I Knew MacBean
Jeremy Sturrock
  The Wilful Lady

Farm/Stables/Ranch/Estate

Catherine Aird
  Harm's Way
Delano Ames
  Murder Begins at Home
Jeffrey Ashford
  The Burden of Proof
  To Protect the Guilty
  Three Layers of Guilt
H.C. Bailey
  Clunk's Claimant
Agatha Christie
  Death Comes as the End
Douglas Clark
  The Libertines
Dick Francis
  Flying Finish
  Blood Sport
  Bonecrack
  Knockdown
Cyril Hare
  He Should Have Died Hereafter
John Buxton Hilton
  Mr Fred
Roderic Jeffries
  The Benefits of Death
Ronald A. Knox
  Still Dead
Jessica Mann
  The Sting of Death
Ngaio Marsh
  Died in the Wool
A.A. Milne
  Four Days' Wonder

Peter Lovesey
  Mad Hatter's Holiday
Ngaio Marsh
  Colour Scheme
Patricia Moyes
  Dead Men Don't Ski
  Season of Snows and Sins
Emma Page
  A Fortnight by the Sea
Ellis Peters
  Death to the Landlords
  Horn of Roland
Jonathan Ross
  Burial Deferred
Patrick Ruell
  The Castle of the Demon
Margaret Yorke
  Silent Witness
  Mortal Remains

Island

Margery Allingham
  Mystery Mile
Delano Ames
  Lucky Jane
  No Traveller Returns
J.R.L. Anderson
  Death in the City
  Death in the Caribbean
Francis Beeding
  The Five Flamboys
Josephine Bell
  The Wilberforce Legacy
Anthony Berkeley
  Panic Party
Gavin Black
  A Big Wind for Summer
John and Emery Bonett
  No Grave for a Lady
Christianna Brand
  Tour de Force

Roy Vickers
  The Sole Survivor
David Williams
  Treasure up in Smoke

Manor House/Mansion

Catherine Aird
  A Most Contagious Game
Michael Allen
  Spence at Marlby Manor
Margery Allingham
  The Crime at Black Dudley
  Look to the Lady
  Dancers in Mourning
  Take Two at Bedtime
Delano Ames
  The Man with Three Chins
James Anderson
  The Affair of the Blood-stained Egg Cosy
  The Affair of the Mutilated Mink Coat
  Assault and Matrimony
Marian Babson
  Tightrope for Three
H.C. Bailey
  Mr. Fortune Finds a Pig
Robert Barnard
  Death by Sheer Torture
  Unruly Son
  Corpse in a Gilded Cage
Josephine Bell
  Fall over Cliff
  A Question of Inheritance
  To Let: Furnished
  Fires at Fairlawn
  Double Doom
  The House above the River
Lionel Black
  Swinging Murder
  The Eve of the Wedding

Nicholas Blake
  Thou Shell of Death
  The Case of the Abominable Snowman
Christianna Brand
  Suddenly at His Residence
  Cat and Mouse
Leo Bruce
  Neck and Neck
W. J. Burley
  Death in Willow Pattern
  Charles and Elizabeth
  The House of Care
Youngman Carter
  Mr. Campion's . . . Farthing
Agatha Christie
  The Mysterious Affair at Styles
  The Murder on the Links
  Dumb Witness
  Hercule Poirot's Christmas
  Sad Cypress
  The Hollow
  After the Funeral
  Curtain
  Sparkling Cyanide
  The Mirror Crack'd from Side to Side
  Nemesis
  Sleeping Murder
  The Sittaford Mystery
  Crooked House
Freeman Wills Crofts
  Inspector French and the Starvel Tragedy
  Crime at Guildford
  Fear Comes to Chalfont
  The Affair at Little Wokeham
  French Strikes Oil
Eilís Dillon
  Sent to His Account
Margaret Erskine
  The Whispering House
  The Disappearing Bridegroom
  Death of Our Dear One
  Sleep No More

The Open House
Appleby's Other Story
Appleby and Honeybath
What Happened at Hazelwood?
A Change of Heir
P.D. James
Cover Her Face
Romilly and Katherine John
Death by Request
C.H.B. Kitchin
Death of My Aunt
Crime at Christmas
Ronald A. Knox
The Body in the Silo
Elizabeth Lemarchand
Alibi for a Corpse
Philip MacDonald
The Wraith
The Rasp
The Choice
R.I.P.
Ngaio Marsh
A Man Lay Dead
Death and the Dancing Footman
Final Curtain
False Scent
Tied up in Tinsel
A.A. Milne
The Red House Mystery
Anne Morice
Nursery Tea and Poison
Murder in Mimicry
Hollow Vengeance
Patricia Moyes
Murder Fantastical
Ruth Rendell
A Guilty Thing Surprised
Put on by Cunning
A Judgement in Stone
John Rhode
The Claverton Mystery

Dorothy L. Sayers
  Busman's Honeymoon
Julian Symons
  The Blackheath Poisonings
Josephine Tey
  Brat Farrar
Henry Wade
  Too Soon to Die
  Diplomat's Folly
David Williams
  Wedding Treasure
Margaret Yorke
  Find Me a Villain

Medical Office/Hospital/Asylum

Francis Beeding
  The House of Dr. Edwardes
Josephine Bell
  Death at the Medical Board
  Wolf! Wolf!
  No Escape
  Death of a Con Man
  A Hydra with Six Heads
  The Trouble in Hunter Ward
Lionel Black
  Outbreak
Christianna Brand
  Green for Danger
Edward Candy
  Which Doctor?
Agatha Christie
  One, Two, Buckle My Shoe
D.M. Devine
  Doctors Also Die
Nigel FitzGerald
  This Won't Hurt You
Francis Iles
  Malice Aforethought
P.D. James
  A Mind to Murder
  Shroud for a Nightingale

Ngaio Marsh
  The Nursing Home Murder
John Rhode
  Death in Harley Street
June Thomson
  Shadow of a Doubt

Movie, Radio, TV Studios

Marian Babson
  Murder, Murder, Little Star
Simon Brett
  The Dead Side of the Mike
  Situation Tragedy
  Dead Giveaway
Edmund Crispin
  Frequent Hearses
H.R.F. Keating
  Filmi, Filmi, Inspector Ghote
Peter Lovesey
  Keystone
Patricia Moyes
  Falling Star
Sara Woods
  The Case Is Altered

Museum/Library

J.R.L. Anderson
  Death in a High Latitude
Edward Candy
  Bones of Contention
Agatha Christie
  Hallowe'en Party
Margaret Erskine
  The Ewe Lamb
Elizabeth Lemarchand
  Step in the Dark
David Williams
  Treasure Preserved

Nature Preserve/Park/Woods

Josephine Bell
  Death on the Reserve
John Bingham
  Deadly Picnic
Nicholas Blake
  The Whisper in the Gloom
Leo Bruce
  Case for Sergeant Beef
R. Austin Freeman
  The Jacob Street Mystery
Michael Gilbert
  Blood and Judgment
Cyril Hare
  The Yew Tree's Shade
Reginald Hill
  Fell of Dark
Alan Hunter
  Gently Where the Birds Are
Elizabeth Lemarchand
  Suddenly While Gardening
Gwen Moffat
  Die Like a Dog
Ellis Peters
  The Piper on the Mountain
Ruth Rendell
  Master of the Moor
Colin Watson
  Broomsticks over Flaxborough

Nightclub/Casino

Herbert Adams
  The Golden Ape
Marian Babson
  Death beside the Sea
Lionel Black
  The Life and Death of Peter Wade
Ngaio Marsh
  Swing, Brother, Swing

Private Club

Anthony Berkeley
  The Poisoned Chocolates Case
V. C. Clinton-Baddeley
  My Foe Outstretch'd beneath the Tree
Reginald Hill
  A Pinch of Snuff
John Penn
  Deceitful Death
Dorothy L. Sayers
  The Unpleasantness at the Bellona Club
Michael Underwood
  A Pinch of Snuff
  Crime upon Crime
  Double Jeopardy
Colin Watson
  The Naked Nuns

Pub/Inn

H.C. Bailey
  The Wrong Man
Leo Bruce
  Case without a Corpse
  Death with Blue Ribbon
Agatha Christie
  The Pale Horse
Martha Grimes
  The Man with a Load of Mischief
  The Anodyne Necklace
Michael Innes
  Appleby Plays Chicken
Ronald A. Knox
  The Three Taps
Philip MacDonald
  Rope to Spare
Ngaio Marsh
  Death at the Bar
Simon Nash
  Dead Woman's Ditch

Ellis Peters
   Death and the Joyful Woman
Patrick Ruell
   Red Christmas
Leonard Tourney
   The Players' Boy Is Dead
Patricia Wentworth
   The Catherine Wheel

Racecourse

Dick Francis
   Odds Against
   Whip Hand
   Dead Cert
   Nerve
   For Kicks
   Forfeit
   Enquiry
   Rat Race
   Smokescreen
   High Stakes
   In the Frame
   Risk
   Reflex
   Banker
   Proof
Anne Morice
   Scared to Death
   Getting away with Murder?
Henry Wade
   A Dying Fall

Research Institute

Margery Allingham
   Traitor's Purse
   The Mind Readers
Henry Calvin
   The Poison Chasers
Agatha Christie
   Destination Unknown

Douglas Clark
  Dread and Water
Peter Dickinson
  Walking Dead
E.X. Ferrars
  Hanged Man's House
  Experiment with Death
Michael Gilbert
  The Empty House
Michael Innes
  Operation Pax
P.D. James
  An Unsuitable Job for a Woman
  Death of an Expert Witness
Jessica Mann
  The Sticking Place
Sara Woods
  This Fatal Writ

Rest Home/Orphanage/Health Retreat

H.C. Bailey
  The Little Captain
Josephine Bell
  New People at the Hollies
Lionel Black
  A Healthy Way to Die
Leo Bruce
  Jack on the Gallows Tree
Agatha Christie
  By the Pricking of My Thumbs
  They Do It with Mirrors
Peter Dickinson
  Sleep and His Brother
  One Foot in the Grave
Eilís Dillon
  Death at Crane's Court
Michael Innes
  Honeybath's Haven
P.D. James
  The Black Tower

H.R.F. Keating
  Inspector Ghote's Good Crusade
Frank Parrish
  Snare in the Dark
Sara Woods
  They Stay for Death

River/Canal

Marian Babson
  Unfair Exchange
Lionel Black
  Breakaway
Nicholas Blake
  Head of a Traveller
  The Worm of Death
W. J. Burley
  Guilt Edged
Freeman Wills Crofts
  The Ponson Case
  The Pit-Prop Syndicate
Detection Club
  The Floating Admiral
D.M. Devine
  The Fifth Cord
Cyril Hare
  Death Is No Sportsman
S.B. Hough
  Sweet Sister Seduced
P.M. Hubbard
  The Quiet River
Alan Hunter
  Gently down the Stream
  Gently Floating
  Gently between Tides
Michael Innes
  Appleby's End
  A Connoisseur's Case
Ronald A. Knox
  Footsteps at the Lock
Peter Lovesey
  Swing, Swing Together

Patricia Moyes
 Death and the Dutch Uncle
Sheila Radley
 Death and the Maiden
Jonathan Ross
 Diminished by Death
 Dark Blue and Dangerous

Ship/Boat

Jeffrey Ashford
 The Loss of the Culion
Marian Babson
 Murder Sails at Midnight
 The Cruise of a Deathtime
Josephine Bell
 The Fennister Affair
Gavin Black
 The Golden Cockatrice
Nicholas Blake
 The Widow's Cruise
Leo Bruce
 Death in the Middle Watch
Agatha Christie
 Death on the Nile
 The Man in the Brown Suit
Freeman Wills Crofts
 Inspector French and the Cheyne Mystery
 Sir John Magill's Last Journey
 Mystery in the Channel
 Man Overboard
 The Loss of the Jane Vosper
 Found Floating
 Fatal Venture
Dick Francis
 Risk
Michael Innes
 Appleby's Ararat
 The New Sonia Wayward
Elizabeth Lemarchand
 Cyanide with Compliments

Peter Lovesey
  The False Inspector Dew
Ngaio Marsh
  Singing in the Shrouds
  Clutch of Constables
Patricia Moyes
  The Sunken Sailor
  Angel Death
  Night Ferry to Death
Simon Nash
  Death over Deep Water

Sidewalks

Marian Babson
  Queue Here for Murder
Gordon Daviot
  The Man in the Queue

Sports Arena/Gymnasium

Peter Lovesey
  Wobble to Death
  The Detective Wore Silk Drawers
Philip MacDonald
  Death on My Left

Stately Home/Palace

Catherine Aird
  The Complete Steel
  His Burial Too
Anthony Berkeley
  The Piccadilly Murder
Agatha Christie
  The Secret of Chimneys
  The Seven Dials Mystery
Peter Dickinson
  A Pride of Heroes
  The Poison Oracle
  King and Joker
  The Last Houseparty

A. Fielding
  The Mysterious Partner
Antonia Fraser
  The Wild Island
S.T. Haymon
  Stately Homicide
Reginald Hill
  A Fairly Dangerous Thing
Michael Innes
  Hamlet, Revenge!
  Lament for a Maker
  The Bloody Wood
  Appleby at Allington
  The Ampersand Papers
  Lord Mullion's Secret
  Christmas at Candleshoe
H.R.F. Keating
  The Murder of the Maharajah
Elizabeth Lemarchand
  Death on Doomsday
  Change for the Worse
Dorothy L. Sayers
  Clouds of Witness

Theater/Music Hall

Robert Barnard
  Death on the High C's
John Bingham
  I Love, I Kill
Simon Brett
  So Much Blood
  Star Trap
  An Amateur Corpse
  A Comedian Dies
  Murder Unprompted
  Murder in the Title
Douglas Clark
  Performance
V.C. Clinton-Baddeley
  To Study a Long Silence

Edmund Crispin
  The Case of the Gilded Fly
  Swan Song
Margaret Erskine
  Dead by Now
J.S. Fletcher
  The Dressing Room Murder
Antonia Fraser
  Cool Repentance
P.D. James
  The Skull beneath the Skin
H.R.F. Keating
  Death of a Fat God
Peter Lovesey
  Abracadaver
Philip MacDonald
  The Dark Wheel
Ngaio Marsh
  Enter a Murderer
  Overture to Death
  Opening Night
  Death at the Dolphin
  Light Thickens
Anne Morice
  Death in the Round
  The Men in Her Death
  Sleep of Death
Simon Nash
  Killed by Scandal
Ellis Peters
  Funeral of Figaro
Jeremy Sturrock
  A Wicked Way to Die
Sara Woods
  Dearest Enemy
  Put out the Light

Train/Bus

Herbert Adams
  The Crooked Lip

Josephine Bell
  Adventure with Crime
  A Pigeon among the Cats
Agatha Christie
  The Mystery of the Blue Train
  Murder on the Orient Express
  4:50 from Paddington
Freeman Wills Crofts
  Death on the Way
  Death of a Train
  The Groote Park Murder
J. Jefferson Farjeon
  The 5:18 Mystery
Michael Innes
  Appleby's Answer
  The Journeying Boy
H.R.F. Keating
  Inspector Ghote Goes by Train
Josephine Tey
  The Singing Sands
David Williams
  Murder for Treasure

University/College/School

Catherine Aird
  Parting Breath
Robert Barnard
  The Case of the Missing Brontë
  Death of an Old Goat
Josephine Bell
  Death at Half-Term
  The Summer School Mystery
Nicholas Blake
  A Question of Proof
  The Morning after Death
Leo Bruce
  Case with Ropes and Rings
  Death at St. Asprey's School
W.J. Burley
  A Taste of Power
  The Schoolmaster

Village Fête/Concert/Rock Show

Agatha Christie
  <u>Dead Man's Folly</u>
E.X. Ferrars
  <u>Unreasonable Doubt</u>
Cyril Hare
  <u>When the Wind Blows</u>
Michael Innes
  <u>Sheiks and Adders</u>
Ruth Rendell
  <u>Some Lie and Some Die</u>

Zoo

Freeman Wills Crofts
  <u>Antidote to Venom</u>
H.R.F. Keating
  <u>Inspector Ghote Plays a Joker</u>

8

Miscellaneous Information

Many writers bring to their novels an expertise in or knowledge of another area; I have therefore listed here novels in which such technical knowledge plays a role, large or small. This list does not include references to a general milieu in which a series character is normally found, such as engineering (Henry Calvin's series characters) or banking (David Williams's series character).

Antiques/Art/Old Books

Delano Ames
  The Body on Page One
Lionel Black
  Ransom for a Nude
W. J. Burley
  Death in Willow Pattern
  Wycliffe's Wild Goose Chase
Douglas Clark
  The Gimmel Flask
V.C. Clinton-Baddeley
  Only a Matter of Time
Margaret Erskine
  The Ewe Lamb
E.X. Ferrars
  Foot in the Grave

R. Austin Freeman
  The Penrose Mystery
  The Stoneware Monkey
Jonathan Gash
  All Titles
Michael Gilbert
  The Etruscan Net
S.B. Hough
  The Bronze Perseus
P.M. Hubbard
  A Hive of Glass
Michael Innes
  A Family Affair
  Appleby and Honeybath
  Honeybath's Haven
  From "London" Far
Anthony Oliver
  All Titles
Stella Phillips
  The Hidden Wrath
  Death in Sheep's Clothing
Sheila Radley
  The Chief Inspector's Daughter
Dorothy L. Sayers
  Whose Body?
Margaret Yorke
  Grave Matters

Archaeology

J.R.L. Anderson
  The Nine-spoked Wheel
Francis Beeding
  The League of Discontent
Leo Bruce
  Death at Hallows End
Agatha Christie
  They Came to Baghdad
Jessica Mann
  The Only Security
Ellis Peters
  The City of Gold and Shadows

Botany

Delano Ames
  Crime out of Mind
J.R.L. Anderson
  Death in the Greenhouse
Lionel Black
  Death Has Green Fingers
Douglas Clark
  Bouquet Garni
James Fraser
  A Cock-pit of Roses
  Deadly Nightshade
Reginald Hill
  Deadheads
Gladys Mitchell
  Death of a Blue Delft
John Sherwood
  Green Trigger Fingers
  A Botanist at Bay
June Thomson
  Death Cap

British Education System

Robert Barnard
  Little Victims
Colin Dexter
  The Silent World of Nicholas Quinn

Bullfighting

Peter Alding
  Six Days to Death
Delano Ames
  No Mourning for the Matador
Francis Beeding
  The Hidden Kingdom
John and Emery Bonett
  The Private Face of Murder

Change-ringing

Dorothy L. Sayers
   The Nine Tailors

Classical Music

Edward Candy
   Scene Changing
Cyril Hare
   When the Wind Blows

Crossword Puzzles

Freeman Wills Crofts
   Enemy Unseen
John Buxton Hilton
   Corridors of Guilt
Patricia Moyes
   Murder Fantastical
   A Six-Letter Word for Death
Ruth Rendell
   One Across, Two Down

History

Francis Beeding
   The Seven Sleepers
Gavin Black
   The Golden Cockatrice
Nicholas Blake
   The Private Wound
Agatha Christie
   Death Comes as the End
   They Came to Baghdad
Peter Dickinson
   A Summer in the Twenties
Margaret Erskine
   Dead by Now
Jonathan Gash
   Spend Game

Michael Gilbert
  The Etruscan Net
Reginald Hill
  A Killing Kindness
John Buxton Hilton
  The Quiet Stranger
  Gamekeeper's Gallows
  Dead-Nettle
  Some Run Crooked
Kenneth Hopkins
  Dead against My Principles
Alan Hunter
  Gently Sahib
  Gently with the Innocents
Michael Innes
  The Weight of the Evidence
H.R.F. Keating
  The Underside
Elizabeth Lemarchand
  Buried in the Past
Peter Lovesey
  Invitation to a Dynamite Party
Jessica Mann
  The Sticking Place
Gladys Mitchell
  Death of a Blue Delft
Ellis Peters
  One Corpse Too Many
  Monk's-Hood
  Saint Peter's Fair
  The Leper of Saint Giles
  The Pilgrim of Hate
  An Excellent Mystery
Patrick Ruell
  Red Christmas
Josephine Tey
  The Daughter of Time
R. J. White
  A Secondhand Tomb
David Williams
  Murder in Advent

Margaret Yorke
  Dead in the Morning

Law (British and Continental)

Margery Allingham
  Take Two at Bedtime (Last Act)
Jeffrey Ashford
  The Burden of Proof
  An Ideal Crime
Marian Babson
  So Soon Done For
Sarah Caudwell
  Thus Was Adonis Murdered
  The Shortest Way to Hades
E.X. Ferrars
  A Legal Fiction
Dick Francis
  Enquiry
Michael Gilbert
  The Crack in the Teacup
  The 92nd Tiger
Cyril Hare
  When the Wind Blows
  The Yew Tree's Shade
  Tragedy at Law
  He Should Have Died Hereafter
  An English Murder
John Buxton Hilton
  Dead-Nettle
P.D. James
  Innocent Blood
Roderic Jeffries
  Evidence of the Accused
  Dead against the Lawyers
  Death in the Coverts
Ronald A. Knox
  Still Dead
Ellis Peters
  The Sanctuary Sparrow
Michael Underwood
  Crooked Wood

Literary Figures

Robert Barnard
  The Case of the Missing Brontë
Edmund Crispin
  Frequent Hearses
Martha Grimes
  The Dirty Duck
Ngaio Marsh
  Death at the Dolphin
Julian Symons
  The Name of Annabel Lee
Colin Wilson
  The Glass Cage

Medicine

Agatha Christie
  Sad Cypress
Douglas Clark
  Sweet Poison
  Sick to Death
  The Longest Pleasure
Nigel FitzGerald
  This Won't Hurt You

Numismatics

Lionel Black
  The Penny Murders
E.X. Ferrars
  Unreasonable Doubt
Jonathan Ross
  Burial Deferred

Opera

Robert Barnard
  Death on the High C's
V.C. Clinton-Baddeley
  To Study a Long Silence

Edmund Crispin
    Swan Song
Ellis Peters
    The House of Green Turf
    The Will and the Deed
    Funeral of Figaro

Sailing

J.R.L. Anderson
    Death on the Rocks
    Death in the North Sea
    Death in the City
    Death in the Caribbean
    Death in a High Latitude
    Reckoning in Ice
    Redundancy Pay
Josephine Bell
    A Hydra with Six Heads
Nicholas Blake
    A Penknife in My Heart
P.M. Hubbard
    Cold Waters
    The Causeway
Alan Hunter
    Death on the Heath
Patricia Moyes
    The Sunken Sailor
    Angel Death

Shipping

Peter Alding
    The C.I.D. Room
J.R.L. Anderson
    Death in the North Sea
    Death in the City
    Festival
Jeffrey Ashford
    The Loss of the Culion
Gavin Black
    The Golden Cockatrice

Freeman Wills Crofts
  The Loss of the Jane Vosper

Sports

Brian Ball
  Death of a Low-Handicap Man (golf)
John Bingham
  Brock (fishing)
  Night's Black Agent (fishing)
Douglas Clark
  The Libertines (cricket)
Dick Francis
  All Titles (horse racing)
Michael Gilbert
  Be Shot for Sixpence (climbing)
Cyril Hare
  Death Is No Sportsman (fishing)
Reginald Hill
  A Clubbable Woman (rugby)
P.M. Hubbard
  The Graveyard (deer stalking/hunting)
Alan Hunter
  Gently to the Summit (climbing)
Roderic Jeffries
  Death in the Coverts (pheasant shooting)
H.R.F. Keating
  A Rush on the Ultimate (croquet)
Peter Lovesey
  Wobble to Death (walking)
  The Detective Wore Silk Drawers (pugilism)
Philip MacDonald
  Death on My Left (boxing)
Gwen Moffat
  Miss Pink at the Edge of the World (climbing)
  Over the Sea to Death (climbing)
  Persons Unknown (climbing)
  Die Like a Dog (climbing)
Anne Morice
  Getting away with Murder? (horse racing)
Patricia Moyes
  The Curious Affair of the Third Dog (dog racing)

Jeremy Sturrock
  The Pangersbourne Murders (cricket)
Julian Symons
  Bland Beginning (cricket)
Henry Wade
  A Dying Fall (fox hunting)

Zoology

Marian Babson
  Murder on Show (cats)
H.C. Bailey
  Mr. Fortune Finds a Pig (pigs)
Freeman Wills Crofts
  Antidote to Venom (snakes)
E.X. Ferrars
  Two at the Bone (falcons)
R. Austin Freeman
  Mr. Pottermack's Oversight (molluscs)
P.M. Hubbard
  The Holm Oaks (birds)
Michael Innes
  Stop Press (pigs)
  Appleby on Ararat (marine life)
  Hare Sitting Up (birds)
P.D. James
  The Skull beneath the Skin (birds)
Roderic Jeffries
  The Benefits of Death (dogs)
Gladys Mitchell
  Spotted Hemlock (pigs)
Gwen Moffat
  Grizzly Trail (grizzly bears)
Jonathan Ross
  Death's Head (lepidoptera)
Sara Woods
  They Love Not Poison (pigs)

9

One Hundred Classics of the Genre

There is an abundance of fine work in the genre of the mystery novel, and any list of the "best" novels in this field will inevitably be in part subjective. Nevertheless, I have listed here one hundred novels that are outstanding for various reasons: some are historically important as well as being well written; some are fascinating stories; and others are ingenious tales that capture and hold the reader until the surprise ending. The novels represent the several categories of this genre without being limited to the strict definition of a subtype. For example, Robert Barnard and Freeman Wills Crofts write police procedurals, but each author transcends that type in different ways. The better the mystery novel, the less useful is the name of a subtype to describe it. I have therefore not defined the novels by subtype, hoping instead that readers of one favorite author will find here, through browsing, other authors of a congenial nature.

Catherine Aird
    The Complete Steel
Margery Allingham
    Black Plumes
Delano Ames
    Corpse Diplomatique
James Anderson
    The Affair of the Blood-stained Egg Cosy
    Assault and Matrimony
J.R.L. Anderson
    A Sprig of Sea Lavender

Marian Babson
  So Soon Done For
H.C. Bailey
  The Bishop's Crime
Robert Barnard
  Death of an Old Goat
Francis Beeding
  The Six Proud Walkers
  Death Walks in Eastrepps
Josephine Bell
  Death at the Medical Board
  A Pigeon among the Cats
E.C. Bentley
  Trent's Last Case
Anthony Berkeley
  The Poisoned Chocolates Case
Nicholas Blake
  The Beast Must Die
  The Case of the Abominable Snowman
  The Whisper in the Gloom
Christianna Brand
  Green for Danger
Edward Candy
  Bones of Contention
G.K. Chesterton
  The Man Who Was Thursday
Agatha Christie
  The Murder of Roger Ackroyd
  Murder on the Orient Express
  Death on the Nile
  The Murder at the Vicarage
  A Caribbean Mystery
Douglas Clark
  The Gimmel Flask
  Dead Letter
Edmund Crispin
  The Moving Toyshop
  Buried for Pleasure
Freeman Wills Crofts
  Death of a Train
  The Cask
  The Pit-Prop Syndicate

Colin Dexter
  The Silent World of Nicholas Quinn
Peter Dickinson
  Skin Deep
Eilís Dillon
  Death in the Quadrangle
Margaret Erskine
  Harriet Farewell
A. Fielding
  The Mysterious Partner
Nigel FitzGerald
  Midsummer Malice
  This Won't Hurt You
J.S. Fletcher
  The Middle Temple Murder
Dick Francis
  Dead Cert
R. Austin Freeman
  The Red Thumb Mark
Michael Gilbert
  Smallbone Deceased
Martha Grimes
  The Man with a Load of Mischief
Cyril Hare
  When the Wind Blows
  An English Murder
Georgette Heyer
  A Blunt Instrument
Reginald Hill
  Deadheads
Fergus Hume
  The Mystery of a Hansom Cab
Francis Iles
  Malice Aforethought
Michael Innes
  Death at the President's Lodging
  Lament for a Maker
  The New Sonia Wayward
P.D. James
  The Black Tower
  Death of an Expert Witness

H.R.F. Keating
  The Murder of the Maharajah
  Inspector Ghote Breaks an Egg
C.H.B. Kitchin
  Death of My Aunt
Ronald A. Knox
  The Footsteps at the Lock
  The Viaduct Murder
Elizabeth Lemarchand
  Cyanide with Compliments
  Step in the Dark
E.C.R. Lorac
  Fire in the Thatch
Peter Lovesey
  Swing, Swing Together
Philip MacDonald
  The Rasp
  The Nursemaid Who Disappeared
  R.I.P.
Ngaio Marsh
  Surfeit of Lampreys
  Died in the Wool
  Opening Night
J.C. Masterman
  An Oxford Tragedy
A.A. Milne
  The Red House Mystery
Gladys Mitchell
  The Saltmarsh Murders
Gwen Moffat
  Over the Sea to Death
Patricia Moyes
  The Sunken Sailor
  Murder Fantastical
Ellis Peters
  Death and the Joyful Woman
  Death to the Landlords
  Never Pick up Hitch-Hikers
Stella Phillips
  The Hidden Wrath

Ruth Rendell
  A Judgement in Stone
  The Lake of Darkness
John Rhode
  Death in Harley Street
Robert Robinson
  Landscape with Dead Dons
Dorothy L. Sayers
  The Unpleasantness at the Bellona Club
  Murder Must Advertise
  The Nine Tailors
Julian Symons
  The Blackheath Poisonings
  The End of Solomon Grundy
  The Man Who Lost His Wife
Josephine Tey
  The Singing Sands
June Thomson
  Death Cap
Glen Trevor
  Murder at School
Michael Underwood
  A Pinch of Snuff
Roy Vickers
  The Sole Survivor
Henry Wade
  The Duke of York's Steps
  Heir Presumptive
Colin Watson
  Lonelyheart 4122
David Williams
  Treasure up in Smoke

10

The Metropolitan Police and Local Forces

The Metropolitan Police, popularly known as Scotland Yard, are responsible for Greater London. The police first had their headquarters, in 1829, at 4 Whitehall Place, where once stood a thirteenth-century palace used by the kings and queens of Scotland when on state visits--hence the name Scotland Yard.

Scotland Yard periodically undergoes administrative changes, prompted by scandal, economics, or new technology. Major administrative changes were made in 1824, 1878, 1933, and 1972. For the mystery reader, this means little more than that the fictional inspector may have new channels for reporting. The commissioner of the Metropolitan Police is appointed by the Crown on the recommendation of the home secretary. With the exception of a period after World War II, the authorities have always relied upon promotion from within to fill the upper ranks. Several writers of police procedurals have referred, with varying degrees of enthusiasm, to the reform measure of bringing in police officers at higher levels from universities or colleges. The rank above superintendent, now listed as commander, was once chief constable. Members of the police are in either the uniformed or the detective branch; the ranks are the same in both branches, with the term detective being added to the titles in the latter. These branches were separate until 1972, when a reform measure enabled members of one branch to transfer to the other. Again, several writers refer to this reform and comment on its consequences. Another reform required members of the detective branch to report to a superintendent in the uniformed branch. Despite the many changes in the titles of the upper ranks and in the channels for reporting, the ranks and duties from constable to superintendent have remained the same over the years.

The City of London (the financial district) has had its own police force since 1839. The top officers are a commissioner, an assistant commissioner, a commander, and four chief superintendents, who are responsible for the six departments. Again, the ranks from constable to superintendent have remained the same over the years.

In a county, city, or borough police force, the highest-ranking police officer is the chief constable, who reports to the Watch Committee of the local governing council. Again, the upper levels may expand as needed, but the ranks from constable to superintendent remain the same. There are two main branches in the local forces, uniformed and detective.

Although Scotland Yard officers tend to show up in every county during a major criminal investigation, Yard men and women stand on an equal, not a higher, footing with their county counterparts. The Yard has the advantages of centralized resources in fingerprinting and other areas, and shares these with other police forces.

Metropolitan Police Force

Crown
Home Secretary
Commissioner
Deputy Commissioner
Assistant Commissioner
Deputy Assistant Commissioner
Commander
Deputy Commander
(Detective) Chief Superintendent
(Detective) Superintendent
(Detective) Chief Inspector
(Detective) Inspector
(Detective) Sergeant
(Detective) Constable

County Police Force

Watch Committee
Chief Constable
Deputy Chief Constable

(Detective) Chief Superintendent
(Detective) Superintendent
(Detective) Chief Inspector
(Detective) Inspector
(Detective) Sergeant
(Detective) Constable

11

The British Class System

Though officially a meritocracy, Great Britain is still very much a nation of classes. Class is a function of many things--birth, education, occupation, and income--and the British are quick to recognize the signs of one class or another in the people they meet. Class consciousness is strongest at the borders between classes, and occasionally a character in a novel will remark on the importance of having broken through the barrier between the classes, most often between the working class and the lower middle class. The intricacies of this system may remain forever a mystery to most Americans, but it is nevertheless possible to have a general overview.

The upper class comprises the royal family, the five ranks of the peerage, baronets, knights, and dames, and the gentry, which includes the large landowners and over centuries has absorbed the most successful members of government, business, industry, and the professions. These are the people who form the county society that seems so impenetrable to the nouveau riche. They are also, the peers in particular, the participants in the London Season.

The border line between the upper and middle classes is populated by successful people in government, business, industry, and the professions. Headmasters, headmistresses, and other members of the best schools and colleges are on the fringes of the upper class by virtue of the class of their students. Teachers in state-supported elementary schools are at the lower end of the middle class, again by virtue of the class of their students. Although most men and women of the cloth fall into the middle class, if they are ranked at all, members of the clergy may appear in the upper class. The highest-ranking members of the Church of England belong properly to the upper class. In general, the Church of England ranks higher than other Protestant groups, which rank higher than the Catholic church. Men and women of the cloth tend to rank near the people they minister to.

The working class comprises workers in agriculture and the trades unions, and skilled, semiskilled, and unskilled manual labor, as well as clerical workers and shop assistants. Below these are the domestic servants, and at the bottom are the down-and-out, prostitutes, and criminals.

It would be almost impossible to write a mystery novel in which the characters came from only one class. For example, the police have for decades recruited from the working class, but officers move up socially with each promotion, with the top ranks (the commissioner and the deputy commissioner) joining the upper class. Lawyers are usually upper middle class, and judges at the higher levels are upper class. Indeed, the education of most of the high court judges is typically upper class: a public school and Oxford or Cambridge. Many of the court personnel and junior lawyers are middle class. Novels written in the 1920s and 1930s often include a character whose family recently lost its money and now faces an economic decline from upper middle class to lower middle class: these characters are often young women who find themselves working in milliners' shops or professional offices with no training but a good education, or the young men from an old family who sell off the estate and pursue a career in banking, beginning at the bottom as a clerk. Although stereotypes abound in this genre as in any other, no character is free of his class origins or entirely bound by them.

The British Class System

<u>Upper Class</u>

the royal family

the peers of the realm

(duke, marquess, earl, viscount, and baron)

baronets

knights and dames

gentry

(landowners, top rank in government, business, industry, and the

professions)

<u>Middle Class</u>

MPs, businessmen, industrialists, stockbrokers, lawyers,

doctors, academics at top schools

managers, provincial businessmen, top-level bureaucrats

bankers, insurance officials

vicar, parson, minister

teachers at midlevel school, salespeople

owners of small businesses

foremen, forewomen, secretaries

teachers in state schools

entry-level office workers

<u>Working Class</u>

clerical staff, shop assistants

skilled, semiskilled, unskilled manual labor

domestic servants

the unemployed, the down-and-out

prostitutes, criminals